DATE DUE

Expert System Applications to Telecommunications

WILEY SERIES IN TELECOMMUNICATIONS

Donald L. Schilling, Editor
City College of New York

Expert System Applications to Telecommunications

Edited by

Jay Liebowitz
Department of Management Science
George Washington University
Washington, D.C.

WILEY
INTERSCIENCE

A Wiley-Interscience Publication
JOHN WILEY & SONS
New York • Chichester • Brisbane • Toronto • Singapore

Library of Congress Cataloging-in-Publication Data

Expert system applications to telecommunications/edited by Jay
    Liebowitz.
        p. cm.
    "A Wiley-Interscience publication."
    Includes bibliographies and index.
    ISBN 0-471-62459-4
    1. Telecommunication systems—Data processing. 2. Expert systems
  (Computer science) I. Liebowitz, Jay.
  TK5102.5.E97 1988
  384--dc 19

Printed in the United States of America

10 9 8 7 6 5 4 3 2 1

To my wife, Janet, and my son, Jason

CONTRIBUTORS

DAVID BAILEY, ICF/Phase Linear Systems, Inc., Washington, D.C.

JOSEPH CHANG, IntelliTek, Inc., Rockville, Maryland

KENNETH DEJONG, U.S. Navy Center for Applied Research in Artificial Intelligence, Naval Research Laboratory, Washington, D.C.

DANIEL A. DESALVO, MCI Telecommunications Corporation, McLean, Virginia

JERALD L. FEINSTEIN, ICF/Phase Linear Systems, Inc., Washington, D.C.

GEORGE W. GARBER, Office of Spectrum Management, National Telecommunications and Information Administration, Washington, D.C.

SHRI K. GOYAL, Knowledge-Based Systems Department, GTE Laboratories, Waltham, Massachusetts

HENRY H. HEXMOOR, IntelliTek, Inc., Rockville, Maryland

ELIZABETH M. HORTON, AT&T Bell Laboratories, Liberty Corner, New Jersey

WARREN T. JONES, Department of Computer and Information Sciences, University of Alabama at Birmingham, Birmingham, Alabama

JAY LIEBOWITZ, Department of Management Science, George Washington University, Washington, D.C.

PATRICIA LIGHTFOOT, Spacecraft Control Programs Branch, NASA Goddard Space Flight Center, Greenbelt, Maryland

DAWN LOWE, NASA Goddard Space Flight Center, Greenbelt, Maryland

JOHN LYCAS, M/A-COM Telecommunications, Inc., Germantown, Maryland

MICHAEL MARRONE, U.S. Navy Center for Applied Research in Artificial Intelligence, Naval Research Laboratory, Washington, D.C.

NADINE MATTESON, Stanford Telecommunications, Inc., Reston, Virginia

STEVE MIKSELL, Stanford Telecommunications, Inc., Reston, Virginia

DICK PEACOCKE, Knowledge Technology, Bell–Northern Research, Ottawa, Canada

FRANK PIPITONE, U.S. Navy Center for Applied Research in Artificial Intelligence, Naval Research Laboratory, Washington, D.C.

JOHN POPOLIZIO, ICF/Phase Linear Systems, Inc., Washington, D.C.

BARBARA A. POWER, M/A-COM Telecommunications, Inc., Germantown, Maryland

ROBERT QUILLIN, Stanford Telecommunications, Inc., Reston, Virginia

RAVI RASTOGI, IntelliTek, Inc., Rockville, Maryland

ROBERT L. SAMUELL III, Division of End User Computing, BellSouth Services, Inc., Atlanta, Georgia

D. J. SASSA, Bell Communications Research, Inc., Red Bank, New Jersey

FREDERICK SIEMS, Booz, Allen & Hamilton, Inc., Bethesda, Maryland

BARRY G. SILVERMAN, Institute for Artificial Intelligence, George Washington University, Washington, D.C.; and IntelliTek, Inc., Rockville, Maryland

GARY M. SLAWSKY, Bell Communications Research, Inc., Red Bank, New Jersey

MIKE SMISKO, Stanford Telecommunications, Inc., Reston, Virginia

WILLIAM SPEARS, U.S. Navy Center for Applied Research in Artificial Intelligence, Naval Research Laboratory, Washington, D.C.

AARON WANG, Booz, Allen & Hamilton, Inc., Bethesda, Maryland

WILLIAM M. WILKINSON, Stanford Telecommunications, Inc., Reston, Virginia

RALPH W. WORREST, Knowledge-Based Systems Department, GTE Laboratories, Waltham, Massachusetts

JON R. WRIGHT, AT&T Bell Laboratories, Liberty Corner, New Jersey

ED ZAKRZEWSKI, Stanford Telecommunications, Inc., Reston, Virginia

JOHN E. ZIELINSKI, AT&T Bell Laboratories, Liberty Corner, New Jersey

PREFACE

Expert systems are one of the hottest topics in computer science today. Expert systems are computer programs that emulate the behavior of human experts in narrow, specified domains of knowledge. They have permeated a multitude of areas ranging from medical diagnosis to mineral exploration to telecommunications.

With telecommunications advancing rapidly into the office and home, there is a growing need for better understanding of these technologies. One way to improve this understanding is to capture the knowledge and professional experience of the telecommunications experts. An expert system provides a convenient vehicle for encapsulating the expert's knowledge, thus building up the corporate memory of the institution. Expert systems might be needed because expertise is scarce, expensive, and/or unavailable. They could be used to allow a practitioner to verify his or her opinion, to help accomplish tasks under time and pressure constraints, to free up time to do less mundane and more interesting tasks, and to help in the training of new employees in a specified domain.

In the telecommunications field, expert systems are beginning to be developed and used in the implementation of various tasks. Fault diagnosis is the major telecommunications application for which expert systems are being developed. Other fruitful areas for expert system application in telecommunications include network and spectrum management, local area network configuration, monitoring and control of networks, and scheduling of satellite experimenter requests.

This book addresses these topics and with contributions by leading authorities in the field of expert system applications in telecommunications. It gives a representative sample of expert systems being built for telecommunications applications. Hopefully, it will serve as a reference or textbook for those already engaged or interested in developing telecommunications expert systems.

It should be noted, however, that even though this book gives a representative sample of telecommunications expert systems, not all telecommunications expert systems could be included here, for one reason or another. Bolt, Beranek, and Newman have developed Designet, an expert system for telecommunications design. Avant-Garde, Inc. has developed Net/Advisor, an expert system for telecommunications management and design. NYNEX is developing an expert system to interpret data from the Mechanized Loop Test. Northern Telecom has developed Meridian SL-1, an expert system that configures node equipment. Bell Laboratories is developing NEMESYS, an expert system used to help fight long-distance network congestion. Also, Bell Laboratories is developing LODE, a domain-independent system that learns rules describing patterns in examples created from databases. Case Communications has developed 5010ES-DCX, an end-user expert system for configuring multiplexer networks.

The goal of the book is to show that expert systems have been developed for telecommunications applications and that telecommunications is an area of great potential for future expert systems development. There are two intended audiences: practitioners in the field of expert systems who are presently developing or considering developing expert systems for telecommunications applications and those telecommunications specialists who would like to move into the expert systems field to build expert systems for telecommunications applications.

The book is divided into three parts. The first part offers case studies of expert systems that have been developed for telecommunications applications. The second part describes methodologies that could be used specifically for building telecommunications expert systems. The third part deals with areas in telecommunications that show potential for future expert systems applications.

I am particularly grateful to the contributing authors for their invaluable time and energy spent in developing interesting and scholarly chapters. I am also extremely grateful to Donald Schilling for giving me the opportunity to put together such an exciting book. George Telecki, Phyllis Brooks, and Veronica Welsh have also been extremely helpful in making this book a reality. My wife, parents, family, students, and colleagues deserve special attention for being kind and understanding during the book's development.

Expert system applications in telecommunications will continue to proliferate. As these systems are developed, the telecommunications field will be transformed and grow into an evermore efficient and exciting technology. This book is just the beginning of many examples of telecommunications expert systems yet to come.

JAY LIEBOWITZ

Washington, D.C.
October 1987

CONTENTS

METHODOLOGIES

FUTURE APPLICATIONS

Expert System Applications to Telecommunications

CASE STUDIES

EXPERT SYSTEM APPLICATIONS TO NETWORK MANAGEMENT

Shri K. Goyal and Ralph W. Worrest

Knowledge-Based Systems Department, GTE Laboratories,
Waltham, Massachusetts

1. INTRODUCTION

Commonly, a telecommunications network is a complex aggregate of electronic gear (switches) and a transmission medium, which together provide a multiplicity of channels over which many customers' messages and associated control signals can be transmitted. The primary function of a transmission system is to provide circuits having the capability of accepting information-bearing electrical signals and delivering related signals bearing the same information to a distant point. The telecommunications network, as a whole, provides access to different types of circuits and services that use them. With the increasing complexity of networks and these services, it has become important that these networks be managed carefully for efficient and reliable operation.

The goals of network management are the following:

- Maintaining efficient, reliable operation both as it is under stress because of overload or failure and as it is changed by the introduction of new equipment and services.
- Increasing the performance of the network in terms of the quality and quantity of service provided to its end users.

These goals drive the decisions of the various functional units that compose network management. Although there are several definitions of the term, network management, for this chapter, consists of the following:

- Traffic management
- Repair and maintenance

- Capacity planning
- Design (engineering) and construction
- Administration

Maintenance and management of networks have always been a challenge. More recently, this domain has begun to be explored for artificial intelligence and expert system applications. Exploration has been slow to start because conventional communication and switching technology forced the design of network architectures that could easily be modeled, centrally controlled, and cheaply maintained. Demands for innovative communication services, new architectures to meet these demands, hardware built to fit in the new architecture, and the requirements of flexibility and reliability have opened the door for nontraditional approaches to network management. Expert system applications are demonstrating a great deal of potential in meeting the challenge.

Today's telecommunication networks are more than a conduit to carry analog voice, video, or digital bit patterns from one place to another. The evolution of the "intelligent network" concept and the proliferation of network services are placing increasing demands on network capabilities. In the following sections, we shall look at the evolution of networks and examine the different network characteristics that demand intelligence.

2. TODAY'S (AND TOMORROW'S) TELECOMMUNICATIONS NETWORK

In the past few years, there have been revolutionary changes in the functionality and architecture of telecommunications networks. Future networks are carefully blending the advanced network technologies that offer inherent flexibility to meet user needs (and increasingly sophisticated demands) for new network services in a constantly changing regulatory environment. Tomorrow, networks will implement open network architecture (ONA), and facilities will be assembled in a modular way by using the equipment from various vendors and a wide variety of intelligent peripherals distributed throughout the network.

In this section, we describe the functions of the telecommunication network and the different views of the network, suggesting the advances that face those managing the network.

2.1. Network Functions

Telecommunications networks are designed to support two major functions: (1) communication of voice/data/video and (2) information services.

2.1.1. *Communication Function.* The basic function of a network is to carry information. The building blocks, switches, transmission links, and terminal equipment provide this basic function. By adding intelligence and knowledge about the end-user equipment, the baseline networks are transformed into "value-added"

networks that support error-free, high-speed communication and protocol conversion and, in general, provide a functionally rich and a more robust end-to-end connectivity.

2.1.2. *Information Services.* Information services are value-added services offered to end-user and network managers on a public or private network. Examples of such services include service, information access, computer processing support, and electronic shopping services. With the advent of integrated services digital networks (ISDN) and the proliferation of these services, there is a need for intelligence in networks. In providing services, one needs to deal with the form and content of the information and the ability to generate, manipulate, and understand the information. Intelligent networks will access, store, and manipulate complex information in a variety of forms, drawing on a myriad of sources distributed throughout the world.

Networks will need to "understand" users and user needs in order to provide a friendly interface to information services. This requires the ability to process spoken and typed commands, understand user commands and intentions, and deal with the different context and profiles of users—accommodating and adjusting to their individual needs.

With the emergence of "intelligent network" concepts, more demands are being placed on network capabilities. To explore these concepts, we shall examine the different views of a network, the different kinds of intelligence that may be applied, and some technology issues that are relevant to network management problems.

2.2. Views of a Network

There are at least five views of the networks. Each view demands certain intelligent behavior from the network.

2.2.1. *End-User's View.* The end user views the network as an interface to intelligent telecommunications and transaction services, as well as a conduit for carrying voice and data. The network must offer a user-friendly interface (with syntactic, semantic, and pragmatic processing capability) to various database services and electronic mail systems. The intelligent interfaces should "know" the user! Purely as a communication medium, the network will be required to offer services such as user selection of allocated bandwidth and transmission quality.

2.2.2. *Network Operator's View.* The objectives of the network operator are to offer a high level of performance and reliability with existing facilities. This requires near-optimum use of network facilities under varying traffic conditions. As such, intelligent subsystems for network fault isolation and recovery, performance analysis, routing and congestion control, network security, and call processing can be valuable in achieving these goals. From the network operator's viewpoint, minimizing operational costs is important provided a certain level of performance can be guaranteed.

2.2.3. *Network Designer's View.*

The network designer wants the network to be robust and easy to maintain, analyze, and expand. From a designer's viewpoint, modeling and analysis, service impact studies, capacity planning, preplan construction, and evaluation tools are most valuable. Expert systems have been employed (speculated and hypothesized) for many of these applications in other domains. Intelligent simulators, which generate simulation algorithms based on the system aspects being studied, are just one of these systems.

2.2.4. *Network Owner's View.*

The network owner, often a telecommunications company, sees the network as the basis of business. Its offering must be in demand by the end users. It must further be competitive with other ways of meeting these demands. The objective of the network owner is to provide as much service as possible while using the smallest investment. This requires careful analysis of the end-users' needs and the network's capability to provide for those needs. The owner will prefer designs that are flexible enough to keep pace with changes in the end-users' demands.

In part, the owner relies on the functions of the operators and designers to meet its own objectives. The owner, in fact, directs and coordinates these groups to keep pace with end-user demands. Intelligent systems that improve this overall function as well as those that support individual business operations, like billing and marketing, are of primary interest to network owners.

2.2.5. *Network Supplier's View.*

Various equipment and system vendors supply owners and designers with components and support systems ranging from individual line cards and modems to fully configured and installed networks. The trend in the industry is toward standard interfaces and open architectures. Intelligent systems will be used by suppliers to assist in the development and design of these components (to allow for the expansion of product line diversity) and to enhance the products they offer. Product enhancement will be accomplished through embedded intelligence and through stand-alone and add-on products to enhance their existing product base.

2.3. Network Management Functions

Network management is a recursive, three-step process, applied to several functions necessary to network operation:

- Data analysis and interpretation
- Situation assessment
- Planning and response generation

The following sections describe the major functions of network management.

2.3.1. Traffic Management.

Traffic management is one of the most demanding of the network management tasks. In a telecommunications network, traffic management is concerned with maximizing network efficiency when the network is under stress because of overload or failure. Traffic management does not itself fix the failure or overload condition (that is the task of repair and maintenance); rather, it provides an interim adjustment until the failure is fixed or the network load returns to its engineered level.

Traffic management is affected by changing the way switching systems handle calls. Such changes are referred to as control. Centralized computer support, including the availability of data from many switches, the processing of raw counts into meaningful measurements, and the ready access to specific data provided by the display system, is fundamental to the way traffic management is done today. However, attempts to automate many tasks have run into difficulties because of the complexity of the problem. Beyond a certain point, current approaches tend to bog down in processing huge quantities of data.

Procedures designed to select appropriate controls break down because a particular set of traffic measurements can indicate different actions depending on the cause of the problem; for example, a traffic manager would implement very different controls depending on whether a problem was caused by a focused overload or by transmission problems. Diagnosing the nature of a problem is itself a complicated procedure involving many different types of information. Such information includes network topology, state of the network subtending a node exhibiting a problem, and the affected traffic. This information also applies to the question of control removal because the decision to remove a control depends on the type of problem the control was intended to relieve.

While traffic managers are able to do these and similar tasks by using their experience and selected pieces of information as keys for sifting through the data, such tasks have not been automated successfully. Expert systems technology may provide a new approach that will help automate them.

The introduction of expert systems technology is especially important because the pool of traffic management expertise is small, and the scope of the job has increased enormously with the introduction of new network architectures and technologies.

Traffic managers are subject to considerable time pressure. They must analyze problems as quickly as possible to prevent the degradation of the network, and they must monitor network controls closely so that the controls can be removed as soon as they become counterproductive.

In order to support traffic managers in these efforts, computer systems have been deployed throughout the network. These systems presently perform a number of tasks:

- They collect data from switching systems, signal transfer points (STP), and other network entities. There are two basic types of data: binary status indicators, which are collected every 30 seconds, and peg counts (register data), which are collected every 5 minutes.

- They process the register data to determine if there are any exceptions (out-of-the-ordinary conditions). They then provide traffic managers access to the data via a set of specially formatted display capabilities.
- They also allow traffic managers to take action by sending messages back to the switching systems, which, in turn, instruct the switches to change the flow of traffic.

2.3.2. *Repair and Maintenance.*

Repair and maintenance is charged with keeping the physical network running and (possibly) in top shape. This task can be broken down into the following:

- Problem detection, which involves using the built-in equipment checks, add-on test equipment, and customer complaints to discover that a problem exists with the network.
- Fault isolation and diagnosis, which seeks to find explanations for the patterns of trouble indications that have been collected and which may involve basic causal reasoning to track down the root of the trouble.
- Repair selection, which requires choosing among all the possible repair actions to get the ones that are likely to solve the problem(s) as quickly, cheaply, and effectively as possible (often also ensuring that the actions will not affect the operating network adversely).
- Repair implementation, which is the skilled completion of the selected repair action.
- Repair certification, which checks that the action taken was correctly performed and that the original problem has been resolved.

2.3.3. *Planning, Design, and Construction.*

The two prior functions are focused on maintaining the network status quo. This collection of functions focuses on sizing the network to meet the demands of the end users (maintaining a performance status quo). Some of the input to this process is shared with traffic management and repair and maintenance, namely, the demand currently on the network and its ability to handle the demand.

The tasks performed in this function are as follows:

- Performance analysis—reviewing the input and looking for areas where expansion is warranted.
- Growth planning—projecting the changes in demand in order to have capacity in service before it is needed.
- Facility design—selecting new equipment and specifying how it is to be incorporated in the network to meet capacity objectives.
- Installation—site preparation and incorporation of the new equipment into the fabric of the existing network.

2.3.4. Administration. Since there are many different tasks and organizations to deal with them, and because they must interact to perform their individual functions, there is an administration function to coordinate the activities of the different groups and make use of common resources.

3. ARTIFICIAL INTELLIGENCE (AI) APPLICATIONS IN NETWORK MANAGEMENT

Traditional approaches to network management are not coping now and will not work in the future. The complexity and diversity of telecommunications systems providers demand experimentation with new approaches to solve these problems—methods that will extend the capability of the network operations involved. One of these methods involves the use of AI techniques.

3.1. Artificial Intelligence

The popular press and many technical journals are heralding the advent of AI . . . again. This is because of successful application of some of the mechanisms that came out of the continuing university research in the processes of intelligence. AI is, among other things, a set of programming methodologies that focus on the techniques used to solve problems rather than on solution algorithms. As such, it provides a new, often successful, way of attacking problems that have not previously been considered solvable by machines. The techniques focus on the use of declarative (factual) knowledge and relatively simple rules of inference for putting that knowledge to work on a specific problem. The systems built in this way are called knowledge-based systems.

The university efforts showed that technical knowledge alone was not enough to get the performance exhibited by most experts. The people performing tasks acquired another kind of knowledge that allowed them to concentrate on the most likely causes of a problem and to adapt and optimize "cookbook" answers to the specific problems. The people that do this well are regarded as experts. The machines that capture their problem-solving strategies and selectively apply them under specific circumstances are called expert systems.

3.2. Place for AI in Network Management

AI is a new, often misunderstood and misapplied, technology. It is a powerful method when applied in the right situation. It is useless and potentially dangerous in the wrong situations.

3.2.1. Cautions in Choosing AI Applications. Expert systems have been
called "amateurishly written and, for the most part, very poorly supported [pro-
grams]'' [1]. Since many expert systems are built by graduate students to meet the
requirements of a semester project or master's thesis, or by a startup AI project to
meet some demonstration goal, one has little basis for disagreement.

Since it is a new technology and few support tools exist, there is a strong
temptation to ignore the lessons learned in software system development. This is
further amplified because the people developing AI systems tend to be young, less
experienced designers (generally fresh out of school). All this leads to many problems in the later stages of systems development and deployment.

It is relatively new and untested technology. There are not many good examples
in existence. Expert systems combine qualities of humans and machines (favoring
the latter). They should be tested to the standards of both. As a machine, they
should be as rigorously tested as any program serving in the same domain. The
inference engine should be "proved correct" to the extent that any compiler is
verified today. The knowledge and support routines should be tested as thoroughly
as any software is today. As an intelligent system, they should be put through a
period of apprenticeship—more rigorous than any human, because expert systems
do not generalize from their experiences. After this period of close scrutiny, they
may be allowed to work autonomously—but not without periodic peer review.

A final caution is to choose the application carefully. Prerau [2] has compiled
a list of criteria that have been used in selecting problems suitable for AI solutions.

3.2.2. Reasons for AI Applications. With proper caution taken, AI provides
many subtle benefits. Some of these are not immediately obvious, but all should
be used to advantage.

- *Software Design Strategy.* ·AI focuses on the techniques of solving problems
  as opposed to traditional focus: solution algorithms. Thus, it is a viable strategy to apply when conventional algorithms are not known—yet someone does
  solve the problem or it seems like there are good and bad ways to go about
  solving the problem. This is also a good approach when the problem is ill
  defined (as a way of finding out the requirements).
- *Rapid Prototyping Process.* By concentrating on the problem and techniques
  for solutions, an understanding of the requirements is built up. Often the
  result of an expert system development process is a system that can now be
  recoded using more conventional software techniques, because the proper
  solution algorithm has been formed from the fragments of knowledge built
  into the system over time.
- *Integration Technique.* An expert system or knowledge-based system can aid
  in the task of performing a complex analytical function by using a collection

of other programs to solve different parts of the problem as humans do today. Another integration role is making sure that changes made to data in one information system are propagated to the other impacted systems and databases.

- *Assistant.* An assistant is one that removes much of the lower-level tedious tasks from the more knowledgeable, experienced expert. The assistant checks details, tracks changes, and suggests alternate solutions. The expert guides the overall solution process according to the guidance of years of similar problem solutions.

- *Colleague.* A colleague is a full partner in a problem-solving endeavor. It must be able to cooperate by sharing *partial* solutions to problems and discuss alternate approaches to solving the problem. When knowledge-based systems are patterned after human reasoning, the human being can make assumptions about the system's reasoning (and vice versa). This improves their interactions.

Most network management applications employing AI chose to do so because they needed either a system to solve a problem or an assistant to some human. As more complex network management systems emerge, the integration, prototyping, and colleague motivations will become more prevalent.

3.2.3. Expert System Tasks in Network Management.
Several generic categories of knowledge engineering applications have emerged in the last several years. Some of the categories of knowledge-based systems relevant to network management capture and use interpretation, diagnosis, monitoring, planning, design, prediction, and control expertise.

Interpretation and diagnosis involves inferring system malfunction from sensor data and observables. This expertise is useful in assessing network performance, network fault isolation, and recovery from an outage by observing sensory information and alarms. The major task in this category may not require real-time response. AT&T's ACE [3] and GTE's COMPASS [4] are expert systems in this category and are among the few network applications.

Monitoring involves comparing observables to predictions and hypothesizing inner states using sensor data and interpreted data. On-line monitoring of observables is used in assessing network performance and in planning corrective actions, for example, rerouting of traffic in the event of an outage or congestion. A network state analyst can be employed to analyze the sensory and traffic information, regional configuration, and problem hypothesis on a continuous basis.

Planning requires designing actions to achieve desired results. Short-term reactive planning may involve certification of a new routing strategy or generation of new routing tables to suit the current traffic patterns. A planning expert system may also provide expertise for capacity planning, network expansion, and multi-network integration strategies.

Design involves configuring network elements to meet acceptable criteria. The design activity may be initiated by a request for service from a customer or design or expansion of a network facility (in collaboration with planning). The design may require physical or logical design steps and actions.

Prediction is anticipating likely consequences of given situations. Prediction can be modeled on the basis of historical data and performance trends. Proactive maintenance and preventive actions may be possible using prediction capabilities to warn of pending failures.

Control involves taking action to bring the system state to the desired level. Control action may be initiated as a result of interpretation of the sensory data to bring the network performance within the acceptable bounds. Control actions include imposing routing changes, network reconfiguration, call blocking, and repair suggestions.

3.3. AI in Network Management: A Survey

In the past few years, several applications and expert systems [3–14] for these applications in network management have emerged. We will examine these systems and applications in this section. Table 1 summarizes examples of network management expert systems. Note the dominance of diagnostic expert systems, particularly for switching system matrices. One reason for this is that diagnostics in this area are quite sparse, almost never pinpointing the exact cause of the problem. Since this leaves the maintenance people with a time-consuming task, which is tractable using AI techniques, the first effort of many companies is to build a diagnostic expert system for network management.

Another point to note is that, while planning has been studied by AI for a long time, there are no planning systems in the list. Planning is a task that has simple functions (that are best handled with conventional techniques) and a reliance on a wide body of diverse knowledge. Thus, building a knowledge-based planning system would be difficult to accomplish.

Finally, note the emergence of the development or delivery of AI systems on microcomputers. The hardware technology has caught up with the demands of AI development tools and the current applications. With this, more systems will be deployed and harder problems will be attempted.

3.3.1. Expert Systems for Interpretation and Diagnosis Applications

3.3.1.1. Advanced Maintenance Facility (AMF). This system does TXE4A fault diagnosis, which comprises 30% of British Telecom's switching base. Written in SAGE and running on a 16-bit microcomputer, it uses a huge knowledge base to perform the expert diagnostic task three times faster than a less experienced human (AMF takes 20 minutes per problem.)

3.3.1.2. COMPASS. COMPASS performs expert analysis of maintenance print-outs of GTE's No. 2 EAX. Faults are identified up to a circuit card, switching relay, or wiring pin level. Field trials have shown accuracy comparable with that of human experts.

3.3.1.3. Switching   Maintenance   Analysis   and   Repair   Tool (SMART). SMART is built by BellCore for diagnoses of 1AESS by isolating certain problems and suggesting repair actions—either hardware or software. Knowledge is based on input from NYNEX, Bell Atlantic, and Southwestern Bell. SMART was built using S.1 and translated for the most part to C.

3.3.1.4. Network Troubleshooting Consultant (NTC). NTC troubleshoots DECnet problems. It is an interactive knowledge-based system analysis of DECnet and Ethernet related problems, geared for use by novice technicians, in conjunction with existing Network Control Program (NCP) network management tools. The knowledge base contains 300 symptoms, 300 conclusions, and about 600 rules connecting sets of symptoms to single conclusions with a confidence factor. It is data driven and uses "procedural findings" to access the real network under consideration.

3.3.2. Expert Systems for Monitoring, Prediction, and Planning Applications

3.3.2.1. NEMESYS. NEMESYS is designed to fight congestion in the AT&T network. It is based on techniques to optimize performance during times of overload and stress. Information on call completions and blocking (and why) is gathered via Network Management Operations Support System (NEMOS) to the expert system, which will make suggestions on actions to take (ranging from "nothing" to re-routing calls).

3.3.2.2. Net/Advisor. Net/Advisor works with the Avant-Garde, Inc. product Net/Command to monitor real-time network status and suggest actions to take to improve situations. It uses PROLOG-based inferencing in parallel with LISP data collection component.

3.3.3. Expert Systems in Design

3.3.3.1. DESIGNET. DESIGNET is an "expert assistant" to help design data networks. Much thought has been given to the user interface that supports many views of the network as well as why and what-if questions. It will be paired with a configurer to configure boards, racks, cables, and so on at each site in the network.

TABLE 1 Examples of Expert Systems in the Network Management Domain

System	Task Performed	AI Method	Type, Status	Environment
Advanced Maintenance Facility (AMF) [8]	Finds faults in TXE4A telephone exchanges	Basically a production system	Diagnostic, field tested	16-bit Micro; UNIX SAGE and LISP
Central Office Maintenance Printout Analysis and Suggestion System (COMPASS) [4]	Finds Faults in GTE's No. 2 EAX telephone exchanges	Mix of frames, rules, LISP, and active values	Diagnostic, field tested	Xerox 11xx KEE and INTERLISP-D
Network Maintenance Expert System [9]	Finds network faults in GTD's No. 5 EAX telephone exchanges	Forward-chaining rules	Diagnostic, research prototype	Xerox 11xx KEE and INTERLISP-D
Switching Maintenance Analysis and Repair Tool (SMART) [13]	Find faults in 1AESS telephone exchanges on demand from SCC personnel	Production system with certainty factors	Diagnostic, field tested	XEROX 1108 → PC-AT S.1 and LISP → S.1 and C
Automated Cable Expertise (ACE) [3]	Troubleshoots telephone company local loop plant	Forward-chaining rules	Diagnostic, commercial product	AT&T 3B2; UNIX OPS4 and LISP → C
Real-Time System (RTS) [6]	Filters 1AESS alarms in a network and passes important ones on to SMART for analysis	Forward-chaining rules	Interpret, research prototype	Symbolics KEE and LISP
Network Management Expert System (NEMESYS) [7]	Reviews traffic completion data and suggests traffic control changes	Mix of rules, procedures, and active values	Monitor, research prototype	Symbolics KEE
Network Troubleshooting Consultant (NTC) [11]	Finds problems in DECnet and Ethernet LANs	Forward-chaining rules with confidence factors	Diagnostic, field tested	VAX EXPERT

Troubleshooter [6]	Finds problems in Datakit Centrex-style LANs	Rules with conditional probability adjustment ("learning")	Diagnostic, research prototype	AT&T 3B2 → PC7300; Franz LISP
Net/Advisor [6]	Monitors real-time network status and suggests actions to take when problems are diagnosed	Back-chaining rules (PROLOG) with LISP interface code	Diagnostic, commercial product	Symbolics PROLOG and LISP
Expert Telecommunications Resource Allocation Consultant (XTRAC) [12]	Allocates available resources in a network according to priority and global maximum of completed circuits.	Combination of frame-based semantic nets and forward-chaining rules	Design, research prototype	(Commercial tools)
DESIGNET [6]	Assists in building a data communications network	Object-oriented programming	Design, research prototype	Symbolics 36xx ZETALISP
COM-NET [10]	Performs fault "sectionalization" of digital data service and analog circuits (fault isolation)	Object-oriented programming (also rules, active values, and multiple worlds)	Diagnostic, research prototype	LASER
Network Control Using AI (NCAI) [14]	A distributed routing function for military packet radio networks	Forward-chaining rules	Control, prototype	OPS5 → OPS83
Communication Network Troubleshooting Expert System [5]	Diagnoses failures on private switching packet networks	Rules	Diagnostic, research prototype	LISP and MORSE

3.4. Some Case Histories

Expert systems are emerging to support both network services and communication functions. Some of the experiences gained during the specific expert system developments, evaluation, and interpretation are discussed in this section.

3.4.1. Intelligent Database Assistant (IDA) Expert System.

IDA is an expert system developed at GTE Laboratories in support of network services. Network services and the network management functions rely on several databases, which have been acquired over time. Traditional database management systems provide the users with fixed-format query languages targeted exclusively to access a single database at a time within one database management system. The distribution of databases in communication networks, using a variety of database management systems ranging from fourth-generation relational systems to IMS-type files, requires automation of many functions currently done by database analysts/ programmers. Research on an IDA [15] system addresses many of these issues. Functionally, the system consists of two parts: the front end and the back end. The front end system provides a natural language user interface and menu selection options for an interactive dialog, controlled through the use of interaction scenarios and user profiles. It also controls and formats the presentation of data. The back end system provides database expert functions such as domain understanding, multiple database selection, data combination and fusion among different databases, query program generation, and communication with distributed databases.

3.4.1.1. The System Architecture and Implementation Characteristics.

The IDA system is composed of three main components: the *user interface processor, database expert system, and network communication processor* as shown in Figure 1. The end-user queries in natural language or in a menu-driven mode are entered into the system, and parsed by the user interface processor by using the knowledge of English and the domain. The knowledge implemented in the system was acquired through extensive interactive sessions with database analysts who serve as the intermediary for the end users and experts in the use of databases for specific applications.

The results of parsing are represented as a network of case frames, which are an input to the next component of the system, the data expert system. The query planner component of this system is a rule-based system that produces a virtual database query. The virtual query has three important features. First, the virtual query is based on a universal relation predefined in the system design. Second, the virtual query refers to domain objects at a general level rather than actual database fields and files level. Third, the virtual query has an abstract syntax, not constrained by the syntactic restrictions of a particular database query language. These characteristics of the virtual query language make the planning process efficient and database independent.

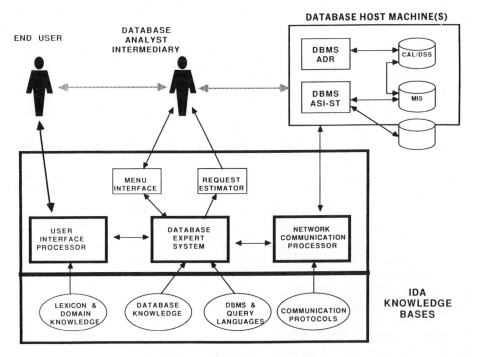

Figure 1. IDA functional diagram.

The transformation from the virtual query to the database-specific query (target query) is performed by the database processor. The query is converted to the target database language by applying a set of database-specific transformation rules. A formalized query is then sent to the target database for processing.

The IDA system is developed using INTERLISP on Xerox 1186 AI workstations. The design and implementation of the main functional components of the IDA system—the natural language processor, database expert, and network communication processor—have been completed and tested with several databases. Figure 2 shows a screen during the system operation. The accessed database management systems include SQL-based systems (DB2, ORACLE, and INGRES), and ADR data query. The system is now being tailored to a marketing application domain for conducting field trials.

3.4.1.2.   Conclusions.   IDA development was undertaken to develop techniques for providing a complete set of functions to an intelligent interface to advanced telecommunication services. The emphasis in the designing was on developing a general-purpose shell, well supported with tools. Efforts have been to build sufficient flexibility into the system so that IDA can be tailored to a new application with modest effort.

Some of the experiences on the project suggest the following:

1. A stand-alone natural language interface does not provide sufficient functionality to create active enthusiasm on the part of an end user. To make it a viable system, expert system applications need to be built around it.

2. An intelligent interface system should offer the needed functionality and sufficiently flexibility so that it can be tailored to specific applications with modest effort. Too much effort needed for customization would be perceived negatively.

3. There are more databases and machine types that the end users would like to see the system work with than one can deal with. Some constraints and selection processes need to be developed to keep the task manageable.

4. Domain knowledge reflects very positively in the system performance. A general-purpose user interface may not seem powerful enough. A powerful interface with good functionality for a narrow application domain is possible using today's technology.

5. During the development and testing, do not underestimate communication interface issues. Reliable intercomputer communication solutions are often very time consuming!

3.4.2. Switch Maintenance: GTE's COMPASS.

COMPASS (Central Office Maintenance Printout Analysis and Suggestion System) is an expert system developed at GTE Laboratories. COMPASS performs an expert analysis of maintenance printouts of a telephone company central office switch (GTE's No. 2 EAX), suggests maintenance actions in expert priority order, and justifies the suggested actions. The faults are identified up to a circuit card, switching relay, or wiring pin level.

A central office telephone switch such as the No. 2 EAX produces thousands of maintenance messages daily. In GTE telephone companies, the output messages from the No. 2 EAX are collected, sorted, and reformatted by GTE's Remote Monitor and Control System (RMCS), as shown in Figure 3. Telephone maintenance personnel analyze the RMCS printout to determine maintenance actions. In the present manual operation, maintenance personnel analyze the day's data in a batch mode and perform the maintenance actions that they deem appropriate. These manual procedures require a high level of expertise. Personnel with greater expertise (with judgment and rules-of-thumb accumulated over years of task performance) and greater ability can perform the analysis significantly better and in substantially less time than those with less expertise.

COMPASS captures the knowledge used by a top switch expert to perform the maintenance printout analysis task. It thus replaces the manual mode of maintenance printout analysis, as performed by maintenance personnel of varying abilities

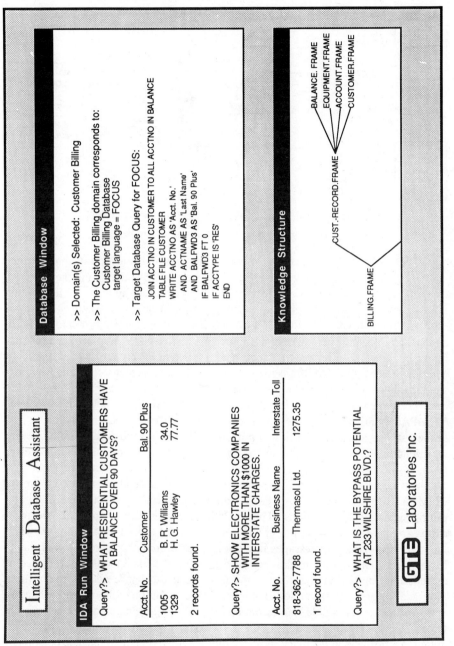

Figure 2. A typical interaction with IDA.

19

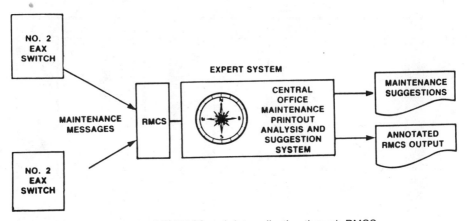

Figure 3. COMPASS and data collection through RMCS.

and experience, with an automatic mode of analysis and selection of maintenance actions, performed at or above the level of a top expert. By automating the expertise of a top expert, COMPASS considerably reduces the time (up to 1 or 2 hours) that is being spent by a nonexpert maintenance person in doing the analysis. Furthermore, it upgrades the results of the analysis, finding switch problems that an average maintenance person may not find. This also saves a good deal of time that might be spent in continually reanalyzing a problem over weeks or months. In addition, since COMPASS ranks the maintenance actions and selects the best possible maintenance action to be performed first, time is saved that would otherwise have been spent performing maintenance actions unlikely to solve the problem. COMPASS thus upgrades the performance of less experienced maintenance personnel. It also allows lower-skilled personnel to perform the task, thereby freeing experienced technicians to tackle the more difficult problems or to learn newer technology. It reduces the need for having experts available around the clock.

There is a large amount of expertise required by an analyst, and therefore by COMPASS to analyze a No. 2 EAX maintenance printout and to determine and prioritize maintenance actions. This includes (1) grouping of maintenance messages, so that all messages in a group are likely to be caused by a common switch fault; (2) analyzing the messages in a group to determine the specific switch faults that could be causing the messages; (3) estimating the likelihood of occurrence of the possible faults; (4) determining the possible maintenance actions to fix these faults; (5) prioritizing the actions list by considering fault likelihood, ease of action performance, and possible risk of the action; (6) merging items on the actions list to combine maintenance actions that can be performed together; and (7) specifying output in a format and language most appropriate for switch maintenance personnel. In the design and implementation, the system consisted of these blocks. Figure 4 shows COMPASS input and output.

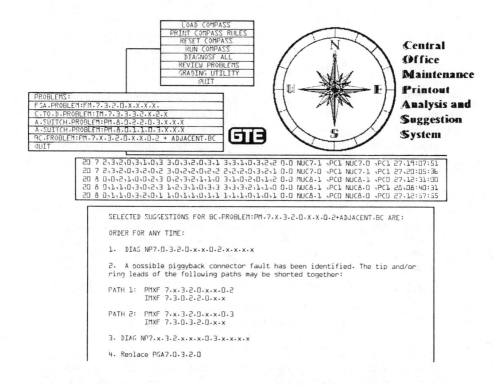

Figure 4. Top-level COMPASS interface with primary output of selected suggestion list.

To obtain the knowledge needed by COMPASS, the development team met with a No. 2 EAX expert (from General Telephone of the Southwest) for 1 week per month for about 18 months. Through these interactions, the procedures and rules the expert uses to analyze an important subset of the No. 2 EAX's maintenance messages were identified and formulated.

3.4.2.1. Implementation and Operational Characteristics. COMPASS is a stand-alone system implemented on Xerox 1108 LISP machines, using Intellicorp's Knowledge Engineering Environment (KEE). It utilizes KEE's rules, frame hierarchies, daemon mechanisms, and object-oriented programming facilities. The system is implemented using 1000 frames, 500 rules, and over 500 LISP functions.

There are seven active knowledge bases: *Communications, messages, patterns, clusters, problems, analyses,* and *suggestions.* These contain information on the switch maintenance messages, the message commonalities that allow clustering, switch faults, possible maintenance actions, and the expert's procedures for executing the different analysis steps.

3.4.2.2. Verification. Evaluation and verification of an expert system are critical elements of expert system development. The COMPASS performance has been evaluated using two techniques: (1) several field trials have been completed and (2) a group of experts (with backgrounds and expertise similar to the COMPASS expert) have reviewed the COMPASS procedures and knowledge. The results of both verification processes have been positive. COMPASS has performed at nearly the level of the domain expert (and in some cases better).

In addition to several field trials, the analyses, rules, and procedures of COMPASS were examined in detail by a group of four No. 2 EAX switch experts (peers of the project's domain expert) from three different GTE telephone companies. They generally came to the same conclusions as COMPASS, though sometimes by a slightly different procedure. In a series of test problems, the group of experts agreed in almost all cases with the COMPASS analyses and suggested actions. In at least one test problem, COMPASS identified a switch problem that none of these top experts had identified in their analysis.

3.4.2.3. Conclusions. The COMPASS development was undertaken as a project to introduce AI technology into GTE's operational environment. An initial system was implemented and demonstrated in a period of 1 year. This system has undergone several verification procedures, including field trials and peer expert review. It is now in the process of being deployed in the various GTE telephone company environments.

Some of the lessons learned from the project experience are as follows:

- Choose the right domain and identify real users who will participate in the project. Plan for the system to be integrated into the existing method of operations. Promote technology awareness throughout the organization beginning in the early stages of the project.

- Plan for expert system verification procedures early on. Review by peer experts and formal field trials are both useful.
- Develop an initial version of the system to demonstrate capabilities, with a Go/No-Go decision point for reimplementation and expansion. A fast turnaround time for early evaluation is essential.
- Consider technology transfer in all phases of the project. Participative design with a central technology organization will help build synergy and common objectives and facilitate smooth transfer of technology to the users.
- Avoid unrealistic expectations by all concerned. Encourage creative applications while maintaining a realistic view of potential payoff.

3.4.3. Network Maintenance: AT&T's ACE.

With switch maintenance well in hand, technologically speaking, attention is turning to the rest of the network—the outside plant or customer access facilities. Based on the early success of AT&T's ACE in patterning intermittent troubles to find sections of cable that need repair attention, several companies have begun similar efforts to assist the cable expert in the detection and diagnosis of problems as they develop in outside plant facilities—before a customer notices that the problem exists.

ACE was first reported in 1983 at an AI conference [16]. The description here will be brief because it is the subject of another chapter in this book. It was originally developed on a DEC VAX 11/780 but has since been ported to AT&T's 3B2 300 supermicro, which sits on a cable analyst's desk. The cable analyst uses a program to call up the diagnoses performed by ACE the previous night. ACE does its analysis by querying the database of daily test results stored in their CRAS system and looks for patterns in the data that indicate where trouble may exist in a telephone company's local loop plant. AT&T has offered ACE as a commercial product since 1984, according to a sales brochure. One key conclusion to be drawn from ACE is that it is not too soon for commercial products to be created with AI techniques.

3.4.4. Traffic Management.

Traffic management is the most time critical function we will discuss in this chapter. It is also one of the more time critical functions in network management. Most information is updated every 5 minutes; some information (alarm status) is updated continuously and summarized every 30 seconds. Except for the switching function itself, nothing in telephony is faster. Hence, it is this application, of all the ones we are describing, that stresses knowledge-based system techniques the most. Several telecommunications companies have efforts to build these systems, but no one has yet reached the prototype stage.

Telephone networks are carefully designed and modified over time to provide a given grade of service to the end users while returning a reasonable percentage of the investment to the telephone company. A century of experience (and a few key studies) have reduced the task of sizing a network's call-carrying capacity to a handful of formulas based on measures of average peak busy hour traffic. Traffic, unfortunately, is never average. There are always coincidental calling patterns that, while they are normal (summed over the entire hour and averaged over several days), cannot be handled by the network or leave most of its capacity idle.

In addition to this, the business concerns of the telephone company require the engineer to install the least expensive (and hence smallest capacity) solution that meets company service objectives. From these efforts, high-use trunk groups and time-of-day routing design models were developed. Therefore, any of a number of failures in the network or extraordinary usage of the network will violate the design models sufficiently to warrant changing the designed routing the network employs.

There are four typical problems facing traffic managers. All the problems are cases where demand for circuits exceeds the networks existing capacity to supply them. They are differentiated by the source, extent, and alternatives available to solve the problem.

- *Routine Capacity Exhaust.* Because networks are engineered with close tolerances and because changing the network is a time-consuming process, there is a period of time (often lasting months or years) when a route is undersized for the demand placed on it. In these cases, the demand placed on the route begins to overflow its capacity regularly. This kind of problem is by far the most frequent handled by the traffic managers.

- *Focused Overload.* A focused overload is a localized demand excess in a network that otherwise has capacity. It is most severe when the facility being overloaded is required for completing the calls—for example, the destination end office. Focused overloads are typically caused by natural disasters such as power failures and floods and mass call-in events such as telethons and radio giveaways.

- *General Overload.* A general overload is the situation that exists when the excess demand is not localized to one region of the network. The major difference between the general overload and focused overload is the extent of the problem and concomitant reduction in control alternatives; the problem is everywhere and so there is no place left to go. While holiday calling patterns constitute the major reason for general overloads, the most feared cause is a poorly handled local problem escalating to involve the entire network.

- *Facility Failure.* Facility failure is the case where demand exceeds capacity because capacity has been reduced through loss of the services of some transport element in the network. Typically, the failing facility is a trunk group or an entire cable and the problem is temporary and corrected by routine, often automatic, action. In the worst case, it is a major loss such as a large cable being broken by falling trees or fallen tower or a central exchange going down. In these cases, the traffic controller must take action to prevent this failure from causing problems throughout the network. Facility failures most resemble focused overloads from the traffic control viewpoint. However, the loss of call-carrying capacity they represent often makes the problem much more severe.

3.4.4.1   Network Controller for Traffic Management.   Most existing public networks today are monitored and controlled by means of a (centralized) National Control Center (NCC). The SMARTS knowledge for traffic management is contained in a traffic controller. Figure 5 shows a general traffic management system in which control actions are determined by analyzing the alarm and traffic data from the network.

The function of a traffic controller is to modify the routing patterns of the network to handle the existing calling patterns more efficiently. There are two reasons for doing this:

1. Limit the automatic use of alternate routes to prevent other calls from being blocked; the first task of the traffic manager is to protect the network from the excess demand.
2. Direct the network to use available capacity it would not otherwise use; if the normal routes from one point to another are all exhausted and another (yes, longer) route has spare capacity, then traffic control actions may be used to direct some of the demand along that route. This is by far the more dangerous task of traffic control.

Any new methods for traffic control or management should be tested off-line— preferably in a simulated network environment. Figure 6 shows a simulated network display interface that is being used in a research project. The link traffic and switching processing load are displayed in the bar gauges.

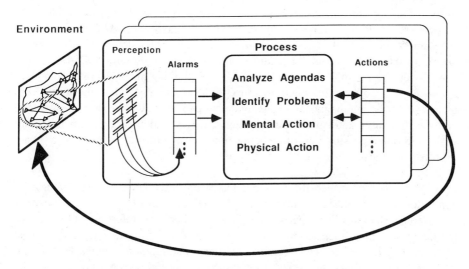

Figure 5. General traffic management.

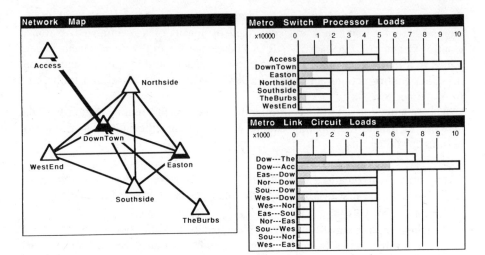

Figure 6. Simulated network display interface.

CONTROL KNOWLEDGE. The (real-time) knowledge-based controller has knowledge about several aspects of the control function. It must be able to diagnose the problem, plan a set of remedial actions, and monitor the network for signs of improvement (or other response.)

DIAGNOSE THE PROBLEM. Traffic managers use knowledge to interpret physical signals, models of network component behavior to trace hypothetical trouble sources to sets of symptoms, and a description of network topology and physical layout to support their reasoning. The diagnostic process takes alarm and severe load messages and searches for problem descriptions that can explain the perceived trouble. Owing to the time-constrained nature of the problem, there are several layers of explanation of the problem—each higher layer explaining the problems of the layer below. In this way, simple diagnoses are produced quickly, while the more complete or illuminating diagnoses are being developed. For example, a processor load alarm is diagnosed and handled immediately as a focused overload at the processor while the other possibilities of it being a transient problem or part of a larger problem are considered.

PLAN THE REMEDY. Once the problem has been classified to some degree, the controller must decide what action to take. Unless the problem is expected or catastrophic, the most likely early reaction is to gather more information to improve the diagnosis. The other actions must be designed carefully to relieve the traffic pressure from the components in trouble without creating more problems elsewhere in the network. Because the information the controller has does not uniquely define the problem, the controller goes through a cyclical reasoning process in which an initial solution is developed, checked against the current state of the network for adverse impacts, and, if the effects are acceptable, the action is taken.

MONITOR THE REACTION. The problem of ensuring the effectiveness of the action taken is complicated by several factors. First, the reporting interval is fixed by the clock, so actions taken in the middle of an interval will only have part of their effect reported. Second, controls do not affect calls that are already in progress, so a control to block new traffic to a trunk group will not immediately reduce the load on that trunk group. Third, the demand is always changing and therefore the effects of the control actions must be weighed against perceived changes in outside demand. And fourth, the quantities used in calculations are always approximations, so the evaluation routines must make qualitative judgments in assessing the effectiveness of the actions taken.

If the evaluation determines that the situation has not improved (or has not improved because of the actions taken), the cycle must be restarted to determine what changes in the control of the network must be made.

3.4.4.2. Reasoning in This Domain. As already mentioned, the difficulty of reasoning in this domain is the result of the time constraints involved. Answers must be reached in a timely fashion and must take into account changes in information since the reasoning process began. To make matters worse, the answers are needed fast and must be well-considered when there is the most data to consider—in times of crisis. Two methods that are particularly suitable for reasoning in network management are the following:

1. *Build a Solution Incrementally from Scratch.* Early work in AI used planning techniques that constructed plans incrementally from basic building blocks. The advantage of this approach is that most situations will be solvable by a reasonably sized set of control and planning rules. The plans will be suited to the current situation because they were invented to handle it. The disadvantage is that these methods tend to be slow. The better answers, particularly in complex situations, take a long time to develop. In network management, because the most common actions of a controller are in reinstalling controls for a repeating problem, this method is inefficient because it does not take advantage of experience.

2. *Build a Solution Based on Past Experience.* This approach attempts to use past solutions directly in solving the current problem. This employs a technique drawn from the reasoning of legal professionals, called case-based reasoning [17, 18]. In this style, the current situation is matched against characteristics of past problems with known (and tried) solutions (with some flexibility). This technique works well when the key characteristics that distinguish the different cases can be organized into a search tree and used to find the match with the current situation. This is an active area of research and much remains to be learned and discovered to match the reasoning

methods with applications. Another useful technique for traffic management in distributed networks is distributed artificial intelligence.

3.5. Distributed Artificial Intelligence

AI systems' solutions and actions are more accessible to human comprehension because a more humanlike approach is taken by the system in producing them; AI systems are often partners in the problem-solving process. Distributed artificial intelligence (DAI) systems are a class of systems that permit several (more or less) autonomous processes, called agents, to perform globally coherent intelligent acts solely through local computation and interprocess communication [19]. Thus, the goal of DAI research is to find mechanisms that can be employed by individual expert systems (or expert system builders) to coordinate the activities of a group into an effective organization for solving problems that the systems share—in whole or in part. It has been noted that DAI research may not just be a subfield of AI, but in fact may be a necessary component of any AI system.

The benefits of DAI are similar to the benefits derived from having groups of people working together to solve problems. Problems that are too large or complex for one person (expert) to solve can be solved by a team. Problems can be solved in parts by people (experts) working in parallel. Better solutions can be produced by collections of people (experts) bringing to bear different expertise and experience. The operation is more reliable when the solution does not rely on the presence of a single individual; the performance of a team degrades more gracefully than that of an individual. By making the AI system a full partner in a cooperative effort, the efficiency of the team is improved.

3.6. The Place for DAI

DAI holds such a large potential payoff that it could lead to major breakthroughs, both for the use of AI in industry and in better understanding of intelligent systems.

3.6.1. Reasons for Using DAI.   There are many reasons for viewing a problem as a DAI problem. By distributing the functionality, one can obtain higher reliability by using distributed, less expansive or specialized hardware.

More Computing Power or Cheaper Total Hardware. This is one of the main reasons for distributing functionality in a system—the available hardware to solve the problem centrally either is not fast enough or is too expensive to purchase. The solution (when an algorithm is known that can make use of it) is to use many smaller or cheaper processors. As with non-AI systems, the chief concern is that the communication needed to coordinate the individual activities is not the bottleneck in the solution process.

Greater Reliability and Fault Tolerance. This too is a standard reason for distribution: if you are not relying on a single processor to solve the problem, then a single processor failure will not prevent its solution. In some DAI systems, several different experts may be asked to solve the same problem with the best timely answer being used as the final solution.

Extends Current Technology. DAI can be used as a means of getting limited single expert systems to solve problems that the technology supporting them would not permit. It allows for partitioning knowledge into individual areas of expertise—each of which is constructible and executable in current hardware/ software systems.

3.6.2. Coordination Techniques for Existing and Future Expert Systems.

One way to have cooperating systems is to build them to work together from the start—much as you would build the subroutines of a larger program. However, this will not produce a system that functions well in novel or dynamic situations: the system will work well only in the problem mix for which it was designed. Nonetheless, this is a viable approach for many applications such as routine office automation, as reported in Chang et al. [20]. A more flexible approach is to give each agent the means and motivation to communicate with and coordinate with other agents. Patterned after the abilities of human beings, this will allow agents to form dynamic organizations for solving problems as they arise. This is a much harder problem because there are many features of the ways humans work together that are still unknown.

3.7. Expert Systems: Value and Potential Risks

A variety of expert systems have emerged for applications in telecommunication systems. It is too early to assess their real impact on the fast changing telecommunication industry, although their presence is beginning to be felt. The potential benefits of these systems are mainly in improving quality of service through optimally (and in a timely fashion) using the resources and in saving cost through automation. This section highlights benefits and potential problems in introducing this technology in the current telecommunication environment.

3.7.1. Potential Benefits of Telecommunications Expert Systems.

There are several potential benefits of telecommunications expert systems. These are listed below.

3.7.1.1. Providing Higher Quality Service

- Substantially increases performance. Routine use of expert systems for network routing, system maintenance, and so on would significantly improve the performance of telecommunications systems. It would allow personnel and computer systems to perform at or above the level of an expert. From the customer's standpoint, it should yield a better product or service with a higher level of reliability.

- Captures knowledge that will be less available in the future. This is an important, though difficult to quantify, benefit. In the dynamic world of telecommunications, expertise is being lost as experienced personnel move to work on new systems or new problems or just leave the company. This generates potential problems in the use of older systems. An expert system can capture the expertise of a top expert while he or she is available and at peak performance and make it available for the future.
- Makes expert performance available at all times in all locations. The expert system performs at the same high performance level 24 hours a day, in all locations.

3.7.1.2. Providing Lower Cost Service by Productivity Improvement

- Significantly increases productivity. An expert system can bring a less experienced person to the level of an expert, allowing tasks to be performed faster and more efficiently. Even experienced personnel can be aided, as they are still not at the level of a top expert.
- Reduces staffing costs and makes top performers available. With an expert system, some high-level jobs could be performed by lower grade (and thus possibly lower paid) staff. This also frees the top (experienced) performers to concentrate on the more important jobs, which may be beyond the reach of the present state-of-the-art expert systems.
- Expert systems can often do better than an expert. Expert systems can combine the capabilities of the computer with the expertise of a top expert. Thus, expert systems can do a complete analysis of a complex situation, which is difficult even for an expert. Being a computer system, an expert system is thorough in all its analyses and will not make many errors that average maintenance personnel may make and that even the best human expert will occasionally make. Also, an expert system can do the detailed, repetitive, or laborious tasks that an expert, though capable, often might disregard if he or she feels that they have only a small chance to help solve the problem.
- Improves worker's general performance by having the presence of an expert review. When the expert system is used to make recommendations related to a worker's task, the worker subconsciously may be more careful in his or her work, so as not to be "caught" doing a poor job by the expert system.

3.7.1.3. Other Benefits

- Provides management and supervisors with greater flexibility in staffing. Since the required skill level may be lowered for certain jobs, management and supervisors, at times, can use personnel with skills in one area to work on a related area, with the assistance of an expert system.

- Expert systems can be a major aid in training. Expert systems often can output explanations and justifications of their analyses, in many levels of detail. This can be a major aid in training inexperienced personnel. In addition, some expert systems have been developed specifically for training, having the expertise of a trainer as well as the application expertise.

3.7.2. Potential Problems in Introducing Expert Systems. Though expert systems offer significant advantages to the industry, those introducing the system must be careful for the following reasons:

- As with the introduction of any automation, expert systems may create a feeling of insecurity among workers. If expert systems are not implemented carefully, it could lead to social problems in changing the way things are done owing to the deviation from the ''business as usual.'' To avoid this situation, the system and the technology should be introduced gradually, in a natural mode.
- Expert systems are not sensitive to political situations. It can sometimes produce results politically damaging to someone and therefore could be the subject of embarrassment. It may be important to employ expert systems in a subordinate role—in a decision support mode.
- Finally, there is a problem with the unrealistic expectations. The area of AI and expert systems has many people expecting too much and others expecting too little.

4. EXPERT SYSTEM DIRECTIONS IN NETWORK MANAGEMENT

As research in AI produces new results, network management applications can be extended to incorporate these advances. Some of the AI techniques that are on the forefront today, such as general causal reasoning, cooperative experts, planning, simple learning, and pattern recognition, will be the basis for the next generation of network management applications.

Diagnostic experts are the most prevalent today. From this base of technology there will be two major lines of effort: (1) broadening the coverage of existing and similar systems and (2) building tools to support the development of such systems.

4.1. More Applications Using Current Technology

The existing systems and their future siblings will be broader in scope, coverage, and more integrated with the control of the systems they monitor. Thus, rather than covering a subset of messages or alarms produced by some piece of equipment, they will cover them all. Similar systems will be built for pieces of equipment not covered today. The knowledge and accuracy of expert systems will be enhanced by incorporating the knowledge from several experts—leading to the creation of corporate knowledge repositories for each subject. All this will free up the brightest staff members to learn newer systems and will allow the company to keep pace with changing network technology.

For example, COMPASS covers all messages relating to failures of a No. 2 EAX's switching matrix but not to problems related to individual electronic components like line cards or the CPU, except as they are indicated by switching problems. The same technology could be used to build diagnostic procedures for these other elements of the exchange. By the same token, COMPASS technology could be used to build diagnostic systems for other switching systems.

4.2. Specialized Tools

Whenever a large number of related activities are to be performed, two kinds of specialized tools are created: tools to perform a central part of all the problems and tools to span the needs of all the problems. The first kind of tool provides a skeleton application or shell onto which the specifics of a given application can be added. The purpose of a shell is to provide representation and inferencing knowledge common to application systems built with it, permitting the knowledge engineers to concentrate on the unique aspects of the current system.

For example, most of the diagnostic systems reported here use a production (rule) knowledge representation, a forward-chaining (data-driven) inferencing method, and pattern matching as the way of locating relevant knowledge. A shell to support development of switch diagnostic systems would have to include these techniques. Furthermore, most of the current systems use some hierarchical structuring in the knowledge that describes the subcomponents and problems of the switch, so a diagnostic shell should include other representation schemes, such as frame representation mechanisms. In addition to these general mechanisms, the diagnostic shell should include knowledge for general causal tracing of symptoms, definitions of common terms, and other domain-specific knowledge.

The other type of tool is often referred to as a toolkit. It does its best to provide an integrated collection of separate mechanisms, each good at supporting the development of some application within the set but not necessarily good for all of them. These systems provide the building blocks for development of expert systems. Rather than have the knowledge engineer learn the use of many different tools, many companies provide integrated toolkits with a choice of inferencing strategies. Major AI companies provide these tools (e.g., KEE by Intellicorp and ART by Inference). The problems in network management are so varied that single paradigm systems like OPS-5 do not provide sufficient power to allow knowledge engineers to solve the range of problems they face. One such system, ESSAI [21], has been developed by ITT to handle the range of problems they face.

4.3. More General Causal Reasoning

A trend in AI is toward more general reasoning. This is possible if the inference engine and the processor it runs on is fast enough to execute the longer reasoning chains and more extensive searches needed to reach a conclusion in time for the answer to be of use. The advantage of this approach is that a smaller body of knowledge can handle a wider range of problems.

One possible application to make use of this approach is *fault isolation*. Fault isolation is a more general problem than diagnosis, in that it is concerned with finding the most likely sources of failure without necessarily finding out what caused the failure. These systems can be used on larger, more complex systems to guide self-healing functionality to the unit that failed so that (1) it can be isolated from the system's operation and (2) it can be diagnosed more carefully by a unit expert. These systems generally are not found today because they rely on more general reasoning (and hence are harder to codify efficiently). New research results make this prospect more likely.

4.4. Cooperative and Distributed Systems

The current technology supports developing expert systems in small, well constrained domains. A group of limited functionality expert systems can be connected to work together in a cooperative mode and solve larger problems requiring multiple expertise.

One example of potential application of cooperative system technology is a project management assistant—a system that understands cooperation and the limits of the various human and mechanical agents and has the patience to follow every detail of scheduling and production would be a powerful tool. This assistant (which may itself be a collection of autonomous intelligent systems) would help in the early stages of project planning, keeping track of the organization, scheduling decisions, and checking for feasibility and success confidence. Its comments would make sense to the project planner because they would be following similar lines of reasoning and using many of the same tools. It would keep track of allocation trade-offs and ensure that schedules were not significantly violated. In addition, it would suggest alternative task assignments based on access to the qualifications of personnel and contractors available and track milestones, alerting the project manager of pending problems. The system can work with the various project managers to plan for contingencies jointly—keeping work crews productive when the delay warrants a shift of emphasis. This approach will be explained later in the book.

Another area receiving some attention in the AI and DAI communities (as well as a growing office automation community) is *office information management*. This is a potentially high payoff, but very complex area with future efforts concentrating on, first, developing and, later, integrating:

- Intelligent mail systems
- Personal secretaries
- Office managers (schedulers, work assigners, operations analysts)
- Database or information management systems

4.5.   Planning

Planning is one of the oldest lines of investigation in AI. Despite this, there are very few deployed planning systems. To a large measure this is because there are too many factors to consider in real planning tasks. One way to gain early success in commercializing AI planning capabilities will be to create planning assistants that leave major decisions and planning direction up to a human and concentrate on consistency checks and filling in detail, and to integrate knowledge-based reasoning with existing operations research and PERT systems in a reasonably sized domain.

One example in planning is a dispatch system for repair and maintenance operations. Operations research (OR) has provided several systems that can schedule, to some degree, a set of activities. Expert systems will grow up around those OR systems to (1) accept and integrate the tasks to be performed from diagnostic trouble-reporting systems, (2) integrate the field reports of work completed and repair status, and (3) adjust the scheduling parameters under the natural language direction of the human dispatcher.

4.6.   Simple Learning

There are two kinds of learning that can benefit the next generation of AI systems supporting network management: parameter adjustment and pattern recognition. Parameter adjustment can be built into all expert systems that use some quasistatistical expectations for the probability of an occurrence. These systems could easily monitor the success of their predictions and adjust this measure to match the current conditions better.

Pattern recognition systems would study the network performance and build recognizers that are of significance to the operation and administration of the system. These techniques enable the system to acquire and adapt knowledge, under some human supervision, to a changing environment. Future systems will involve more sophisticated analyses taking a wide variety of factors into account such as length of service, vendor, weather conditions, usage, and trouble and test reports. Other factors such as existing maintenance and repair plans would also be useful.

Detection of recurring network problems, such as routine capacity exhausts, is another pattern recognition task. The next generation of network management systems will have a module to identify these situations and predict their occurrence so the network manager has more time to create (or reuse) an adequate solution to the problem.

4.7.   Embedded AI

Most AI systems today work off-line, analyzing data after the fact and proposing actions to remedy the situation. If telephone companies are to achieve the maximum return from this technology, it must be developed to the point where it can be incorporated responsibly into on-line applications. The hardware and software tools of AI are just now making this possible; more effort is needed in testing the limits of these tools.

5. NEEDED AI TECHNOLOGY

In addition to the need for developing applications in support of existing and future network management activities, there is a need to support the development of more powerful tools so that problems beyond the reach of the current state of the art may be addressed in a timely fashion. We have already suggested many of these needs; this section summarizes and extends those discussions.

5.1. General Knowledge Representation and Inferencing

AI has produced some major advances and yet has still not solved what seem to be some of the simplest problems—representing specific, limited, technical knowledge about objects and relations between them. AI techniques work well in areas where highly formal and well-defined concepts dominate the thinking of the practitioners, such as electronics and medicine. AI systems have been created that solve problems very few humans can—in some cases, better than the best experts.

AI, however, is surprisingly weak in domains where nearly every human does well, e.g., in so-called ''common sense'' problems. These problems are difficult because ''common sense'' deeply engrained in our basic, everyday reasoning: they are not explicitly learned and thus are difficult to separate out. Much of the research effort in AI is focused on the task of getting machines to reason in the ''simple'' domains of time, geography, physics, and qualitative analysis. Of note is the effort of Doug Lenat at MCC in Austin, Texas, where, in the CYC project, his team is attempting to address all these dimensions simultaneously by encoding the knowledge necessary to read and understand the contents of a typical desk encyclopedia.

5.2. Learning and Adaptation

The bottlenecks in creating any intelligent system are filling the system with the knowledge it needs to solve the problems it will face and adjusting that knowledge to keep pace with changes in the domain and new experience. Research into learning techniques is addressing this problem by creating systems that take an active role in the knowledge acquisition process. There are several different approaches to learning, ranging from very fine-grained connectionist approaches to higher-level cognitive skill acquisition (e.g., algebraic manipulations). The field is currently trying to understand the power and limitations of the various methods so that they may be applied successfully to real-world situations.

5.2.1.   Crucial Issues.   The major problems facing learning researchers are the following:

- Recognizing an example (something to be remembered as prototypical) from an exception (which merely modifies a basic class).
- Selecting the aspects of an example that are to be generalized into a rule for behavior.
- Determining, in unsupervised learning situations, which elements used in reaching a correct answer to reward and which were irrelevant.

5.3.   Embedding AI Systems

Embedded AI systems imply that these are integrated as an individual component in a larger system. As such these systems can transparently access data, analyze and communicate control information with the other components of the system. In this section, when we talk of embedded expert or knowledge-based systems, we are distinguishing certain characteristics of them from other systems, which we will refer to as *add-on equipment*. Add-on equipment is something you roll-up, plug in, turn on, and then use.

The key features of embedded systems are the following:

- *Continuous Operation.*   Embedded systems tend to operate continuously with the system in which they are embedded. This often leads to real-time or at least time-constrained requirements on their operation. If their operation is not continuous, it is often automatically triggered by an alarm to invoke some analysis or control function.
- *Dedicated, Autonomous Activity.*   Embedded systems tend to have a dedicated function and the autonomy to perform it. This may not be an essential feature with embedded knowledge-based systems working in a decision support mode.
- *Inseparable Operation.*   Embedded systems tend to be indistinguishable from the rest of the system when they are performing their function. They use the same user interface as the rest of the system and get their information from the same places as the rest of the system.
- *Access to Internal Data.*   Embedded systems use the same internal pathways and representation of information as the rest of the system.

5.3.1.   Reasons for Embedding

5.3.1.1.   Intelligent Activity Is Part of an Integrated System.   If the system must interact with the data (or another system) during the problem-solving task, an embedded implementation is required. If a complex system must be monitored (and perhaps controlled) by an intelligent process (usually a human being), the support systems must be integrated so that there is no apparent boundary between them.

So embedding is indicated when (1) intelligence is an assistant in complex analysis, (2) intelligence is a data filter, (3) intelligence is a command interpreter/executor, and (4) intelligent agents must work closely together.

5.3.1.2. *Intelligent Activity Is Time Dependent.*

Another reason for having the system embedded is that the solution must be presented in a time-constrained fashion. An example of this constraint would be a noise mitigation diagnostic system, which must begin testing at the first sign of a problem because of the transitory nature of the faults. If the system waits for more evidence, the problem disappears. Most complex control tasks are real time and the intelligence supporting or performing the control decisions must be an integral part of the overall system.

Intelligence should be embedded in cases where (1) real-time analysis and response are needed, (2) a dynamic world exists, (3) the system has large inertial mass, that is, the effects of an action are not immediately perceived but can only slowly change the state of the system, and (4) the system must be monitored continuously.

5.3.2. *Crucial Issues in Embedding Expert Systems.*

The issues facing developers seeking to embed AI into their application are the following:

- *Data Sharing.* Techniques for expert systems to share information they possess with existing databases to avoid wasteful and sometimes dangerous duplication of information.
- *Memory Reclaiming.* The general process of reclaiming memory that has not been used in a while and does not appear to be relevant in the future. The simplest, most elementary example of this is garbage collection. But, knowledge representations and inference engines generate a series of intermediate results with enough "live" references to prevent their being swept up by the garbage collection process. This has the same performance-robbing effect as poor garbage collection—as the problems are more complex (and probably more critical) the system slows down. Inferencing methods are needed that either limit the volume of intermediate results created or provide mechanisms for intelligently eliminating the data that are no longer (likely to be) needed.
- *Performance.* Components must be fast and operate consistently (or nearly so) across the range of problems they are asked to solve. Many tools exist to monitor the run-time performance of software as an aid in discovering the bottlenecks in the process and to isolate the areas where optimizations can most fruitfully be applied. Similar tools are needed for the knowledge structures used in embedded intelligent systems as an aid in discovering the bottlenecks in the inferencing process and to isolate areas where restructuring the inferencing flow can improve performance.

- *Error Recovery.* Some mechanism is needed to force the expert "back into the real world" if it fails to come up with an answer (or simply takes too long before reaching one). The system must have built-in safeguards against "reasoning failures" in addition to the normal software safeguards. Some of this may be taken care of by adopting a refinement approach to problem solution where a quick (and less accurate) solution is created first and is successively refined as time permits. If multiple processors are available, several competing techniques may be applied at once and the best answer chosen when the time for action arrives.

5.4. Distributed Artificial Intelligence

Just as an expert system needs to be embedded in the system with which it works, so expert systems need to be integrated in the teams with which they work. This is the goal of research in DAI. Distributed intelligent systems will be able to handle problems that are larger or more complex than those single expert systems can handle today. The chief problem facing these teams is keeping the communication overhead down while maintaining global coherence of action. This is becoming a major discipline within the AI community, its sixth annual workshop having been held in 1986.

Of course, the network management assistant will have to interact productively with a human network manager (or several network managers). One approach is to make the exchange more dynamic and adaptive to the situational demands by viewing the assistant and the manager(s) as a team. We gain an independence of activity that will allow each to concentrate on a part of the overall problem, working in parallel. Properly executed, a team is a very effective organization for handling a crisis. Poorly executed, there is nothing worse.

5.4.1. DAI Techniques.
The techniques identified thus far for coping with the problems of distributed reasoning and coordination focus on single aspects of the problem. Game theory has been applied to the problem of coordinating decisions with minimal communication (by using shared knowledge) [22]. Business negotiations have been used as the basis for developing a task allocation and scheduling protocol [23]. Business management theories of organization and control are being explored for their utility in structuring systems of intelligent agents.

One of the most prevalent architectures used for DAI systems is the blackboard system. The chief components of a blackboard system are the following:

- The *blackboard*, a repository for working knowledge about the current problem and the state of its solution.
- The *knowledge sources*, single function procedures that scan the blackboard for relevant patterns of data and take some action to further the solution.

- The *agenda*, which evaluates the list of knowledge sources ready to run and selects the one to execute next.

Since the reasoning performed by a blackboard is inherently distributed, it works quite well in an environment where data are passed among independent agents to coordinate activity and partial solutions to shared problems.

5.4.2. *Crucial Issues in DAI.*

There are several issues [24] that serve to separate DAI from the rest of the field. The whole issue of interagent communication is the one that separates DAI from non-DAI. Other than general categories of commands, requests, and data, what do agents say to one another? What language do they use? When do they volunteer information? What must they describe? For example, in solving problems, humans often have the choice of doing "it" themselves or teaching someone else how. Cooperative, planning systems will have this ability just to do their job. What must agents know about each other to be able to communicate and cooperate?

Organizations are restrictions of choice made to speed up joint activity. Communication protocols are perhaps the simplest organizations. Can individual agents build organizations to meet problem demands? Can they tear them down when they become counterproductive? And, how do you find out that organizations are counterproductive?

One issue DAI shares with AI is that of evidential reasoning. What factors should go into the weighing of evidence in arriving at a conclusion? How do you discover the worth of another agent's conclusions? How do you keep reasoning about evidence from overshadowing the cost of reasoning with evidence?

6. THE FUTURE: AN AUTONOMOUS NETWORK

The two essential functions of a network are to provide connectivity and communication facility. By the year 1990 and beyond, with the introduction of (limited) ISDN and proliferation of advanced network services, there will be an increasing demand for intelligence in the network to support reliability, flexibility, and end-user control of the network.

The primary objectives of network management are more completed calls, higher return on network capital investment, and better network performances and customer service. The principles on which network control actions are based are "keep all trunks filled with messages, give priority to single-link connections, use all available trunking, and inhibit switch congestion." Methods to accomplish this will include real-time traffic monitoring, collection and analysis of network performance data, identifying abnormal situations, determining reasons for traffic flow problems, activating network controls, and coordinating with facilities maintenance to minimize the impact of outages.

The role of the network maintenance is to monitor component performance by real-time surveillance of alarms and comprehensive remote control and to react when failures occur.

6.1.   A Closer Look

Consider an integrated intercity network providing circuit-switched and packet-switched transport with distributed processing power supporting enhanced services, consisting of five conceptual subnetworks whose names and major functions are as follows:

- Network Services: information processing to provide enhanced services.
- Bearer: switching and transmission services.
- Signaling: translation, validations, out-of-band signaling, and related network control functions.
- Information Management: transaction systems (e.g., customer billing, account administration, and facilities management) not requiring real-time response.
- Operations, Maintenance, Administration, and Control (OMAC): network management and control, surveillance, maintenance, database management and distribution, and data transport.

The overall performance of the network is determined by these functions although network management resides in the OMAC subnetwork.

In some sense, such a network is self-contained, having measurables—that is, traffic data, reports on the success or failure of the equipment base, and hardware sense points—and controls, which manipulate the system's response. To meet the needs of identified patterns of usage, preplans based on extensive analysis and simulation are invoked to control the system as a whole.

Network management is a recursive, three-step process, distributed through the various levels in the network management hierarchy:

- Data analysis and integration
- Situation assessment
- Planning and response

Network control, maintenance management, and all facets of this activity deal with data, hypotheses, and plans, all of which are subject to being imprecise, incomplete, untimely, irrelevant, or incorrect.

Control of this highly variable entity is a complex inference and planning task that, because of the need to operate in near real time, can be more than a team of controllers can handle adequately. It is data driven and situation dependent. Solutions are based on broad knowledge of the task domain and the conflicting purposes being served, experience in dealing with situations and responses, and appeal to mathematical modeling. Moreover, operating the network at a given time is not enough; as customers, equipment, and services are added, network control must evolve as it is done. Offering computer-based assistance to network management is a challenge to computer science research.

6.2. The Ultimate Network and Its Evolution

An obvious way to deal with such a complex network is to build automatic controls in the network by providing sufficient numbers of control and sensory points—a task much easier said than done! It is still a long way before we can take this goal seriously, but limited automatic control functionality is beginning to appear in the present systems.

Several generic categories of knowledge engineering applications have emerged in the last several years. Some of the categories of knowledge-based systems relevant to network management capture and use design, planning, interpretation, diagnosis, monitoring, prediction, and control expertise. The intelligent system applications for networks can be mapped into two broad conceptual categories. The first category deals with design and planning issues in establishing and providing network facilities. Flexibility of the network is built into this phase. The second category supports operations, management, administration, and control (OMAC) functions and reflects on the reliability aspect of the network. There are strong pressures to integrate the existing optimizing and algorithmic methods and tools with the emerging intelligence in the network. A variety of stand-alone knowledge-based systems are in field trial or in commercial use in the network. Also, algorithmic design and planning tools such as EFRAP (The Exchange Feeder Route Analysis Program), cashflow, and traffic engineering tools are available today to the network designers. There is a need for building intelligent planning tools and integrating them with currently used databases, so that the same system can be used by different groups, including fundamental planning, network engineering, and implementation planning. Expert system front ends will be providing the consolidated data environments for these groups to make intelligent decisions.

Network management and traffic control systems are currently used in decision support mode to manage networks. As traffic control expert systems become closely integrated with alarm surveillance systems and are tested sufficiently to verify the accuracy of their decisions, they can be trusted to make simple traffic rerouting decisions and to install controls, thus making networks more automatically controlled (autonomous). At the same time, as the systems are extended with more knowledge about operations and alternative controls, they will more closely support human experts in making complex decisions.

6.3. An Autonomous Network Scenario

In an autonomous network, error-free operation is provided by hardware flexibility and redundancy and intelligent diagnostic functions embedded into the network components and into the network management system. The network management system continuously monitors traffic demand and facility operation adjusting the normal flow of traffic as needed. This system also has a learning component to permit it to come to anticipate the routine overloads and adjust to the slower shifts (hopefully growth) in traffic demands. One function of this system is to report on the capacity of the network to handle the demands and to warn the planning group when problems seem due to design mismatch rather than temporary demand anomolies. Operators now work with the system to solve long term operational threats—the system itself handling the small problems. The autonomous network will also request and direct repair and maintenance functions. Figure 7 gives a conceptual view of a network management command and control system. The overall system has a wide variety of sensors and status display systems integrated and distributed in the network. The actions are taken by a collection of processors, with some of the monitoring and analysis functions being performed at switch level, along with some repair and maintenance actions; the reset of the repair actions will take place at regional centers serving a subset of the network (and a single roving repair crew) along with more monitoring and analysis and facility error detection and diagnosis. Regional centers will also be the first line of attack on traffic management functions. For the sake of improved reliability and load sharing, the regions covered by a center will overlap. The centers will be individually responsible for coordinating their actions so that work is not duplicated and that answers to requests from other functions are complete. For the major operational functions, such as diagnosis of networkwide problems and overall coordination of complex problem solutions, there may be one or more central coordination centers. The function of these centers is to monitor the overall performance of the network and the other control centers and initiate action when it seems appropriate and is lacking. For this reason, the line between operation and design is less distinct. Operation and design are merged into one process directing the hardware and software evolution of the network. These centers will also be responsible for interacting with the network owner to provide needed information on network

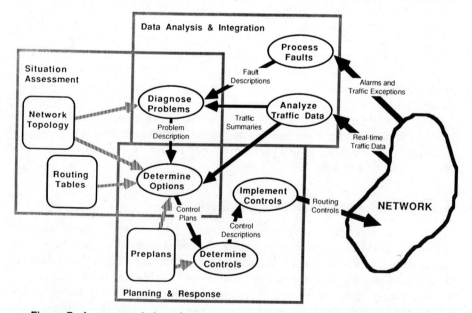

Figure 7. A conceptual view of network management command and control system.

operation and performance. The network owner is now a strategist, orchestrating the decision priorities to meet business objectives.

The other function of the autonomous network is that of advanced service provider. This functionality requires intelligent user interfaces—interfaces that can understand user needs and adjust to their profiles. Other functionalities (and technical issues) related to network services are in providing a variety of services (e.g., transaction, marketing, and computing library), security, and reliability. Network services also draw heavily on advanced database technology.

7. SUMMARY AND CONCLUSIONS

Artificial intelligence offers network management a collection of methods for implementing new services and support tools that have eluded more conventional approaches and that will increase the utility of new networking hardware. AI built into network components will assist network managers and end users to run the system better and to use the services. Expert systems developed in the past few years have demonstrated the feasibility of intelligent network concepts. Responding to this, almost every major telecommuications company has efforts developing new support systems using AI techniques. Research laboratories, both industrial and university, are extending the techniques available for network management applications.

Can there be an autonomous network or network without a central control center? By relinquishing a central control, can a nonhierarchical network generate and control communication between its intelligent nodes and provide a quality communication facility? Can a communication network control itself effectively using its own intelligence? Where is the limit? There are interesting questions whose answers will emerge through further research. For now, integration of expert systems in network management and operations is paving the way for more reliable, functionally rich, and intelligent networks.

REFERENCES

1. G. Martins, AI: The Technology that Wasn't, *Defense Electronics*, pp. 56–59, December 1986.
2. D. Prerau, Selection of an Appropriate Domain for an Expert System, *AI Magazine*, Vol. 6, No. 2, pp. 26–30, Summer 1985.
3. P. Zeldin, F. Miller, E. Siegfried, and J. Wright, Knowledge Based Loop Maintenance: The ACE System, *ICC'86*, pp. 1241–1243, June 1986.
4. D. Prerau, A. S. Gunderson, R. E. Reinke, and S. K. Goyal, The COMPASS Expert System: Verification, Technology Transfer, and Expansion. In *Second Conference on Artificial Intelligence Applications*, pp. 597–602, IEEE, Washington, D.C., 1985.
5. J. Brossier, B. Faller, A. Fron, G. Garcia, and P. Kirsch, "A Communication Network Trouble-Shooting Expert System. In *International Communications Conference*, pp. 1238–1240, IEEE, Washington, D.C., 1986.
6. L. Mantleman, AI Carves Inroads: Network Design, Testing, and Management, *Data Communications*, pp. 106–123, July 1986.

7. S. Guattery and F. Villarreal, NEMESYS: An Expert System for Fighting Congestion in the Long Distance Network, *Expert Systems in Government,* IEEE, October 1985.

8. M. Thandasseri, Expert Systems Application for TXE4A Exchanges, *Electrical Communication,* Vol. 60, No. 2, 1986.

9. K. Macleish, S. Theidke, and D. Vennergrund, Expert Systems in Central Office Switch Maintenance, *IEEE Communications Magazine,* Vol. 24, No. 9, September 1986.

10. Y. Reddy and S. Uppuluri, Intelligent Systems Technology in Network Operations Management, *ICC'86,* pp. 1220–1224, June 1986.

11. J. Hannan, Network Solutions Employing Expert Systems, *Phoenix Computers and Communications Conference (PCCC-87),* pp. 543–547, IEEE, Washington, D.C., 1987.

12. D. Chuang and S. Gross, Telecommunications Resource Allocation: A Knowledge-Based System, *Expert Systems in Government,* IEEE, pp. 666–675, 1985.

13. M. Sutter, The Smart Project: An Approach to Expert System Integration and Evaluation in the BOCs,'' *ICC'86,* pp. 1230–1232, June 1986.

14. P. Benson, Artificial Intelligence Assisted Packet Radio Connectivity, *Electrical Communication,* Vol. 60, No. 2, November 1986.

15. G. Jakobson, C. Lafond, E. Nyberg, and G. Piatetsky-Shapiro, An Intelligent Database Assistant with Expert System Capabilities, *IEEE Expert,* Vol. 1, No. 2, pp. 65–78, 1986.

16. G. Vesonder, et al., ACE: An Expert System for Telephone Cable Maintenance. In *8th International Joint Conference on Artificial Intelligence,* pp. 116–121, AAAI, Menlo Park, CA, 1983.

17. J. Kolodner, R. Simpson, Jr., and K. Sycara-Cyranski, A Process Model of Case-Based Reasoning in Problem Solving, In *Proceedings IJCAI-85,* AAAI, Menlo Park, CA, 1985.

18. S. Goyal and L. Kopeikina, The Evolution of Intelligent Network, ICC '87 Workshop on the Integration of Expert Systems into Network Operations, June 11–12, 1987, Seattle, WA.

19. V. Lesser and D. Corkill, Functionally Accurate, Cooperative Distributed Systems, *IEEE Transactions on Man, Systems, and Cybernetics,* Vol. 11, No. 2, pp. 24–33, January 1981.

20. S. Chang, H. Chen, L. Leung, L. Liang, and G. Stefanek, "An Intelligent Message Management System," ICC'85, pp. 842–847.

21. J. Harvey, "ESSAI Expert Systems Toolkit," *Electrical Communications,* Vol. 60, No. 2, pp. 109–114, 1986.

22. J. Rosenschein, "Rational Interactions: Cooperation Among Intelligent Agents," Ph.D. dissertation, Stanford University, Stanford, CA, October 1985.

23. R. Smith and R. Davis, "Frameworks for Cooperation in Distributed Problem Solving," *IEEE Transactions on Systems, Man, and Cybernetics,* Vol. 11, No. 1, pp. 61–70, January 1981.

24. S. Goyal and R. Worrest, "Expert Systems in Network Maintenance and Management," *ICC'86,* pp. 1225–1229, June 1986.

EXPERT SYSTEMS DEVELOPMENT: THE ACE SYSTEM

Jon R. Wright, John E. Zielinski, and Elizabeth M. Horton

AT&T Bell Laboratories, Liberty Corner, New Jersey

1. INTRODUCTION

In this chapter, we describe Automated Cable Expertise (ACE), a knowledge-based system that assists telephone company engineers in maintaining the local loop. ACE began at AT&T Bell Laboratories in 1981 as an applied research project, became a development project in the fall of 1983, and has been commercially available since September 1985. ACE has been through all stages of software development—prototype, experiment, field test, deployment, and product maintenance. It continues to be enhanced and extended at the direction of its user community.

By almost any measure, ACE is a successful application of AI (artificial intelligence). It is a mature system by expert system standards and has a large, enthusiastic, and growing user population. Because ACE has been through all phases of software development, we are in a position to comment on the life cycle of an expert systems project, how it differs from or is similar to the life cycle of other software projects.

ACE is not a typical expert system. Unlike, for example, MYCIN [1] or MOLGEN [2], ACE is not a consultant. It is probably best described as an *automatic* or *background* analysis system. Its chief distinguishing feature is that it interacts with a conventional database system called Cable Repair Administrative System (CRAS) that maintains records on maintenance activities in the local telephone loop. Telephone company engineers use CRAS to locate trouble spots in the local loop, to forecast work force requirements and to drive plant rehabilitation decisions. ACE emulates the activities of an experienced engineer or manager working with CRAS to uncover maintenance problems and then summarizes its findings for a human user.

Before ACE, human experts analyzed local loop problems using the CRAS report generation language and standardized CRAS reports. A complete analysis of the geographical areas over which a single engineer was responsible was very time consuming as well as tedious. ACE relieves the human expert of much of the paperwork and think time needed for a complete geographical analysis of local loop maintenance, while at the same time giving the expert a significant amount of control over the operation of the program.

The system is not interactive in the sense of most expert consulting systems. Rather, it takes over a portion of the human expert's job as its own, does its best to proceed without intervention by the user, and reports back to the user when serious problems are uncovered. This has led to our view of the system as a *background data analyzer*.

ACE's independent nature has proved to be an important selling point for the system. It takes over an area of responsibility with which the human expert no longer need be concerned. Its performance is sufficiently effective so that human experts never have the desire to reanalyze ACE results. In fact, within the narrow domain it addresses, ACE is probably much superior to that of any human analyzer simply because it is more persistent and complete than any person could hope to be.

ACE has both monitoring functions and diagnostic functions. Although the time scale is greatly slowed down with respect to most monitoring systems, the system keeps track of repair activity in the local loop by studying repair records and alerts users when serious problems are found.

On the other hand, ACE does not stop with simply notifying its users that a problem exists. Accompanying each notification is a classification or diagnosis of the problem along with detailed evidence from the CRAS system that supports its conclusions. As much as possible, ACE tries to assemble all the key information about a local loop problem into one package. This package of information has proved useful not only to the human analyzers but also to a variety of people in local loop maintenance.

ACE's programming techniques were originally modeled after those used by R1/XCON, Digital Equipment Corporation's computer configuration program reported by McDermott [3]. Although the problem domain of ACE appears fundamentally different from that of R1, there are enough common characteristics of both domains to suggest that a program organization similar to R1 is also suitable for ACE. As it turns out, the problem of locating maintenance problems in the local loop is mainly one of locating a few critical patterns among many database records. Consequently, many of the design decisions faced in the development of ACE were guided by the methods used in R1/XCON.

The main type of program organization used by ACE is the *production system*. The ACE production systems are written in a special LISP-based language called OPS4 [4]. OPS4 is one of a family of production system languages; others are OPS5 [5] and OPS83 [6], which are faster with improved debugging environments. However, OPS4 is a highly extensible language, and the project has a considerable investment in language extensions. Whereas R1/XCON was reworked in OPS5 when it became available, ACE is still an OPS4-based system, partly because of the importance of retaining ACE's OPS4 extensions.

Like R1/XCON, ACE uses a *forward-chaining* production system architecture and the *match* problem-solving paradigm [7]. Match is a good method of organizing a production system when the overall problem can be broken cleanly into subproblems and the subproblems do not interact. Each subproblem can therefore be solved independently and the results assembled into a complete solution. The problem space of analyzing loop maintenance records fits these requirements well.

ACE is not just one production system, rather it is a collection of production systems each of which is somewhat independent of the others. In this respect, ACE followed the lead of the human experts who had several different methodologies for accomplishing their job and tended to think of each method as a separate task. All the production systems use forward chaining and match and have a similar subproblem organization. They differ mainly in the specific knowledge each of them encodes.

A production rule architecture is so frequently adopted for expert systems that their complexity is often described in terms of the number of production rules. ACE currently has about 500 production rules and probably should be classed as a medium-scaled expert system.

The most unique feature of ACE is the use of an external database, CRAS, as a source of data. ACE is fundamentally an intelligent interface to the CRAS system. As a side effect of the actions taken by the ACE production systems, database queries are sent to CRAS and loop maintenance records are received in return. The ACE production rules use these records to infer patterns in the mass of repair activity taking place in the local loop. Users need to know little about the CRAS query language and they need to review only the critical records presented to them by ACE.

The importance of this service to local loop maintenance should not be underestimated. The geographical areas for which individual loop engineers are responsible are quite large—covering many square miles—and every engineer has thousands of maintenance records to be tracked and analyzed each month. Without ACE, even the best experts get lost in the amount of data that must be handled. ACE can analyze virtually every maintenance problem within a user's area of responsibility and provide updated reports daily. This capability is unmatched by any human expert.

Most efforts to merge AI techniques and database systems are mainly aimed at providing a natural language or a logical interface in place of a standard query language (e.g., see Kellog [8]). This can be viewed as an attempt to bringing the database query language closer to the actual language used by experts in the application domain.

ACE, on the other hand, bypasses the need for the user to be concerned with database queries. It has encoded knowledge about the application domain beyond the CRAS query language and uses this knowledge to assemble and package data in a form meaningful and useful to loop maintenance experts. In a sense, ACE itself is a user of the CRAS database system and could be described as representative or agent of a human expert specializing in CRAS database analysis. In the hands of a sophisticated user, it is a potent productivity enhancer, allowing the best loop engineers to take on more responsibility and new tasks.

2. SOME ACE HISTORY

We think of ACE as having passed through three stages. The first was a prototype stage in which ACE existed only for demonstration and discussion within AT&T Bell Laboratories. Next was an experimental stage in which the prototype was tested in field conditions. Finally, ACE underwent a significant transformation in a project stage on the road to becoming a genuine software product. Secure communications, a user interface, management of the conclusions and results it produced, administrative functions, and substantial rule base enhancements were all completed in this last stage.

The prototype versions of ACE were written in Franz LISP [9] and the OPS4 production system language and ran under the UNIX* operating system. There was one production system of about 100 rules. The CRAS database system resided on the same computer as ACE so that communication problems between the two systems were minimized.

The ACE prototype was developed by one person with the help of several consultants, both internal and external to AT&T Bell Laboratories. The use of consultants was instrumental in getting the prototype working and establishing credibility for the project. It also gave time for others who assumed ultimate responsibility for ACE to gain valuable experience. Time from conception to a working prototype was approximately 1 year.

After feasibility of the system had been sufficiently demonstrated, an experiment was arranged with telephone company users at several outside locations. A CRAS database was still maintained on the ACE machine, located at AT&T Bell Laboratories, and there were special arrangements to send live database updates overnight from the user's local CRAS machine to ACE. ACE processed these data and then sent conclusions or results to end users at remote locations via electronic mail. ACE developers managed the database updates and monitored the ACE system daily. The entire process was managed with UNIX shell utilities written and revised as the need arose.

This experimental ACE is roughly the system whose architecture was reported in the early ACE papers [10]. It demonstrated the feasibility of AI applications and received very high marks from the end-user community. When the initial ACE experiments were completed, ACE had become such a significant part of the user's workday that the experimental sites requested arrangements for continued ACE support. ACE, in that early configuration, continued to run in these experimental sites for several years.

The ACE field experiments were fundamental in shaping the future of the proj-

---

*UNIX is a registered trademark of AT&T Bell Laboratories.

ect. Most of the work on ACE since that time, in one way or another, has been based on ideas formulated during the field experiments. One of the key decisions coming out of that period was to relocate ACE from a centralized computer center to the office of the end user. The prevailing view on the project at that time was that each ACE system would be customized to the decision methodology of an individual user.

It also became clear during the experiments that analyzers frequently used different methodologies, sometimes having several active at the same time, depending on the specific problems they experienced in their areas. Furthermore, the experts with whom we worked during the experiment were quick to realize the potential ACE had for automating additional analysis methods, and there were recommendations that ACE accommodate other methods. Once they gained an understanding of expert system technology, they began suggesting new ways in which it might be used—techniques that were not previously part of their cable analysis methods. It was this activity that led to the development of one of the ACE production systems—Pair Transposition Analysis.

In this way, ACE evolved to become a collection of production systems each addressing different problems in the local loop. ACE currently has four production systems, each embodying a different analysis methodology.

We have previously emphasized the gulf between having a working expert system prototype and something that has genuine value for end users [11]. Much of the work during ACE's project stage can be seen as providing the proper support environment for the ACE production systems. Our view is that it has been no less challenging to provide the right support environment than it has been to collect, understand, and encode knowledge about cable analysis in the ACE production systems. In this effort, the UNIX operating system has been fundamental to ACE's success.

Numerous domain experts have been relied on, both inside and outside Bell Laboratories. Reliance on multiple experts raises some difficult issues, such as what to do when experts disagree. Ultimately, conflicts among experts over knowledge issues were resolved by the ACE developers, relying on their own understanding of the application domain.

Typically, during ACE's history one developer assumed the role of principal knowledge engineer. This individual did not write production systems but instead took on the responsibility of learning as much as possible about the application—in effect, becoming a local expert free to consult with the developers. The specialized knowledge provided by our local expert gave us an important perspective during critical choice points on the project.

3. THE APPLICATION DOMAIN

The people for whom the ACE system is targeted are specialists called *cable analyzers* who are responsible for preventive maintenance and rehabilitation in the local loop. The local loop is the part of the telephone network that connects residential or business telephones with a local switching machine. In the simplest case, the local loop is nothing more than a twisted pair of copper wires. However, new technologies such as digital loop carrier systems are making the local loop an increasingly complex domain in which to work. One of ACE's strong points is that its rule base reflects the use of these new technologies.

Considerable resources are dedicated to maintenance of the local loop. It is the most accessible and exposed part of the telephone network and the most likely to suffer deterioration and failure. Maintenance cost is therefore relatively high and, by necessity, there is a significant emphasis on cost control.

Cable analyzers play a key role not only in cost control but also in the general quality of telephone service offered at the local exchange level. Their job is to identify areas of either high maintenance cost or poor telephone service and then order either preventive maintenance or plant rehabilitation to correct the problem.

One of their main weapons in this task is the study and tracking of maintenance records and maintenance trends. At one time, paper records and accounting reports were used by cable analyzers to keep track of maintenance trends in the local loop. These methods have largely been replaced with modern computer database systems. CRAS is one such system that is specialized to handle loop maintenance records for the cable analyzer.

Because database systems provide data in significantly more quantity and detail than the paper record methods they replaced, users are sometimes overwhelmed by the massive amounts of information they are able to generate. A typical cable analyzer, for example, might be responsible for geographical areas large enough to generate 15,000–20,000 maintenance records per month in the local loop. In addition, each CRAS record is a rich source of information, containing a high level of detail about the individual tasks carried out during repair work. Although human assistants are often used, it is difficult for an analyzer to gain the full benefits of the CRAS system because of the sheer volume of information.

Cable analyzers usually have extensive experience in local loop construction and maintenance, and it is experience that distinguishes good from poor or average cable analyzers. In other words, the knowledge these people possess is largely experience as opposed to theory based. Typical analyzers will have 10–20 years experience in loop maintenance.

Although individual analyzers will disagree over some of the finer points, there is actually very little about local loop maintenance that is not well understood. Both the technology and the methods of repair and detection are all quite well documented.

Cable analyzers have available extensive training material—usually in the form of short courses and self-paced manuals. These courses tend to assume that the trainee is already well grounded in loop technology and concentrate on methods of detecting maintenance problems by studying maintenance trends and maintenance records.

Methods or practice documents are an equally good source of domain knowledge on loop maintenance. A methods document describes a standard way of accomplishing a task or a job. For example, there are methods documents describing the way to repair the different kinds of equipment in the local loop. Similarly, there are methods documents for cable analyzers describing different methodologies, the kinds of data that should be studied, and how to extract and arrange these data in a meaningful form.

These training and methods documents are extremely rich sources of information. They are especially useful for imparting the flavor of what it is like to do cable analysis. Figure 1 shows some excerpts from an early training document developed using a case study approach [12]. The references to specific wire centers and districts are from a training database used to teach cable analyzers about CRAS. Ignoring some of the jargon (e.g., code 4s refer to a particular kind of loop repair), there are several important things to note about Figure 1.

First, cable analysis involves studying multiple levels of data, starting fairly high and then proceeding into progressively more detail as the characteristics of the specific problem are unraveled. Figure 1 shows at least three levels—wire centers, geographical areas (geoids), and the specific problem level—but there are follow-up methods used by cable analyzers that could easily add more levels. The analyzers work through these levels in what amounts to a fixed sequence of sub-problems, at first selecting high-level data to pick out likely trouble spots, then using detailed maintenance records to study a geographical location and to identify faulty equipment.

Next, much of the language in Figure 1 is ambiguous. For example, the term *commonality* is poorly defined, yet it is critical in understanding how cable analyzers identify serious problems out of a mass of maintenance records. Any attempt to emulate this process, no matter what programming methods are used, must develop the meaning of such words in significantly more detail than is provided by the training or methods documents. Cable analyzers themselves have difficulty describing what they mean by such words as commonality with any real precision even though they seldom have trouble communicating among themselves. Considerable work on the part of a knowledge engineer is needed to root out what is really meant by the ambiguous language frequently used by experts.

Figure 1 also contains frequent references to time intervals or time variables—long and short time frames, trends, and so on. The occurrence of events (failures in the telephone network) over time is a highly salient attribute of doing cable analysis. Both the frequency and the sequence of repair activities over time is important in the interpretation of maintenance problems.

Finally, because there are never enough resources to cover all the maintenance problems in a geographical area, there is a constant shifting in the focus of attention. This week's most pressing problem may be downgraded because of intervening events; more serious problems may appear in the interim. Cable analyzers are constantly changing their opinions and revising their work schedules. The ability to provide updates on previously issued reports and to give new information on problems as they occur is part of ACE's strong attractiveness to the human experts.

There is no one single methodology for cable analysis. Rather, cable analyzers tend to employ a collection of methods based on what works best for them. The training material in Figure 1 is based on a methodology informally known as *Found*

Case Problem
CODE 4 ANALYSIS (INITIAL)

Situation:

The district is exceeding the year-to-date objective for code 4s. You have been asked to identify the primary causes of the missed objective. Assume that the problem is physical plant and identify specific areas that are candidates for rehabilitation work.

Problems:

1. Find the wire center that has the greatest code4 deviation from year-to-date objective.

2. Obtain a CRAS output report that displays all geoids in any wire center that had 15 or more total code4s for the most recent 6 months.

3. Using the report from problem 2, identify the geographic areas with high numbers of code4s for short time frames (1 month).

4. Using the same report, select the four (4) geographic areas that in your opinion appear to have the worst code4 trend.

5. Obtain a CRAS output report that displays in detail all cable troubles that occurred in the four identified geographic areas during the time period having the heaviest activity.

6. Using the report from problem 5, identify a specific commonality in each of the four geographic areas identified in problem 4.

7. Obtain CRAS reports on a wire center level that shows how each communality affects the year-to-date objective.

8. State your conclusions and recommendations.

Figure 1. Example from a training document on cable analysis.

Trouble Analysis, and there are others. The ACE software organization, as we shall see, tends to reflect this fact.

Using the taxonomy of problem domains described by Stefik et al. [13], we classify the telephone cable maintenance problem in the following way:

- The large volumes of data are temporally based. Cable analysis is based on the interpretation of data that is essentially failures over time.
- The knowledge of the domain is reliable. Loop maintenance is a well-understood topic on which there is no significant disagreement.
- The data are reliable. The CRAS database provides rich detail and is essentially complete for the task.
- There is a fixed sequence of subproblems.
- The subproblems do not interact.

4. PRODUCTION SYSTEMS AND HOW THEY ARE USED BY ACE

The fundamental program organization used by the ACE system is the *production system*. Production systems are generally thought of as having three major components: a collection of production rules sometimes called *production memory*, a global database often referred to as *working memory* (not to be confused with the CRAS database), and a *control system* of some sort.

Each production rule has a left-hand side and a right-hand side. The left-hand side is a description of elements that may or may not be present in working memory. The right-hand side is a description of either a simple or compound operation on working memory. Legal operations are additions, deletions, and updates to working memory. A right-hand side may also contain various side effects such as input–output operations.

If the description on the left-hand side of a rule is satisfied—in other words, the conditions represented by the left-hand side are present in working memory—then that rule is said to become eligible to fire. When a rule fires, the operations described on its right-hand side are performed on the elements in working memory. The resulting changes to working memory may cause new rules to become eligible to fire and may disqualify others.

More than one OPS4 production rule may be eligible to fire at any one time. In addition, one rule may have several *instantiations*, meaning that several different sets of working memory elements satisfy the left-hand side of a single rule. The control system determines which rule actually fires and the specific working memory elements it affects through a process known as *conflict resolution*.

Working memory can be thought of as representing the state of the production system. The production system proceeds through a series of states until a solution state is reached, in which case the production system halts. In some cases, temporary data structures and intermediate results of computations are written to working memory to be picked up by other rules in a subsequent state. In fact, rules can only pass information to other rules by writing information to working memory.

ACE is a forward-chaining production system, meaning that the left-hand sides of its production rules are basically the IF part of an IF–THEN rule, and the right-hand sides are the THEN part. In other words, ACE's production rules can be thought of as IF ⟨condition⟩ THEN ⟨action⟩ rules. Because the sequence of rules that fire is controlled by the data present in working memory, writing production rules is sometimes described as *data-driven programming*.

ACE is appropriately described as a *knowledge-based system*, and it is fair to ask where the knowledge in ACE resides. In the main, expert knowledge for ACE is represented by its production rules, although some of ACE's knowledge is represented by data structures kept in working memory.

The production rule base is structured along the lines of the match strategy. In particular, the rules are divided into groups of rules, each group capable of solving one subproblem. Each subproblem is taken on in a fixed sequence. When one subproblem is solved, a transition rule fires that activates a different group of rules to solve the next subproblem. Accompanying a transition to a new subproblem may be a reorganization of or additions to working memory. When all subproblems are solved, they are assembled into an overall solution in a form suitable to communicate to the end user.

A perfectly valid design for production systems is to place data structures representing expert knowledge in working memory [14]. ACE employs no special techniques for representing expert knowledge in working memory such as tables or decision trees. Working memory mostly records the state of the production system and the intermediate results of computations. However, certain kinds of data structures are maintained in working memory. Mainly these are historical records on what ACE has reported or how it has previously interpreted a loop problem. ACE has special rules to extract information from these historical records.

The main requirement for applying the match problem-solving strategy is that there be no interaction among the subproblems. In other words, the outcome of one subproblem cannot affect the solution for another. For ACE, there is never any backtracking to rework a subproblem once it has been solved. Nothing ACE discovers in a later stage ever requires a previous subproblem to be reworked.

At the rule level, the interface to CRAS is quite simple. Some of the ACE rules have side effects that result in queries being sent to the remotely located CRAS system. These records are returned to ACE and placed in working memory. Other ACE rules detect meaningful patterns among the records and report them to the human expert along with an interpretation of the pattern.

5. THE ACE SYSTEM

5.1. System Organization

Figure 2 shows a block diagram of the current ACE architecture showing the major pieces of the system along with the information flow at each point. The ACE

ACE SYSTEM   CRAS SYSTEM

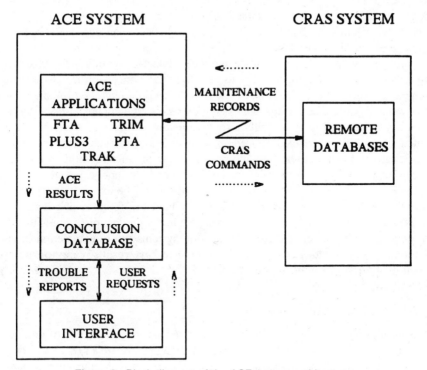

Figure 2. Block diagram of the ACE system architecture.

hardware is a supermicro computer (an AT&T 3B2) running UNIX System V and typically is located in an office environment on the desk of an end user. The users tend to view the ACE system as their personal workstation, and it is typical of them to run other applications when the supermicro is not being used by ACE.

The major feature to notice in Figure 2 is that the CRAS database exists remotely from the ACE system. To do its work, ACE must have some way of gaining access to that database. ACE uses the switched network to log in to the CRAS system just as any user would. Each ACE system has its own CRAS user account. Once logged in, ACE issues queries to the CRAS database and receives in return maintenance records for the local loop. Of course, communications software on each side is required for secure data transmission.

Figure 2 shows five separate applications. Four of them, Found Trouble Analysis (FTA), Trouble Report Improvement Methodology (TRIM), PLUS3, and Pair Transposition Analysis (PTA), are production systems and are written in the OPS4 programming language and Franz LISP. The fifth, TRAK, is a C language application. Although the ACE developers chose to implement TRAK in C, from the user's point of view it is no different from the other ACE application programs. TRAK is commonly referred to as a "production system" by the user community.

The five ACE applications are run in sequence, each of them making use of the link through the switched network to CRAS. When a production system has thoroughly analyzed a problem, it sends results to a repository appropriately called the *Conclusion Database*. ACE uses a relational database manager, UNITY [15], to manage the results it produces.

The final component is a menu-oriented user interface written in the C programming language. The interface accesses results in the Conclusion Database using C language calls to UNITY routines. The ACE users, although comfortable in their own areas of expertise, are far from being experienced computer users. The menu interface has proved to be a highly attractive feature of the ACE system. We have found that a new user, experienced in loop maintenance but never having seen ACE, can sit down at a terminal and become quite productive within a few hours. In our experience, this is unusual for complex computer applications.

ACE usually is scheduled to begin work during off hours, most often at night after the CRAS database is updated. Users also have the option to demand an ACE analysis at any time they desire and can schedule the production systems to run on different days. Together, the ACE production systems run to completion in about 4 hours, which provides enough time for ACE to have results ready for the users when they arrive for work in the morning.

5.2.   The Production Systems

ACE is unusual for an expert system in that it consists of a collection of production systems that are only loosely tied together. Although there are a few cases in which one production system knows about the results of another, the chief means of integrating output for the user is through the menu interface and UNITY database queries. The reasons for this are partly historical, but also because, in the minds of our experts, each represents a conceptually separate methodology.

Although the problem organization of each production system is highly similar, each one has a slightly different perspective on maintenance problems in the local loop. They have different units of analysis, they analyze different classes of data, they have different pruning heuristics, and they encode different kinds of knowledge.

FTA is an enhanced version of the first ACE production system. In one form or another, FTA has been in active use by cable analyzers since mid-1982. It currently has about 225 rules, which cover comprehensively the different kinds of problems analyzers see in the local loop. FTA can diagnose problems in about 60 categories of local loop equipment.

The chief concept underlying FTA is known as the *trouble block* or *trouble cluster*. FTA attempts to locate all instances where maintenance jobs have been issued on what appears to be a common problem in the local loop. This happens more often than one might think. In many cases, where the emphasis is on returning service to an out of service customer, telephone companies prefer short-term techniques that work around serious problems in the network, as opposed to fixing them outright through lengthy repairs. The trick is not to let such short-term repairs get out of hand.

In associating common cause trouble, FTA adjusts its unit of analysis depending on the nature of the data with which it is working. In some cases, this may be a particular piece of equipment in the local loop, it may be a geographical area, or it may be a specific street address. For example, problems might be spread across a series of cable terminals located on the same run of cable. This would be likely to appear in FTA as a cluster of cable terminal problems all with the same street name, but with nearby address numbers. However, if the cable run cuts across several streets, the problems would not have a common street name. Still, FTA might be able to locate the problem through the use of CRAS geographical identifiers, which sometimes can narrow problems down to a small area.

TRIM refers to a highly comprehensive collection of formalized methods used by cable analyzers. The TRIM production system is actually an implementation of only part of the TRIM methodology known as TRIM phase I. Like FTA, TRIM is quite comprehensive in that it is geared to find most maintenance problems that might crop up in the local loop. It currently consists of about 190 production rules. In a sense, TRIM is a competitor to FTA. Human experts seem to prefer either FTA or TRIM: it is unusual for them to use both. A TRIM production system was the first major enhancement requested by the user community.

The TRIM methodology was formalized a few years before ACE came into being. It is, to some extent, a common language for cable analyzers in different parts of the country, something everyone can relate to and understand. It is also a more rigid methodology than FTA, relying on a unit of analysis—the 100 pair cable complement—that was chosen partly because it made conventional database reports easy to write. Nevertheless, the methodology caused something of a revolution in loop repair. ACE has a rather faithful rendition of TRIM, staying as close as possible to the methodology as defined in the formal documents.

The core concept underlying TRIM is known as *not-found trouble*. Some trouble reports (usually initiated by customers) are closed without a technician ever having made a repair; some troubles are simply intermittent in nature. If test equipment or on-site inspection shows that nothing is wrong, the report may be closed without action. In other cases, customers may still have telephone service problems even after one or more attempts to repair faulty equipment. Both kinds of situations fall into the *not-found trouble* category. TRIM is based on the idea that clusters of these not-found troubles will lead an analyzer to chronic and difficult service problems. Once an area with high numbers of not-found troubles has been identified, TRIM prescribes study methods to determine the underlying cause. These study methods frequently entail on-site inspections of the suspect cable plant.

Both TRIM and FTA are very much oriented toward problems that are likely to cut across many different customers. For example, problems in a cross connect box (a type of loop equipment) or a digital loop carrier device are quite likely to affect several customers. FTA and TRIM are rather insensitive to problems that affect only a single customer. It sometimes happens, however, that problems are localized to a single customer.

PLUS3 is actually a part of the TRIM methodology that was selected for implementation as a separate production system. PLUS3 has a substantially different approach to cable analysis. For one thing, the basic unit of analysis for PLUS3 is the individual customer. A PLUS3 analysis is triggered by repeated customer complaints, and the production system has rules geared toward the special problems of single customers.

PLUS3 goes into action when a customer calls the telephone company repeatedly to report service problems, and nothing is fixed as a result. Such reports are referred to as *not-fixed troubles* by cable analyzers. Not-fixed troubles most frequently occur when test gear used to analyze the electrical state of the loop finds no fault on the customer's line. Problems related to transmission noise, although they represent real service problems, may have this characteristic. In a real sense, PLUS3 is a monitor and analyzer of the quality of service given to the individual telephone customer.

Records of each not-fixed customer report are kept by the telephone companies in a large database that is available to ACE through the CRAS system. Normally, three reports are required, but PLUS3 can be set to analyze problems that show only two reports. PLUS3 analyzes these conditions and reports to the user its results along with a summary of related repair work obtained from the TRIM production system.

PTA was not a formalized methodology before ACE. Rather, it was an idea that occurred to one of our experts during the ACE experiment. It was at least partly inspired by the capabilities demonstrated by the FTA production system. The idea proved to be useful enough to become a production system in its own right. It is especially interesting in that it represents something that probably would not have been possible in the manual environment that preceded ACE.

Cable analyzers often remark that many cable failures do not take place all at once. Instead, they occur slowly over a period of many months, failing a line at a time. The reasoning behind this remark is that the technology used to construct modern telephone cables is capable of functioning under extremely adverse conditions. For example, in the not so distant past, penetration of a buried cable sheath allowing water to enter would cause a sudden disaster, putting many telephone customers out of service. However, new methods of insulating individual telephone lines inside the cable sheath enable the telephone cable to continue functioning for long periods of time even under the worst conditions. Although this is a highly desirable attribute, it presents a difficult detection problem for cable analyzers, since the pattern of failures in such a cable may occur slowly over many months.

Except for emergency conditions, repair technicians typically work around a bad section of buried cable, putting the customer back in service by using a variety of short-cut methods, one of which is called a pair transposition, which bypasses the bad section by using a second cable pair. Pair Transposition Analysis monitors such repairs, allowing the analyzer to determine when the situation may be out of hand and helping to determine when a replacement should be scheduled. PTA makes heavy use of ACE's street address matching capabilities, since street address is frequently the only common thread in this kind of analysis.

The final ACE application is called TRAK, and it is a C language application, not a production system. However, it clearly belongs in this section as one of ACE's core applications. If ACE does its job effectively, plant rehabilitation projects are identified, scheduled, and worked. Many rehabilitation projects may be ongoing at any one time, and many others may be scheduled for work in the near future. TRAK, as the name suggests, keeps track of the various loop rehabilitation projects, when they are scheduled for completion, and, to some extent, what effect they have on maintenance cost and servce. It has proved to be a highly effective way for the ACE users to understand the impact of their efforts, how ACE is helping them, and most importantly, how they can improve. It is an important part of ACE and is a useful complement to the ACE production systems.

5.3. Subproblem Organization

Each of the four production systems has a very similar subproblem organization. Table 1 shows the main stages through which each production system proceeds. The stages correspond to the structuring of rules following the match problem-solving strategy. There are supporting functions written in LISP that help improve performance and cut down on the number of rules needed to solve each subproblem. One of the main objectives of writing supporting LISP code has been to keep the OPS4 rules as close as possible to the knowledge as expressed by human experts.

ACE works by first examining the flow of trouble reports on a daily basis. High-level data are collected from CRAS and integrated with records kept from previous days. After irrelevant records are filtered from the input, these data are used to select areas for detailed analysis. Then the appropriate detailed records are drawn from CRAS and analyzed to produce a trouble diagnosis.

ACE uses different search methods in different subproblem areas. In effect, the search of the CRAS database is exhaustive. However, heuristic methods are used in other phases of the program. For example, the production systems have their own thresholds that determine when an outside plant problem should be studied, thus pruning the number of cases that a production system must consider. Also, ACE does not exhaustively consider every possible solution for an identified problem.

Stage six, the stage in which trouble diagnosis is performed, deserves a few additional comments. There are essentially three things that ACE tries to provide

TABLE 1 Subproblem Organization for an ACE Production System

Stage	Description
High-level query	A block of new records is requested from CRAS
Filter stage	Irrelevant data are filtered from input
Assimilation stage	Filtered data are merged with historical records on loop maintenance
Detection stage	Trouble conditions are detected in the updated records
Specific data queries	Detailed CRAS data are requested
Diagnostic stage	Trouble conditions are diagnosed from specific CRAS data
Report assembly	Findings with supporting data are assembled for users

in a diagnosis. First, ACE attempts to cluster together all records related to a single problem in the loop for confirmation by the human expert. Second, it tries to determine a physical location for the underlying trouble—usually a street address. Third, ACE attempts to identify the type of loop equipment involved and makes a guess at a cause for the trouble.

Each of these aspects of trouble in the network is quite difficult and complicated by the fact that address information in CRAS is entered in a free textual format. One collection of rules is solely concerned with determining whether two addresses such as *WASH & 5* and WASHINGTON AND FIFTH might refer to the same address.

5.4. Support Modules

Surprisingly enough, the language of choice for an ACE developer is C. C programs account for slightly more than 50% of all the code written for ACE. Another 20–25% of ACE code is written in shell or some other UNIX software tool such as awk or sed. Only about 20% of the ACE system is actually written in LISP or OPS4. The reason is that the core ACE applications require various support modules to function without a sophisticated user. Because ACE is based on the UNIX operating system, these support modules are written using a variety of UNIX software tools—as is appropriate for any software application based on the UNIX operating system.

There is a relatively clean division between the ACE support modules and the application programs. The support modules and utilities are written in either the C language or some UNIX software tool, while the applications are LISP and OPS4 programs. TRAK, as a C language application program, is the one major exception. This has been an effective way of organizing the ACE system since it allows each module to be written in a language that fits its function the best. In particular, the UNIX operating system provides a strong base for developing and testing the support modules.

ACE is basically a single user system located in the office of an end user that knows little about computers. We expect the user to be able to log in to his or her system, start up the user interface, and follow the menu selections. We feel this is a reasonable assumption since we want the user to concentrate on the application domain—that is, be an expert in loop maintenance as opposed to being an expert in the use of the UNIX operating system. This one fact has had a truly significant effect on the ACE project. Much of the work done on ACE has been aimed at making the system friendly and easy to use, without requiring sophisticated administration.

Table 2 shows the major software modules for the project, the language in which each is written, and a brief description of their functions. The *Scheduler* is a C program that organizes and coordinates an ACE run. The Scheduler knows when to invoke each ACE production system, when to establish communications with CRAS, when to terminate CRAS communications, and so on. It also takes steps to ensure that the various ACE applications do not interfere with one another.

TABLE 2   Major Support Modules for the ACE Production Systems

Module	Language	Function
Scheduler	C language	Management and coordination of application programs
Hygiene	UNIX system command language, C language	Administration of critical application files
Sanity	C language	Administration of UNIX system resources
Digester	UNIX system command language, UNITY	Database processing for Conclusion Database
Rex	C language	ACE to CRAS communications
Utilities	UNIX system command language, C language	Administrative tasks, status reports, error message interpretation, etc.
ACE applications	LISP, OPS4, C language	FTA, TRIM, PLUS3, PTA, and TRAK modules

Hygiene and *Sanity* are ACE's two main administrative programs. Hygiene performs many administrative functions on behalf of both the user and the ACE application, such as trimming log files, checking for electronic mail, and file cleanup. Sanity examines the status of various UNIX system resources such as free file space and checks on the integrity of various critical and mandatory files. Sanity has modes specific to each application, and these modes are called before a production system is permitted to proceed.

CRAS to ACE communications are managed by *Rex (Remote execution)*. Rex has the job of establishing communications over the switched network and uses a protocol similar to *uucp** to ensure secure communications. It does a good job of handling the many exigencies of CRAS communications. For example, under extremely noisy conditions, Rex will automatically seek a clean line, and it will survive unexpected CRAS down time without allowing the ACE applications to become affected.

ACE logs in at the beginning of a run and maintains that link until CRAS data are no longer needed. The profile of an ACE session is bursty, like that of a real user—and also like a real user, the queries have a dynamic character. It is impossible to predict beforehand precisely the sequence of commands ACE will send over the CRAS link. ACE requests some data, analyzes it for periods ranging from a few seconds to several minutes, then requests additional data based on the outcome of that analysis.

Each production system starts off with a rather high-level pass over the CRAS database, trying to locate areas that seem to be generating unusual amounts of maintenance activity. When a trouble spot is located, more detailed requests are sent as ACE tries to diagnose the problem and assemble supporting data that the user will want to view a confirmation. The dynamic nature of ACE's interaction with CRAS precludes use of standard UNIX file transmission utilities such as *uucp*.

*UNIX to UNIX Copy Program.

Management of the Conclusion Database is assigned to the *Digester* module. The Digester accepts new results, formats them, and places them in the proper place. The Digester also removes results when they become too old to be interesting and performs various housekeeping duties associated with database management.

There are numerous utilities that report on ACE status, communicate errors, interpret error messages, do backups, and so on. There is no overriding theme to this collection of programs, but they are critical to the success of the project and are quite important to the user's feeling that the system is performing as advertised.

Finally, there are the ACE application modules—the four OPS4 production systems and TRAK. Overall, these applications comprise about 25% of the total system. In other words, about 25% of the system is devoted to its core application, and about 75% is devoted to software that supports the application programs, keeps it running during all reasonable conditions, and communicates its results in a friendly way to the human user.

The 25 : 75 ratio, although surprising to many, is a key point. In particular, it validates our choice of the UNIX operating system as a development base. We rate the UNIX operating system as an especially strong development environment for the ACE support modules, which in the final analysis accounted for most of the development work on the project.

5.5.   ACE Rule Examples

Figure 3 shows English language translations of two ACE-like rules. Although neither rule is used in the current versions of ACE, both were part of the ACE prototypes. They illustrate, at least in a simple way, what programming in a production rule language is like. Both rules are concerned with trouble address matching, a feature that has been a critical part of ACE since the early prototypes. Certain complexities are left out of the examples, but we will point out where the rules would be affected by the added complexity. Both rules in Figure 3 are part of the diagnostic stage.

Because ACE is a forward-chaining system, it is convenient to think of the production rules as IF ⟨condition⟩ THEN ⟨action⟩ rules, where ⟨condition⟩ specifies types of elements in working memory, and ⟨action⟩ specifies something to do to the elements in working memory.

The first rule in Figure 3 is called *TERMINAL__REPAIRS* and it has two condition elements in the IF part of the rule. These are shown as *IF* and *AND__IF* conditions in TERMINAL__REPAIRS. By convention, the first condition element of each ACE rule designates the subproblem of the match strategy on which the production system is working.

All the production systems use the concept of a *trouble block*, which is simply a group of maintenance records that are related to a common problem in the outside plant. The second element, the AND__IF part of TERMINAL__REPAIRS, indicates another condition of the rule that requires a majority of the records in the trouble block to be of type *terminal repairs*, of which there are about ten subtypes or subcategories.

FIND_TERMINAL_ADDRESS

IF
    the subproblem is trouble_block_diagnosis

AND_IF
    most of the work in the trouble block
    was of type terminal_repairs.

THEN
    find the common_trouble_address

TROUBLE_ADDRESS_1

IF
    the subproblem is trouble_block_diagnosis

AND_IF
    the subgoal is find a common_trouble_address

AND_IF
    more than 50% of the repair work in a
    trouble block was at the same street address

THEN
    make that address the common_trouble_address

Figure 3. English language translations of two ACE rules.

The action or THEN part of TERMINAL__REPAIRS is simple: it merely establishes the subgoal of finding the common trouble address for the trouble block in working memory. Other rules would then be enabled to perform the actual work of finding the common trouble address.

One of these rules, called TROUBLE__ADDRESS__1, is also shown in Figure 3. It represents the simplest case in which a majority of the maintenance records were all done at a single trouble location. This rule has three elements in the IF part: the production system must be in the diagnostic stage, the diagnostic rules must have established the subgoal of finding a common trouble address, and the trouble block must have one address occurring in more than 50% of the maintenance records.

The OPS4 code for the TROUBLE__ADDRESS__1 rule is shown in Figure 4. Although we will not go into detail on OPS4, note that even without knowing much about OPS4, it is possible to pick out the main components of the rule. The left-hand side and right-hand side are separated by the $\rightarrow$ symbol. By convention, the first element in a rule description represents the subproblem state—in this case, trouble block diagnosis. The subgoal is clearly identified as the second element in the rule, and the main condition of the rule is found in the third element. Variables in OPS4 are designated by the use of an $=$ sign preceding a variable name. The construction $\&$ =pat1 in TROUBLE__ADDRESS__1 binds the entire working memory element to the variable =pat1. In the third element, ⟨greater-than⟩ is an OPS4 language extension known as a *left-hand-side function*. For TROUBLE__ADDRESS__1 to become eligible to fire, a *block__addresses* element must be present in working memory indicating that 50% or more of the trouble block addresses are common.

TROUBLE_ADDRESS_1

(

   (diagnose trouble block)

   (find common trouble address) & =pat1

   (block-addresses =block =address (<greater> 50)) & =pat2

   -->

   (<delete> =pat1 =pat2)

   (<add> (common-trouble-address =block =address))

)

Figure 4. OPS4 code for the TROUBLE__ADDRESS__1 rule.

The right side of TROUBLE__ADDRESS__1 accomplishes two things. First, it deletes the working memory elements associated with the subgoal *find common trouble address*. Both the *block__addresses* element and the element representing the subgoal itself are deleted from working memory by the ⟨*delete*⟩ action. Since the subgoal has been accomplished, there is no reason to keep its representation in working memory. Second, the common trouble address for the block being analyzed is recorded in working memory using the ⟨*add*⟩ function. Both ⟨*add*⟩ and ⟨*delete*⟩ are examples of *right-hand-side* functions in OPS4. Right- and left-hand-side functions are the major kinds of language extensions in the OPS4 language.

Although the examples shown in this section are realistic, several important complexities are left out. For example, calculation of a common trouble address and its frequency is no simple achievement. The CRAS database system handles trouble address as a free form narrative field and the users have no standard way of entering address information. About a dozen OPS4 rules as well as some specialized language extensions handle this aspect of the diagnostic subproblem.

5.6.   A Sample ACE Message

Figure 5 shows one of the output messages from the user interface. Although no real data are displayed, Figure 5 is based on a real analysis performed by FTA and is typical of the kind of results produced by FTA. The figure contains too many details and too much telephone company jargon to discuss completely, but we will cover the main points. Most of this section will concentrate on the specifics of FTA, but similar comments could be made about all ACE production systems.

At the top of Figure 5 is a header, showing from which production system the message came, and some general information, such as how many customers have reported problems associated with this item and how many times ACE itself has notified the expert of this particular trouble. *WC* stands for *wire center*, which is best thought of as a building containing telephone switching machines. Typically, telephone cables originating from a wire center have administrative numbers such as 4, 16, 1012, and so on. However, the use of numbers is simply a naming convention and a telephone cable could just as easily be named something like *main street cable*. In the header, ACE reports the trouble to be in wire center 11123, cable 4.

The part of Figure 5 labeled *ACE TROUBLE BLOCK* summarizes the inferences ACE has made about the trouble. ACE gives a brief diagnosis of the problem in the field labeled *ACE's DIAGNOSIS*. In this case, ACE concludes that the problem is *ready access aerial*, meaning a ready access aerial terminal, which is simply a type of equipment where repair technicians can access the actual telephone wires contained in a cable. Although there are some exceptions, an ACE diagnosis is usually an attempt to name the particular type of loop equipment that is faulty.

In the cause field, ACE guesses at a possible cause for the trouble. *Probable craft action* means that a technician, while working in a ready access terminal, probably has damaged the telephone lines of several customers. ACE also attempts to give a location for the trouble—in this case, it gives the street name *northern*

```
ACE TROUBLE MESSAGE  initial  ANALYSIS: fta  WC: 11123   CA: 4

Sun Aug 3 (YEST)  6  SA CTTS ANALYZED AND  0  fta  REPORTS IN PAST  30  DAYS
```

ACE TROUBLE BLOCK

RANGE: 102-193   PERIOD: 06/04/86 TO 08/02/86

DIAGNOSIS: ready access aerial
TR CAUSE: probable craft action   SHEATH: p   INSLN: pc
TROUBLE ADDRESS: northern blvd   GEOID: 413a

DETAILS

PAIR	NEW	DISP	CAUSE	CLRDATE	TN	FNCA	FNPR	ID SRC
102	*	431	145	7/9/86	453-4622			924 SAX

addr: mh rear of 242 central
rmks: open faceplate

| 112 | * | 431 | 600 | 7/10/86 | 453-7832 | | | 931 SAX |

addr: northern blvd p50
rmks: came clear while work was grd

| 154 | * | 431 | 145 | 7/31/86 | 453-9823 | | | 924 COP |

addr: northern blvd p50
rmks: dried insulation

see 11 next lines

previous menu   first ACE menu   copy   help   quit

Figure 5. Sample output from Found Trouble Analysis.

blvd. All inferences are strictly based on the information contained in the CRAS database records. ACE knows essentially nothing about the actual layout of telephone cables.

FTA is capable of giving about 70 different kinds of diagnoses and about 30 different cause interpretations. Although new technology is being introduced into the local loop at a rapid rate, these cover fairly comprehensively the kinds of equipment and most common problems. FTA is probably the most comprehensive, but the other production systems all have a similar capability.

ACE's address matching features are quite important. Local loop records make extensive use of street addresses to name the location of different kinds of loop equipment. Ready access terminals are simply one kind of loop equipment that is recorded by street address. Although ACE uses several different kinds of addresses, the *trouble address* is the most important.

When technicians complete a repair job in the loop, they report the street address where they are working. This address is recorded in the CRAS maintenance record as the *trouble address*. By using the trouble address, ACE can determine when repairs are repeated at the same location and therefore can help the human expert determine when further repair or rehabilitation methods are needed to resolve the underlying problem. Figure 5 shows a trouble that was uncovered by FTA through matching trouble addresses for many CRAS records. All ACE production systems make use of address matching to some extent, although it is especially fundamental to FTA.

The *Details* section shown in Figure 5 gives the supporting information for the inferences reported in the trouble block section. As much as possible, ACE tries to assemble all the important information related to each trouble it uncovers so the analyzer can confirm that ACE's assessment of the situation is correct.

An interesting point about the ACE messages is that they appear to have functions unforeseen by their original designers. For example, ACE messages have proved to be quite useful to repair technicians and their supervisors troubleshooting in the field. First, ACE can often send a repair technician to a specific trouble address, which avoids a lengthy process of sectionalizing or locating a trouble with test equipment and field inspection. Second, ACE gives a report on the type of equipment at fault and a likely cause so that technicians begin with a good notion about what the trouble is. Finally, both field technicians and their supervisors are more correctly able to gauge the seriousness and extent of the problem and thus make better decisions about the appropriate repair strategy.

An ACE analyzer frequently obtains hard copy of an ACE message to send to the technician selected to work on a particularly hard problem. The ACE messages may be supplemented by other information, such as information on insulation testing of the telephone lines involved, but technicians find the messages to be convenient and informative for troubleshooting. In most areas, use of the ACE messages by repair technicians in the field is standard practice.

6. KNOWLEDGE ENGINEERING

ACE does not represent the knowledge of a single expert: rather, we have used many sources of knowledge in building ACE. The main sources have been the following:

1. Textbook knowledge developed from training material and other documents on telephone cable analysis.
2. Expert advice from the developers of CRAS.
3. Expert advice from theoreticians of cable analysis both in AT&T Bell Laboratories and in the local operating companies.
4. Local analysts from the operating companies and users of CRAS, who perform the actual analyses.

In general, the ACE production systems were built by first constructing a skeleton system from whatever textbook knowledge could be obtained. This was sufficient to get a first-cut working prototype established. The developers of CRAS had acquired considerable knowledge about cable analysis, and their comments on the early prototypes were instrumental in getting the ACE prototype off the mark.

One of the important lessons we gained from ACE is that human experts often have a great deal of difficulty describing what they know unless they are provided with some kind of structure. Having a working prototype available early on turned out to be very significant in this regard. In essence, the prototype itself provided the structure the experts needed to begin expressing themselves.

ACE knowledge engineering was very much a case-oriented approach centered around the performance of the prototype. The experts were able to study output from the prototype and found it very natural to describe what they would do differently in specific situations. In general, their remarks were concrete enough for the ACE developers to make adjustments to their programs. There was an iterative nature to the process, with discussions of specific cases followed by a period of modifications to the ACE production systems, then a return to the cases for further elaboration.

Many experts provided input to ACE. Although cable analysis, as previously discussed, is not a highly theoretical discipline, there are some acknowledged theoreticians both inside and outside AT&T Bell Laboratories. These people were either authors or consultants to authors on analysis methods. Some of them ran training centers for cable analysts, and all were quite helpful in ACE knowledge engineering. By far the most valuable resources for ACE knowledge engineering, however, were the actual practitioners of cable analysis. They were closest to the real-world problems ACE was trying to address and gave us the best insights into what cable analysis was all about.

The use of multiple experts raises the issue of what to do when experts disagree. In general, there have been few cases on the project in which experts had outright disagreements over knowledge issues. This is at least partly due to the fact that cable analysis is a rather well-understood discipline. In each instance where there was such disagreement, the ACE developers tried to understand the underlying issues and then proceeded to make their own decisions. To the extent that the project has been clear in describing its rationale and the users have been made to understand what ACE is doing in these special cases, this method of settling disputes has been well accepted by our user community. Expert disagreement, then, has not been a troublesome issue for the ACE project.

However, we have found considerable variability in the kinds of loop problems encountered across geographical areas. There has been a desire on the part of many ACE users to have what are essentially local rules tailored to the special problems in their areas. Although this has nothing to do with having disagreeing experts, it has a similar impact. Completely resolving the issue would require each user to have their own rules for local customization. Thus far, the problem has been handled satisfactorily by rooting out the kinds of local customization that are desired and designing options directly into the ACE software. Additional methods of providing local customization may be needed in the future.

7. DISCUSSION

The key to understanding ACE is its relation to CRAS. Unlike many other expert systems, ACE is not a consultant, and it is not truly interactive—features that most expect to be present in an expert system. ACE does not require these features largely because of its relation to CRAS. ACE is a *background data analyzer* for the human experts, working independently, retrieving data when needed, and reporting only when a serious problem in the local loop has been uncovered. Part of ACE's attractiveness to the users is that it significantly reduces the complexity of their work environment without consuming much of their time.

ACE does not continuously interpret signals, nor does it work in real time: basically, the time critical aspects of the ACE problem space are minimal. Nevertheless, ACE does serve some genuine monitoring functions for local loop maintenance. At least part of the reason why ACE is able to provide a true monitoring function without facing difficult time critical aspects is that the time scale of the application is greatly slowed down compared to most monitoring systems. The plant rehabilitation projects resulting from ACE's analyses require preparation that may take several weeks. Beyond that, the job itself may require as long as a week to complete. One might compare this response environment to that required of process control or patient monitoring [16]. In the ACE time scale, a monitoring system that wakes up and scans a database once a day is adequate.

The ACE project has also been fortunate in that the knowledge base has been relatively stable. By and large, the ACE rules have required little modification. Most of the changes have fallen into the category of enhancements, such as providing certain local customization features, better street address matching, and so on. Maintenance of the knowledge base has therefore not been a very serious issue for ACE. ACE's success is partly the result of the selection of an application that fits very well the state of the art in AI.

By and large, our orientation is applications development, and therefore we tend to evaluate technical issues in terms of their impact on the end user. Nevertheless, it is instructive to consider if there is anything fundamentally different about ACE when compared with other software systems.

ACE is really part of a network of computer systems built by AT&T Bell Laboratories to support local loop maintenance [17]. Like ACE, these systems are highly customized software systems. Some of these systems do jobs similar to ACE but have been built without explicitly using expert system methods. For example, the Predictor system [18] processes messages generated by switching machines that suggest trouble in the local loop. The amount of data generated by a switch is surprisingly large, far more than a human analyzer could hope to comprehend all at once. Predictor proceeds through a series of stages, roughly corresponding to the steps human analyzers use, in the process of bringing the total message mass down to a few critical pieces of information that a person can understand and act on. This bears at least a superficial similarity to the organization of an ACE production system.

An important difference between Predictor and ACE is that ACE uses specific techniques for encoding and organizing what is known about its application domain. It is possible to isolate in ACE specific chunks of code that represent knowledge about cable analysis. Although we feel two systems have a similar impact on the user, ACE goes significantly farther in emulating the activities of a human expert simply because the organization of its application programs permits it to do so. The rule representation used by ACE for the purposes of emulating human experts is inherently more understandable and more modifiable than traditional ways of organizing application programs.

These comments reflect our underlying feeling that there are many similarities between expert systems and so-called conventional or traditional methods of software development.* Most of the development for ACE, if measured by lines of code, is in fact conventional in nature. We expect this to be a common experience as AI becomes viable for a broader range of computer applications. Making the core application work is only part of the job of building a working software system.

Looking back on the experience, ACE has been managed principally the same as other software projects with which we are familiar. Requirements specification, use of design documents, design reviews, and other techniques of software engineering have had important roles in the project. Our perception of similarity between the life cycles of conventional software and expert systems is so strong that we frequently find it more economical to comment on the ways they differ.

One important difference is that while working on an expert systems project, one is more willing to admit not knowing exactly what to do in the early stages of a project. Consequently, there is planned overlap between requirements and development simply because the character of the application domain is not fully clear until someone designs software in sufficient detail to model it. There is also a trial-and-error aspect to knowledge engineering. Experts cannot always tell you what they know in precise terms, but they generally know if something is right or wrong when they see it in action.

These characteristics heavily favor the use of prototypes as a means of seeking out and refining the expert's notion of how a system should perform and what it should do. The development process therefore tends to have a bottom-up flavor as opposed to the top-down methods implied by following a staged requirements-specifications–development model. The use of prototypes allows the interaction between a domain expert and a real working system to clarify requirements where they are hazy or poorly articulated. In the current state of the art, prototyping methods appear to be the style of choice for expert systems development.

8. PRESENT STATUS

The first ACE software generic was released in September 1985, and a second software generic was made available in December 1986. As of this writing, there

---

*We use these words guardedly with the understanding that much software development for the UNIX system, while not AI related, can hardly be described as traditional or conventional.

are 40 ACE systems deployed in six of the seven Regional Bell Operating Companies. ACE is still a growing project, and its potential impact goes beyond the specific numbers cited here. Users have been quick to recognize the potential of this technology and there have been plenty of good ideas on possible enhancements and extensions to ACE.

ACKNOWLEDGMENTS

Many people have contributed to the success of the ACE project. About ten people have been members of the ACE development team off and on since the project's inception in 1981—although the developers seldom numbered more than four at any one time. The project has been fortunate to have had so many people who kept the needs of the project as their first priority and who really cared for its success. Of course, ACE would not have been possible without the many subject matter experts in the local operating telephone companies who gave their time to educate us about cable analysis. Support by our line of management, especially in the early days when the ACE project was risky and vulnerable, has been no less important. Most of all, we owe a debt to Gregg Vesonder, who conceived the project, did the original research on which it is based, and guided it through prototype and experimental stages.

REFERENCES

1. E. H. Shortliffe, *Computer Based Medical Consultations: MYCIN*, American Elsevier, New York, 1976.
2. M. Stefik, Planning with Constraints (MOLGEN Part 1). *Artificial Intelligence*, Vol. 16, pp. 141–169, 1980.
3. J. McDermott, R1: The Formative Years, *AI Magazine*, Vol. 2, pp. 21–29, 1981.
4. C. L. Forgy, *The OPS4 User's Manual*, Technical Rept. CMU-CS-79-182, Computer Science Department, Carnegie–Mellon University, Pittsburgh, PA, 1979.
5. C. L. Forgy, *The OPS5 User's Manual*, Technical Rept. CMU-CS-81-135, Computer Science Department, Carnegie–Mellon University, Pittsburgh, PA, 1981.
6. C. L. Forgy, *The OPS83 User's Manual*, Production Systems Technologies, Pittsburgh, PA, 1986.
7. A. Newell, Heuristic Programming: Ill-Structured Problems. In *Progress in Operations Research*, Vol. 3, A. Aronofsky (ed.), pp. 360–414, Wiley, New York, 1969.
8. C. Kellog, Knowledge Management: A Practical Amalgam of Knowledge Base and Database Technology, *AAAI-82*, pp. 306–309, 1982.
9. J. K. Foderaro, *The Franz LISP Manual*, Computer Science Department, University of California, Berkeley, 1979.
10. G. T. Vesonder, S. J. Stolfo, J. E. Zielinski, F. D. Miller, and D. H. Copp, ACE: An Expert System for Telephone Cable Maintenance, *IJCAI*, Vol. 8, pp. 116–120, 1983.
11. J. R. Wright and E. M. Siegfried, ACE: Going from Prototype to Product. In *Expert*

Systems and Knowledge Engineering: Essential Elements of Advanced Information Technology, Thomas Bernold (ed.), pp. 121–131, North-Holland, New York, 1985.

12. *Cable Repair Administrative System—CRAS Analyst Job Aids*, AT&T Standard Training Course—ND 448, 1980.

13. M. Stefik, J. Aikins, R. Balzer, J. Benoit, L. Birnbaum, F. Hayes-Roth, and E. Sacerdoti. The Architecture of Expert Systems. In *Building Expert Systems*, F. Hayes-Roth, D. A. Waterman, and D. B. Lenat (eds.), pp. 89–126, Addison-Wesley, Reading, MA, 1983.

14. A. Pasik and M. Schor, Table-Driven Rules in Expert Systems, *SIGART Newsletter No. 87*, pp. 31–33., January 1984.

15. D. T. Chai and P. D. Ting, Unity: A Microcomputer DBMS for Stand-Alone and Distributed Environments. In *Proceedings of IEEE Electronics '79*, pp. 1–10, IEEE, New York, 1979.

16. L. M. Fagan, J. C. Kunz, E. A. Feigenbaum, and J. Osborn, Representation of Dynamic Clinical Knowledge: Measurement Interpretation in the Intensive Care Unit, *IJCAI*, Vol. 6, pp. 260–262, 1979.

17. Automated Repair Service Bureau, *The Bell System Technical Journal*, Vol. 61, No. 6, p. 2, 1982.

18. P. S. Boggs and J. R. Wright, Knocking Potential Problems for a Loop, *AT&T Bell Laboratories Record*, pp. 22–26, January 1985.

THE FIS ELECTRONICS TROUBLESHOOTING PROJECT

Frank Pipitone, Kenneth DeJong, William Spears, and Michael Marrone

U. S. Navy Center for Applied Research in Artificial Intelligence, Naval Research Laboratory, Washington, DC

1. INTRODUCTION

FIS, short for Fault Isolation System, is an ongoing research project at the Navy Center for Applied Research in Artificial Intelligence, a branch of the U.S. Naval Research Laboratory. The focus of the work is a model-based expert system shell capable of acquiring from a user a description of a piece of electronic equipment, called a unit under test (UUT). This description is later used by FIS to perform such diagnostic functions as recommending the next "best" test to make on the UUT during a fault isolation sequence and estimating fault probabilities after each test is made. These and other capabilities make FIS a powerful tool that can be used in a variety of diagnostic settings, as discussed in Section 1.2. FIS has been developed primarily with large-scale analog–hybrid electronic systems such as radar and sonar systems in mind, but it is applicable at least in principle to any human-engineered system with discrete replaceable components. FIS is written in LISP and has been under development for several years. Earlier versions of the FIS prototype system are described by Pipitone [1,2].

1.1. The Need for Artificial-Intelligence-Based Diagnostic Systems

The maintenance of electronic equipment has drawn increasing attention during the past decade as a potential artificial intelligence (AI) application, particularly in the military. This has been motivated by the increasing complexity of military electronic systems and the resulting high maintenance costs as well as the scarcity of highly trained technicians.

The Navy has been particularly interested in and supportive of the development

73

of fault isolation expert systems that can improve the quality of their maintenance and troubleshooting activities. As an example, Navy technicians on aircraft carriers may be responsible for troubleshooting several hundred different (sub)systems for which they have had varying amounts of training (frequently little or none). To compensate, the Navy has and continues to invest heavily in automatic test equipment (ATE) to aid or replace these technicians. The quality of the "test programs" that drive these ATE stations varies dramatically in spite of a uniformly high cost to acquire them.

Although it is tempting to leap to the conclusion that one could significantly improve this sort of troubleshooting activity with reasonably straightforward applications of current expert system technology, there are several aspects to the problem that raise significant technical issues. First, with several hundred different systems to maintain, it seems infeasible to think in terms of independently developed expert systems for each one. Rather one thinks in terms of a more general fault isolation shell providing a common knowledge acquisition–representation scheme for use with all subsystems. However, even with this level of generality, there are still several hundred knowledge bases to be built, debugged, and maintained in a context in which there can be considerable overlap and/or similarity in the content of many of the knowledge bases. These observations strongly suggest the development of a sophisticated knowledge acquisition system that can be used to facilitate the construction of a new knowledge base for a specific system in a variety of ways including reusing and/or adapting existing knowledge modules.

Compounding the problem of applying current expert system technology is the fact that, for many of the subsystems being maintained, there is little human expertise in the traditional sense of finding someone who is good at fixing a particular subsystem and capturing his or her knowledge in a set of associative rules. Rather, technicians depend heavily on the structural and functional descriptions contained in the technical manuals of the many subsystems they attempt to maintain. This suggests that simple rule-based architectures are not likely to be sufficient for the task at hand.

For the past few years, we have had the opportunity to explore the use of AI and expert system technology in this setting. We have built (and discarded) several prototype fault isolation shells in the process of understanding how this technology can be usefully applied. We feel that we have now evolved an architecture (FIS) that directly addresses the issues discussed above.

1.2. Maintenance and Troubleshooting Applications

Before diving into the details of FIS, it is important to understand how FIS might be used in maintenance and troubleshooting applications. The following paragraphs discuss what we feel are the most promising modes of use.

The first and most obvious use of FIS is as a technician's aid. The model we have in mind is a cooperative effort in which FIS and a technician *together* fault isolate complex systems. To be most effective in this mode, a tool must have a "mixed initiative" interface in the sense that it must be willing to accept and integrate actions taken by a technician as well as being capable of recommending actions of its own when asked by a technician.

A second obvious use of FIS is as the controller of automatic test equipment (ATE). There are many continuing efforts to reduce maintenance and troubleshooting costs by removing humans as much as possible from the diagnostic loop. This is accomplished by developing ATE stations that are capable of making tests, interpreting test results, and making replacement recommendations. In the electronics world, such stations consist of a battery of signal generators and measurement devices that are controlled by a test program running on a small mini- or microcomputer. After an operator loads the appropriate test program and attaches the test gear to the UUT, the ATE system runs through a sequence of diagnostic tests in an attempt to fault isolate.

For the most part, these test programs fault isolate by following a decision tree designed by a test engineer at some point in the past. When these decision trees are accurate and up-to-date, they provide an efficient form of fault isolation. However, they are also notorious for their development costs, their rigidity, and the cost of keeping them up-to-date.

FIS can be applied to the ATE world in several ways. First, if a particular application requires the flexibility of *dynamic* decision making, FIS can be run directly on ATE gear with sufficient computing capability. However, if that is not possible or desirable, FIS can be used by test engineers to reduce significantly the cost of developing the required decision trees.

Even with the most sophisticated ATE stations, fault isolation can be hampered significantly by equipment that was designed without testability considerations in mind. Such problems arise for a variety of reasons including a lack of interest by design engineers and the effort involved in evaluating a design for testability. By applying FIS during the design cycle to generate fault isolation trees, many testability problems can be identified easily and inexpensively.

There are many contexts in which it is not possible or desirable to remove technicians from the fault isolation process. Rather, the emphasis is on providing fast, cost-effective training programs to improve technician skills. Here again we feel FIS can be used as an effective training tool by providing an environment in which simulated faults can be introduced and the fault isolation activities of trainees can be monitored and compared with those made by FIS.

1.3. Current Focus of FIS

Although the underlying architecture of FIS is general enough to support all the application areas discussed in Section 1.2, the Navy has been particularly interested in its use as a technician's aid and as a test tree generator for ATE stations. As a consequence, the first two interfaces actually implemented have been for these two application areas. Figure 1 illustrates how FIS is used in these contexts.

To be successful in either of these applications, the diagnostic components of FIS depend heavily on the quality of the underlying causal model of the UUT developed by a design/test engineer using the knowledge acquisition components

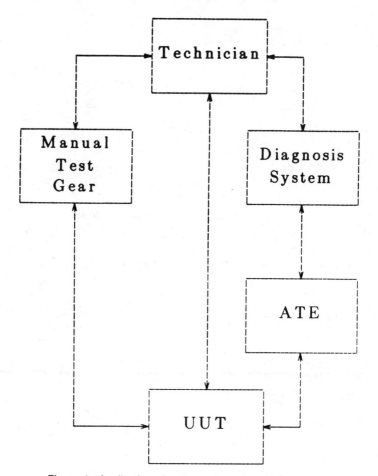

Figure 1. Application of a diagnosis system such as FIS.

of FIS. Ideally, one would like to start with the CAD/CAM database used by most manufacturing systems today. However, such databases are frequently proprietary or in highly nonstandard formats. As a consequence, we currently assume only that a design/test engineer has access to documentation describing the UUT. This includes schematic and functional block diagrams, specified values of measurable parameters at various test points, theory of operation, some notion of the relative failure rates of the replaceable components (modules), and the cost (in time) of various test operations with available test gear.

Given the above information, an engineer uses the knowledge acquisition interface of FIS to create a qualitative causal model of the UUT. FIS later uses this model in some diagnostic setting to recommend repeatedly a next best test for maximal informativeness per unit cost and to analyze the results of tests made until faulty replaceable modules are identified. These capabilities can be used to generate a test decision tree automatically. Also, FIS can answer queries about the UUT or about the diagnostic process. Typical queries include what is the merit of a given test, what causal path led to the suspicion of a given module, what are the modules affecting a given test, what is the current probability of a given fault combination, and what are the causal rules describing a given module.

The initial focus of the FIS system can be summarized as follows:

(a) Provide the facilities for acquiring with minimum effort a UUT description suitable for diagnosis.
(b) Provide the reasoning mechanisms for recommending the next best test to make or the module to be replaced.
(c) Maintain good estimates of fault probabilities after tests.
(d) Respond to queries about the UUT model or explain (b) or (c).
(e) Automatically generate a test tree using (b) and (c).

1.4. Our Approach and Related Work

The basic approach to diagnosis used in FIS is that of capturing the important part of the behavior of a UUT for diagnostic purposes by describing each replaceable module with local causal rules and specifying the connectivity of the modules. The system then uses this network of causal rules to determine the set of possible causes (ambiguity set) of any failed test and which modules to certify in what manner when a test passes. This information is used in conjunction with a priori fault probabilities by an efficient Bayesian algorithm to estimate posterior probabilities of module faults and test outcomes. These are used along with test cost data and module replacement costs to make next best test or replacement recommendations. The next best test is found using a combination of fast heuristics to screen the available tests and information theoretic entropy (Shannon entropy) calculations to evaluate further the remaining candidates. No single-fault assumption is made. Also, we do not acquire global, empirical symptom–cause associations such as "frequency high at terminal7 implies module3 or module4 bad" during knowledge acquisition. FIS computes such relations from module descriptions and connectivity. The choices of method were strongly driven by the need to minimize knowledge acquisition cost. Effective automatic diagnosis can be achieved in many ways, but most approaches require much data about the UUT. Section 3.1 discusses some of the major alternatives.

The following is a summary of some of the more novel features of the FIS fault diagnosis system:

(a) The ability to do accurate diagnosis using a qualitative behavior model of a complex analog–digital UUT without simulation.
(b) An efficient UUT knowledge acquisition capability.
(c) An efficient evidential reasoning method specialized for device troubleshooting based on Bayesian principles.
(d) A natural treatment of multiple faults.

(e) An efficient method for computing the entropy of a complex system for use in best test selection.

Notable recent work has been directed at some of the same problems FIS has addressed. For example, DeKleer [3] gives a clear analysis of the problems of computing fault hypothesis probabilities, test result probabilities, and using entropy for test recommendation. However, this approach requires a strong UUT model; one must be able to predict module output values from module input values. It is often impractical to provide such a model for analog systems, although for digital systems it may be appropriate. Also, computational efficiency is not addressed. For the results to be applied, one needs fast probability and entropy algorithms and module simulations. Another recent work [4], based on Bayesian belief networks [5], provides a powerful mathematical approach to treating the joint statistics of component faults and signal abnormalities.

Much previous related research deals only with digital circuitry [6,7]. Most work on reasoning about analog devices is restricted to simple components because of the demands of performing detailed circuit analysis [8–10]. One that treats a complex analog system (a radio receiver) [11] requires considerable knowledge acquisition effort. Another [12] uses only a shallow functional model. Systems that have general analog–digital applicability [13,14] use only topological (connectivity plus directionality) knowledge about the UUT and therefore are forced to suspect all upstream modules from a failed test. Also, such systems cannot handle passed tests well because they cannot know to what extent each module upstream of a given passed test can be certified as good, lacking functional modeling. King [15] gives a survey of some previous work.

2. ARCHITECTURE OF THE FIS SYSTEM

The major components of FIS, as well as its two principal users, are illustrated in Figure 2. We will describe the components chronologically as they are used. First, the knowledge engineer, whose principal expertise is a detailed understanding of the type of equipment to be diagnosed, describes the UUT to the computer. He or she does this at a computer terminal via the knowledge acquisition interface (KAI), producing the UUT description, which is then stored in a file. A principal concern in the design of the KAI is to maximize the ease with which a user with a good electronics background but little familiarity with computer science can generate a description of the UUT that will yield acceptable diagnostic performance in FIS. This description contains such information as a priori rates of failure of the replaceable modules, costs (primarily in time) of setup and test operations, connectivity and qualitative functional descriptions, a set of allowed tests, and a graphics description for displaying a block diagram of the UUT.

The electronics library is primarily intended to store partial or complete qualitative functional descriptions of modules that occur frequently in the UUTs being described. The electronics library is to be referred to whenever possible while using

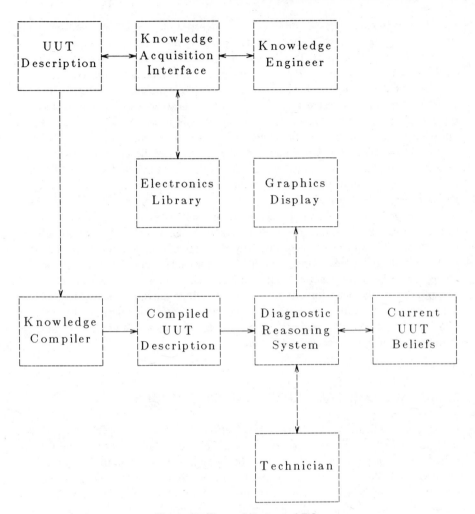

Figure 2. The architecture of FIS.

the KAI to enhance speed. The resulting approximate module descriptions can then be edited using the KAI. Also, the KAI can be used to add, delete, or modify items in the library. After its completion, the UUT description is processed by the knowledge compiler. This produces a file containing the compiled UUT knowledge.

The purpose of the knowledge compiler is simply to transform knowledge from a form suitable for editing to a form suitable for efficient diagnostic computation. The knowledge compiler is run after the UUT description is completely finished and stores the compiled UUT description in a file.

Once we have compiled UUT descriptions available, the diagnostic reasoning subsystem can be invoked to perform a variety of diagnostic tasks. The diagnostic reasoning subsystem uses a compiled UUT description to construct and maintain dynamically a belief model about what is properly and improperly functioning as test results become known. This belief model in turn is used to find the best test to make next or recommend the replacement of some module of the UUT.

We currently provide two user interfaces to the diagnostic subsystem. The first is a "mixed initiative" interface intended to be used by a technician as an aide during a diagnostic troubleshooting session. In this mode, FIS is capable of (1) updating the current beliefs about the UUT based on a technician's entry of test results; (2) responding to a technician's query regarding the probability of a fault hypothesis, the merit of a test, the UUT description, or the belief state of FIS; and (3) making suggestions and/or recommendations about the next best action to take (further tests or replacements).

The second mode of use is to use the diagnostic subsystem to produce a traditional test tree by invoking the next best action generator, following its advice (hypothetically), and recursively invoking the next best action generator for each of the possible outcomes of the previously recommended action. In this way, large, complex test trees are generated automatically with no human intervention.

Both the knowledge acquisition subsystem and the diagnostic subsystem of FIS are complex entities that are not easy to describe in a few paragraphs. In the next two major sections, we describe in more detail the motivations behind and the current state of both of these subsystems.

3.   KNOWLEDGE ACQUISITION CONSIDERATIONS

In most AI applications, knowledge acquisition is a crucial consideration because it typically has a high cost in work-hours. Fault diagnosis is no exception. To create a computer program that can troubleshoot a piece of equipment with useful accuracy and efficiency, one must invest a considerable amount of effort in knowledge acquisition. The diagnostic reasoning methods chosen must be able to use a UUT description that is easily obtainable by the knowledge engineer and of sufficiently small size. Also, the KAI must allow the fast and accurate transfer of these data to the computer.

3.1.   Knowledge Acquisition Trade-offs in Diagnostic Systems

Let us briefly consider some different approaches to achieving some of the diagnostic functions described in Section 1.3 in the light of the relative ease or difficulty of the knowledge required to support them. First, consider the approach of directly writing a test decision tree. This corresponds to the conventional practice of writing programs to control ATE gear in which the burden of diagnostic reasoning lies primarily on the human technician, and what he or she enters into the computer is essentially a decision tree that is to control the ATE autonomously or with minimal human interaction. Although converting such a decision tree into computer code is usually not very labor intensive, much labor is usually involved in producing the decision tree, because the technician needs to consider many things at each decision point in the tree. The technician must consider what modules are currently suspected of being faulty, in what manner they are suspected, to what degree various modules are certified by previous passed tests, what cost in time or other risk is incurred by performing a certain test, what tests are available to the system, how these tests depend on various faults in various modules, and many other matters. This decision tree approach therefore has high knowledge acquisition cost. It also has the disadvantage of limited fault coverage, inflexibility, lack of explanation capability, and susceptibility to human error and suboptimal decisions.

At another extreme is the approach of entering into the computer a detailed model of the structure of a UUT (e.g., schematic diagrams) and behavior models of the individual components and placing on the computer the burden of deducing enough of the behavior of the replaceable modules and of the whole UUT to do diagnostic reasoning. This approach also requires that the human specify in some way the intended function of the UUT. That is, the diagnosis system must know what part of the UUTs full range of behavior must be tested to certify that the UUT has completely acceptable performance. This approach has the potential of allowing automated diagnosis with low knowledge acquisition cost, since CAD/CAM data could in the future be used to provide the model of the structure of the UUT in computer readable form, and only the intended function (performance specifications) would need to be largely human specified.

Intermediate between these two extremes is the approach of providing to the diagnostic system a simplified model of the qualitative behavior of the replaceable modules and the structure (connectivity) of the UUT, as well as UUT performance specifications. The diagnostic system then can deduce the qualitative relations between test results and possible faulty modules. This then enables it to perform the functions of Section 1.3. Within this paradigm, which is the one adopted by FIS, there are trade-offs. Consider the issue of how detailed a model is needed of each replaceable module. In our current implementation of FIS, we have decided to represent it by a set of *causal rules* describing what signal abnormalities at terminals of the module can be caused by the module failing or by signal abnormalities at other terminals of the module (see Section 3.2). The module's failure statistics are represented by a single number, its failure rate relative to the other modules. We do not require joint statistics of the different ways the module can fail (*failure modes*) because providing them is often infeasible. Indeed, even the module failure rates must often be grossly approximated.

The lack of failure mode statistics makes things difficult for a diagnostic reasoning system. For example, suppose a diagnosis system currently suspects that one of two modules m1 and m2 contains a fault. Then it might be able to determine which is likely to be faulty by finding a test dependent on m1 but not on m2. If the test fails, m1 is faulty, and if the test passes, m1 is less suspect than it was, and m2 more suspect. However, if a human interpreted that passed test, he or she would think about what failure mode of m1 tested okay. If it were the same failure mode that made m1 initially suspect, m1 would be exonerated. If the passed test depended on a completely independent failure mode of m1, then m1 would be only slightly certified.

Thus, a diagnosis system could benefit from knowing the complete joint statistics of the failure modes of each module and the qualitative relation between these and measurable abnormalities at the terminals of the module. However, since providing such data is often infeasible, we have considered and implemented various approximate methods for handling the certification of modules after passed tests without using failure mode statistics (see Section 4.4).

3.2. The UUT Description Used in FIS

The knowledge required to describe a specific UUT type includes the following:

(a) A graphics description for display of a block diagram of the UUT.

(b) A list of module (component) names.

(c) Causal rules for each module.

(d) Connectivity description.

(e) Module replacement costs.

(f) Relative a priori module and UUT failure probabilities.

(g) A list of performance tests for the UUT.

(h) A list of additional tests available for fault isolation.

(i) Test cost rule set.

The graphics description (a) is generated automatically by FIS from the connectivity description (d) and consists of a block diagram with the modules labeled by their names and current fault probabilities. The user then edits this diagram to optimize its appearance.

The most interesting UUT-descriptive knowledge is (c) above. It consists of causal rules relating measurable (at least in principle) parameters among various terminals of each module. These are intended to describe the behavior of each module in its context. Thus, where loading and other effects of Kirchhoff's laws affect behavior, these are assumed taken into account. We are not restricted to unidirectional modules with fixed input–output voltage behavior. For the common case in which this behavior is independent of context, the library module descriptions, when available, can be invoked without modification. These rules contain both information about the correct behavior of UUT modules and about fault modes of modules, as discussed later. The rules are of the following two forms, called through rules and fault rules, respectively:

1. Given *precondition, parameter1 abnormality1* at *terminal1* can cause *parameter2 abnormality2* at *terminal2*.

2. Faulty *modulename* can cause *parameter abnormality* at *terminal*.

Here a precondition is a predicate on the state of the UUT inputs (or input history). Preconditions are optional and are used primarily to model devices such as multiplexers and devices with enable inputs in which a causal path is present or absent depending on some signal conditions. Although we have experimented with elaborate precondition schemes involving estimating probabilities of control signal values, we have found it quite adequate simply to refer to the stimulus data associated with the current test to see if the input stimuli correspond to those named in a precondition. An abnormality is a qualitative value such as high or low. For example, a rule of type 1 is "Given that power supply 3 is in the on state, DC voltage high at t3 can cause the frequency to be low at t4," in English paraphrase. This might describe the way a voltage-controlled oscillator propagates a voltage error, given that its power supply voltage is in spec. In the case of a module with two inputs both affecting the same output parameter, such as a summing junction, a problem can arise. Suppose two of the rules are "input1 DC high can cause output DC high" and "input2 DC high can cause output DC high." Then, if "output DC high" is suspected, both inputs are to be suspected high. However, one might be very high and the other slightly low, and the latter would be missed. However, if such a case occurs, the system will find a fault leading to the high input, and the ensuing repair may even cure the slightly low input. Otherwise, a second diagnostic pass can search for it. Each causal rule is associated with the module immediately connected to the terminals appearing in the rule.

Rules of type 1 represent the correct behavior of a module in context in the form of qualitative relations among quantities at its terminals. Rule type 2 represents limited knowledge about how a given module can fail. Note that even if we had no such fault model knowledge available, we could allow the system to include all conceivable rules of type 2 by default and still have a viable diagnosis system. That is, we could assume that any abnormality at a terminal could have been caused by the failure of any directly connected module. This would lead to somewhat larger ambiguity sets (suspect sets) than with a more minimal set of type 2 rules, but most of the diagnostic power of FIS comes from rules of type 1, since it is largely by chaining them that we determine what portion of the UUT affects a given measurement. When in doubt about the inclusion of any rule, we must include it or else we risk missing some faults.

The connectivity description [item (d) above] is given in terms of triples (module1 terminal module2). Note that in the connectivity description there are always two modules connected to one terminal. This is because metal conductors are modeled as modules themselves to capture their open-circuit fault behavior. Thus, three module terminals connected together in a Y become three UUT terminals connecting six module terminals as shown in Figure 3. The connectivity knowledge is also represented redundantly in the causal rules, which refer to terminals and are each associated with a module.

Item (e), the module replacement costs, are used to recommend the replacement of a module when that action minimizes the expected total cost of testing and replacement (see Section 4.6). These costs are manifested primarily in time and risk of equipment damage and are represented in time units. Item (f) is to be obtained ideally from statistics of actual failures of each module in the current UUT type. If that is unavailable, failure rates for the most specific generic class

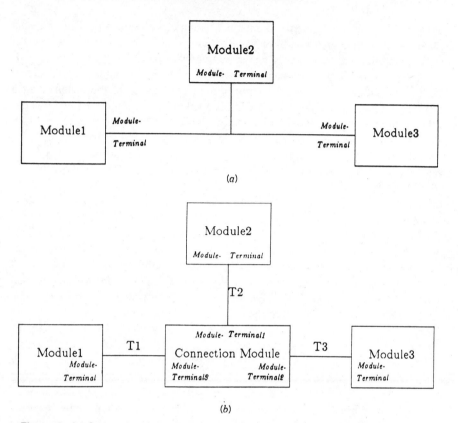

Figure 3. (a) Conventional drawing of a connection and (b) our model of a connection.

to which a module belongs and for which statistics are available should be used, with equal probabilities the last resort. The a priori UUT failure probability is simply the estimated probability that the UUT has any faulty module. Item (g) is a list of tests that, if all were made and passed, would imply that the UUT is for practical purposes certified as fully functional. Item (h) is a list of tests that are potentially useful for fault isolation but that are not needed to certify the UUT as fully functional.

A test of either type consists of several items of data, as illustrated in Figure 4 by the small sample of tests from a radar UUT. Each has a unique test number, a terminal to use as test point, a parameter to be measured, a set of qualitative test outcomes and the quantitative specifications defining them, the units of measurement of the specifications, the test type (performance or diagnostic only), and cost-code data. In the case of analog parameters such as frequency, the specifications would be numerical ranges. In the digital case, they would be values of bits or words. The test cost code gives a prescribed state or mode of use for each of the stimulus or measurement instruments or other hardware involved in each test. z is the "don't care" condition and 1 is the "off" state. Item (i) is a small and simple

Test#	Terminal	Parameter	Qualvals & Specs	Units	Type
t0300a	outbus	d-reply	(ok (ecl-1) bad (ecl-0))	logic	p
t0300b	outbus	ovrtemp	(ok (ecl-1) bad (ecl-0))	logic	p
t0300c	outbus	reply	(ok (ecl-1) bad (ecl-0))	logic	p
t0302a	outbus	d-reply	(ok (ecl-0) bad (ecl-1))	logic	p
t0302b	outbus	ovrtemp	(ok (ecl-1) bad (ecl-0))	logic	p
t0302c	outbus	reply	(ok (ecl-0) bad (ecl-1))	logic	p
t0386	outbus	agcpar	(ok (ecl-1) bad (ecl-0))	logic	p
t0388	outbus	agcpar	(ok (ecl-0) bad (ecl-1))	logic	p
t0390	outbus	sdipar	(ok (ecl-0) bad (ecl-1))	logic	p
t0392	j9bus	g-off-par	(ok (ttl-1) bad (ttl-0))	logic	p
t0394	outbus	sdipar	(ok (ecl-1) bad (ecl-0))	logic	p

Test#	Test Cost-Code Information												
	m	p	d	sc	pw	fq	am	fm	anl	tmr	dvm	arr	dd
t0300a	z	1	1	z	z	z	z	z	z	z	z	z	z
t0300b	z	1	1	z	z	z	z	z	z	z	z	z	z
t0300c	z	1	2	z	z	z	z	z	z	z	z	z	z
t0302a	z	1	2	z	z	z	z	z	z	z	z	z	z
t0302b	z	1	2	z	z	z	z	z	z	z	z	z	z
t0302c	z	1	3	z	z	z	z	z	z	z	z	z	z
t0386	z	1	6	z	z	z	z	z	z	z	z	z	z
t0388	z	1	7	z	z	z	z	z	z	z	z	z	z
t0390	z	1	10	z	z	z	z	z	z	z	z	z	z
t0392	z	1	11	z	z	z	z	z	z	z	z	z	z
t0394	z	1	12	z	z	z	z	z	z	z	z	z	z

Figure 4. Description of available tests.

set of rules giving the cost (in time units) of using each test instrument in a current test given the previously made test. For example, if the timer (tmr) were in the "off" state (tmr = 1) in one test and in state 23 in the next test, we would capture the fact that the timer needs a 50-second warm-up time with the rule "(timer 1 to x) implies cost = 50." This compact approach was motivated by the fact that there are n^2 possible transitions from one of n tests to a second one, and therefore n^2 costs, a prohibitive amount of data to be acquired explicitly.

3.3. Knowledge Acquisition Strategies

The description of a new UUT is developed by a user with the aid of the KAI in Figure 2. In the future, it may be possible to replace the user at least partially with a CAD/CAM database describing the UUT. For the most part, the UUT descriptive data described in Section 3.2 are acquired in a direct manner from the user via a menu system in the current implementation of FIS. The largest data items are the lists of tests and the causal rules of the modules. For the latter, the user needs to transfer to the computer his or her understanding of each module's behavior. This requires a large number of causal rules for a typical UUT (30 rules per module is typical). Therefore, efficient transfer of knowledge is important. For this reason, we have experimented with several means of specifying causal rules for a module:

1. Entering individual causal rules.
2. Entering several causal rules at once by expressing them in a compact form; for example, "The DC voltage at all terminals of module3 can cause the failure of any parameter at terminal6," in English paraphrase.
3. Obtaining a complete rule set of a familiar module from the library by specifying the UUT-specific module name, the generic module name, and the associations between UUT terminal names and library module terminal names.
4. Modifying the current rule set for a module of the UUT by naming properties (partial descriptions of a module rule set) from the library and giving the associations between UUT terminal names and property terminal names. This leads to both additions and deletions of rules.

Item 2 can take advantage of various patterns in the rule set of a module. The example given causes the generation of all combinations (the "outer product") of the given causes and the given effects. Such notation is useful for a complex module for which any abnormality at one terminal can, under some circumstances, cause any abnormality at some second terminal, or for which the user has an incomplete understanding. Another example is "All abnormalities at terminal5 of module3 can cause the failure of the same parameter at terminal6," in English paraphrase. This yields a one-to-one correspondence between causes and effects. Various other compact notations have been tried. The KAI can expand these immediately to yield individual rules that can be edited further, if desired, by the user.

Every rule for each UUT module carries a label of "mandatory" or "forbidden" for use during editing. After compilation, only the mandatory ones survive and the label is dropped. The reason for this feature is evident from item 4. Rules obtained by invoking a property are of both the mandatory and forbidden types, whereas all rules obtained by method 1, 2, or 3 are mandatory. Thus, when a new rule is obtained by any of the four methods, if it is mandatory and not present in the UUT module rule set, it will be added. If it is mandatory but already present and marked mandatory in the UUT module rule set, nothing is changed. If it is mandatory and present but marked forbidden in the UUT module rule set, then the user is called on to resolve the conflict. The case of dealing with a forbidden new rule is handled exactly symmetrically. Thus, when there is a conflict, the user resolves it, and when there is not, the new rule is "unioned" into the UUT module rule set.

Besides speed of acquisition, in the case of the causal rules it was found useful to assist the user in ensuring that the rule set is a good one. This means that the rule set has upstream causal paths from each possible failed test result to a set of modules that is sure to contain a faulty one. At the same time, each such ambiguity set should not contain any module that we know could not cause the test result. To facilitate enforcing this, FIS can sort the rule set by effects (right-hand sides) and give the causes of all the rules having each effect. Figure 5 shows a sample of such a list. This enables us to follow the causal paths upstream quickly by eye to evaluate the rule set. FIS also can display the computed ambiguity sets for each possible test. This is a useful tool in validating the causal rule set.

3.4. The Knowledge Compiler

The UUT descriptive data described in Section 3.2 are processed by the knowledge compiler to produce data structures allowing fast diagnosis time processing. For example, the *ambiguity sets* of each test are computed and stored; that is, for each abnormal qualitative value of the test, the causal rules associated with the terminal and parameter tested are obtained. The right-hand sides (effects) are matched against the failed test result. The left-hand (causes) sides of the matching rules now represent possible causes of the failed test. These are now matched recursively against rules until all culpable modules are found. Also, for each of these modules, those rules having that module as cause and having an effect on the causal path to the test result are recorded. These are called *immediate effects* and are used in performing module certification after a passed test (see Section 4.4).

The compiler also sorts the set of tests in several ways so that we can quickly look up the set of available tests at a given terminal, measuring a given parameter, dependent on a given module via a given fault rule, and so on. These data structures will be used by the best test heuristics (Section 4.6).

4. DIAGNOSTIC REASONING

The diagnostic functions of FIS are illustrated in Figure 6 by the menu FIS displays when ready to be used in the technician's aid mode. The major functions are *make-test* and *best-test*, which we will describe in detail. Also of interest is *forget-last*, which allows the user to retract the last make-test he or she performed. This is useful for considering hypothetical sequences of tests and test results.

4.1. Beliefs About Faults in the UUT

The updating of beliefs about faults after a test is a crucial function in a diagnosis system. Poor selection of tests can delay the diagnosis, but inaccurate use of their

Effect	Cause	Precondition
(agcpar logic b)	adc	t
(bit-rf freq hi)	(lo-out freq hi)	t
	(ifosc2 freq hi)	t
(bit-rf freq lo)	(lo-out freq lo)	t
	(ifosc2 freq lo)	t
	(td-cnt any b)	t
(bit-rf pulsespread hi)	tdrive	t
	(td-cnt any b)	t
(bit-rf pulsespread lo)	(td-cnt any b)	t
	tdrive	t
(bit-rf pwr hi)	(td-cnt any b)	t
	tdrive	t
(bit-rf pwr lo)	tdrive	t
	(lo-out pwr lo)	t
	(td-cnt any b)	t
	(ifosc2 pwr lo)	t
(cagc1 logic b)	adc	t
(cagc2 logic b)	adc	t
(cagc3 logic b)	adc	t
(first-lo freq hi)	l-osc	t
	(locnt any b)	t
	(refout freq hi)	t
(first-lo freq lo)	l-osc	t
	(locnt any b)	t
	(refout freq lo)	t
(first-lo pwr lo)	l-osc	t
(fmr dc hi)	pwr&cnt	t
(fmr dc lo)	pwr&cnt	t
(fmr noise hi)	pwr&cnt	t

Figure 5. Sorting the UUT rules by effects.

results can cause erroneous diagnosis. When a test is made in FIS (see Sections 4.2–4.4), the result is processed along with the compiled UUT description and the current beliefs, and produces as output updated beliefs. This deterministic data can then be processed (see Section 4.5) to obtain probabilities of fault hypotheses. The beliefs consist of five types of data and represent what FIS currently knows about the state of the UUT:

INITIALIZATION	INSPECTION	TROUBLESHOOTING	CONTROL
	sh: show-history	rc: repeat-command	li: lisp
	al: active-list	bt: best-test	cu: change-uut
	du: draw-uut	fa: forget-all	hu: hardcopy
	tt: trace-tpt	fl: forget-last	qt: quit
	ut: untrace-tpt	mt: make-test	un: unix
	ct: console-trace		
	gt: graphic-trace		
	ft: file-trace		
	tn: trace-net		
	as: amb-set		
	ss: show-specs		
	sp: show-probs		
	w: window		

Enter command or ? -->

Figure 6. The menu appearing when FIS is used as a technician's aid.

1. Quantitative and qualitative values of tests made.
2. The set of current *ambiguity sets*, that is, the sets of modules each of which is believed to contain at least one faulty module. This accrues one new ambiguity set per failed test.
3. The current setup of the UUT–ATE system, represented by the *test cost code*, corresponding to the last test made (see Section 3.2). This is needed for comparison with the test cost code of the following test to compute its cost.
4. Certification numbers for each immediate effect of each module. These indicate the number of passed tests dependent on the given module via the fault rule whose cause is the module and whose effect is the *immediate effect*.
5. The certification factors to be multiplied by the a priori relative failure rates a_i of the modules when calculating fault probabilities (see Section 4.5). These are initially 1.0, indicating no evidence from tests that module i is good. Complete certification is indicated by 0.0. These factors are computed from the certification numbers as described in Section 4.4.

The five types of belief information described in this section together with the a priori module failure probabilities include all the important information about the possible faults in the UUT at a given time. However, this information is most useful both to a technician and to the routine that computes the next best test if it is converted into the form of probabilities of fault hypotheses, as described in Section 4.5.

4.2. Making a Test

When a technician (or ATE) makes a test on a UUT, the result is reported to FIS as a quantitative or qualitative value of the parameter measured. Figure 7 illustrates

*Enter command or ? -->***mt**

*Enter terminal at which this test was made-->***rf-out**

TEST	PARAMETERS
rf-out	pwr
	pulsespread
	noise
	freq

*Enter parameter which was measured-->***pwr**

TEST	SETUPS
rf-out	52-1-7
pwr	51-2-3
	20-21-1-1

*Enter setup under which this test was made -->***52-1-7**

TEST	QUALVAL	SPEC
rf-out	ok	((-inf -65))
pwr	hi	((-65 inf))
52-1-7		

*Enter measured value or qualval -->***hi**

Figure 7. Making a test in FIS.

the process of making a test in the technician's aid mode. A test can be specified by naming the terminal, parameter, and setup (part of the test cost code) of the desired test, as shown, or by naming the test number. If a quantitative value is entered, FIS converts this to one of the qualitative values for that test, such as high, low, or okay for an analog measurement, by comparing it with the specified values. In processing the test result, FIS first makes a new copy (using constructive LISP operations for compactness) of the current UUT state so that it can undo tests if desired. Then it updates the test cost code to the one reported with the test. Failed and passed tests are processed differently.

4.3. Processing Failed Tests

If the specification is violated, the ambiguity set for the particular qualitative value (such as low or high) of the particular test taken is found. This set is then appended to the set of ambiguity sets. The ambiguity set is found by lookup, since all such sets are precomputed by the knowledge compiler. In previous versions of FIS, the ambiguity sets were computed when a test was made. This was more time consuming and was done because various deductions about qualitative values of electrical parameters were made while processing a test result [2], which required following the rules at diagnosis time. However, we have decided to abandon these deductions because they are marginally useful. The important information gleaned from a set of failed tests is the corresponding set of ambiguity sets.

The simple cascade network of Figure 8 illustrates the small size of ambiguity sets computed with FIS. Note, for example, that if a test shows the DC voltage to be high at T6, only the highpass filter can be the cause. The reader can readily see how the ambiguity sets were found by mentally chaining through the given rules from right to left from a test result.

Having added the ambiguity set of the current failed test to the UUT beliefs, FIS now proceeds with the probabilistic computations described in Section 4.5, as indicated in Section 3.1.

4.4. Processing Passed Tests

In the case of a passed test (qualitative value okay), FIS first notes for each module on which the test depends how many of the abnormalities that it can immediately cause (at its terminals) lie on the causal path to the failed (e.g., low or high) outcomes of the test. It finds these *immediate effects* by direct lookup of precompiled *ambiguity sets* for the test (see Section 3.4). Then it must determine how much to reduce the suspicion (fault probability) of the modules involved.

As indicated in Section 3.1, the manner in which a passed test results in reducing the suspicion of a module needs careful consideration. We have experimented with several schemes for certification. In all cases, we convert the information gained from the various tests into a single certification factor for each module, as described in Section 4.1. In earlier versions of FIS we tried a simple linear scheme. For example, if a module has ten *fault rules* and four of the rules have right-hand sides on the causal path to the test, then the certification factor for the module is $1 - \frac{4}{10} = 0.6$. This rough approximation was used because the a priori statistics of the various modes of failure of a given module are seldom available. Thus, the a priori fault probability of the module would be multiplied by 0.6 before being used in the probability calculations of Section 4.5. However, two problems were found with this. First, the different ways a module can fail are often not mutually exclusive. Thus, the first passed test should have a greater effect than later ones. Second, if a module is currently strongly suspected of being faulty because one or more tests depending on it failed, then it should be certified more strongly by some passed tests than by others (see Section 3.1).

To alleviate these difficulties while still avoiding requiring joint statistics data for the failure modes of a module, we are currently experimenting with the following scheme. We keep track of how many of the tests that depend on a given failure mode of a module have been made and passed. Then we take the sum s of these

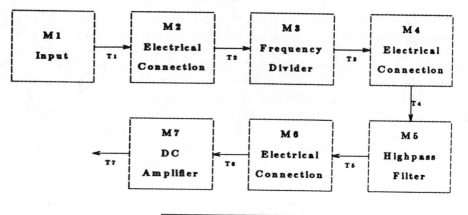

Test Result	Ambiguity Set
T6 freq high	M1, M3
T6 dc low	M5, M6, M7
T6 dc hi	M5

Rules Fired in Propagation of above Test Results

Cause	Effect	Comments
T5 freq high	T6 freq high	
T4 freq high	T5 freq high	
T3 freq high	T4 freq high	
T2 freq high	T3 freq high	
M3	T3 freq high	M3 not dividing
T1 freq high	T2 freq high	
M1	T1 freq high	M1 has high frequency
T5 dc low	T6 dc low	
M6	T6 dc low	M6 open, M7 pulls low
M7	T6 dc low	M7 input grounded
M5	T6 dc low	M5 output has offset
M5	T6 dc high	M5 output has offset
T5 dc high	T6 dc high	

Figure 8. Simple examples of the propagation of a test result.

and compute exp $(-ks)$ as the certification factor for the module, with the constant k chosen empirically to optimize performance. This addresses the first problem, the requirement that successive passed tests reduce the fault probabilities by progressively lesser amounts. Now if the module in question is contained in any ambiguity set then exp $(-ks - k_a s_a)$ is taken as the certification factor, where s_a is the number of passed tests that depend on those particular immediate effects of the module that are responsible for that module being in an ambiguity set. The constant k_a is chosen empirically to optimize performance. This addresses the second problem mentioned above.

4.5. Calculating the Fault Probabilities

In problem domains that are complex and for which deep models relating structure and function are incomplete, such as medical diagnosis, it is often impossible to do evidential reasoning in a precise manner, since the relevant joint statistics are unavailable. Therefore, approximate methods have been found useful such as those in MYCIN [16] and PROSPECTOR [17] and the Dempster–Shafer [18] formalism. However, in the domain of diagnosis of human-engineered systems constructed from discrete modules, it is possible to use more precise probabilistic methods exploiting the regularities of this domain. One regularity is that the information gleaned from a failed test can often be described as an ambiguity set, a set within which at least one faulty module must lie. Another is that it is often an acceptable approximation to assume that the replaceable modules fail independently of one another with their own a priori probabilities.

A fault hypothesis is defined here as a Boolean combination of assertions that individual modules are good or faulty. For example, x_1 & $\overline{x_2}$ & x_3 is the hypothesis that modules 1 and 3 are bad and module 2 is good, without regard for the other modules. FIS contains a program that computes the probability of a fault hypothesis in light of the test results to date. We make the assumption that the individual module fault propositions x_i are statistically independent of each other with relative a priori probabilities a_i, so that $a_i a_j$ is the relative a priori probability of x_i & x_j, for example. We are thus ignoring the case of one component failing first and stressing a second component so that it fails also. This will cause some error in probability calculations, which will affect primarily the selection of tests, and therefore the cost (e.g., time and money) of diagnosis, and not its accuracy. Barring this coupling, we can view double faults as independent events—the second of which occurred by chance in the time between the occurrence of the first and the time of testing.

For clarity, we will first describe how the program processes the results of failed test results only. Then we will treat the case of some failed and some passed tests and, finally, the case of all passed tests. As described in Section 4.3, each failed test gives rise to an ambiguity set containing all modules that could have caused that abnormal measurement. The set of these ambiguity sets corresponds to a Boolean conjunctive normal form expression in the module fault propositions x_i: at least one member of the first ambiguity set is faulty and at least one member of the second ambiguity set is faulty, and so on. Let T denote this expression and H denote an arbitrary Boolean function of the x_i and their complements, describing a hypothesis whose current probability is desired. From Bayes' rule the current probability of H is given by

$$P(H|T) = \frac{P(H \& T)}{P(T)} . \tag{1}$$

$P(B)$ is defined for an arbitrary Boolean function B as the a priori probability of the proposition B, that is, the a priori probability that the fault state of the UUT is consistent with B.

The problem is now reduced to that of computing $P(B)$ for an arbitrary Boolean function of the literals x_i. The strategy is to manipulate B so that all terms of conjunctions are statistically independent (involve no common x_i) and all terms of disjunctions are nonoverlapping (mutually exclusive). We can then replace the x_i with the corresponding a priori component failure probabilities a_i and the three Boolean operations with arithmetic operations using the following three laws from probability theory:

(A) If $P(X) = p$, then $P(\overline{X}) = 1 - p$.

(B) If $P(X) = p$ and $P(Y) = q$, then $P(X \vee Y) = p + q$ iff $X \,\&\, Y = 0$.

(C) If $P(X) = p$, $P(Y) = q$, and X and Y are statistically independent, then $P(X \,\&\, Y) = p \times q$, prior to the use of a_i in the above paragraph.

We have developed an efficient algorithm for performing the computation of Equation (1) outlined above. For those interested we give a concise trace of its behavior on an example problem. Suppose that three tests have failed and our current ambiguity sets are $\{m_2, m_3, m_4\}$, $\{m_4, m_5, m_6\}$, and $\{m_7\}$. Let us compute the probability of the hypothesis x_7 that module m_7 is faulty. The ambiguity sets overlap interestingly (at least two faults are present) and make a good illustration. We define the shorthand notation $\overline{P(B)} = 1 - P(B)$ and x_i is denoted by i. Then the numerator of Equation (1) becomes

1. $P(H \,\&\, T) = P\big[(2 \vee 3 \vee 4) \,\&\, (4 \vee 5 \vee 6) \,\&\, (6 \vee 7) \,\&\, 7\big];$

2. $\qquad\quad = P\big[(2 \vee 3 \vee 4) \,\&\, (4 \vee 5 \vee 6) \,\&\, 7\big]$ Boolean absorption;

3. $\qquad\quad = P\big[(\overline{2} \,\&\, \overline{3} \,\&\, \overline{4}) \vee (\overline{4} \,\&\, \overline{5} \,\&\, \overline{6}) \vee \overline{7}\big]$ DeMorgan's law;

4. $\qquad\quad = \overline{P}\big[(\overline{2} \,\&\, \overline{3} \,\&\, \overline{4}) \vee (\overline{4} \,\&\, \overline{5} \,\&\, \overline{6}) \vee \overline{7}\big]$ law (A) above;

5. $\qquad\quad = \overline{P}\big[(\overline{2} \,\&\, \overline{3} \,\&\, \overline{4} \,\&\,(5 \vee 6) \,\&\, 7)$

$\qquad\qquad \vee (\overline{4} \,\&\, \overline{5} \,\&\, \overline{6} \,\&\, 7) \vee \overline{7}\big]$ disjunction overlap removal;

6. $\qquad\quad = 1 - P(\overline{2} \,\&\, \overline{3} \,\&\, \overline{4} \,\&\, (5 \vee 6) \,\&\, 7)$

$\qquad\qquad - P(\overline{4} \,\&\, \overline{5} \,\&\, \overline{6} \,\&\, 7) - P(\overline{7})$ law (B);

7. $\qquad\quad = 1 - P(\overline{2})\, P(\overline{3})\, P(\overline{4})\, P(5 \vee 6)\, P(7)$

$\qquad\qquad - P(\overline{4})\, P(\overline{5})\, P(\overline{6})\, P(7) - P(\overline{7})$ law (C);

8. $\qquad\quad = 1 - \overline{P}(2)\, \overline{P}(3)\, \overline{P}(4)\, P(5 \vee 6)\, P(7)$

$\qquad\qquad - \overline{P}(4)\, \overline{P}(5)\, \overline{P}(6)\, P(7) - \overline{P}(7)$ law (A)

9. $P(5 \vee 6)$ becomes $P(\overline{\overline{5} \,\&\, \overline{6}})$ DeMorgan's law;

10. $P(H \,\&\, T) = 1 - \overline{P}(2)\, \overline{P}(3)\, \overline{P}(4)\, \big(\overline{\overline{P}(5)\, \overline{P}(6)}\big)\, P(7)$

$\qquad\qquad - \overline{P}(4)\, \overline{P}(5)\, \overline{P}(6)\, P(7) - \overline{P}(7).$

The $P(i)$ are simply the a_i. The denominator of Equation (1) is treated similarly.

The above method is used to compute the current fault probabilities of the individual modules after each test. It can also be invoked by the user to compute the probability of any fault hypothesis, even one including some fault states inconsistent with T.

Now we will treat the case of having at least one passed test and at least one failed test. As described in Section 4.4, for each module m_i, FIS computes a certification factor c_i that represents the evidence from passed tests. Thus, module m_i is regarded as certified by the amount c_i and the a priori failure rate a_i is simply replaced with $c_i a_i$ in the probability calculations above.

Finally, if all tests have passed so far, then there are no ambiguity sets and the probability algorithm above is not used. Instead the a priori module fault probabilities are renormalized using the a priori UUT fault probability P_0 and the certified a priori module probabilities $c_i a_i$.

4.6. Next Best Test and Replacement Decisions

The problem of finding the "best" test to make next in troubleshooting is analogous to that of playing a game against an opponent who responds randomly. The test result is the opponent's move and the test selection is our move. The object of our side is to minimize the cost of finding the faults. We could think of the opponent as confounding our efforts by giving test results that sometimes further our goal and sometimes do not. Applying a mini-average algorithm to the "game tree" [13] yields an optimal solution but is infeasible for large branching factors. In FIS, selecting a test amounts to choosing three things—setup, test point, and parameter measured. Thus, the number of available tests can be large. At the next level of the game tree, there can be several test results, one for each of its qualitative values, for example, low, high, and okay. We take the approach of first heuristically screening the set of possible tests to reduce their number significantly and then examining only one level of the game tree to pick the best of the remaining candidate tests. Specifically, we find the screened test that maximizes the ratio of the expected information gain to the estimated test cost. The expected information gain is a weighted average of an entropy-based evaluation function over the several possible test results, where the weights are the estimated test result probabilities.

In earlier versions, we screened the tests by simply exhaustively computing the initial (opening move) evaluation function values at compilation time and then taking the best n of these as our screened candidate tests during diagnosis. This is not very satisfactory, however, since the initial ordering of the tests by their merit is often very different from their ordering after one or more tests have been made. Therefore, we are currently experimenting with heuristic screening techniques that are highly dependent on the current UUT beliefs. This is expected to result in a small set of high-quality candidates, allowing rapid evaluation by the entropy–cost routine. One source of good heuristics is the observation that tests dependent on some but not all of the highly suspect modules are powerful. Another is that tests made under the same UUT stimulus conditions as some failed test are more likely to fail and thus contribute significantly to fault isolation. Tests that have low cost are to be preferred to tests of otherwise equal merit but with higher cost. If no tests have failed thus far, those with greatest estimated failure probability are preferred.

Reasonably accurate estimates of the probabilities of test results are needed for use in the best test calculations. The probability of an abnormal (such as high or low) result is computed by looking up the ambiguity set for that result and the associated *immediate effects* of each module m_i. Then an estimate is made of the fraction f_i of the current probability P_i that m_i is faulty that is causally related to those immediate effects, using the certification information for m_i. Then the estimated test result probability is $1 - \Pi_i(1 - f_iP_i)$. More simply put, we estimate the amount of the probability mass of various possible faults that causally lies upstream of the hypothesized test result.

The entropy-based evaluation function mentioned above can be expressed as the change in the following information expression (the negative of the entropy of the system):

$$\sum_{i=1}^{2^n} p_i \log p_i, \tag{2}$$

Here p_i is the current probability of the ith fault hypothesis and n is the number of modules in the UUT. Expression (2) is not in a suitable form for efficient computation because its complexity increases exponentially with the number n of modules. For only 20 modules, $2^{20} = 1,048,576$ terms would need to be computed. Therefore, we compute this quantity more efficiently by the drastic automatic simplification of Equation (2) after expressing the p_i in terms of the a priori fault probabilities a_i using the methods of Section 4.5. This procedure introduces no approximations but greatly improves running time.

The strategy for deciding whether to invoke the best test calculations above or to recommend the replacement of some module is to estimate the expected total cost (time) of testing in the two cases and take the minimum. Thus, if we have so far expended a time T in testing, the expected cost of replacing module m_i is $(1 - P_i)T$, where P_i is the current probability that m_i is faulty, since if m_i is good, retesting will probably yield the same behavior, taking time T. On the other hand, making another best test incurs the known cost T' of that test plus $(1 - P_i')(T + T')$, where P_i' is the average value over the possible test results of the maximum module fault probability.

4.7. Automatic Generation of Test Trees

Much conventional automatic testing is done by encoding a decision tree in a computer, which in turn controls ATE gear. Such a decision tree, or *test tree*, can be generated automatically by FIS, as discussed in the first application in Section 4.7. FIS performs the task of automatic test tree generation by alternately executing the best-test or replacement function and the make-test function, always doing the recommended test. For each test recommended, all qualitative values for its result are tried. That is, a make-test is done for each. Each result represents a branch in

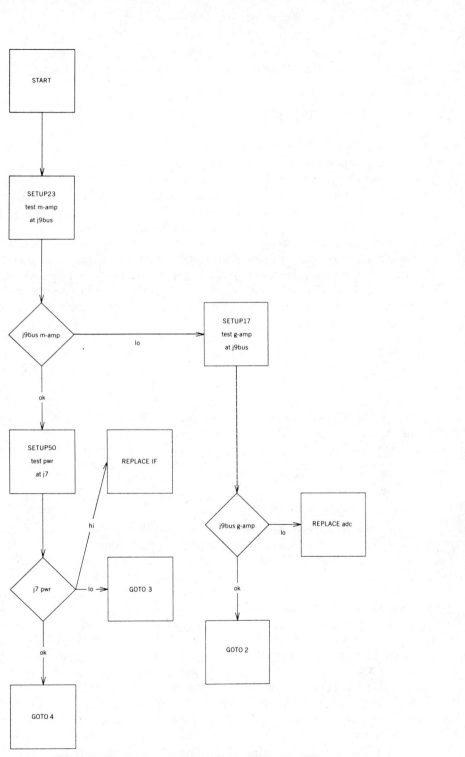

Figure 9. Partial diagnostic flowchart produced by FIS.

the test tree. Each test or replacement recommendation represents a node in the test tree. Figure 9 shows a sample of output from the automatic test tree generator.

5. CURRENT APPLICATIONS OF FIS

We have been testing and refining FIS on real analog UUTs to assess its performance and practicality and to provide ideas for improvements. We have been modeling a radar receiver–exciter subsystem with the goal of generating test trees (called diagnostic and functional flowcharts) that are comparable in quality to those written by test programmers. As a second application, we have recently begun applying FIS to a Navy sonar system as a technician's aid.

In the radar application, the goal is to demonstrate that FIS can relieve the human test programmer of part of the labor of producing a *test program set* (TPS), which is a program that controls ATE gear in the automatic execution of a test tree. It is the automatic test tree generation capability of FIS (see Section 4.7) that is used here. The part of the human effort that is relieved is the sequencing of the possible tests and the determination of when some modules warrant replacement and which ones. In exchange for this, FIS places a modest knowledge acquisition burden on the user, primarily in the form of causal rules and test cost information. Other parts of this task that we leave under human control are the choice of test equipment and the determination of what constitutes a sufficient set of tests to certify that the UUT is performing correctly and to do fault isolation. Figure 10 shows a hardcopy version of the more detailed CRT color graphics display of the radar unit. This is useful during the development of the UUT description, when the technician's aid mode is invoked to test interactively the diagnostic performance before test trees are generated. We are currently making refinements in FIS to make it practical for the TPS application. This includes primarily the improvement of the speed and accuracy of the best-test computation and the more intelligent handling of passed tests.

The second application involves the use of FIS as a maintenance advisor to a technician. It will be installed in a rugged portable computer and will direct or assist a technician in the troubleshooting of a complex, primarily analog sonar subsystem consisting of 105 replaceable modules, using manual test equipment. The primary functions will be the recommendation of a next best-test and the reporting of the FIS beliefs after a test is made.

The applications brought into focus the issue of computational complexity, since they require speedy operation even for large UUTs. The computational complexity of the propagation of test results through the causal rules appears to be approximately linear in the number of terminals in the UUT, since during the finding of an ambiguity set the number of rules invoked at each terminal depends only on the complexity of the immediately connected modules, not on the size of the UUT, and each terminal is visited at most once for each parameter. However, this is done at compile time, and so it need not be fast. In both technician's aid applications and test tree generation applications, most of the computation consists of make-

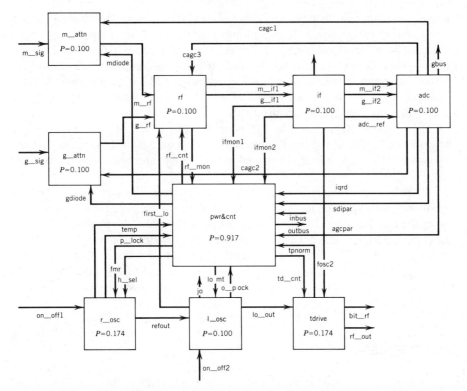

Figure 10. A model of a radar receiver/exciter in FIS.

test operations and best-test operations. The latter is the more computationally costly. The best-test selection procedure is too complex to perform a rigorous complexity analysis easily, but its complexity has two major contributions—one from the heuristic screening of available tests and one from the entropy calculations on the remaining candidates. The latter currently takes on the order of a few seconds for typical UUTs but is expected to be improved considerably by implementation changes. Since this is invoked once per candidate test, it is important that the heuristic screening procedures produce a small number of candidates. We expect that the heuristics described in Section 4.6 will lead to no more than ten candidate tests when they are fully implemented. The running time for the heuristic procedures is expected to be less than that of the entropy calculations.

6. CONCLUSIONS

The FIS project has resulted in an expert system shell that can efficiently acquire a causal model of the behavior of a UUT adequate for diagnostic reasoning and use that model in a variety of diagnostic settings to recommend tests and replacements and to interpret test results. Even with relatively small UUTs, the qualitative causal modeling of components clearly shows its power in the correctness and small size of the ambiguity sets resulting from each test, as compared to a topologically based troubleshooting system such as those of Cantone et al. [13] and Simpson and Balaban [14]. In the example of Figure 8, a purely topological troubleshooting system would miss the loading problem of M7 at T6 and suspect all the upstream modules for any failed test. There is no known nontopological system with which we can directly compare FIS.

The causal model required by FIS is modest in size and in our experience can be generated efficiently using the methods of Section 3.3. This suggests that our approach will allow efficient knowledge acquisition and accurate diagnosis for larger UUTs.

We plan to continue refining the FIS prototype, using lessons learned from the radar and sonar applications. Most of the additional improvements are expected to be in the user interface, for example, to make the graphics more suitable for large UUTs in the technician's aid application and to improve the efficiency of knowledge acquisition. We will also further refine the best test calculations (Section 4.6) to achieve as much speed and accuracy as possible and make other improvements to facilitate the transition of this technology into further development and eventual use in the field.

REFERENCES

1. F. Pipitone, An Expert System for Electronics Troubleshooting Based on Function and Connectivity. In *Proceedings of the IEEE First Conference on Artificial Intelligence Applications*, pp. 133–138, IEEE, Washington, D.C., 1984.

2. F. Pipitone, The FIS Electronics Troubleshooting System, *IEEE Computer Magazine*, pp. 68–76, July 1986.

3. J. DeKleer and B. C. Williams, Diagnosing Multiple Faults. In *Artificial Intelligence*, North-Holland, Amsterdam, 1987.

4. H. Geffner and J. Pearl, Distributed Diagnosis of Systems with Multiple Faults. Technical Report R-66 CSD-8600, UCLA Computer Science Department, Los Angeles, 1986.

5. J. Pearl, Distributed Revision of Belief Commitment in Multi-Hypotheses Interpretation, In *Proceedings 2nd AAAI Workshop on Uncertainty in Artificial Intelligence*, pp. 201–209, AAAI, Menlo Park, CA, 1986.

6. M. R. Genesereth, Diagnosis Using Hierarchical Design Models. In *Proceedings of the National Conference on Artificial Intelligence*, pp. 278–283, AAAI, Menlo Park, CA, 1982.

7. R. Davis, H. Schrobe, W. Hamscher, K. Wieckert, M. Shirley, and S. Polit, Diagnosis Based on Description of Structure and Function. In *Proceedings of the National Conference on Artificial Intelligence*, pp. 137–142, AAAI, Menlo Park, CA, 1982.

8. J. S. Brown, R. Burton, and J. DeKleer, Pedagogical, Natural Language and Knowledge Engineering Techniques in SOPHIE I, II, and III. In *Intelligent Tutoring Systems*, D. Sleeman and J. S. Brown (eds.), pp. 227–282, Academic Press, London, 1982.

9. R. M. Stallman and G. J. Sussman, Problem Solving About Electrical Circuits. In *Artificial Intelligence: An MIT Perspective*, P. H. Winston and R. H. Brown (eds.), Vol. 1, pp. 31–91, MIT Press, Cambridge, MA, 1979.

10. J. DeKleer and J. S. Brown, Foundations of Envisioning. In *Proceedings of the National Conference on Artificial Intelligence*, pp. 434–437, AAAI, Menlo Park, CA, 1982.

11. A. L. Brown, Qualitative Knowledge, Causal Reasoning, and the Localization of Failures, MIT AI Lab AI-TR-362, Ph.D. thesis, November 1976.

12. D. McDermott and R. Brooks, ARBY: Diagnosis with Shallow Causal Models. In *Proceedings of the National Conference on Artificial Intelligence*, pp. 370–372, AAAI, Menlo Park, CA, 1982.

13. R. R. Cantone, F. J. Pipitone, W. B. Lander, and M. P. Marrone, Model-Based Probabilistic Reasoning for Electronics Troubleshooting. In *Proceedings of the Eighth International Joint Conference on Artificial Intelligence*, pp. 207–211, AAAI, Menlo Park, CA, 1983.

14. W. R. Simpson and H. S. Balaban, The ARINC Research System Testability and Maintenance Program (STAMP). In *Proceedings of the 1982 IEEE Autotestcon Conference*, IEEE, New York, 1982.

15. J. J. King, Artificial Intelligence Techniques for Device Troubleshooting. Computer-Science Laboratory Technical Note Series, CSL-82-9 (CRC-TR-82-004), Hewlett Packard, Palo Alto, CA, 1982.

16. E. H. Shortliffe, *Computer-Based Medical Consultations: MYCIN*, Elsevier, New York, 1976.

17. R. O. Duda, P. E. Hart, K. Konolige, and R. Reboh, A Computer-Based Consultant for Mineral Exploration. Artificial Intelligence Center, SRI International, Menlo Park, CA, 1979.

18. G. Shafer, *A Mathematical Theory of Evidence*, Princeton University Press, Princeton, NJ, 1976.

EXPERT SYSTEM FAULT ISOLATION IN A SATELLITE COMMUNICATIONS NETWORK

Steve Miksell, Robert Quillin, William M. Wilkinson, Nadine Matteson, Mike Smisko, and Ed Zakrzewski
Stanford Telecommunications Inc., Reston, Virginia

Dawn Lowe
NASA Goddard Space Flight Center, Greenbelt, Maryland

1. INTRODUCTION

This chapter discusses the application of expert systems as decision aids to support the operation and control of communication networks. Specific functions to be addressed include performance monitoring, status assessment, trend analysis, anomaly detection, fault isolation, and problem resolution. A case study for the development of a communication network control fault diagnostic support tool is presented. The case study network is NASA's Tracking and Data Relay Satellite System (TDRSS) Space Network (also known as the SN). The diagnostic tool is the Fault Isolation Expert System for TDRSS Applications (FIESTA). This network control decision aid is being developed at Stanford Telecommunications, Inc. (STI) to support operators at the Network Control Center (NCC) at the Goddard Space Flight Center. Functional application areas being addressed by FIESTA involve providing automated support to manually intensive performance monitoring and fault isolation functions of the NCC.

Section 2 describes the company development approach, which has been employed (and has evolved) in applying expert systems technologies within STI's Communication Support Group. Section 3 presents the case study of the FIESTA project. The FIESTA case study is followed by a brief section describing other areas in which the development team members are applying the technology of expert systems. Where applicable, the manner in which these other applications either support or benefit from the FIESTA experience is discussed. A glossary of terms is provided at the end of the chapter.

2.   A GENERAL METHODOLOGY

2.1.   An Overview

Figure 1 presents an overview of the various stages of development for a typical operator support aid for communication network control. These development stages are often preceded by preliminary studies assessing the applicability of expert systems. The subtasks that define the methodology as well as a description of the underlying preliminary study are described briefly in the following subsections.

2.2.   The Preliminary Study

A fundamental driving force behind the consideration of expert system techniques for a particular application is a need or desire to replicate or automate a specific function, which is performed well by a human but does not appear readily amenable to conventional automation techniques. The success of an expert system project depends heavily on a match between the targeted application area (including requirements and resources) and the applicability of these items to knowledge-based techniques. An initial study is often required to provide the analysis to make such a distinction and is an important predecessor to any software development effort or commitment to a knowledge-based design strategy.

The initial study effort examines the type and availability of knowledge that is involved in the task. It assesses the degree of availability of this knowledge on which the success of the expert system will depend. The success or failure of the expert system will be dictated by the amount of application knowledge that can be ascertained and appropriately harnessed in the system's knowledge base. The objective of the initial study is to evaluate the problem to be solved in light of existing solutions and the tools available for development. Such a study also determines the applicability of the methodology and provides recommendations incorporating feasibility, cost, and potential benefits and identifies additional knowledge and application experts that will be required.

2.3.   Requirements and an Operational Concept

Clearly stated requirements and operational concepts are just as important for expert systems as they are for conventional software, despite differences in obtaining, organizing, and exercising requisite knowledge. As a minimum, requirements describe the domain, while operational concepts describe system roles. Such requirements are needed for project focus and to allow tracking of project status.

Expert system projects frequently have requirements and operational concepts that are less detailed than those of conventional projects, especially in initial phases.

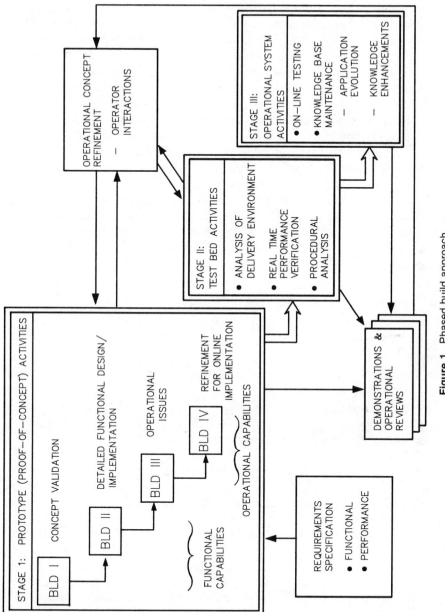

Figure 1. Phased build approach.

Requirements for conventional software are usually written with a more detailed understanding of the nature of the problems and an implicit understanding of how the problems will be solved for any and all circumstances. In conventional software, this understanding results in detailed software design documents before code generation begins. For these detailed requirements to be developed, a detailed functional procedure for all possible inputs must be identified and the number of possible procedures must be manageable. One must also assume that all data drivers required for program execution are available to the system in a relevant time frame, represent valid data, and allow unambiguous selection of the correct procedure. To the extent that one or more of these factors are absent (e.g., corrupted, inconsistent, or missing data coupled with an exponentially exploding list of possible conditions), a knowledge-based system design becomes more appropriate.

As the system evolves, procedures can be expected to become further defined and the initial requirements can be refined appropriately. In a similar manner, the operational concept can be expected to evolve as the system develops. As it becomes better understood how experts do their jobs, the optimum role for an expert system can be defined more accurately.

2.4.   An Iterative Build Approach

Elements that are often present in the application of expert system technology to support the control of communications networks include the following:

- Evolving system functional and performance requirements as the operational system develops.
- Effective problem resolution techniques that are employed by experts but often are poorly documented and have been developed through a rich history of operational refinement and evolution.

These factors often dictate an evolutionary development environment. Iterative builds and demonstrations of the interim approaches and results are supported by the development environment of a knowledge-based system and help to refine problem understanding and solutions in the process. Interim demonstrations provided by an iterative build approach also allow timely assessment of resolution techniques and the presentation of results, directly supporting the operational personnel who will use the system. Iterative builds allow this feedback to be incorporated immediately in the evolving system.

A key factor in meaningful demonstrations is the use of realistic situation data. Such data allow direct comparison of system behavior with expert behavior under identical circumstances and support increasingly expert performance as differences are recognized and the system is modified appropriately.

2.5.   Development Stages

Figure 1 also indicates various stages of development. Stage I is a proof-of-concept development effort often performed in an off-line environment that simulates the eventual deployment scenarios. During phase 1 (BUILDS I and II) of the stage I activities, the basic functional capabilities of the system are defined and implemented. Operational questions are also identified and addressed in a prototype environment. Assuming that operational constraints prevent the system from being developed in the environment in which it is to be fielded, operational questions (e.g., real-time performance issues) are addressed and resolved during phase 2 (BUILDS III and IV) of stage I. Phase 2 includes refinements to the simulation environment to ensure increased realism. Stage II involves testing of the system in an environment more tailored to the expected idiosyncrasies of the delivery environment. During this stage, a full operational testbed is often developed and the performance is evaluated and validated within the testbed. Operational refinements and changes necessitated by the environment are implemented in this stage also. Stage III stresses the use of the system as an operational tool. As also indicated in the diagram, the development suites established for the preliminary stages are retained to support further system growth and modification.

2.6. Development Support

2.6.1. Use of Software Tools.

Two factors that have influenced the current explosion in the application of expert system technology are (1) successful implementations that have spurred interest in knowledge-based technologies and (2) commercially available (and supported) knowledge engineering tools.

Knowledge engineering tools are currently available from companies like Inference Corp., Intellicorp, the Carnegie Group, Teknowledge Inc., Software A&E, computer manufacturers including DEC™ and IBM™, and universities that have begun direct marketing of their research and development efforts.

Capabilities of these tools range from providing a convenient language in which to write production rules, to full-blown inference engines with graphics capabilities, strong debugging aids, and natural language processors. Selecting the appropriate tools involves a comparison between the capabilities offered by the tools and the system requirements identified in the preliminary study. The more closely these capabilities and requirements match, the less time will be required for tool augmentations (e.g., hand-coded LISP functions) or time-consuming software workarounds. Such activities diminish the primary benefit associated with the tool—the ability to apply expert system technology directly to solve engineering problems.

2.6.2. Use of Specialized Hardware.

The major commercial offerings in the preceding section are available on either dedicated computers or specialized hardware such as LISP machines (e.g., SYMBOLICS™ and LMI™) developed specifically for symbolic processing. Tools available on these specialized machines include KEE™ from Intellicorp and ART™ from Inference Corp. An example of a dedicated computer would be a VAX™ 11/780 running an OPS5 application.

The expert system development tools were originally available only on the hardware where they were developed. The current host environment of fielded applications reflects this fact, and selection of a tool virtually dictated the hardware requirements. At the present time, tools are being actively ported to alternative hardware environments (including PCs). As this occurs, the hardware selection process will become more complex and additional cost benefits can be realized by careful trade-offs in this area.

2.6.3.   Situation Data: Real and Simulated. A tenet that has emerged as gospel from expert system developments (successful and otherwise) involves the importance of realistic test cases both for evaluation and for the development itself. For engineering applications, this concept needs to be extended to incorporate presentation of the test cases (the situation data) to the expert system. To be deployed effectively in an operational environment, the expert system needs access to the data that will drive the analysis and reasoning.

Development efforts undertaken without incorporating realistic interface concepts for data access in the overall design run the serious risk of requiring significant redesign before deployment can occur.

3.   FIESTA: A CASE STUDY

3.1.   The Problem Domain

FIESTA is being developed as a fault isolation expert system for NASA's Space Network. The Space Network, using geostationary satellites as relay stations, provides communication support to orbiting spacecraft as shown in Figure 2. As an aid to understanding the role of FIESTA, we first present a description of the Space Network itself.

3.1.1.   Space Network Overview. NASA's Space Network is the primary communications gateway for connecting NASA spacecraft with their respective ground support facilities [1]. The Space Network (SN) combines space and ground segments to provide high-availability tracking and data acquisition services for spacecraft in near-Earth orbit. Examples of current Space Network "users" include the Space Shuttle, Landsat-4 and -5, and the Earth Radiation Budget Satellite (ERBS). Future users will include the Space Telescope and eventually the Space Station.

The space segment of the baseline Space Network will consist of two operational geostationary satellites, Tracking and Data Relay Satellite East and West (TDRS-E and TDRS-W), as well as one spare satellite. From their geosynchronous orbit, the two operational satellites will be able to provide service to user spacecraft in near-Earth orbit (200–12,000 km) 85–100% of the time [2]. The TDR satellites are monitored and controlled from the White Sands Ground Terminal (WSGT) in White Sands, New Mexico. Space-to-ground links include a composite forward link for TDRS command and for relay of commands to user satellites and a composite return link for TDRS telemetry and for relay of data from user spacecraft.

Collocated with WSGT is the NASA Ground Terminal (NGT), which provides

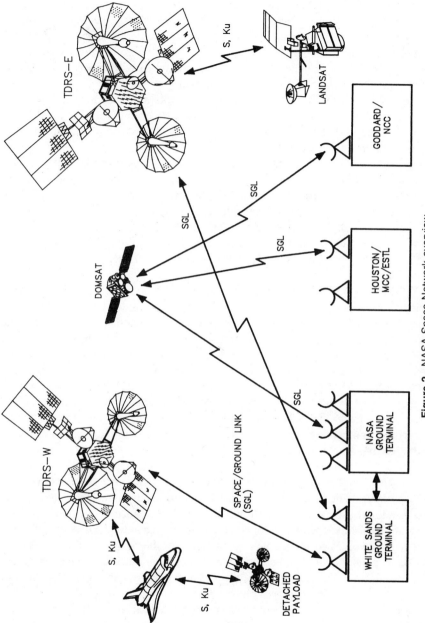

Figure 2. NASA Space Network overview.

the communications interface for the transfer of digital, TV, and analog data from WSGT to the other Space Network elements and users, via the NASA Communications (NASCOM) network. The NGT is responsible for many functions including data quality monitoring, which is performed through the use of frame analyzers. The statistics that they produce are compared with expected values and thus provide the basis for data quality evaluation.

NASCOM consists of a global system of circuits and switching and terminal facilities, operated by NASA to provide long-haul communications capabilities. All communications (voice and data) between Space Network elements and user spacecraft facilities are via NASCOM.

The Network Control Center (NCC) is the operations control facility for the entire Space Network. It serves as the focal point for network elements and user spacecraft facilities for coordination of all network support and resolution of problems. Its prime functions include scheduling of network resources, equipment configuration direction, and service quality monitoring and assurance. Thus, it coordinates isolation and resolution of faults when they occur. Figure 3 illustrates the NCC's place in the Space Network and the role of FIESTA in the NCC.

3.1.2. Space Network Telecommunication Services.
The Space Network provides both forward and return telecommunications service between low Earth-orbiting spacecraft and their control centers and data processing facilities. Several types of service are provided, depending on the data rate and duration of service period required, as well as the user spacecraft's telecommunication system design. The services can be divided into two general categories: multiple access (MA) and single access (SA). Multiple-access return services on the TDR satellite can be provided for up to 19 spacecraft simultaneously, using an electronically steered phased array. Each TDRS has two high-gain, parabolic antenna systems for K-band and S-band single-access services [2]. Generally, multiple services are combined to form a single schedule "event."

3.1.3. The Problem: Space Network Monitoring and Fault Detection and Isolation.
The extensive orbital coverage provided by the Tracking and Data Relay Satellite System (TDRSS) allows for increased real-time operations by user spacecraft. Real-time operations, together with the high bandwidth data flow through the Space Network, accentuate the critical nature of the NCC's fault detection and isolation responsibilities. It is essential that problems are detected immediately and service outages are resolved quickly, to minimize data loss and impact to the user mission. This function requires continuous monitoring of network performance indicators and comparison of expected versus actual values to detect anomalies. The NCC does not monitor user spacecraft command, telemetry, and tracking data directly. Rather, the NCC receives network performance data (related to user services) in the form of high-speed electronic messages from the Space Network elements.

The operations data messages (ODMs) [3] are received periodically from WSGT (approximately every 5 s), indicating the status of all ongoing services through the

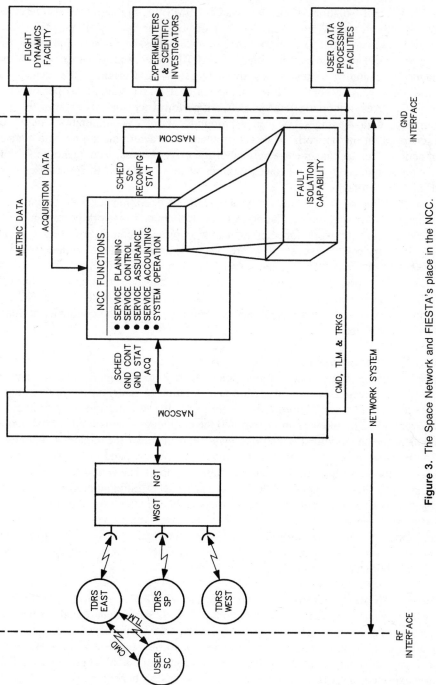

Figure 3. The Space Network and FIESTA's place in the NCC.

TDRSS. Fault Isolation Monitoring System (FIMS) [4, 5] reports are also received periodically from NGT (if requested), indicating the quality of the data being transferred from WSGT to the user spacecraft facilities. In addition, multiple types of operational performance messages (OPMs) [3] are employed to report on dynamically changing system states and configurations. Currently, the contents of these messages are combined and displayed on CRTs to operations personnel in the NCC. Network controllers and network performance analysts monitor the performance data messages, as well as ground control (reconfiguration) messages exchanged on the network, to detect problems and determine appropriate courses of action. This task is an extremely labor-intensive process. The quantity of information contained in the messages requires at least one (and in some cases two) display screen per service.

At the time of this writing, only one TDRS is operational, supporting a small number of user spacecraft. The network controllers and network performance analysts are able to work together in teams to provide complete coverage of all ongoing services. However, they are reaching an information saturation point. When the second TDRS is launched and the number of user spacecraft increases, the manual approach to network monitoring and fault detection and isolation will be inadequate. Some form of automation will be needed in order for the NCC to satisfy its mission-critical requirement to assure the quality and continuity of Space Network services.

3.1.4. The Solution: An Expert Assistant. Automating Space Network monitoring and fault detection and isolation presented a significant challenge. It was quickly recognized that detection and isolation of faults on the SN was not a deterministic process. Nominal values for performance indicators vary from event to event based on the user spacecraft and the equipment chains used. Furthermore, nominal and nonnominal conditions may often manifest the same "symptoms." For example, a nominal return service handover from S band to Ku band exhibits some of the same characteristics as an acquisition loss. The controllers and analysts in the NCC have developed substantial expertise in differentiating nominal and anomalous situations. This experience is accumulated in the form of heuristic "rules of thumb" that they apply to their task. The same knowledge must be captured and formally represented in order to automate the Space Network monitoring and fault detection and isolation functions. Consequently, a knowledge-based, expert system approach was pursued.

3.1.5. Expected Benefits. The objective of FIESTA is to provide an intelligent assistant to the Space Network controllers and performance analysts that will continuously monitor selected services, detect faults, bring these faults to the attention of the controller and analyst, and isolate the source of a problem to the major system component level. Based on the success of the initial prototype system, it is expected that FIESTA will provide the following benefits:

- Substantial increase in controller and analyst productivity. FIESTA will monitor multiple events (each of which may involve multiple services) simultaneously and direct the operator's attention when necessary. Thus, each controller and analyst will also be able to manage multiple events. This contrasts sharply with the current limitation of two or three services (i.e., at most one event) per operator.

- Permanent retention of the expertise accumulated by the most experienced controllers and analysts.
- Historical account of Space Network services. Currently, the NCC relies heavily on handwritten logs from the controllers and analysts for records of problems and their causes. This places an additional burden on the operations personnel. With FIESTA, complete, accurate, and standardized records of all problems and their known and suspected causes will be maintained automatically.
- A realistic training environment for new operations personnel. FIESTA's abilities to explain its conclusions and to operate in a stand-alone mode (using previously recorded data messages) will provide an ideal training environment for new operators.

3.2. System Architecture for an Expert System Solution

3.2.1. Architecture Overview. From a system architecture perspective [6], FIESTA falls within the class of real-time decision aids because it involves three unsynchronized elements. These elements are as follows:

- A source of real-time situation data
- A reasoning/inferencing expert
- A human operator of the system

Problems inherent in driving an expert system from external data sources in real time, while simultaneously reasoning about the incoming data and responding to operator requests for data and advice (without restricting the timing of those requests), must be addressed by the system architecture. The architectural design of FIESTA incorporates various features of the software development environment selected for this system. ART, the Automated Reasoning Tool from Inference Corporation, provides much of the structure through which the architectural characteristics are realized.

The FIESTA system architecture features three-way asynchronous operation of data handling, reasoning, and operator interaction to coordinate the elements involved. This asynchronous operation is accomplished by interfacing all components through a central knowledge base. Figure 4 provides an overview of the system architecture. The FIESTA front-end processor serves as a gateway for automatically obtainable situation data (AOSD), which are arriving from external data sources in real time. The FIESTA reasoning expert combines the situation data with its prestored knowledge base of rules, propositions, and frames to derive conclusions about the health of the system. Finally, the run-time monitor sends alerts and

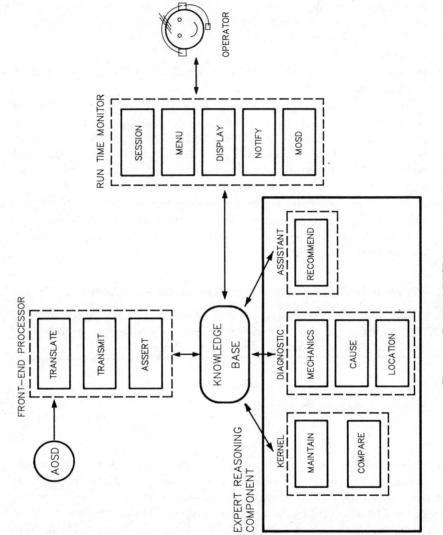

Figure 4. Detailed FIESTA system architecture.

114

requested displays to the operator. It also enables the operator to request more information or enter any manually obtainable situation data (MOSD) that may be available. These data provide further information (via voice, special console, or hardcopy report) beyond that available automatically through high-speed message traffic.

The synchronization necessary to coordinate these components is provided by the ART fact database. The front-end processor, FIESTA expert, and run-time monitor consist of processes and rules that maintain and monitor this fact database. The rules nominate themselves for execution whenever their conditions are satisfied. Various mechanisms available in ART can then be used to sort through the nominated rules and select one for immediate execution. By exploiting the capabilities provided by expert system development tools in the rule nomination and selection process, the knowledge engineer is provided with a powerful and easily adjusted mechanism for arbitrating between the competing needs of the expert reasoner and human–machine interface components when resource contention occurs.

3.2.2. FIESTA Subsystem Descriptions.

The expert reasoning portion has been subdivided into three parts (kernel, diagnostic, assistant), as shown in Figure 4, reflecting the specific fault-reasoning functions in the end-to-end Space Network. This results in a total of five subsystems (dotted boxes), which communicate via the common knowledge base and consist of a total of 14 individual modules (solid boxes). Each subsystem and module are described below.

Front-End Processor. The FIESTA front-end processor obtains AOSD for assertion to the KB once every AOSD input cycle. External interface to the AOSD is in standard NASA high-speed message formats. The front-end processor consists of three modules:

- Translate: translate contents of AOSD to knowledge base format.
- Transmit: move data from hardware or software point of origin to point of use.
- Assert: "assert" AOSD into FIESTA database.

Kernel. The FIESTA kernel contains rules that must process (fire or be eligible to fire) every AOSD input cycle. It monitors incoming AOSD to detect anomalies and maintain system memory variables (SMVs) describing the AOSD stream. The kernel consists of two modules:

- Maintain: maintain SMVs for event, service, and anomaly life cycles and initiate diagnostic episode (DE) life cycle.
- Compare: compare AOSD/SMVs to SMVs/static standards for value, range, trend, correlation, and timing.

Diagnostics. The FIESTA diagnostics subsystem interprets available situation data and SMVs. It determines whether faults have occurred, isolates and diagnoses them, and keeps a record of its reasoning to support explanations and justifications to the operator. The diagnostics subsystem must cover its domain and provide sufficiently accurate results in a reasonable time frame. Diagnostics consists of three modules:

- Mechanics: maintains DE life cycle, including current values for certainty factors.
- Cause: determines whether a fault has occurred, diagnoses cause, and requests MOSD if needed.
- Location: determines location of data/control network fault and requests MOSD if needed.

Assistant. The FIESTA assistant subsystem determines what operator actions are needed to improve service at any given time for each active service:

- Recommend: recommends testing, repairs, or other actions that the operator can take to improve service.

Run-Time Monitor. The FIESTA monitor provides the operator with a "window" on the evolving Space Network, by providing data automatically as well as on request. Operator interface is provided via the keyboard, the mouse, and the menu system. The monitor consists of five modules:

- Session: initialize FIESTA session from operator log on through termination.
- Menu: provide menu trees, error control, and on-line help.
- Display: manage terminal workspace and window inventory and refresh static and dynamic data.
- Notify: monitor knowledge base and decide when to issue notifications and alerts to the operator.
- MOSD: process system requests for MOSD and operator requests to provide MOSD.

3.2.3. FIESTA Subsystem Interfaces.
The FIESTA system has two external interfaces. The AOSD interface is defined in standard NASA high-speed message formats including schedule orders (SHOs), operational messages (OPMs), operational data messages (ODMs), and fault isolation monitoring system (FIMS) messages. The operator interface is provided using commands, menus, a mouse, graphics, and text and has evolved throughout the multibuild process of developing FIESTA based on feedback from operators and human factors personnel.

The FIESTA system has seven key internal interfaces. Each interface is a defined communication path from one FIESTA subsystem to one or more of the other FIESTA subsystems. The data-driven nature of the processing directly supports implementation of the interfaces. Rules within a source subsystem assert facts in the ART knowledge base. Corresponding rules in the sink subsystems will be "instantiated" and then executed by this fact assertion, thus completing the pathway.

The interfaces employed in FIESTA are as follows (arrows indicate sources, crosses indicate sinks):

	Front-End Processor	Kernal	Diag-nostics	Assistant	Run-Time Monitor
HSM interface	→	×	×	×	×
Service interface		→	×	×	×
Anomaly interface		→	×		
DE interface		→	→	×	
Certainty factors interface			→		×
Recommendations interface				→	×
MOSD interface			×	×	←

3.3. Representative Subsystems and Interfaces

The preceding section provided an overview of the FIESTA solution to the fault isolation problem. In the following sections three areas of FIESTA are examined in detail:

1. Simulation of the NCC environment and the FIESTA front-end processor.
2. Knowledge representation approaches and the underlying knowledge engineering task for the expert reasoning component.
3. Realization of the operational concept as shown in a typical dialog session.

3.3.1. Simulating the NCC Environment

3.3.1.1. Situation Data. FIESTA's primary source of information about the situation of the TDRSS Space Network is a series of control and status messages that are passed around the network [6, 7]. The sources, sinks, and types of data are rigidly defined in a series of interface control documents. NASA calls these data *high-speed messages* or HSMs. To allow for possible enhancements to the data available via electronic means in the NCC, we divide all situation data into automatically obtainable situation data (AOSD) and manually obtainable situation data (MOSD). Currently, AOSD consists of HSMs only.

MOSD is not as well defined as AOSD, but it can be viewed as data that are accessible and useful for fault diagnosis but not available on-line in the NCC. This definition changes as the knowledge engineering process proceeds and the uses of additional data are uncovered. Since new HSMs or changes to existing HSMs cannot be introduced readily into the operational network, FIESTA incorporates this information as MOSD. MOSD currently used are data that are typically passed through special closed-circuit displays or via telephone conversations between operators at various points in the network, for example, weather conditions at White Sands Ground Terminal, locally recognized system failures, and unscheduled equipment outages. Telephone and face-to-face conversations and comparisons of data are currently used in manual fault isolation and will continue to be helpful in reducing fault ambiguities. They are not a new "operations concept" imposed by FIESTA.

MOSD can be requested by FIESTA or volunteered by the operator. MOSD are requested only when needed for diagnosis and isolation of a particular fault. This is done to minimize the operator's workload. MOSD are taken directly from the operator's console via an asynchronous process to avoid delay in other processing.

AOSD bear more discussion in terms of the contents and treatment in the FIESTA development process. Four types of HSMs are currently used in FIESTA. More are available in the NCC and may be used later. Note that FIESTA views network operations in terms of services, so the following HSMs will be discussed in terms of FIESTA's service viewpoint. Services are instances of simplex communications to or from a given user over a specific channel. For SHOs, the actual organization of the messages is in terms of "events." An event is defined in terms of support for a single user for a specific continuous time period. It consists of one or more services that are provided during this period.

An example of an event would be Space Shuttle support (a single user) consisting of Sa-band return, Sa-band forward, and Ku-band return, all single access (multiple services), from 11:00:00 until 11:52:00 (the time period). Such scheduling is necessary because the Space Shuttle is often required to communicate over multiple channels simultaneously both to and from its Project Operation Control Center (POCC).

While SHOs are organized around events, the major organization of ODMs and FIMS messages is in terms of TDRS satellites and radio-frequency bandwidths. OPMs are organized by service. FIESTA uses the following message types:

- *SHO*. Scheduling orders [3] originate in the NCC to allocate network resources to given users. They are typically broadcast well before those resources are to be used. FIESTA uses them to remember to look for services to start and stop at given times and to characterize services by user, type of service to be provided, bandwidth, antennas, channels, and other resources to be used. Normally only one SHO is transmitted per event.

- *OPM*. Various operations messages [3] are defined. Some are for normal occurrences such as the end of a service, while some notify various entities for exceptional occurrences or are requests and approvals for activity needed only in exceptional circumstances. The latter are events such as requests for reconfigurations or reacquisitions of signals. FIESTA uses a subset of the available OPM types.

- *ODM.* Operations data messages [3] are reports on the health and status of every ongoing service every 5 seconds. The data to generate them originates on board the TDRS and at White Sands. Contents vary by type of service, containing such things as indicators for synchronization and carrier lock and bit error rate status. Most fields are quantized to only a few possible values. ODMs are the primary source of data for detecting the occurrence of faults.
- *FIMS.* Fault isolation monitoring system [4, 5] messages are produced by frame analyzers located at the NGT. These messages contain data such as flags for clock/data present at White Sands, number-of-frames-in-lock count, and frame synchronization. These are also sent every 5 seconds for each ongoing service that schedules their use.

Figure 5 depicts the TDRSS Space Network and the data paths of several HSMs. FIESTA has potential to see all messages that originate in or go to the NCC.

FIESTA is purely passive as seen by the rest of the TDRSS Space Network. It only listens to these messages and never generates any. Any diagnoses made are presented directly to the operator. Thus, keeping the human-in-the-loop remains a critical element for outputs as well as inputs. This is especially important to encourage user acceptance of FIESTA as a tool to help the operator, not as a replacement threat.

3.3.1.2. *Hardware and Software Environments.*
The FIESTA prototype is currently being built in an off-line environment outside the NCC. This parallels conventional software development in which on-line validation occurs after off-line development and thorough system testing.

Magnetic tapes of HSM traffic are made available to developers. The data contained on these tapes are taken from the live network and from a set of simulations run expressly for the purpose of creating test data sets. STI has accumulated a library of historic faults along with many hours worth of nominal network operation.

The off-line development environment is made to look as much as possible like the NCC in terms of the data available and the software environment. A decision was made early on to isolate interface and NCC simulation functions in a front-end processor for development and possibly for fielding purposes. This provides a separation of the preprocessing and interface functions from the knowledge-based functions that are the primary interests of the project and makes the hardware and software required for the interface function cheaper to redefine if required. The rest of this section will deal with the prototype testbed system developed at STI's facilities in Reston, Virginia.

The FIESTA prototype consists of two computers and two bodies of software that communicate over commercially available networking tools. The fault isolation expert system component runs on a dedicated Symbolics 3640 LISP machine. Much of the expert system application is written in ART from Inference Corp. The FIESTA front-end processor (FFEP) has been prototyped on a VAX 11/730. Figure 6 illustrates STI's AI Laboratory, some of which is exercised for this testbed.

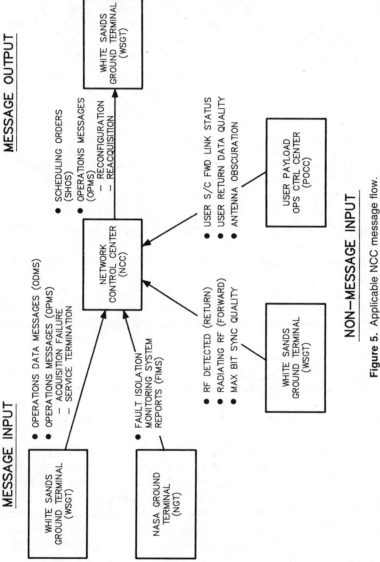

Figure 5. Applicable NCC message flow.

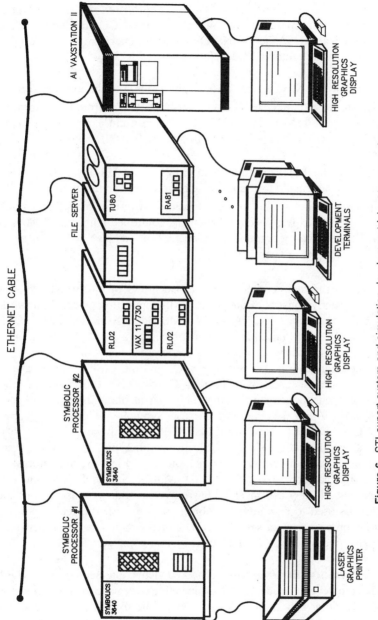

Figure 6. STI expert system and simulation development laboratory overview.

121

3.3.1.3.   The NCC Simulator and AOSD Transformer. This section presents an overview of the purpose and functionality of the NCC simulator and AOSD transformer software (NSAT). The NSAT was built to perform the following functions for the FIESTA prototype's development:

- To simulate the NCC insofar as providing AOSD to the rest of FIESTA.
- To isolate the expert system components of FIESTA from the preprocessing functions performed in the NSAT to provide a close representation of the actual delivery environment and to isolate NCC interface functions in a preprocessor.
- To offload the LISP machine, translating coded HSM values to symbolic expressions amenable to use by the expert system application.
- To provide a tool useful in development and testing of FIESTA—one for ''feeding'' the expert system components controlled amounts of data at controlled times; the programmer needs a tool to ''replay'' a given scenario to test and debug the expert system.

Figure 7 depicts the main components and data flows of the FIESTA prototype. The system currently consists of one VAX/VMS application process and two LISP machine application processes. The VAX/VMS side also makes use of the NCP and VMS. Several LISP machine system processes are also used (the garbage collector processes, mouse and keyboard processes, network processes, screen manager). Communications between the VAX and the LISP machine take place over a one-way Chaosnet stream connection. Chaosnet is a LISP machine protocol providing communications over Ethernet and other media. (Chaosnet will soon be replaced by DECnet in the prototype because Symbolics is dropping support of their VMS Chaosnet systems with release 7.0 of their software.)

The NSAT reads and translates AOSD from a disk file, transmitting it to the LISP machine under user control. A ''synchronizing'' LISP machine process reads AOSD over the net and makes the AOSD available in the LISP world for the FIESTA process. (The LISP machine has only one address space so that global symbols can be used to pass arbitrary objects between LISP machine processes.) The FIESTA process then parses the AOSD and asserts it as a set of facts into the ART database, ready for use by the expert system components.

3.3.2.   Knowledge Engineering. The knowledge engineering process [6] for the FIESTA project consisted of two baseline efforts germane to all expert systems: *knowledge definition* and *knowledge collection*. The overall goal of this process was to analyze, identify, and define the knowledge structures that encompass NASA's TDRSS Space Network fault diagnosis domain. The definition phase determined the scope and complexity of the task at hand by identifying where the knowledge resided, what form it was in, and how difficult it would be to acquire. The collection phase focused on an all-out effort to tap the wide range of resources identified in the definition phase.

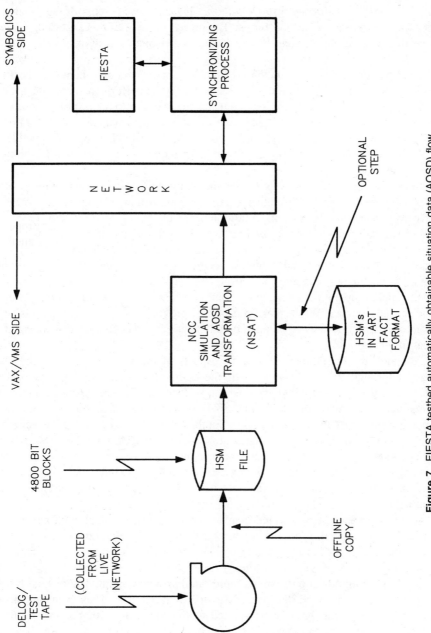

Figure 7. FIESTA testbed automatically obtainable situation data (AOSD) flow.

123

3.3.2.1.   FIESTA Knowledge Definition. TDRSS Space Network fault diagnosis expertise existed in varying forms. The primary source of this knowledge came from the experts who currently perform the fault isolation task at the NCC. The current operational environment highlights a definite need for a further level of automation. Fault detection remains a highly manual function where the operator visually monitors two or more video screens displaying performance data and action and information alerts. A voice loop connects the operator to the rest of the network elements by providing a conference style forum for other element operational personnel to notify the NCC of anomalous conditions, for the NCC operators to query other network operators to aid in further fault diagnosis, and for coordination of resolution procedures.

Since no automated analysis of the incoming performance data is made, the responsibility to (1) visually detect a parameter transition, (2) determine whether the current value indicates a fault condition or merely a routine or expected dropout, and (3) initiate a diagnostic session rests solely with the operator. Fundamental to all the diagnostic work is a basic knowledge of the TDRSS Space Network: its topology, message flow and contents, relations between parameters and specific signal processing equipment, and aspects unique to each user. On top of that, the expert applies operational procedures outlined in a variety of handbooks, user's guides, and courses. While these procedures provide a set of possible tools, the operator relies most heavily on operational experience to decide what is wrong and what to do about it.

Although the operational experience aspects of the knowledge could only be gleaned through direct observation of the operator in action or in face-to-face interviews, the fundamental knowledge was well documented but spread throughout numerous documents. High-level TDRSS Space Network operational concept documents provided a convenient overview but the fine detail was found in the element-to-element interface and data format control documents (ICDs and DFCDs), which defined the data flows and message contents and low-level ground communication equipment specifications that described in detail the ground equipment and its relation to specific parameters, different user services, and equipment chains and topologies.

Additional expertise was found in areas outside the operational environment. In particular, the network testing group provided an entirely different perspective and gave some much needed insight into problem areas that they had become familiar with through years of network testing. Further knowledge sources were located in the form of communications experts more familiar with communications hardware in general than the TDRSS Space Network in particular. They provided deep knowledge that could broadly be applied to the localization of communications system hardware faults in general. By searching out pockets of knowledge beyond that of the expert(s) whose thought process was being modeled, STI was able to complement the operational expertise to provide a stronger, more powerful tool in the end.

The depth and breadth of the knowledge identified in this initial analysis dictated an appropriate adjustment of the scope of FIESTA's application domain. Instead of focusing on all users of the network, the FIESTA prototype was developed for Space Shuttle applications. A wide base of knowledge had evolved for Shuttle operational support and centered around a select group of experienced operators brought in specifically for Shuttle events. Since initial proof-of-concept was more important than full operational coverage at the prototype stage, the focus on Space Network fault diagnosis during Shuttle support provided a stepping stone toward support for all network users.

3.3.2.2. Knowledge Collection. Having defined what kind of knowledge existed, the next step entailed collecting these data. For NCC operational personnel, primarily the Shuttle operational support team at the NCC, knowledge collection best took place during real-time mission observation. It was extremely important to observe directly the expert operating in a real-time, hands-on environment because the expert was often unaware of the assumptions he or she made, the steps skipped, or the many other obvious problems routinely conquered but not considered important. Through a combination of direct observation coupled with one-on-one interviews, the knowledge engineer identified the heuristics, assumptions, tricks, and underlying logic that would eventually make up the knowledge base from which FIESTA could draw its inferential power.

3.3.3. Knowledge Representation.

Knowledge representation requires translating collected knowledge into a working software unit. Two efforts comprised the task of knowledge representation: *diagnostic strategy design* and *knowledge structure design*. The design of the diagnostic strategy determined how the diagnostic rules would be represented in software form. The knowledge structures defined the internal format of symbolic facts in FIESTA, both background knowledge and input facts.

3.3.3.1. Diagnostic Strategy Design. The concepts behind acquisition determination, fault detection, and fault diagnosis make up the core of FIESTA's diagnostic methodology.

ACQUISITION DETERMINATION. The concept of acquisition plays a major role in FIESTA's diagnostic approach because of signal behavior differences during and after acquisition. An important differentiation must first be made between signal acquisition and data acquisition. Signal acquisition is determined through monitoring of appropriate demodulator lock and bit error rate indications. Data acquisition keys on bit synchronizer lock and frame sync lock indications. This differentiation is necessary for several reasons:

- Signal acquisition can occur without data acquisition.
- Shuttle may schedule data on channels for an entire event but only transmit on that channel for a portion of that event.
- Positive signal acquisition without data acquisition points the problem to different diagnostic areas than combined negative signal and data acquisition.

Prior to full fault detection and diagnostic processing for a specific service, FIESTA must first determine that positive signal acquisition has occurred for that service. FIESTA monitors signal quality parameters and determines positive acquisition when these parameters have remained nominal for 2 consecutive minutes.

The rationale behind this buffered 2-minute monitoring is based on the erratic behavior of the signal and its indicators as the Shuttle comes into line-of-sight of the TDR satellite. Sporadic dropouts are common in this stage of the service, and FIESTA should not waste resources running down this expected behavior pattern. FIESTA will not consider that an acquisition anomaly has occurred until 4 minutes have passed since the beginning of service and a nominal signal quality 2-minute buffer count has not been initiated.

Since the Shuttle nominally acquires on SSA (S-band, single access) return utilizing the SSA forward for a coherent frequency reference, FIESTA determines positive SSA forward acquisition upon SSA return acquisition determination (given SSA return is configured for coherent service). This provides a more reliable determination of SSA forward acquisition since there is a scarcity of useful performance data available on the SSA forward link (e.g., SSA forward link status is set to active at the start of an event and merely indicates that White Sands Ground Terminal equipment has been allocated for that service).

Data acquisition determination is a challenging problem for the Shuttle support. Reasoning takes place in two different areas for Shuttle data acquisition: SSAR/KSAR channel 1 acquisition and KSAR channel acquisition (channels 2 and 3). The complexity of the problem stems from a lack of high-speed message notification of actual versus scheduled support. To be more precise, the Shuttle will frequently schedule data on all KSAR (Ku-band, single access) channels for a whole event but only transmit data for a portion of that event. No indication of when the data will start or stop is made. In another case, since SSA return and KSA return channel 1 provide mutually exclusive services, only one is up at any one time, but handovers back and forth occur without high-speed message notification. These situations present a dilemma for FIESTA. With dropouts (handovers or data termination) occurring without notice and lack of data on channels where it was scheduled, FIESTA needs a philosophy and methodology to handle these conditions.

FIESTA currently will not monitor for data quality anomalies until data acquisition has been determined for that channel. Data acquisition is determined positive when nominal bit-sync-lock and frame-sync-lock indications have been detected for more than 10 consecutive seconds following signal acquisition. Once data acquisition has occurred, a data-related anomaly will cause a fault to be detected and a diagnosis to follow. A possible cause of the fault will include an unannounced termination of data by the user. When handovers occur between the KSAR channel 1 and SSAR services, FIESTA detects a dropout on one of those services but is able to diagnose the problem as a handover with a high degree of certainty. In certain cases, FIESTA can detect handovers prior to detection of the dropout, recognize that this is not a fault, and hence not initiate a diagnostic episode.

FAULT DETECTION. A major goal of FIESTA is the detection of all detectable anomalies. This is addressed through the use of an independent set of anomaly detection and data filtering rules to allow for anomaly detection independent of fault isolation. In other words, fault detection takes place with no prior knowledge of whether or not the fault can be isolated. Thus, FIESTA addresses all anomalies regardless of fault diagnosis potential. An alternative approach would pattern match only on performance and status data patterns that correspond to known fault conditions. This strategy violates the first goal and unnecessarily restricts the scope of the FIESTA prototype. Hence, the first strategy discussed provides us with a capability to handle all detectable anomalous scenarios.

Four areas within fault detection warrant discussion:

- Nominal value and range definitions
- Initial fault detection
- Secondary fault detection
- Service normalization.

Fault detection rules provide an independent source of network status information to the diagnostic rules. Diagnostic rules rely on this network status data to reason about current conditions. The detection rules monitor for anomalous conditions, detect non-nominal parameters and initiate diagnostic episodes based on detected conditions, continue to monitor and provide network status information to the diagnostic rules through a diagnostic episode, and determine when the diagnostic episode can be terminated.

The definition of what is nominal varies among different services, events, and conditions within an event. FIESTA determines the nominal range for all signal strength parameters and will not monitor for data-related faults when it has been determined no data are on a particular service or channel (in line with the rules concerning data acquisition). FIESTA continually tracks the signal strength parameters and decides on a nominal value when the service is acquired (i.e., signal acquisition has occurred) and the appropriate signal strength indication has remained steady (at one level) or fluctuated within one unit less of that level for a period of 1 min. At this point, FIESTA determines the nominal value and then defines the lowest acceptable bound in line with operator-defined heuristics.

Following positive acquisition determination for a particular service, FIESTA will subsequently monitor that service to detect fault conditions. The first out-of-tolerance condition detected on incoming performance reports for a particular service will initiate a "diagnostic episode." FIESTA will only monitor for signal-related faults (e.g., out-of-tolerance conditions in link status, demodulator locks, bit error rate, and signal strengths) when signal acquisition has occurred. Likewise, once data acquisition has occurred, FIESTA will monitor for data-stream-related faults (e.g., symbol/bit-sync locks and clock present, data present, frame-sync-lock, and frames-in-lock counts).

Thus, the first detection of such an anomaly opens up a diagnostic episode. A diagnostic episode is defined as an effort to diagnose an anomalous condition on a given service. FIESTA can have as many simultaneous diagnostic episodes as there are services ongoing at any one time. Diagnostic episodes can share information to search for commonalities among simultaneous fault conditions on different services. Once a diagnostic episode has been started, FIESTA continues to monitor the service. It will detect status changes from nominal to anomalous and vice versa. FIESTA detects problems at both the element and equipment levels (if possible). For example, given detection of a subcarrier-lock status of no-lock, FIESTA asserts (anomaly-detected-element WSGT) and (anomaly-detected-equipment medium-rate-demodulator). FIESTA closes out diagnostic events after 2 minutes of consecutive nominal service. All parameters must return to their nominal values for this entire 2-minute stretch.

FAULT DIAGNOSIS. The fault diagnostic approach developed for FIESTA can be described under two primary areas: *hypothetical reasoning* and *certainty factors*. These interrelated concepts form the backbone of the overall system diagnostic methodology.

Hypothetical reasoning attempts to parallel the thought pattern of an expert by selecting the most likely fault from a pool of known possibilities. This process involves hypothesizing all known faults (at a high level), immediately ruling out some, and pursuing others to a lower level of detail. Although there are a finite number of fault possibilities in the TDRSS Space Network, it is far more logical and computationally efficient to form a hierarchy of faults and work down the tree in a structured manner.

The highest-level hierarchical breakdown in a diagnostic episode occurs between fault location and fault cause. Both branches provide significant information on fault conditions in the network. While the fault location identifies where the anomaly occurred, the fault cause explains why the anomaly occurred at a particular point. These two forms of reasoning can be separated because fault localization involves significantly different rules from fault cause reasoning in that the location of a fault is a data flow/data blockage problem while the fault cause is a much more inferential and heuristic exercise in diagnosis. The two branches can be viewed as two independent experts, a fault location expert who determines the point at which data were lost and a fault cause expert who explains why. Following their analyses, the two experts confer and present the most likely fault location and cause to provide a twofold explanation of the anomaly.

Using the natural hierarchy of the TDRSS Space Network fault causes and fault locations provides FIESTA with the flexibility to diagnose locations and causes as low as possible. In some cases, the available data may not be sufficient to pin down a specific piece of equipment or a particular network operator, but the data may be sufficient to isolate the location to a network element (e.g., a specific ground terminal), set of elements (e.g., either the Shuttle or the relay satellite), or isolate the cause to an operational type of error at a high level. Thus, this structure attempts to give the diagnosis as much flexibility and depth to accommodate varying levels of operator experience and skill and to adapt to a variety of data availability conditions.

Next, we discuss *certainty factors*. A fundamental design characteristic of an expert system is its uncertainty management approach. The inferences humans make are often uncertain; certain conditions may "suggest," "sometimes result in," or "may mean" a corresponding conclusion. Thus, a mechanism must be developed to (1) represent probabilistic statements, (2) gather and combine evidence for and/or against a certain hypothesis; and (3) present this hypothesis and its "certainty" to the user. Various alternatives exist for representation of uncertainty (Dempster–Shafer theory of evidence, fuzzy logic, Bayesian inference). The technique chosen for FIESTA was the MYCIN CF Model [8].

The original MYCIN CF (Certainty Factor) Model was published in 1975 as part of the Stanford University Heuristic Programming Project. MYCIN is viewed as "the granddaddy of expert systems" and one of the primary milestones toward the launching of the expert system field. It was developed to diagnose bacterial infections, prescribe treatment for the diagnoses, and operate as a physicians' consultant. The following reasons form the basis for our choice of the CF Model: (1) the MYCIN CF Model is a standard in the field in that it has withstood the test of time, scrutiny, and numerous implementations outside its original application. (2) The MYCIN domain was diagnostic as is FIESTA's: FIESTA monitors incoming symptoms (network performance data), detects and diagnoses the problem, and acts as an operational consultant. (3) This model is easily implementable via LISP and ART code. Another feature we have found through our prototyping efforts is that the CF Model is easily understandable and integrates well into the operational psyche of its intended user community.

Through interaction with experts, inferential patterns are developed and translated into ART rules, and the diagnostic conclusions are assigned a degree of certainty. Thus, when a specific diagnostic rule fires, it asserts a positive or negative certainty toward a specific hypothesis. Let us define the following notation in line with MYCIN:

- $MB[h, e] = x$: the measure of increased belief in the hypothesis h based on the evidence e is x.
- $MD[h, e] = y$: the measure of increased disbelief in the hypothesis h based on the evidence e is y.

MB and MD are between 0 and 1 and represent a measure of belief or disbelief with 1 being totally certain and 0 as no support at all. A prototypical rule could work as follows (in ART):

```
(defrule sample-positive-rule
    (symptom-1)
    (symptom-2)
```

$\rightarrow$

```
(assert
  (positive-evidence hypothesis-h 0.5
    (hypothesis-h is a potential problem based on symptom-1 and symptom-
    2)))).
```

This rule assigns an MB of 0.5 to hypothesis h based on the two symptoms on the left-hand side. In addition to assigning a measure of belief (positive evidence for a hypothesis), each diagnostic rule asserts a justification in English syntax as part of the evidence that can provide a traceback capability to explain why a certain hypothesis is believed at a certain level. This structure is consistent for MD assertion, negative evidence toward a hypothesis.

Since numerous rules can contribute both positive and negative evidence toward one single hypothesis, a methodology to combine these MBs and MDs is needed. The MYCIN CF Model defines a value termed CF, the overall certainty factor. The net CF is derived as follows:

$$
\mathrm{CF}_{\mathrm{combine}}\,(X,\,Y) \equiv
\begin{cases}
X + Y\,(1 - X), & X,\,Y\ \text{both} > 0; \\[2mm]
\dfrac{X + Y}{1 - \min\left[\,|X|,\,|Y|\,\right]}, & \text{one of } X \text{ or } Y < 0; \\[2mm]
-\mathrm{CF}_{\mathrm{combine}}\,(-X,\,-Y), & X,\,Y\ \text{both} < 0.
\end{cases}
$$

This is the technique FIESTA uses to combine multiple pieces of evidence relating to a specific fault cause or fault location into an overall net-certainty factor. X and Y above can be either an MB term (positive sign) or a $-$MD (negative sign) term (since both MB and MD as defined above are greater than 0). In analyzing this combination technique, some interesting insights can be made. When a positive net certainty (X) already exists for a hypothesis and another piece of positive evidence (Y) is asserted, that new positive evidence is applied proportionately only to the level of nonbelief still remaining: $Y(1 - X)$. The positive–negative combination rule ensures that one single piece of negative evidence does not overwhelm several pieces of positive evidence (or vice versa). This is accomplished through softening the effect of a piece of evidence of a lesser magnitude on a net-certainty factor of the opposite sign and greater magnitude. FIESTA also combines the net certainty for overall fault location and fault cause to use in an explanation window for notification, explanation, and justification purposes. The highest positive fault location net certainty is combined with the highest fault cause net certainty by taking an average of the two and presenting that number to the user. Individual CFs for separate fault location and fault cause hypotheses are available through an alternative hypotheses menu option.

ADDITIONAL FEATURES. Various ancillary features of the FIESTA system warrant discussion in their relation to the overall diagnostic methodology. As discussed above, the system presents the top fault cause and fault location to the operator in a textual notification–explanation–justification scheme. Also available to the operator is a listing of the alternative hypotheses and their relative CFs. These alternative fault cause and fault location hypotheses are available in menu form and allow the operator to request justification for a specific alternative cause or location and also to request presentation of the next lower hierarchy of fault alternatives (from a particular ground terminal fault location the operator may display all the CFs associated with the different equipment at that ground terminal).

The system also contains goal-oriented rules that request the operator to enter in particular pieces of data (MOSD) that are not available to the system but that the operator can ascertain via voice or special console. The requests are made only when there is a diagnostic rule(s) waiting for a specific data item to be entered into FIESTA. In addition to this facility, the system will also provide recommended actions to help resolve the anomalous condition. The recommendations key off the diagnostic results to give appropriate and coordinated advice. The procedures outlined by FIESTA essentially step down a series of options that branch off in various directions depending on the success or results of the previous recommendations.

3.3.3.2. Knowledge Structure Design. The discussion in this subsection will cover various aspects of the mechanics used to implement the above diagnostic strategy. The highlighted features include rules, relations, and viewpoints.

RULES. FIESTA, as a rule-based system, uses both forward and backward chaining in ART to perform its monitoring, detection, and diagnostic functions. The majority of the rules reason forward from situation data to detect anomalies, characterize network conditions, track and trend service status, and match conditions to suspected fault locations and causes to assign levels of certainty to each conclusion. Backward-chaining rules provide an excellent vehicle to structure a data request facility. Since it would be unwise to request all the data available to the operator, the backward-chaining rules pick up goals for specific facts, which indicate that the conditions preceding the fact in another rule have been matched (implying a need to know the status of the fact to complete the diagnostic conditions). In other words, the system will only request facts that will assist in the diagnosis for that particular diagnostic episode. The system knows that the facts will assist the diagnosis because other diagnostic rules are waiting on those facts and have asserted goals to that effect.

RELATIONS. The symbolic representation of facts and their relations among one another form a key structural baseline for an expert system. Examples of important FIESTA relations include the following:

- (nominal-parameter-value ?parameter ?value);
- (nominal-parameter-range ?parameter ?upper-value ?lower-value);
- (element-on-user-satellite-side-of ?upwind-element ?downwind-element);
- (comes-from-this-element ?message ?element);
- (comes-from-this-equipment ?parameter ?equipment).

These example relations define nominal values and ranges for fault detection, topology relations for fault localization, and message characteristics defining where messages come from and what their parameters mean.

VIEWPOINTS. The FIESTA structure uses viewpoints to partition both the monitoring and diagnostic reasoning flow. Viewpoints in ART essentially provide a means to systematically organize FIESTA's database to assist in diagnostic hypothetical reasoning along multiple paths and allow for monitoring of various communication services independently of one another. One Shuttle event, defined as a single pass in line-of-sight of the TDR satellite, normally consists of three services that FIESTA monitors and reasons on independently through the viewpoint mechanism. Upon detection of a fault, FIESTA initiates a diagnostic episode in a new hypothetical viewpoint branching off the appropriate service viewpoint. From the diagnostic episode viewpoint, alternative fault locations and causes are hypothesized in individual viewpoints where evidence supporting or detracting from the particular conclusion is asserted. Lower-level hypotheses branch off from the first-level hypotheses to determine the next-level conclusion based on the fact that upper hypotheses were true. Inheritance from upper viewpoints to lower viewpoints facilitates data organization but requires extra care to assure data integrity through the analysis.

3.3.4. An Operational Scenario Example.

A key to the development and refinement of the operational concept was the ability to prototype the initial concepts rapidly, to demonstrate them, to evaluate the results, and to incorporate feedback in the evolving system. A sample diagnostic session is presented to illustrate the operation of FIESTA, its human–machine interface, and diagnostic interaction.

A Sample Dialog. This session is driven by real data produced by an actual fault that occurred during a *Challenger* mission in October 1985. The data were logged off the live network onto a tape in real time and later replayed to FIESTA, creating the following dialog.

The dialog opens with Figure 8. A single event consisting of three services is in progress. All three services are up and operating nominally (top center window): K-band single-access return (KSAR), S-band single-access forward link (SSAF), and S-band single-access return link (SSAR). The current time is 9:43:56, about 6 min into the event as indicated by the service start times in the service window. (Note that, for this event, all services have been scheduled for the full duration.)

The main operations menu tree has been traversed to bring up three monitoring displays all dealing with service S-2, the KSAR service. Two are trending displays, which show subcarrier signal strength and various key parameters in the ODM. The third display is a cockpit type display showing the key parameter values of the current FIMS message. Channels 1 and 3 are in inverse video indicating that data acquisition has not occurred on these channels and thus FIESTA is *not* mon-

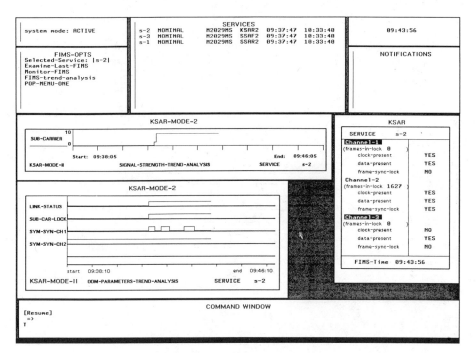

Figure 8. Nominal operation.

itoring these channels for faults. Data acquisition has occurred on channel 2 though, and it is being monitored. This figure represents nominal operating conditions.

Figure 9 illustrates what happens when a fault does occur. The first indications FIESTA gives the operator of a problem are threefold. First, the monitoring displays can indicate anomalous values. One method is through the use of inverse video in cockpit displays as seen for channel 2 in the KSAR FIMS monitor display. A drop in the trend display, as in the subcarrier signal strength, can also be indicative of a problem.

At the same time, FIESTA issues notification N-1 in the notifications window, while the current status of S-2 (KSAR) is changed to nonnominal in the services window. Selecting N-1 in the notifications window (which has already been done here) brings up the explanation window in the lower right corner. Note that N-1 states that a service interruption has been detected in KSAR as indicated by a low frames in lock count in the FIMS message. The first notice will always alert the user to a problem, while subsequent notices for the same fault will provide possible diagnoses. The presence of notification N-2 in Figure 9 shows that the first diagnosis notice has been issued.

Selecting N-2 in the notifications window displays the initial fault diagnosis in the explanation window. The explanation, as shown in Figure 10, states that the most probable explanation for the problem is an antenna anomaly at the Shuttle. It is 65% sure of this diagnosis.

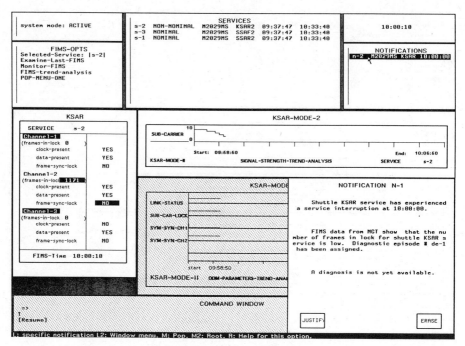

Figure 9. Fault detection.

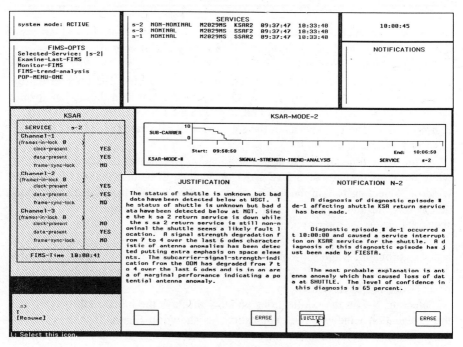

Figure 10. Initial diagnosis.

If the operator desires more information as to how the system arrived at this diagnosis, he or she may mouse on the justify box in the explanation window. This action opens another window, called justification, which provides the evidence supporting this diagnosis. This evidence is pooled together from a number of separate rule firings, each contributing to the overall confidence factor score.

The operator can receive even more information on a fault by selecting the alternative hypothesis display shown in Figure 11 from the main operations menu. This display shows all possible fault locations and fault causes that the system has considered, along with the relative certainty of hypothesis. Negative certainty factor values indicate certainty that this particular hypothesis is *not* the fault location or cause. Clicking on the left mouse button for a location or cause presents the positive and negative evidence in support of this hypothesis in the lower windows. Clicking right on an option brings up the lower-level causes or locations associated with the selected hypothesis, bringing up individual pieces of equipment to which faults can be traced.

Finally, Figure 12 illustrates what happens when the operator elects to enter the extended mode (upper left corner). This mode allows the FIESTA system to query the user for more information, which the user may be able to obtain but to which the machine does not have automatic access. These queries are presented in the MOSD data request window and may be answered by opening the data entry menu through the main operations menu system and defining values for relevant param-

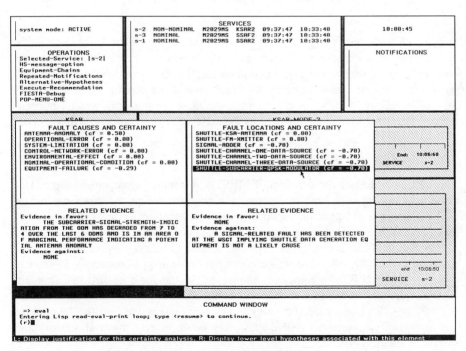

Figure 11. Alternative hypotheses.

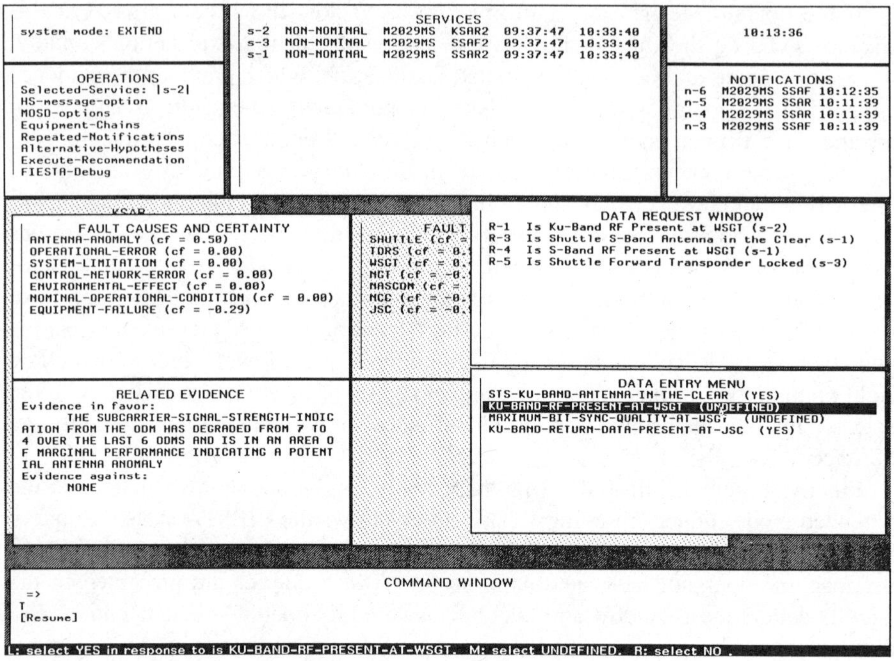

Figure 12. Manually obtainable situation data.

eters by clicking left (for yes), right (for no), or middle (for unknown) on each. This additional information can then revise diagnoses and cause new notifications and/or changes in the alternative hypothesis display. However, the system always continues to operate, monitor, and diagnose, even if the user does not respond to the queries. Thus, the system can monitor and diagnose problems totally independent of the user, or it can supplement its database through interaction with the user.

3.4. Testing and Evaluation

This section addresses the problem of FIESTA system developmental testing. Development testing is a stage in system refinement in which test cases are run to evaluate general and specific capabilities and to generate feedback from experts and potential users. The testing of any expert system is driven by the availability of test data and the accuracy of expected results. The majority of FIESTA test cases were available off log tapes consisting of recordings of messages flowing in and out of the NCC. Documented anomalies, in the form of network problem reports, were matched with their respective data logs and made available to FIESTA through the NSAT software. To provide a clearer perspective on FIESTA testing, the following two sections will discuss the nature of test material sources and system evaluation criteria.

3.4.1. Sources of Test Material. The FIESTA project benefited from an abundance of testable material, and an extensive effort was undertaken to take advantage of this "luxury." FIESTA was designed to operate off network performance and configuration messages as input. The NCC logs these messages as they pass in and out of the NCC front end, providing a historical record of traffic flows during network support. By matching written anomaly reports to log tape segments, STI built up a set of recorded anomalies to test FIESTA against and provide a point of reference for future development. An important benefit derived from the archiving of test cases was the definition of standards to ensure good performance and functionality while either correcting bad performance or extending functionality.

Since FIESTA also functions as a monitor and detection tool, log tapes provided an ample supply of test material to evaluate these capabilities. Monitoring function tests required a wide range of scenarios to account for the various communications services and their interaction among one another. System monitoring performance through nominal scenarios, with no anomalies present, was evaluated as was monitoring performance through known faults. Fault detection tests presented a tougher obstacle. Preliminary system testing indicated FIESTA was able to detect all faults that could be identified off the test data. Unfortunately, FIESTA also detected many more either unknown faults or nonfaults all together. This early system testing redirected our effort to make the fault detection function as "expert" as the diagnosis function. In other words, the fault detection function had to know when to ignore seemingly anomalous behavior to eliminate or minimize false alarm conditions. Of course, many anomalies detected on log tapes by FIESTA were true faults that had not been documented because of their unimportance or because of reasons related to the nature of the fault (e.g., too short in duration or anticipated or predicted).

Another source of test material was based on log tapes consisting of recorded network simulation tests (opposed to live user support). Although difficult to schedule and obtain test time, these simulations provided a controlled environment where it was much easier to trigger certain anomalies or events. In conjunction with Bendix Corporation personnel, scenarios were set up prior to the simulation and executed on the network to allow explicit control over test case production.

3.4.2. System Evaluation Criteria. Evaluation of FIESTA had to be based on how well it met its most basic goals: to provide diagnostic consultation and act at least as intelligently as an expert could given the equivalent amount or level of information. This complicates the "grading" of FIESTA performance since most historic faults were solved with the aid of voice-loop conference information and other manually obtainable situation data. Nonetheless, given only the automatically obtainable performance and status data, FIESTA uses certainty factors to express the accuracy of its results and will request this manually obtainable data to increase confidence and resolve ambiguity. Therefore, for tests involving known faults, an evaluation can be made of the fault detection function and the accuracy of the

FIESTA diagnosis: whether FIESTA fault cause and location were correct, whether other positive/negative alternatives were correct and properly ranked, and whether these diagnoses matched that of the expert (if the expert's diagnosis differed from that of the actual fault). Additional comparisons are necessary to track the diagnostic realignment when further information is entered into the system to reflect the data manually available.

A difficult aspect of FIESTA testing is that FIESTA does not always deal with deterministic problems for which there is clearly a right or wrong answer. Although test cases reflecting documented fault occurrences expect a certain solution, it has become apparent that performance data patterns are not unique among faults. In other words, different fault scenarios can produce identical data patterns. FIESTA can only be evaluated from the standpoint of including the appropriate faults as positive possibilities and guessing in line with operator heuristics (which is one of the fundamental benefits and also drawbacks of an expert system).

Any discussion of expert system evaluation should emphasize the importance of iterative testing at all stages of development. By breaking development into individual builds that emphasize particular areas of domain expertise, testing can be focused and a foundation can be laid for future development with documented system performance at each build. Realistic goals on system performance are necessary to decide what is "expert" performance. It is then useful to evaluate the experts against these standards to gauge expected system performance correctly.

4. RELATED APPLICATIONS

The FIESTA project is one among a number of expert system applications that STI is pursuing. Other areas have included jamming detection and characterization, control of simulation and modeling tool configuration and execution, distributed expert systems, and control of satellite-based communication networks. Some of these projects have been initiated under internal research and development funds, while others have been supported through NASA, the Air Force, and the Navy.

In the area of detection and diagnosis (the general domain of FIESTA), we have begun working on a project for jammer detection. This project, called IDAC (Interference Detection and Characterization), consists of specialized hardware, designed by STI, working in conjunction with a commercially available microprocessor and an expert system. The role of the expert system is to validate the detection of interference by the hardware and characterize its nature (e.g., RFI, pulsed jamming, or broadband noise) through the use of appropriate analytical or heuristic techniques. In addition, it initiates further testing by the specialized hardware.

We are also addressing the use of expert systems in the control elements for military satellite systems. EXACT (Expert System Autonomous Control Testbed) is in its second development phase for the Air Force. It is a support tool for application of expert systems in the area of TT&C processing. One phase of the project entails the development of two expert systems to provide a specific group of satellites and mobile ground stations with more autonomous functioning capabilities, and the other phase tests these capabilities within a simulation environment. As it would be impossible to test, debug, and refine an expert system deployed on a satellite, it must be studied through the use of simulations. EXACT not only examines how well the expert system performs itself, but it also determines the expert system's effect on the rest of the system in terms of data and traffic throughput, connectivity requirements and vulnerabilities, and system survivability in stressed environments.

5. SUMMARY

This chapter has focused on the case study expert system named FIESTA. The presentation began with a survey of the methodology employed in that development. This was followed by a description of the problem domain and an overview of the structural organization of the expert system.

The simulation drivers for testing the system were discussed next, followed by a detailed description of the knowledge organization and knowledge engineering task. Then, an example operational scenario was presented to illustrate the operational concept of the current implementation. Finally, a description of the testing and evaluation efforts for FIESTA was provided.

The chapter concludes with a brief description of other expert systems that are being developed by STI. These projects were developed in parallel with the FIESTA project and use similar strategies. Functional likenesses include direct (in terms of diagnostic techniques) and indirect (in terms of testing needs) compatibilities. They illustrate applications of the general methodology of applying communication anomaly diagnostics using knowledge-based engineering tools to solve real-world engineering problems in both the military and nonmilitary environment.

As these projects (and others) are initiated and continue toward their individual goals, FIESTA is progressing on its planned objective of becoming an operational support tool. Toward this end, the following milestones have been established:

- Development of an enhanced expert system. The current stand-alone prototype includes most of the essential functional features required to support monitoring, fault detection, and isolation of faults during TDRSS Space Network support of the Space Shuttle. The expert system segment will be enhanced to improve performance and incorporate new problem domains, that is, knowledge of non-Shuttle spacecraft support by the TDRSS Space Network on a routine basis (e.g., Landsat and ERBS).
- Development of a front-end processor to interface the NCC computer system (that receives and processes all messages from the TN) to the expert system.
- Implementation of an on-line testbed in the NCC, integrating the front-end processor and expert system with the NCC computers to allow for operational evaluation and feedback of the system functions and performance and to allow for evaluation of the hardware and software implementation.

- Refinement of requirements and implementation of the operational system based on results of the on-line testbed evaluation.

ACKNOWLEDGMENTS

FIESTA development has been undertaken by Stanford Telecommunications, Inc. as a subcontractor to the Bendix Field Engineering Corporation (BFEC). Project support has been provided by the National Aeronautics and Space Administration under Contract #NAS5-27600.

The overall support and encouragement of Paul Ondrus and Anthony Maione of NASA/GSFC are particularly appreciated and acknowledged. The knowledge engineering effort was fortunate to have the operational expertise and cooperation of Joe St. John and Bill Webb of BFEC. Testing materials and network insights, which have proved invaluable in development efforts, have been provided both directly and indirectly by Tom Gitlin (BFEC). The administrative and logistics efforts of Hugh Bath (BFEC) and his technical staff were most supportive.

GLOSSARY

AOSD	Automatically obtainable situation data
ART	Automated reasoning tool
CF	Certainty factor
DE	Diagnostic episode
ESTL	Electronic Systems Test Laboratory
EXACT	Expert system autonomous control testbed
FFEP	FIESTA front-end processor
FIESTA	Fault Isolation Expert System for TDRSS Applications
FIMS	Fault Isolation Monitoring System
HSM	High-speed messages
IDAC	Interference detection and characterization
KSAR	Ku-band, single-access, return link
MA	Multiple access
MB	Measure of belief
MCC	Mission Control Center
MD	Measure of disbelief
MOSD	Manually obtainable situation data
NASCOM	NASA Communications (Network)
NCC	Network Control Center
NCP	Network control program
NGT	NASA Ground Terminal

NSAT   NCC simulator and AOSD transformer

ODM   Operations data message

OPM   Operations message

POCC   Project Operations Control Center

SSAF   S-band, single-access, forward link

SSAR   S-band, single-access, return link

SEC   Special events controller

SHO   Scheduling orders

SMV   System memory variable

SN   Space Network

S/C   Spacecraft

TDRS-E/W   Tracking and Data Relay Satellite (East and West)

TDRSS   Tracking and Data Relay Satellite System

WSGT   White Sands Ground Terminal

REFERENCES

NASA Documents

1. Space Network 10-Year Plan, STDN No. 132, NASA Goddard Space Flight Center, Greenbelt, Maryland, August 1985.
2. Space Network Synoptic Description, STDN No. 134, NASA Goddard Space Flight Center, Greenbelt, Maryland, January 1986.

Interface Documents (Detailed Specification of High-Speed Messages)

3. TDRSS Operational Support Interface Document (OSID), WU-02-17C, Revision C, Spacecom, 20 February 1985.
4. Interface Control Document for the Network Control Center/NASA Ground Terminal, STDN No. 220.7, Revision 1, NASA Goddard Space Flight Center, Greenbelt, Maryland, October 1984.
5. Data Format Control Document Between the Goddard Space Flight Center, NASA Ground Terminal, and the Network Control Center, STDN No. 230.7, NASA Goddard Space Flight Center, Greenbelt, Maryland, May 1982.

FIESTA Documents (Technical Reports)

The referenced sections in this report have been adapted from corresponding sections of the documentation developed for the FIESTA project.

6. FIESTA Project Development Folder, Volume IV: Design and Knowledge Engineering Notebook, TR860151, Stanford Telecommunications, Inc., 10 October 1986.

7. FIESTA Project Development Folder, Volume IV/Appendix A: NSAT Users Manual and Source Code Comments (TR860151).

Books

8. B. G. Buchanan and E. H. Shortliffe, *Rule-Based Expert Systems: The MYCIN Experiments of the Stanford Heuristic Programming Project*, Addison-Wesley, Reading, MA, 1984.

ON-LINE EXPERTISE FOR TELECOMMUNICATIONS

Dick Peacocke

Knowledge Technology,
Bell–Northern Research, Ottawa, Canada

1. INTRODUCTION

There has been a recent upsurge of interest in the use of knowledge-based systems for different kinds of applications. This chapter examines some of the reasons for exploring such systems for telecommunications and mentions some projects that are being carried out at Bell–Northern Research (BNR). One of these projects is building an advisor for maintenance of a digital switching system. Progress is described with emphasis on knowledge-base development and operation of the advisor in a realistic setting. Some future plans are outlined.

There is an inevitable urge to use new technology. Artificial intelligence (AI) techniques—expert systems in particular—are rapidly maturing as viable software development methods although they are also surrounded by much unjustifiable hype. Many people are starting to assume that whenever we interact with computers, it will be through expert systems that will solve all our problems on a routine basis. How much of this enthusiasm is well-founded?

It is a long way to the dream of having neophyte users interacting naturally with expert systems which understand problems fully, having amassed the wisdom and practical experience of scores of experts, yet are also able to reason from first principles when necessary, and learn from their own mistakes. For the nearer term, what tasks are compatible with what expert systems can achieve today, and are likely to achieve soon, and what benefits do expert systems bring?

At BNR we believe that many of the tasks involved in establishing and operating telecommunications networks can be done using expert systems, and indeed that these types of system will soon be essential in helping people perform the complex network tasks required of them. Examples of such tasks are:

- Planning and design
- Engineering
- Operations
- Maintenance
- Administration

Complexity of the telecommunications network is increasing rapidly with the introduction of new functions and services, increased connectivity, and the advent of new components. This means that fewer and fewer tractable algorithms exist for the tasks listed above. Expert systems allow implementation of procedures where more emphasis is placed on our experience and what we know about situations and events surrounding them, rather than on formal sequential algorithms. By articulating and transforming our knowledge of the network and its operation into suitable representations, we can then apply that knowledge to the tasks. Our objective is to enhance their scope and effectiveness, increasing the quality of work performed and reducing the effort required. This in turn has an impact on documentation and training, and it will increase the ability to absorb new technology. The telecommunications network is a particularly fertile area for applying expert systems because the network and its equipment form a highly structured synthetic domain. This compares with domains such as medicine or geology, where the underlying rules of operation are based on natural phenomena and extensive descriptions of these phenomena are required, often as visual descriptions.

In telecommunications, we have begun by building prototypes for configuring node equipment (Northern Telecom's Meridian SL-1), for configuring private data networks [1], and for the generation of functional test cases based on software design input [2]. We have also made significant progress in building an expert system for maintenance [3]. It is called the Maintenance Advisor, or MAD for short, and this paper focuses on its development and operation. The maintenance domain lends itself readily to expert system development for a number of reasons in addition to those in the previous paragraph:

- It is a knowledge-intensive domain, as opposed to a numeric or algorithmic one; human experts draw on vast amounts of knowledge about switch architecture, maintenance strategies, and past experience to cope with new problems.
- There is a clear distinction between experts and novices in this domain; there is a good deal of expertise possessed by relatively few people, and this expertise can be distributed profitably to a much larger number of users.
- Because of the unpredictability of failure modes and their significance in the different operational situations, the maintenance task involves some degree of "fuzziness" and inevitably requires cooperative problem-solving and strong human like communications between the system and its user.

- Because of the complexity of the task and the diffusion of knowledge across a number of experts and organizations, it is not practical to produce accurate or complete specifications before starting development; a strong need exists for an incremental development and testing approach—a task that is greatly simplified by expert systems tools and methodology.

2. FUNCTIONS OF THE MAINTENANCE ADVISOR

MAD is designed to assist operating company personnel clear alarms on the DMS* family of digital switches—potentially a complex task because of the size of a DMS system and the complexity of hardware and software components involved. A DMS switch can connect calls between tens of thousands of lines and trunks, and it can consist of hundreds of hardware modules, each serving various functions, such as line scanning, signaling, circuit connection, or control. Information about various events in the switching system may appear as module status data, alarms, and operational measurements, among other things. Good switch maintenance therefore depends on the accessibility to information that has been collected from many different sources. This information has to be processed and transformed into maintenance solutions. It is here that we find out what knowledge bases and inference engines really produce in practice. So far we are enthusiastic about the results.

Switch maintenance is carried out by both on-site and centralized craftspeople, with the assistance of Northern Telecom Practices manuals for switch maintenance. Problems that cannot be corrected automatically by the switch's sophisticated built-in maintenance software and hardware [4], or that go beyond those described in the maintenance manuals, are referred to either senior colleagues or to the operating company's emergency assistance support organization.

The MAD concept provides a faster and more cost-effective alternative. It emulates some aspects of the dialogue between the craftsperson and a highly experienced and knowledgeable human expert who helps interpret switch alarm data. Interactions with MAD involve symptom descriptions, information requests, recommendations, explanations, and conclusions. During sessions with MAD, the full-screen Maintenance and Administration Position (MAP) associated with the DMS provides the necessary background information on switch operations and status. Figure 1 shows components of the system.

The user may report status information displayed on the MAP to MAD, run tests from the MAP and report the results back to MAD, or perform physical maintenance on the switch, such as replacing cards or resetting tripped breakers. MAD may also request the craftsperson to provide such information as current traffic, or MAD may ask whether a colleague has been working on part of the switch. A typical session with MAD begins with the advisor requesting such information as the identity of the switch, the types and severity of current alarms,

---

*Trademark of Northern Telecom.

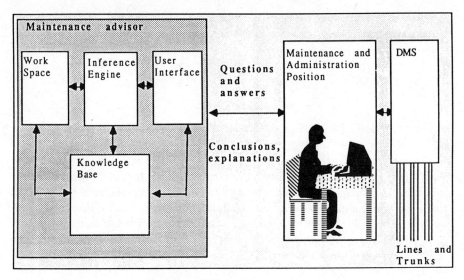

Figure 1. MAD and its components.

and the characterization of major observable symptoms. Based on the craftperson's responses, MAD applies appropriate inferencing rules to hypothesize possible causes and propose remedies for the problem. The system ranks these hypotheses according to cost, effort required, and the likely success of solving the problem. Figure 2 presents a sample interactive session using the question and answer format of the first MAD prototype.

3. BUILDING THE KNOWLEDGE BASE

Despite the availability of advanced tools for building expert systems like MAD, the technology is by no means off the shelf. In particular, two challenges stood out in the development of MAD:

1. How could a working subset of switch maintenance knowledge be acquired, and which sources could provide it?
2. How could a knowledge base be designed to apply this knowledge effectively?

The first source of maintenance knowledge was a 2300-page set of flowcharts—Northern Telecom's Performance-Oriented Practices (POPs)—designed to aid craftspeople in clearing alarms. Although a large undertaking, we developed an effective and systematic methodology that simplified the task of transforming the knowledge from the procedural paper form to rules in the knowledge base. The flowcharts were analyzed to isolate the symptoms and actions to be taken and the preferred ordering of remedial actions. This was a decompilation of the documen-

1>   **What is the problem?**

-->
SYSB
(The DMS has detected a problem in one or more modules and is

not processing calls through them.)

2>   **What kinds of modules are in the SYSB state?**

-->
LM (*line module*), TM (*trunk module*)

We will work on the Line Modules as they are more critical to service...

3>   **Find out which LM is SYSB and post it. Please enter the module's ID.**

-->
HELP

Type: DISP SYSB at the MAP. A list of SYSB modules should appear on the MAP.

If there is more than one SYSB LM, choose one of them to work on.
Type: POST LM <module ID> at the MAP. Please enter the module ID.

-->
BANK 3 0

4>   **Busy BANK 3 0 and test it. What is the test result?**

-->
NO WAI RECEIVED FROM PM

(*The remote LM is not communicating with its parent module*).

5>   **Have there been any log messages in the last few minutes indicating problems with the links to the parent module of BANK 3 0?**

-->
UNKNOWN

6>   **Listed below are several actions that might fix the problem. It is recommended that you try the one at the top of the list first:**

   • Reload the module software
   • Swap the interface cards
   • Check the parent module
   • Swap the main processor card
   • Check the links to the parent module

Please choose one...

-->
Check the parent module

Figure 2. Sample consultation.

7>   **What is the state of the DCM (Digital Carrier Module) serving LM BANK 3 0?**

-->
ISTb *(in-service trouble) (The switch has detected a problem in the*

DCM, although it is still processing calls.)

8>   **Is traffic on the switch high right now?**

-->
WHY?

I ask whether traffic on the switch is high right now in order to determine whether working on the parent module will have an effect on service.

-->
NO <0.8>

(The user is not certain, but is fairly sure - certainty of 80% - that

traffic is not high.)

9>   **I suggest that you busy the DCM and test it. What is the test result?**

-->
INVALID CHECKSUM

10>   **Reload the DCM's software and try returning it to service... Does the DCM return to service?**

-->
YES

11>   **Test the LM again... What is the test result?**

-->
OK

You should now be able to return LM BANK 3 0 to service. The LM SYSB state was caused by a problem in the parent DCM, which was corrected by reloading the DCM's software.

Figure 2. *(Continued)*

---

tation so that the knowledge could be restated in the more natural, extensible rule language of the knowledge base.

Next, MAD system designers met on an ongoing basis with DMS troubleshooting experts from Bell Canada and Northern Telecom to create and enlarge the knowledge base. Through informal discussions and later detailed technical sessions, system designers sought specific information to expand particular areas of the knowledge base. Using a debriefing technique, the system designers translated the experts' knowledge into a set of rules and procedures. Interviews culminated in concentrated joint testing and critique of the advisor at various stages. At this point in the process, one of the advantages of building MAD using an expert systems approach emerged.

Unlike the conventional software approach, which starts with a lengthy specification stage followed by months or even years of development, the growth of MAD has been rapid and directly responsive to user demands. For example, the need for incremental knowledge acquisition required engineers to bring updated versions of the program back to the experts on a regular basis. These contacts led to a more useful knowledge base, which was critically reviewed by the experts as development progressed. In addition, experts participated in testing sessions, both in early development work and later in the verification stage, and these sessions resulted in many recommendations for expansion and change to the program's knowledge. The expert system's knowledge has already gone well beyond the POPs documentation.

4. KNOWLEDGE BASE ORGANIZATION

The key to performance in an expert system is knowledge—its depth, breadth, appropriateness, and organization for effective use. Organizing and representing maintenance expertise in a program are difficult tasks. In the MAD design, we have followed two principles of AI research to great advantage: (1) knowledge should be represented as explicitly as possible and (2) control knowledge should be separated as much as possible from other types of knowledge. These principles not only enabled the use of a "generic" inference engine but also resulted in a system that is more modular and thus more extensible. AI research has developed several representation formalisms and control schemes, supplementing standard computer science practice, to apply the two principles. Several companies and institutions have developed expert system development environments, or "shells," that implement these formalisms [5]. These shells include languages for knowledge representation, interpreters for these representations that embody some automatic logical inferencing, and editors, browsers, and debuggers that are designed to encourage rapid prototyping and flexible design. To build our first prototype we selected and used one of these shells, S.1* produced by Teknowledge [6] and running on Xerox 1109 LISP machines.

We developed models for representing the different types of knowledge required for MAD's task: the necessary knowledge for asking the appropriate questions, describing possible repair actions, and instructing in their execution. The representation includes dynamic information about the state of the switch and the state of the current maintenance session and a static knowledge base with switch configuration facts and maintenance techniques. The switch knowledge base includes DMS architecture, particular office parameters, and knowledge of how the switch's

*S.1 is a trademark of Teknowledge, Inc.

state can change under given actions, called "state transforms." Lastly, the expert knowledge about maintenance—what to do in various situations—is of course the most important. It is divided into *strategic* control procedures, *diagnostic* rules of varying certainty and priority, and detailed *procedural* code for the execution of basic maintenance actions. Figure 3 depicts this taxonomy of MAD's knowledge and shows how the reasoning process uses that knowledge as input for producing solutions to problems.

We begin with the simplest type of knowledge: the physical composition of the switch and the interrelation between the components—facts essential to an understanding of the maintenance strategies. We used a classic model of AI research for representation of physical structures: composition (PART-OF) and specialization–generalization (IS-A) hierarchies. The PART-OF hierarchy of MAD represents the facts that a switch is composed of several subsystems, that a subsystem is a set of computing modules, that a computing module is composed of a set of circuit cards and their backplane, and that, for example, a line concentrating module (LCM) is composed of two processor cards, two line group controller (LGC) interface cards, two power converters, several line drawers (see Figure 4), and so on. More abstract concepts, such as the flow of power from the electrical supply through various conversions and circuit protection to the cards, and the flow of system messages between different modules of the switch, have also been represented as forms of composition. The use and advantage of the PART-OF hierarchy are increased steadily as we expand the knowledge base to deal with more problems and hence more switch components.

The IS-A hierarchy for MAD contains information like the fact that a 2X06 card is a type of power converter and that a power converter is a type of circuit pack

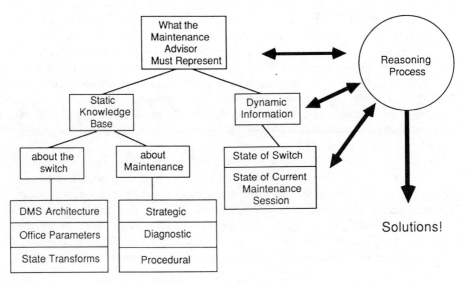

Figure 3. MAD knowledge base.

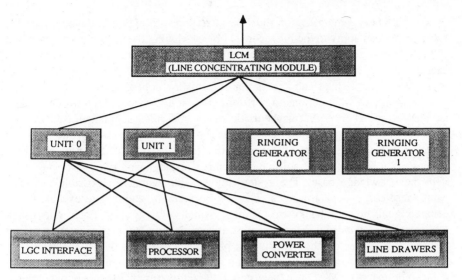

Figure 4. A fragment of the PART-OF hierarchy.

(see part of the hierarchy in Figure 5). IS-A hierarchies provide a simple, intuitive, and efficient way of grouping similar objects in a representation. This grouping leads to an easy way of generalizing code initially written to apply to only one type of object: change the references to the object so that they refer to an object higher up the hierarchy. For example, a rule originally written for just 2X06 power converter cards can be generalized and applied to all types of power converters.

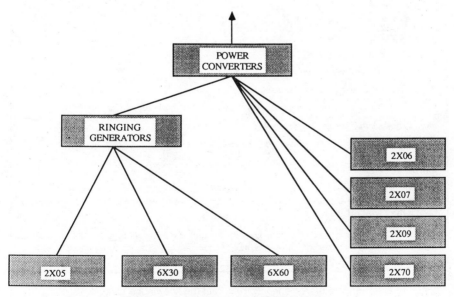

Figure 5. A fragment of the IS-A hierarchy.

Of course, every generalization must be in response to expert knowledge that the rule does indeed apply to the higher-level object. Having the IS-A hierarchy explicit in the system also makes code that uses those relations more perspicuous and thus easier to modify. The amount of switch information is large, but our model makes it possible to implement and access that information coherently.

Knowledge of what actions to perform, given a history of symptoms and earlier actions, is coded in MAD as heuristic diagnostic rules supplemented by small amounts of detailed procedural code. Using a few initial symptoms, the top-level strategic code of the system determines the general nature of the problem. This defines a "context" which will have a number of diagnostic rules associated with it in the knowledge base. The system initiates the search for possible remedies using these context-specific rules. The inference engine attempts to execute them, using a goal-directed backward-chaining search strategy [7]. Each rule has a "premise" or "condition" that is a logical specification for a set of symptoms and history of activities on the switch. If a premise is satisfied, the "conclusion" of the rule asserts a corresponding remedial action, with a certainty factor. The strategic components of MAD use these certainty factors to rank the recommendations, having the inference engine handle the lower levels of certainty factor calculation and storage. Thus, under control of "strategic" code from the knowledge base, the execution of all the diagnostic rules for the given context yields a top recommendation for action and a set of ordered alternatives. A sample diagnostic rule from the knowledge base is shown in Figure 6. (The rule is actually taken from

```
prelim [P2_5 check[power] _module 95] :-
    [
    alarm [ext fsp _ _]
    module [_module]
    not [unit[_module]]
    symptoms [_module]
    if [ state[_module _state]
        then _state :: [istb cbsy sysb]]
    [ housing[_module _frame]
    not [power_fault_checked[_frame]].]

Explanation:

An EXT FSP alarm indicates a possible power problem in the office.
The power problem could be the source of the PM problem and so should
be investigated first.

Note:    The power problem could be on the module's frame, on a frame
         to the cside of the module (especially if module is CBSY), in
         wiring between frames, etc.
```

Figure 6. A diagnostic rule from the knowledge base.

the current MAD prototype which uses PROLOG in its implementation, so the rule's syntax is based on PROLOG and not on S.1. The implementation change is discussed in Section 7). Much of our development effort has gone into the generalization, expansion, and refinement of the rule premises. Accurate descriptions of problem situations are in key focusing the search for effective solutions.

5. QUALITY ASSESSMENT

The quality of a large software system is usually assessed by running the program on a set of test cases generated from a functional specification of the system. As an expert system typically has no well-defined specification, the generation of test cases and the assessment of the expert system's performance on them are necessarily more subjective. This subjectivity, coupled with the fact that the number of unique cases that could be run on a sizable expert system is extremely large, makes testing a difficult problem.

The modularity of MAD somewhat simplified the problem, allowing individual testing of smaller, more manageable segments of the system. The testing was further organized by dividing it into two major phases. The first phase was extensive internal testing to remove obvious program errors and to ensure that the knowledge obtained from documentation was correctly represented in the program. The second phase was an overall assessment of MAD performance by switch experts from BNR, Northern Telecom, and Bell Canada. The overall performance was assessed by having the experts present MAD with a variety of real and hypothetical switch problems and comment on MAD's ability to handle them.

During both phases, records were kept of the system's performance. The basic measurement was the number of items per hour; the items included both programming errors and expert comments on the advice presented. An hour was the length of time typically required for a consultation of about 50 questions. In the early weeks of testing, items were found at a rate of about 10 per hour. At that time we set a target for the prototype of 1.5 items/hour. Four months of testing and modification brought the rate down to under 1 item/hour. As well as counting the items, we analyzed and categorized them according to type and severity in order to determine which ones indicated necessary modifications of the MAD code. Furthermore, typescripts of all the sessions were saved, and after 4 months of testing, they formed a comprehensive set of regression test cases.

6. FIRST TECHNICAL TRIAL

Analysis of MAD performance during a technical trial in a busy Bell Canada maintenance center indicated that within the domain of peripheral alarms clearing the system was capable of solving most novice-level problems in addition to providing correct advice on more complex ones. Trial users recognized and pointed out the system's enormous potential, especially in the areas of training, aiding novice users, and advising on new, unfamiliar, or forgotten problems. In addition, they provided useful comments regarding human–machine interface and the scope and features of the system.

MAD solved problems well in the technical trial and also performed robustly for an experimental system. Introduction and training took only 10 minutes or so on average, and craftspeople found it easy to use. The question and answer format was easy to follow, especially so because menus could be brought up for choices of response. Nor did full words have to be typed, because recognition took place on the unique front part.

But several users expressed concern about the interaction style. Instead of having MAD attempt to solve the problem from scratch, they wanted it to provide assistance with their own style of problem solving. We believed that we had supplied an assistant and not a taskmaster since there were clear decision points for users to control choice of problem-solving activity, "help" features could be invoked when required, explanations could be sought, and so on. But this did not seem to be enough for some of the users.

The chief rationale for providing an advisory capability is to help users become more successful and effective [8]. This does not necessarily mean handing over the problem for the advisor to solve entirely on its own. Coombs and Alty [9] point out that human experts are more often asked to provide guidance to others so that they can solve problems for themselves rather than acting as "wise men" called on to produce solutions to complex, but essentially well-defined, problems.

Users do not want to be guided by the system all the time; sometimes it is just the reverse and they want to guide the system. An effective advisor needs to allow partnership with different individuals' problem-solving styles. And their styles vary with level of experience and training. Some of the different functions that an advisor may carry out are shown in Figure 7. Users may just want a check to be run on what they are doing, they may want alternative possibilities suggested, they may expect the advisor to start from scratch, or they may already be well into a problem before they want to seek any advice at all. Some users do wish to put complete onus on the advisor, of course.

7. THE NEXT DESIGN OF MAD: AWAY FROM QUESTION AND ANSWER

Based on results from the technical trial, we decided to investigate a completely different form of human–machine interface and concurrently switch our implementation from S.1 to PROLOG (and Pascal). The implementation change was made with potential delivery and interworking with current products in mind. The current prototype uses a forms-based human–machine interface, and the prototype runs on proprietary hardware. We have transferred control to the user so that he or she can choose a personal style of problem-solving.

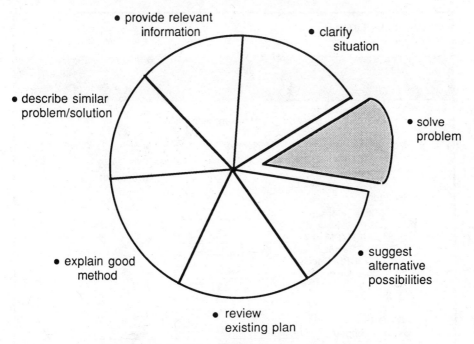

Figure 7. Some of the different functions of an advisor.

In the current prototype, we are using a ''describe–recommend'' cycle as the main problem-solving component, and we have supplemented it with several other mechanisms. The cycle is simple in concept. The craftsperson fills in a form on the screen (Figure 8, in some circumstances additional forms may be used) with selected problem symptoms and then asks for MAD's recommendations. These are of two types:

1. Preliminary actions to be taken, which may include requests for further information from the craftsperson.
2. Repair actions to solve the problem.

The recommended actions are ordered using factors of likelihood of success, cost of taking the action, and possible impact on working parts of the system. At the moment, all these factors are compounded into a single measure and actions are then rank ordered on it for presentation in a menu. The craftsperson takes an action or performs a test and may then recall the previous form and change or add symptom descriptions. Recommendations can be asked for again and the cycle repeated as many times as needed. At any point in the consultation, the user is able to request and get a variety of information; we have removed the tight coupling between requests for information and problem-solving flow to give the craftsperson the majority of control over the session.

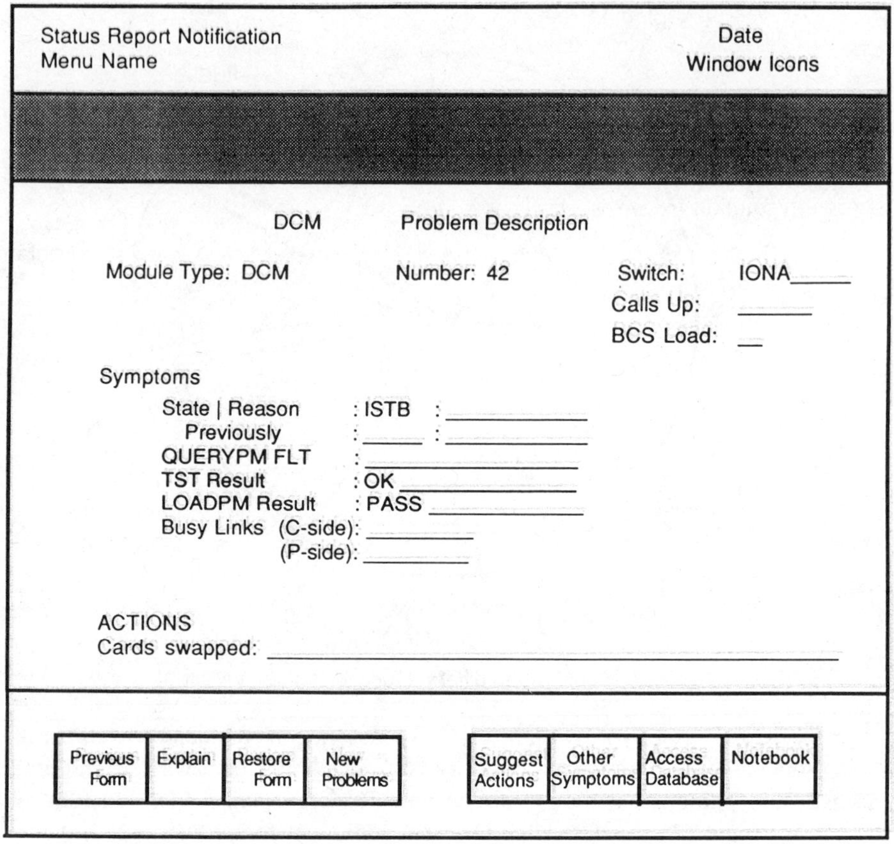

```
+-----------------------------------------------------------------------+
| Status Report Notification                              Date          |
| Menu Name                                               Window Icons  |
+-----------------------------------------------------------------------+
| ░░░░░░░░░░░░░░░░░░░░░░░░░░░░░░░░░░░░░░░░░░░░░░░░░░░░░░░░░░░░░░░░░░░░░░░░ |
+-----------------------------------------------------------------------+
|                                                                       |
|                    DCM        Problem Description                     |
|                                                                       |
|       Module Type: DCM            Number: 42        Switch:    IONA___ |
|                                                     Calls Up:  _____   |
|                                                     BCS Load:  __      |
|                                                                       |
|     Symptoms                                                          |
|           State | Reason    : ISTB  : _____                    |
|               Previously    : _____ : _____                    |
|           QUERYPM FLT       : _____                      |
|           TST Result        : OK _____                       |
|           LOADPM Result     : PASS _____                       |
|           Busy Links  (C-side): _____                             |
|                       (P-side): _____                             |
|                                                                       |
|                                                                       |
|     ACTIONS                                                           |
|     Cards swapped: _____  |
|                                                                       |
+-----------------------------------------------------------------------+
|                                                                       |
|  +--------+-------+-------+--------+  +--------+--------+--------+---------+|
|  |Previous|Explain|Restore| New    |  |Suggest |Other   |Access  |Notebook ||
|  | Form   |       | Form  |Problems|  |Actions |Symptoms|Database|         ||
|  +--------+-------+-------+--------+  +--------+--------+--------+---------+|
+-----------------------------------------------------------------------+
```

This example shows symptoms for a problem with a Digital Carrier Module (DCM).
Softkeys at the bottom of the screen allow the user to control the session.

Figure 8. Input screen for problem description.

8. TWO NEW INFORMATION RETRIEVAL FEATURES

Two major methods of accessing information have been added—a switch database
feature and a notebook feature. These features provide assistance for some of the
aspects of maintenance problem solving shown in Figure 9. The switch database
provides the user with screens of information about the physical composition of
the switch (e.g., layouts for individual cards, block diagrams, and card connections) and on detailed procedures for carrying out various maintenance actions.
Selection of items is made through a hierarchical set of menus, but the detailed
way in which these are presented depends on the current problem context. If there
is a problem under investigation, the first menu will be the one that contains the
module on the symptom description form. The craftsperson can then retrieve in-

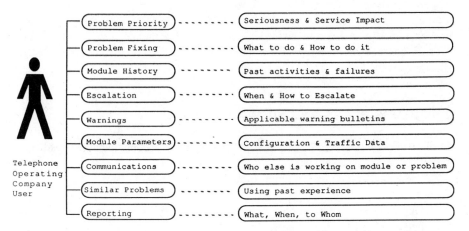

Figure 9. Various aspects of maintenance problem solving.

formation about this module more quickly. If no problem is currently being worked on, a default top menu is displayed first.

The screens are made up of text, graphics, or both. Information on other switch items may be included in the database: for example, MAP usage, customer features, operational measurements, and LOG descriptions. A major advantage of the switch database feature is that it provides a different access path for reuse of parts of the knowledge base and contextual retrieval. In our initial prototype, the craftsperson had to go through a session that recommended a particular repair action, and only then could the craftsperson ask for details about that particular procedure. The current version allows the craftsperson to get details, whether or not such a repair action has been recommended.

The notebook feature is named after the individual notebooks kept by many maintenance technicians. The feature is available throughout a consultation and provides filing and retrieval for various types of information. These are particularly useful for setting up local variations and operating policies:

1. Warning bulletins.
2. Previous switch problems and solutions.
3. Maintenance history of particular hardware components.
4. Local maintenance procedures, including authorization and reporting.
5. Local configuration information.
6. Phone numbers of important contacts.
7. Local mail messages about maintenance.

Templates are used for matching against items to be retrieved in any of the seven categories. The template for access is defined by filling in a screen form, except for the first two categories. For warning bulletins and previous problems and solutions, a template is constructed dynamically during the describe–recommend cycle. For example, if a recommended action to reload a maintenance trunk module (MTM) has been selected, warning bulletins about reloading MTMs can be retrieved by one softkey stroke.

9.   FUTURE PLANS AND SUMMARY

At the time of this writing we are preparing for a second technical trial in a telephone operating company.

Several factors have contributed to the success of MAD so far.

- Our choice of using an expert system shell, with its many built-in features, helped to get the initial prototype off the ground quickly.
- Knowledge acquisition, traditionally a bottleneck in many expert system projects, has been simplified by the availability of Northern Telecom's detailed maintenance documents and flowcharts.
- Working on an application that is vital to switch and network operations has generated the support and enthusiasm of DMS troubleshooting experts.
- Because MAD works as a front end to the existing maintenance facilities of the DMS switch, the building of MAD was simplified. The built-in switch software provides a clean and well-defined high-level interface to MAD.

These points have all worked to our advantage, and our progress has produced growing interest and optimism regarding the potential of expert systems. MAD now handles problems in peripherals, where the initial symptoms are alarms generated by the switch. We are increasing and refining the maintenance knowledge to handle problems with different initial symptoms, such as customer service reports or abnormalities indicated by switch operational measurements, and problems in other areas of the switch, such as the central control. We are also exploring methods for tailoring MAD to local operating company policies, including partitioning the knowledge base. A similar requirement for customization exists in automating large computer center operations [10]. We plan linkage to the switch so that data can be taken directly, and we also plan eventual linkage to other operations support systems. We are also exploring monitoring methods for problem detection and a loose coupling between monitor and advisor components.

In each AI application at BNR, the methodology is the same: careful application selection and planning are followed by incremental development and refinement with the aid of human experts. The process ends in testing and validation by potential users in their working environment. System designers and users alike are excited by the prospects of expert systems technology. By mapping out critical procedures and building support system tools like MAD, we are demonstrating the potential of expert systems to contribute to productivity and future product enhancements. It is a natural and logical progression. Although the dream of expert systems described at the beginning of this chapter may be a long way off, it is only a matter of time before today's expert systems expand into a host of marketable applications.

REFERENCES

1. I. Ferguson, S. Rabie, J. Kennedy, and R. Peacocke, A Knowledge-Based Sales Assistant for Data Communications Networks. In *IEEE International Conference on Communications,* IEEE, New York, 1987.

2. R. Aubin, R. Peacocke, and D. Zlatin, From Specifications to Test Cases: AI in Software Quality, In *IEEE International Conference on Communications,* IEEE, New York, 1986.

3. T. Bult, R. Peacocke, S. Rabie, and V. Snarr, An Interactive Expert System for Switch Maintenance. In *International Switching Symposium*, IEEE, New York, 1987.

4. *Telesis* special issue, DMS-100 Family of Digital Switches, *Telesis,* Vol. 7, No. 4, December 1980.

5. J. Gilmore, and K. Pulaski, A Survey of Expert System Tools. In *Second Conference on Artificial Intelligence Applications,* pp. 498–502, IEEE, New York, 1985.

6. F. Hayes-Roth, Rule-Based Systems, *Communications of the ACM,* Vol. 28, No. 9, pp. 921–932, 1985.

7. R. Davis, B. Buchanan, and E. Shortliffe, Production Rules as a Representation for a Knowledge-Based Consultation Program. In *Artificial Intelligence 8,* pp. 15–45, North-Holland, Amsterdam, 1977.

8. J. Carroll, and J. McKendree, Interface Design Issues for Advice-Giving Expert Systems, *Communications of the ACM,* Vol. 30, pp. 14–31, January 1987.

9. M. Coombs, and J. Alty, Expert Systems: An Alternate Paradigm. *International Journal of Man–Machine Studies,* Vol. 20, pp. 21–43, 1984.

10. K. R. Milliken, A. V. Cruise, R. L. Ennis, A. J. Finkel, J. L. Hellerstein, D. J. Loeb, D. A. Klein, M. J. Masullo, H. M. Van Woerkom, and N. B. Waite, YES/MVS and the Automation of Operations for Large Computer Complexes, *IBM Systems Journal,* Vol. 25, No. 2, pp. 159–180, 1986.

XTEL: AN EXPERT SYSTEM FOR DESIGNING THEATERWIDE TELECOMMUNICATIONS ARCHITECTURES

Jerald L. Feinstein

ICF/Phase Linear Systems, Inc.
Washington, DC

Frederick Siems

Booz, Allen & Hamilton, Inc.,
Bethesda, Maryland

John Popolizio and David Bailey

ICF/Phase Linear Systems, Inc., Washington, DC

Aaron Wang

Booz, Allen & Hamilton, Inc., Bethesda, Maryland

1. OVERVIEW

1.1. The Problem

The Defense Communications Agency (DCA) oversees the design of Joint Service military telecommunications networks for the U.S. government. The United Commanders-in-Chief of U.S. military forces are responsible for ensuring adequate network architecture design. The task of approving a communications network architecture ultimately falls on their shoulders. Their communications designers must satisfy strict requirements for operational design. Thus, the job of architecture development is not taken lightly.

The current European Theater Command Communications Architecture description consists of 700 communications nodes, 1200 connecting links, 800 separate network users, and 30,000 user requirements to fulfill. The number of network components makes this a sizable design problem. The experts estimate there are more than 10,000 possible upgrades for this particular telecommunications infrastructure. Their task involves developing recommended design changes or upgrades to produce the most survivable, cost-effective architecture. Clearly, the conventional approach, a manual element-by-element analysis over the network is often out of the question. The cost in terms of personnel, money, and time is prohibitive.

The design of a theater communications architecture (TCA) focuses on three primary considerations: components, media, and requirements. The components are the communications facilities and equipment that make up each site. The media are the methods (e.g., high-frequency and microwave) of communications, the links, between one or more sites. Requirements are the basic mission-driven communications needs of the users on the network. The design must provide the users with communications service as per their requirements in benign as well as conflict situations. Therefore, the proper set of components and media must be made survivable and robust. Since conflict situations stress and degrade the performance of a military communications network, that is what drives the design problem.

The telecommunications architecture must survive in the face of external threats. Threats include conventional, nuclear, and biochemical weapons as well as sabotage. During times of crises, vital defense communications can be disrupted or lost if any irreplacable network components are damaged or destroyed.

The importance of user communications requirements motivates the desire to design survivable architectures. This goal may be achieved by mitigating threats to the architecture and by using mobile communications resources to replace lost components. Sites and links can be hardened physically and electronically against damage. Architecture redundancy reduces the chances of destroying an important communications path. In this fashion, the network service receives minimal conflict-induced degradation. Mobile assets constitute the network's recovery elements. When sites or links are lost, they may be replaced by a functionally equivalent asset. This combination of preventive protection and real-time replacement enables a communications architecture to satisfy its most important requirements for the duration of a conflict.

Each point mentioned above must be worked into the network design. To do this, expert designers must examine each component in the network sequentially. Local threats and user requirements drive the evaluation process. Threats expose component weaknesses, while user requirements serve to define the relative importance of protection. Each media element is examined to see if it is appropriate and sufficient to support the communications requirements. By executing the study in this manner, sets of design recommendations evolve a survivable architecture meeting the users' needs and supporting their missions.

These recommendations establish a baseline architecture for further analysis. New sets of recommendations can be made by recursively applying the same process to the old network with the enacted recommendations. However, each complete cycle needs staff-years of effort, owing to the limitation of ''by-hand'' analysis. This is impractical and not cost effective. A better, faster method is needed.

1.2. The Solution

Fortunately, there is another method of designing telecommunications architectures that reduces development time and increases peformance. By using the software methods of expert systems technology coupled with modeling and simulation, intelligent tools can be made to assist the network designer. This application is new but not untried; silicon chips are now designed using expert systems [1]. This form of network design on a chip is not altogether different from designing large-scale communications networks.

In choosing how to assist communications designers, using expert systems, we first analyzed the process they go through, sorting out those aspects that can readily be automated. This was not easy. When we interviewed designers and asked them "how they do it," each one had a different order of approach—compounding not only the representation of the process but the execution of "helping hands" for each type of problem. We created a roadmap for each view of the process and flagged departure points, that is, conflicting views. This process was necessary because of our use of multiple experts. It was completed prior to applying classic knowledge engineering disciplines.

1.3. What Is XTEL?

XTEL emulates a telecommunications system architect's activities in designing a military communications network in a specified theater of operations. XTEL was developed as part of a larger set of automated tools that support the development of telecommunications architectures for U.S. forces in military theaters of operation. These architectures are being developed by the Defense Communications Agency for the Unified Commanders-in-Chief of U.S. forces in both the European and Pacific theaters.

XTEL is currently being used to develop a European theater communications architecture meeting the communications requirements of the U.S. European Command through the course of a NATO/Warsaw Pact conflict. In building the architecture, files of site and link information are first created for U.S. and Allied communications networks. A *vulnerability assessment tool* then applies enemy threat assets against these communications networks, computing survivability values for sites and links.

Specific user-to-user communications requirements are derived for U.S. forces to meet their mission objectives. An automated file of these is created, each record characterizing a communications "needline" with associated supporting data. Using the resulting probabilities of survival for network sites and links, a *survivability router* routes the needline requirements over the "damaged" networks choosing the path that maximizes survivability. This is the starting point for the architecture design process.

XTEL employs rules derived from military telecommunications system design experts to develop design alternatives to improve both performance and survivability of network sites and links. The decision as to which specific types of improvements are best suited to a particular site or link depends on a variety of factors and constraints. These include message traffic, location, susceptibility to attack, type of threat element likely to be applied, physical characteristics of the site or link, and a variety of technical, political, and programmatic constraints. XTEL incorporates this knowledge into a set of production rules to assist the network designer in formulating design alternatives.

1.4.   Why an Expert System Approach?

As military communications needs and available technologies expand, the task of designing telecommunications architectures becomes an increasingly expensive and time-intensive effort. This complex design process demands the scarce expertise of seasoned military communications planners and network architects. Using knowledge gained from years of practical experience, these experts apply ''rules of thumb'' to data describing existing network parameters as well as information gained as a result of exercising communications network models, simulations, and other architectural design tools. However, design costs grow nearly exponentially as almost routine changes in assumptions or design philosophy force cycles of lengthy rework. These changes often result in significant architectural modifications. As the rework process continues, the supporting rationale of justification for each design action is often clouded or lost entirely.

To address these problems, we developed XTEL—an expert system to design theaterwide telecommunications architectures. This expert system approach significantly reduces the time and cost needed to design architectures and at the same time improves the design quality. Once an architecture is designed using XTEL, changes in assumptions or design philosophy can be tested quickly by changing one or more rules. Thus, months of work are compressed into only several days. Next, the justification module allows questioning on the rationale supporting any design action. A typical question might be, ''What is the basis for the recommendation to locate tropo equipment at site *xyz*?'' These questions are answered employing a user interface consisting of pleasingly colorful screens coupled with a powerful natural language interface incorporating recognition of synonyms, pronouns, and possessives.

1.5.   XTEL Operation

1.5.1.   Using XTEL.   XTEL operates in four stages. First, threat assessment tools are used on initial network and threat data to produce site and link survivability measures. Second, the survivability measures, along with user communications requirements, are input to network routing models, producing network performance scores for satisfying communications requirements. Third, network parameter data and network performance scores from the second stage are analyzed by the inference engine. The rules in the knowledge base act on the resulting information to produce a recommended architectural design. Figure 1 depicts the XTEL architecture design process.

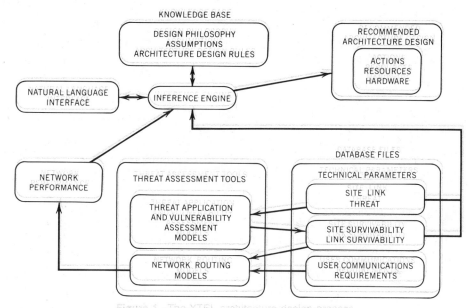

Figure 1. The XTEL architecture design process.

1.5.2.   Knowledge Structure. XTEL emulates a telecommunications analyst through the use of expert architecture design knowledge. Once the preliminary information is read in, XTEL structures it into nested files. Once the file structure is complete, the rules are applied, producing the recommendations. The recommendations specify design actions for both links and sites. Figure 2 shows the structure of knowledge within XTEL.

1.5.3.   XTEL's User Interface. The interface between XTEL and a user consists of a natural language parser and colorful graphic display screens. Once the system is run, the user can examine and validate the recommendations through simple ''show me'' commands. A request for explanation applies to both recommendations and rule formats. A user can see just how each recommendation was derived. The elements in the knowledge base also can be examined through the interface. A request is sent to XTEL to view the knowledge base, and XTEL replies with the appropriate material.

Graphics screens and windows are used visually to structure all output from XTEL. Error handling and notification are handled by the natural language parser and displayed through graphics. Figure 3 shows the structure of the user interface.

1.5.4.   Inference Engine. XTEL's inference engine uses forward chaining and the technique of direct referencing [2] (a software implementation of content addressable memory methodology) to decrease response time for large real-world problems. The rules are accessed using non-Boolean indices. Thus, inferencing time is dramatically reduced over that for conventional methods and is independent

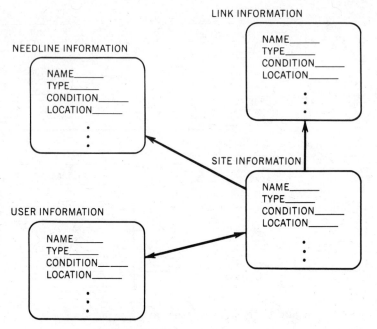

Figure 2. XTEL knowledge structure.

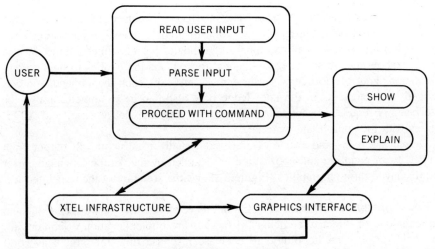

Figure 3. XTEL user interface.

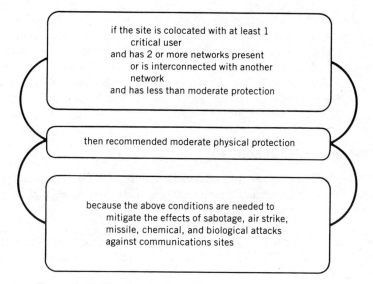

if the site is colocated with at least 1
    critical user
and has 2 or more networks present
    or is interconnected with another
    network
and has less than moderate protection

then recommended moderate physical protection

because the above conditions are needed to
    mitigate the effects of sabotage, air strike,
    missile, chemical, and biological attacks
    against communications sites

Figure 4. XTEL rule, recommendation, and justification triplet.

of the number of rules in the knowledge base. A sample rule, recommendation, and justification triplet is illustrated in Figure 4.

2. SYSTEM DEVELOPMENT

2.1. Development Steps

XTEL's development followed a classic pattern. The process included knowledge engineering, software engineering and testing, and validation of the system's recommendations.

Knowledge engineering involved close interaction between a group of telecommunications architecture design experts and several knowledge engineers. The team began by partitioning the knowledge into smaller, more manageable modules. Each module represented the knowledge required to perform a single facet of the task. The set of modules and rules were then given to the software engineers on the team. The software engineers encoded the pseudocode into rule sets. Modularization served as a basis to divide the rules into related sets. The control structure–inference engine emulated the module structure by ensuring the rules were applied in the correct order. The software engineers set the datatypes for the system. The datatypes reflected a combination of stored information and a set of procedures to deduce missing information from existing data.

The test and validation efforts for XTEL consisted of applying XTEL to a small network and comparing its output with output produced by the TCA experts. During the course of these experiments, XTEL reached a point where it generated a superset of the telecommunications designer's expert output. Initially, rule conditions were written in as general a fashion as possible; then, more clauses were added to existing conditions to limit the number of excess recommendations produced by the system. Exceptions to the new general rules then were added.

With each successive test, the number of rule modifications to XTEL decreased. Eventually, the system was run on larger, more complex networks, and its recommendations were accepted by the experts.

2.2. System Organization

2.2.1. *Overview.* Four software modules comprise XTEL. Understanding the operation of these modules and their interactions leads to a conceptual understanding of the entire system.

2.2.2. *System Modules.* The natural language interface enables users to communicate freely with XTEL. The system allows for default choices by recognizing English pronouns. An understanding of possessives enables users to access pertinent information efficiently within XTEL. Complex queries are created using conjunctions with complex objects. A complex object refers to a series or collection of network components such as "nodes 1 to 5" or "All Recs." Once the natural language interface parses the query XTEL takes all appropriate actions.

The knowledge–inference module contains two submodules incorporating the inference engine and the rules bases. Rules are stored in the traditional "IF 〈condition〉 THEN 〈action〉" format. Rules from the same rule base are commutative, meaning that rule application order does not affect the final results.

2.2.3. *Module Interaction.* By functionality, the modules handle knowledge representation, inference, input data transformation, and user interaction. The modules interact in the following manner. Input data transformation takes the output from the conflict simulation producing facts to be operated on by the rules contained in the knowledge–inference module. The knowledge–inference engine modifies the knowledge representation. The user interaction module enables users to view the knowledge base, recommendation, and information describing the architecture.

2.2.4. *The Rule Base.* Physical node hardening pertains to actual facility protection. This protection defends the communications site against direct attack. These attacks can range from terrorist bombing to an infantry assault. Protective measures include burying the facility, installing protective fences, and reinforcement. Generally, protection upgrades for the node should match the level of protection for the node's most important user. A typical physical protection rule states:

IF	the node is colocated with one surviving critical user
and	the node is a member of two or more networks or
and	the node is an interconnect with another network

and   the node has less than moderate protection

THEN   recommend the installation of moderate protection.

Network electronic protection has been divided into two rule bases: link electronic protect and node electronic protection. Together, they recommend measures to mitigate the effects of jamming and high-altitude nuclear bursts against the communications links and nodes.

XTEL gives advice to increase the robustness and redundancy of the network. These route diversity measures lessen the vulnerability of a node to a single threat. If a node's links are all high frequency, then it is more susceptible to jamming. A rule for new installation fires when a crucial node has less than a specified number of neighboring nodes. A simple rule determines the node for terminating the new link. The rule picks the closest surviving node in the same network. New links are added to diversify the node's capabilities for communication. If this recommendation remains unimplemented, the node would fail to satisfy its requirements when one of its neighbors is destroyed. These design measures enable the architecture to reroute around damaged central communications facilities.

After new links are recommended, XTEL applies its media diversity rules to recommend the appropriate link type. Judgment is based on a combination of distance, voice capacity requirements, and other communications links present at the link's end nodes. All link media types satisfying the voice capacity and distance constraints are recommended. They are recommended in reverse order of their similarity to the end nodes' existing media links.

XTEL performs a simple cost analysis as each recommendation is produced. An estimate of the cost for implementing each recommendation is generated.

The reconstitution rules enable XTEL to provide useful advice during modeling and simulation. These rules apply to the sections of the network needing rapid replacement. They are activated when XTEL encounters a destroyed node.

The first set of reconstitution rules determines the importance of the node, the need to reconstitute it, and the means of reconstitution. The node may be reconstituted with spare parts and mobile assets or reconnected to a backbone node. When a mobile asset solution is suggested, another set of rules is run to determine the type of mobile asset to recommend.

2.3. Lessons Learned

In building XTEL, we learned that most of the important factors that led to success were tied to good knowledge engineering practices. Two areas were most evident: (1) motivating and securing the wholehearted support of the experts and (2) recognizing that systems developed from multiple experts require an approach different from those developed from a single expert.

Getting the communications designers to understand and appreciate the rule developing process of knowledge engineering had the immediate effect of accelerating the rule development rate. At first, progress was slow. Then as the experts began to understand the process, they were able to generate many of the rules alone, without a knowledge engineer being present.

Systems developed from multiple experts suffer from problems not found in single-expert systems. For example, overlapping clusters of rules developed by different experts may, in some cases, actually interfere with each other so as not to produce the desired consequences. One example is looping. Each expert may develop clusters of rules where each cluster alone would be "loop-free." Yet, when the clusters are combined via overlay, looping can often result. Other similar problems can result from combining rule clusters developed by different experts but will not be discussed here. In all cases, we solved the problem using a consensus approach. All rules submitted by individual experts were reviewed and accepted by the group prior to entering the knowledge base.

As XTEL grew, we were ever careful to maintain knowledge base integrity through precise application of proper knowledge engineering principles. This effort paid off in a system requiring only very minor logical corrections within its knowledge base.

3. SYSTEM DESCRIPTION

3.1. Overview

An overview of XTEL can be pictured by understanding the internal modular configuration and the way in which the modules interact.

3.2. System Components

XTEL is composed of four basic parts, including modules to accept information and create an internal image of the telecommunications network, to apply the rules and make recommendations, to provide a user interface to display the results, and to support the other three parts of XTEL with utilities and data abstractions. Each module is described in more detail in the following paragraphs.

Build rep is the component that reads in information from files and creates an internal image of the telecommunications network. First, basic node information is read in from node survivability and node availability files. This information is then converted into the proper format and stored as a node variable in the global node array. Second, link information is extracted from the link survivability, link availability, and link utilization files. Link information is stored as a link variable in the global link array. Third, link information that is important to the node data type (e.g., whether or not any links have antijamming protection) is stored with the appropriate node in the node array. Fourth, build rep reads in the user and mission data from the user location–survivability file. These data are subsequently stored in the user array. Fifth, user information relevant to nodes is stored in with the node variables. An example of user information that is needed by the node abstractions is whether or not the user is critical and/or buried. Finally, the needline information is read from the user requirements file. Once this process is completed, XTEL is finished creating the network's internal image and is ready to apply its design rules to generate recommendations.

Recommendations to improve the connectivity and survivability of a communications network are made using design rules. The rules check for certain conditions, and if the conditions exist the rules generate recommendations. Recommendations are inserted in the fifth and final global array, the recommendation array. The rules are applied to all the links and nodes. First, the link rules are applied, with resulting recommendations placed in a recommendation array. Next, the node rules are applied. These rules deal with physical protection, route and media diversity, reconstitution, and reconstitution media. When this process is finished, a text version of the recommendations is written to an external file. After writing to the text file, XTEL reactivates the user interface.

The user interface contains two parts, a limited domain natural language processor for input and a multicolored graphics screen for output. The natural language front end allows users to enter queries to XTEL in a free format. These queries are then converted into a request to XTEL, and the result is displayed on the graphics screen. The interface allows the user to view all parts of the network, as well as XTEL's recommendations.

XTEL displays an object's information in the print window. The print window is the largest of the three windows and is placed in the upper left corner of the screen. Explanations are printed in plain text, while database information is shown in template form. In a template, the system tag is displayed in bold print; variable information is in plain print.

XTEL queries the user for appropriate input and output files. After the files are specified, XTEL reads the data. When the system is satisfied that the inputs are correct, the rules are applied. During this time, XTEL writes all recommendations to the user specified output module.

When XTEL is finished, the user can view the data and the results by using the natural language window-based interface. The interface screen contains three windows. The command window occupies the bottom two lines of the screen and is used to accept queries.

If a query is acceptable, XTEL processes it. A processed query has the form of a series of operations over a set of objects. The system executes the query by applying the operations to the objects. The status window displays information on the current state of a query's execution. The current operation is printed at the top, while the objects are listed in order below the operation. The current object being displayed is highlighted in blue. The status window is located in the upper right of the screen.

The parser makes the system easier to use. It recognizes such English features as synonyms, pronouns, and possessives. Complex objects may be specified by the use of conjunctions and prepositions. The system replaces pronouns with the last semantically matching object entered. The system replaces possessives by expanding the field associated with that object. Objects are currently specified by their codes, but in the future this will be changed to a call by name format.

3.3.   The Natural Language Parser's Context-Free Grammar

⟨command⟩	→ ⟨operations⟩⟨objects⟩
⟨operations⟩	→ ⟨operation⟩, ⟨operations⟩
⟨operations⟩	→ ⟨operation⟩ and ⟨operation⟩
⟨operation⟩	→ ⟨Run|Print|Show|Display|Explain⟩
⟨objects⟩	→ ⟨complex object⟩, ⟨objects⟩
⟨objects⟩	→ ⟨complex object⟩ and ⟨complex object⟩
⟨complex object⟩	→ ⟨simple object⟩
⟨complex object⟩	→ from ⟨noun⟩⟨int⟩ to ⟨noun⟩⟨int⟩
⟨complex object⟩	→ from ⟨noun⟩⟨noun⟩⟨int⟩ to ⟨int⟩
⟨complex object⟩	→ ⟨noun⟩⟨int series⟩
⟨complex object⟩	→ all ⟨noun⟩
⟨simple object⟩	→ ⟨noun⟩⟨int⟩
⟨simple object⟩	→ ⟨noun⟩⟨poss⟩⟨noun⟩
⟨simple object⟩	→ ⟨pronoun⟩
⟨int series⟩	→ ⟨int⟩, ⟨int series⟩
⟨int series⟩	→ ⟨int⟩ and⟨int⟩
⟨pronoun⟩	→ in|them⟨det⟩⟨noun⟩
⟨pos⟩	→ ˆ | ˆs
⟨noun⟩	→ node|link|user|rule|hardness|protection|XTEL
	|geoloc|interconnect|type|capacity

3.4.   The Architecture Design Process

XTEL's design recommendations take the form of actual architectural initiatives. These initiatives fall into four broad categories: physical protection, electronic protection, route and media diversity, and extension and reconstitution.

Physical Protection. These consist of measures to mitigate effects of sabotage, air strike, missile, chemical, and biological attacks. Four levels of physical protection are considered: minimal, light, moderate, and heavy. Some examples are:

- Minimal: fences, intrusion sensors, lighting
- Light: controlled access, revetments, protected tower legs, auxiliary power
- Moderate: guards, concrete buildings, concrete towers, hardened waveguides, filtered air controlled water supply, buried fuel supply
- Heavy: buried operations

Electronic Protection. These are measures to mitigate effects of jamming and high-altitude nuclear bursts. Two types of electronic protection are considered: antijamming and EMP protection. Some examples are:

- Antijamming: high frequency (4 channels), satellite (JRSC)

- EMP: Aboveground facility in buildings, aboveground facility in vans, buried operations

Route and Media Diversity. These are measures to enhance system capacity, coverage, and survivability. Examples of actual implementations by type include:

- Fiber optic cable buried: 1 fiber pair multiplexed at DS3 (672 channels), 3 fiber pair multiplexed at 2 DS3 (1344 channels), and 5 fiber pair multiplexed at 3 DS3 (2016 channels)
- High frequency (HF) link: 4 channels with multiplex
- Millimeter wave link: 24 channels with multiplex
- Microwave LOS link: 384 channels with multiplex
- Tropospheric scatter link: 132 channels with multiplex
- Satellite link: DSCS II with 384 channel multiplex
- Lease: PTT single voice circuit (4kHz) and conditioned 9600 Bps within Greenland, Iceland, Norway, Denmark, United Kingdom, Belgium, Netherlands, Luxembourg, France, Germany, Switzerland, Austria, Portugal, Spain, Italy, Greece, and Turkey
- Transmission interconnect equipment for 24 channels
- DSN end office: 600 lines, 50 trunk ports
- DSN dual function switch: 1200 lines, 100 trunk ports
- I-S/A AMPE
- DDN C30 processor

Extension and Reconstitution. These are measures to enhance system coverage and survivability. Some examples are:

- Mobile HF system: 1 link at 4 channels with multiplex
- Mobile millimeter wave system: 1 link at 24 channels with multiplex
- Mobile microwave LOS system: 2 links at 192 channels each with multiplex
- Mobile tropospheric scatter system: 1 link at 132 channels with multiplex
- Mobile satellite ground terminal: AN/TSC-93, AN/TSC-94 each with 24 channel multiplex
- DSCS-GMF gateway terminal rack: 20 with 24 channel multiplex
- Mobile DSN end office: 600 lines, 50 trunk ports
- Mobile DSN dual function switch: 1200 lines, 100 trunk ports
- Mobile DDN C30 processor
- Spare equipment tower sections, parabolic dish, waveguide, HF radio, millimeter wave radio, microwave radio, tropospheric scatter radio, multiplexers at group and supergroup level

4. TRACE OF SYSTEM OPERATION

One of the most effective ways to gain an appreciation of XTEL's power is to design a small telecommunications architecture. For this purpose, we provide a sample design session recreating the user–terminal dialogue that would be involved in a small, yet interesting, network design exercise.

In this exercise, we apply XTEL to a small network consisting of 20 nodes, 35 links, and 20 users. During the session, we ask questions about the network's nodes and links and solicit design recommendations as well as the reasoning behind some of the recommendations or "recs" as they are called in XTEL.

An XTEL session can be divided into three logical steps.

Step 1: Data to build the internal image of the network is drawn from resident arrays. This includes information defining the physical network as well as the user communications requirements needing to be satisfied.

Step 2: A simulated conflict allocates an enemy threat, which results in maximum damage to an existing architecture. During the course of conflict, communications requirements are routed over the rapidly degrading architecture, finding paths that maximize their survivability. The number and kinds of requirements satisfied are used as a metric or score to grade the architecture's merit.

Step 3: Steps 1 and 2 are ordinarily carried out by analysts who prepare the results of the modeling exercise for use by military architecture designers with many years of experience. These designers analyze data from computer runs and make design decisions, such as which nodes to harden physically, over which links to put antijam protection, where to increase capacity, where to add additional links, and what is the best media to use. In XTEL, these design rules form the knowledge base used to generate an architecture. The knowledge base used in the sample exercise is listed following this discussion.

Now, we start the session at the point where a simulated conflict has destroyed an existing communications infrastructure. XTEL, as would a human designer, now applies its design rules to design and recommend an architecture that would meet communications needs and survive the simulated conflict.

To view the first XTEL screen, we enter the command "XTEL" from the terminal. The response is presented in Figure 5.

XTEL is now initializing its database to build an internal image of the network, users, conflict-induced damage, simulation statistics, and so on. A blue background color is turned on behind each functional listing on the status screen while being carried out and turned off when completed.

To initiate the architectural design process, RUN XTEL is entered at the " >>> " prompt at the lower left of the screen. See Figure 6.

XTEL is now applying its rule base to the current architecture design problem and is generating design recommendations. Prior to going on to show XTEL's design recommendations, we illustrate XTEL's *browser*. Using the natural lan-

Done.	Initializing...
	Node Objects
	Link Objects
	User Objects
	Needlines
	Availabilities
	Utilizations
| Hit Any Character to Continue |	
Print Screen	Status Screen

XTEL
>>> Run XTEL.

Figure 5. XTEL initializing network and requirement data.

Done.	Running...
	XTEL
| Hit Any Character to Continue |	
Print Screen	Status Screen

XTEL
>>> Run XTEL.

Figure 6. XTEL applying its rules to design an architecture.

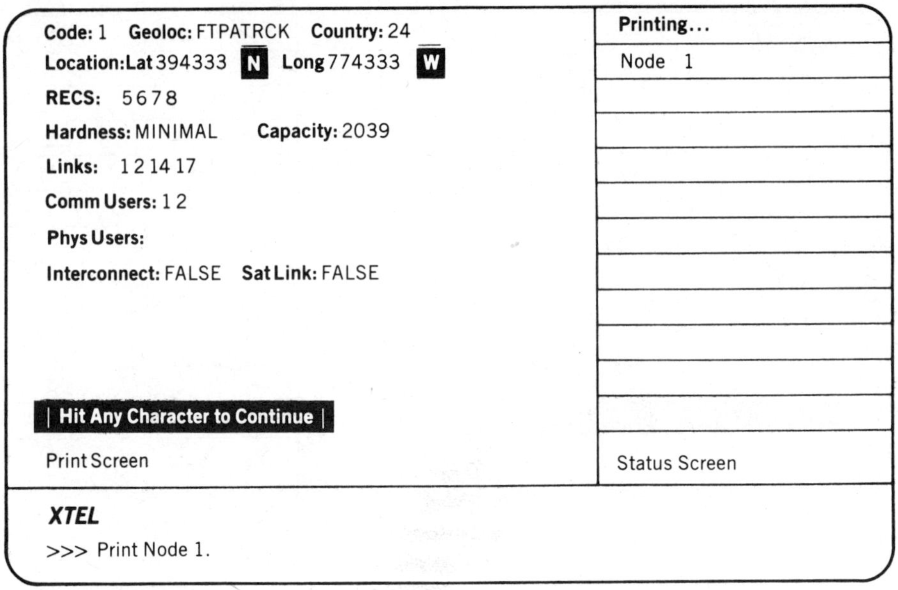

```
Code: 1   Geoloc: FTPATRCK   Country: 24          Printing...

Location: Lat 394333 [N]  Long 774333 [W]         Node  1

RECS:  5678

Hardness: MINIMAL      Capacity: 2039

Links:   1 2 14 17

Comm Users: 1 2

Phys Users:

Interconnect: FALSE   Sat Link: FALSE




   | Hit Any Character to Continue |

   Print Screen                                   Status Screen
```

XTEL
>>> Print Node 1.

Figure 7. XTEL providing important node-related information.

guage parser, we can ask XTEL questions about the network as well as results of the simulated conflict. We enter at the prompt, ''Print Node 1'' (we could have entered, ''Show Node 1'') to get some information about the first network node. A node name other than a number could have been used. See Figure 7.

As a result of this request, certain highly useful information is printed about the node: first its code, then its geographic location at Fort Patrick, a country code for the United States, its position in terms of latitude and longitude, four design recommendation codes that have been generated for that node, a note that the node is relatively soft in that it has only minimal hardening, a number to indicate the degree to which the node had a message transfer shortfall, the code numbers of links associated with the node, codes of the communications users tied into the node, the number of users physically located at the node, an indication of whether the node is used as a connecting point between two different networks, and finally if it can function as a satellite earth station.

Next, at the prompt we enter ''Show its links''. Note in Figure 8 that we used the possessive form of a pronoun here.

XTEL responds with highly important information on each link associated with node 1. The status screen shows which item is being displayed by changing the screen background to blue for that item only. The following are shown: First the link code and ID, then the code number identifying the single recommendation associated with link 1, an indication that link 1 uses troposcatter as the media, an indication of a capacity shortfall over this link, that this link has no antijamming protection, and that this link is used to connect node 1 with 9.

Code: 1 Link ID: T0001	Printing...
RECS: 8	Link 1
Type: Troposcatter Capacity: 92	Link 2
Link Protect: NONE	Link 14
Nodes: 9, 1	Link 17
	Hit Any Character to Continue		
Print Screen	Status Screen

XTEL
>>> Show its links.

Figure 8. XTEL providing important link-related information.

Next, we desire to view recommendations for all the links (1, 2, 14, and 17) associated with node 1. We enter at the prompt, "Show the links' recs." Here we use the possessive form of a plural noun. See Figure 9.

For the four links, there are only two recommendations. The first recommendation, 8, is shown. It is for link 1, and its purpose is to increase the link's capacity. The next screen (Figure 10) shows the second recommendation, which is associated with link 14. It is to install antijamming protection. This is a result of a shortfall induced by communications jamming rather than physical destruction.

XTEL has two levels of explanations in its explanation facility. First, a top-level explanation is given if, at the prompt, we enter, "Explain rec 1." If this is insufficient, we have the option to examine the more detailed rule by entering, "Explain rule 2." This feature is illustrated in the next four screens.

To explain recommendations 8 and 2, we enter, "Explain them." First recommendation 8 is explained (Figure 11), then recommendation 2 (Figure 12).

If additional detail is desired, we enter "Explain the recs' rules." Then, the more detailed actual design rules are shown (Figure 13). Note that recommendation 8 involved rule 7.

Rule 7 is one of the media diversity rules. In this case, XTEL implicitly uses cost to arrive at a recommendation.

Next, XTEL shows rule 2 (Figure 14). This rule embodies the logic that system elements should be at least as well protected as the users they serve.

Next is an example of a design recommendation to upgrade the physical protection at a site. First, we prompt XTEL to show node 9 (Figure 15). This is a

```
┌────────────────────────────────────────────────────────────────┐
│  Recommendation: 8                          │ Printing...        │
│  Code: 8                                    │ ▌Rec  8▐           │
│  Recommend increase existing Link Capacity  │  Rec  2            │
│  For                                        │                    │
│  Node Code: 1      and                      │                    │
│  Link Code: 1                               │                    │
│                                             │                    │
│                                             │                    │
│                                             │                    │
│                                             │                    │
│  ▌Hit Any Character to Continue▐            │                    │
│  Print Screen                               │ Status Screen      │
├────────────────────────────────────────────┴────────────────────┤
│  XTEL                                                            │
│  >>> Show the links recs.                                       │
└────────────────────────────────────────────────────────────────┘
```

Figure 9. XTEL displaying a design recommendation for link 1.

```
┌────────────────────────────────────────────────────────────────┐
│  Recommendation: 2                          │ Printing...        │
│  Code: 2                                    │  Rec  8            │
│  Recommend Antijamming protection           │ ▌Rec  2▐           │
│  For                                        │                    │
│  Link Code: 14                              │                    │
│                                             │                    │
│                                             │                    │
│                                             │                    │
│                                             │                    │
│                                             │                    │
│  ▌Hit Any Character to Continue▐            │                    │
│  Print Screen                               │ Status Screen      │
├────────────────────────────────────────────┴────────────────────┤
│  XTEL                                                            │
│  >>> Show the links recs.                                       │
└────────────────────────────────────────────────────────────────┘
```

Figure 10. XTEL displaying a design recommendation for link 14.

178

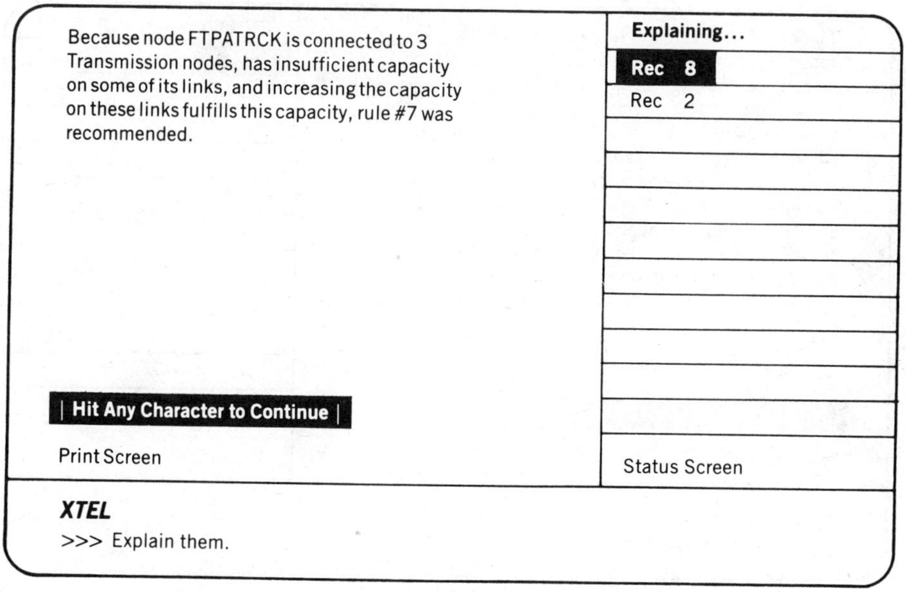

Because node FTPATRCK is connected to 3
Transmission nodes, has insufficient capacity
on some of its links, and increasing the capacity
on these links fulfills this capacity, rule #7 was
recommended.

Explaining...

Rec	8
Rec	2

| Hit Any Character to Continue |

Print Screen

Status Screen

XTEL

>>> Explain them.

Figure 11. XTEL explaining recommendation 8.

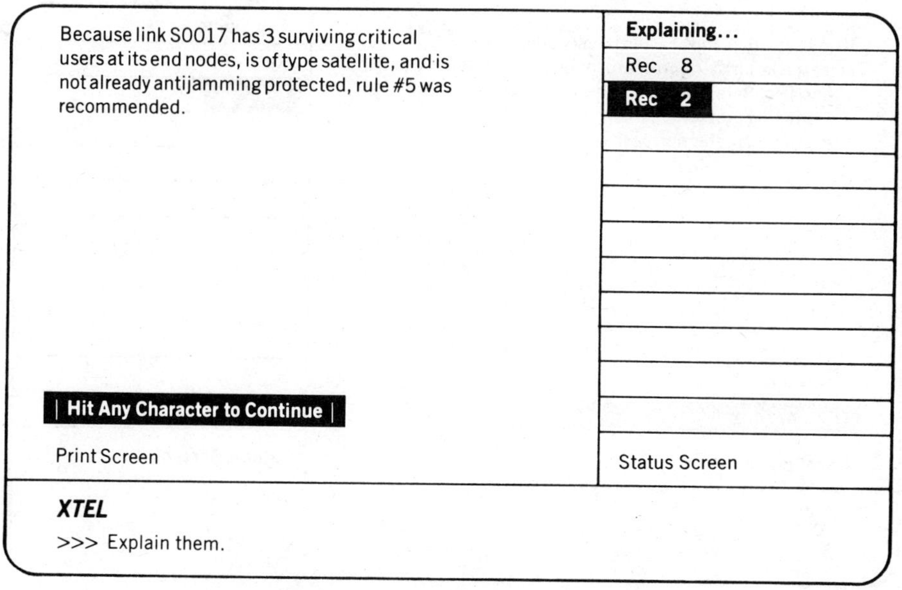

Because link S0017 has 3 surviving critical
users at its end nodes, is of type satellite, and is
not already antijamming protected, rule #5 was
recommended.

Explaining...

Rec	8
Rec	2

| Hit Any Character to Continue |

Print Screen

Status Screen

XTEL

>>> Explain them.

Figure 12. XTEL explaining recommendation 2.

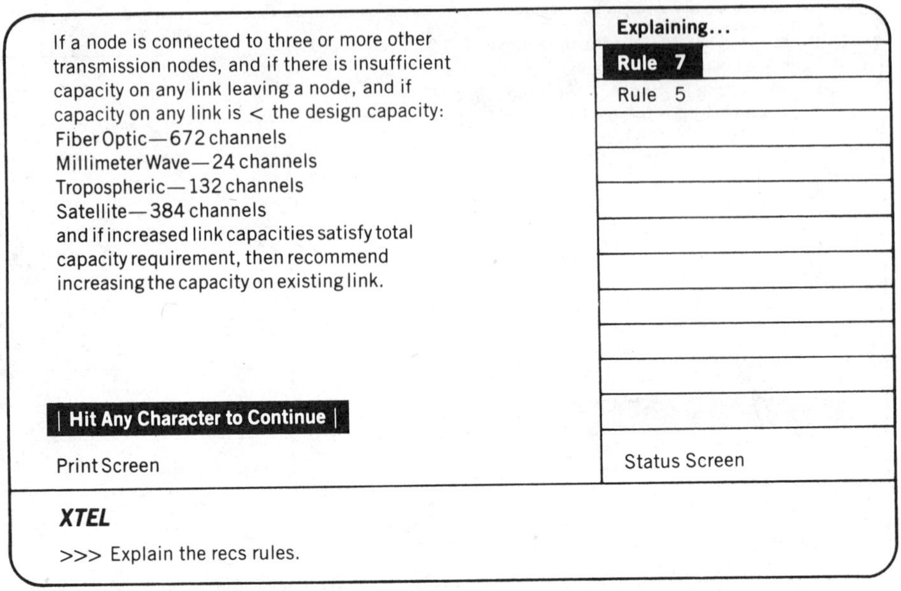

```
┌─────────────────────────────────────────────────────────┐
│ If a node is connected to three or more other │ Explaining... │
│ transmission nodes, and if there is insufficient │ ▐ Rule 7 ▌ │
│ capacity on any link leaving a node, and if │ Rule 5 │
│ capacity on any link is < the design capacity: │ │
│ Fiber Optic—672 channels │ │
│ Millimeter Wave—24 channels │ │
│ Tropospheric—132 channels │ │
│ Satellite—384 channels │ │
│ and if increased link capacities satisfy total │ │
│ capacity requirement, then recommend │ │
│ increasing the capacity on existing link. │ │
│ │ │
│ ▐ Hit Any Character to Continue ▌ │ │
│ Print Screen │ Status Screen │
│ ─────────────────────────────────────────────────────── │
│ XTEL │
│ >>> Explain the recs rules. │
└─────────────────────────────────────────────────────────┘
```

Figure 13. XTEL explaining rule 7.

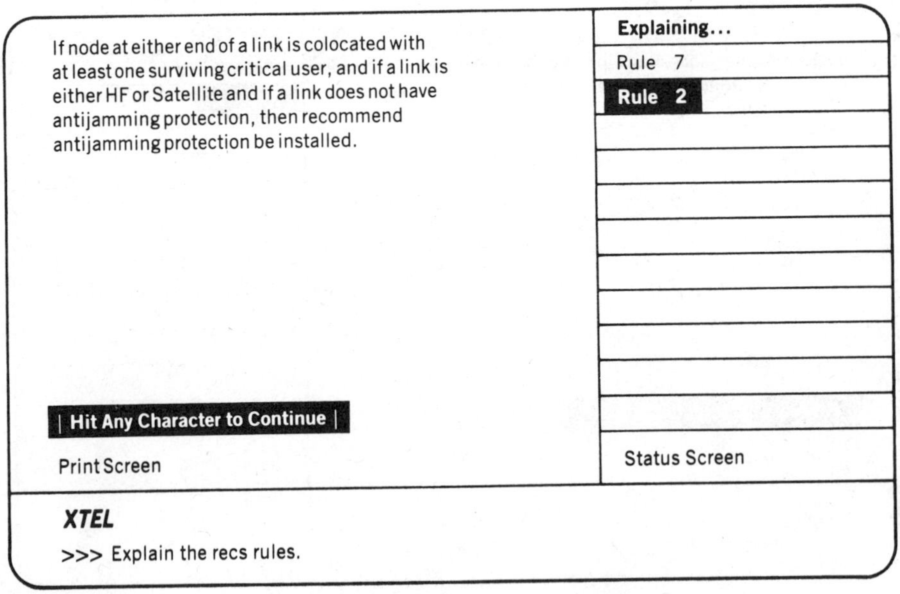

```
┌─────────────────────────────────────────────────────────┐
│ If node at either end of a link is colocated with │ Explaining... │
│ at least one surviving critical user, and if a link is │ Rule 7 │
│ either HF or Satellite and if a link does not have │ ▐ Rule 2 ▌ │
│ antijamming protection, then recommend │ │
│ antijamming protection be installed. │ │
│ │ │
│ ▐ Hit Any Character to Continue ▌ │ │
│ Print Screen │ Status Screen │
│ ─────────────────────────────────────────────────────── │
│ XTEL │
│ >>> Explain the recs rules. │
└─────────────────────────────────────────────────────────┘
```

Figure 14. XTEL explaining rule 2.

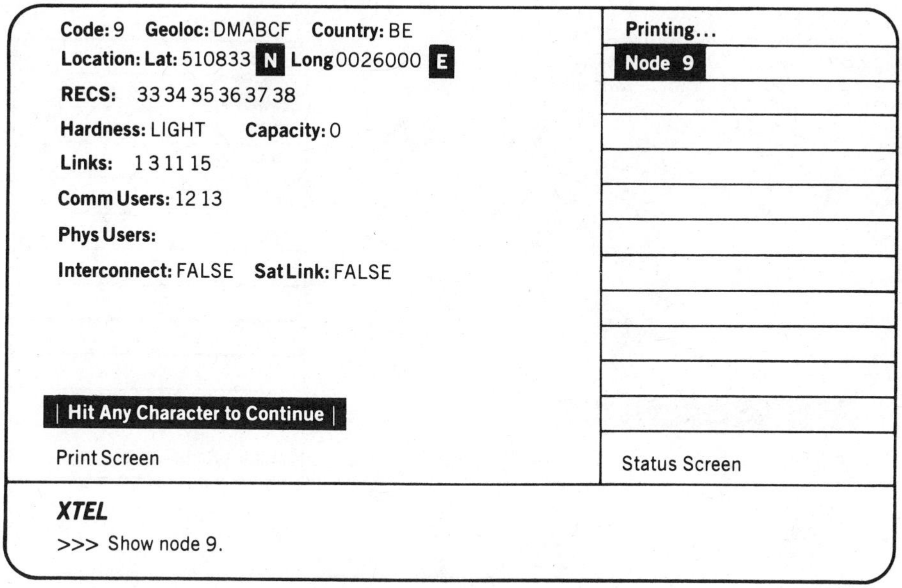

```
Code: 9   Geoloc: DMABCF   Country: BE          Printing...
Location: Lat: 510833 N  Long 0026000 E         Node  9
RECS:   33 34 35 36 37 38
Hardness: LIGHT        Capacity: 0
Links:   1 3 11 15
Comm Users: 12 13
Phys Users:
Interconnect: FALSE   Sat Link: FALSE


| Hit Any Character to Continue |
Print Screen                                    Status Screen
```

XTEL

>>> Show node 9.

Figure 15. XTEL displaying important information on node 9.

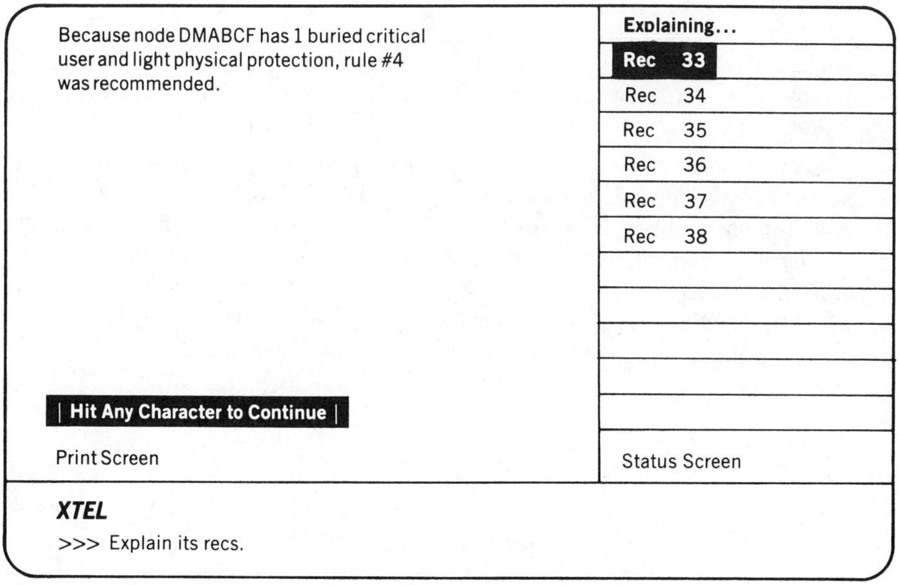

```
Because node DMABCF has 1 buried critical       Explaining...
user and light physical protection, rule #4     Rec    33
was recommended.                                Rec    34
                                                Rec    35
                                                Rec    36
                                                Rec    37
                                                Rec    38




| Hit Any Character to Continue |
Print Screen                                    Status Screen
```

XTEL

>>> Explain its recs.

Figure 16. XTEL explaining recommendation 33 on node 9.

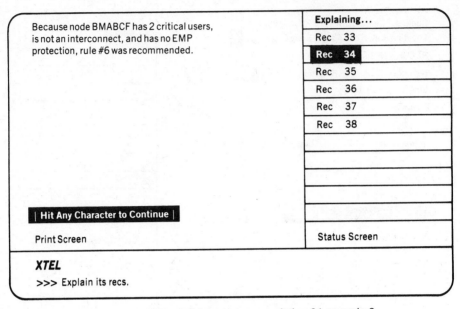

Figure 17. XTEL explaining recommendation 34 on node 9.

communications node destroyed during the simulated conflict. There are six design recommendations for this node.

Next, XTEL is prompted to ''Explain its recs.'' First, recommendation 33 is for increased physical hardening (Figure 16).

Recommendation 34 is for increased hardening to the EMP (electromagnetic pulse) (Figure 17.)

Recommendation 37 is to reconstitute a node if destroyed (Figure 18).

Next, is a recommendation to establish a new communication link to a DFF (distant foreign facility). Each time a new link is suggested, a cluster of media diversity rules determines the proper media. In Figure 19, recommendation 35 suggests that either a high-frequency or troposcatter link would be appropriate. Here, XTEL is running in an advisor mode where a number of options are suggested rather than a mode where only one recommendation is generated.

When finished, we enter, ''Exit'' at the prompt sign (Figure 20).

4.1. The XTEL Example Knowledge Base

The rule base for the Sample exercise is separated into four sections according to design function: physical protection, electronic protection, route and media diversity, and extension and reconstitution. The content of the sample rule base is shown here in a compressed form. Its meaning should be evident.

```
┌─────────────────────────────────────────────────────────┬──────────────────────┐
│  Because the node does not survive, and                 │  Explaining...       │
│  supports needlines serving critical users,             ├──────────────────────┤
│  rule #20 was recommended.                              │  Rec   33            │
│                                                         ├──────────────────────┤
│                                                         │  Rec   34            │
│                                                         ├──────────────────────┤
│                                                         │  Rec   35            │
│                                                         ├──────────────────────┤
│                                                         │  Rec   36            │
│                                                         ├──────────────────────┤
│                                                         │  ▐Rec   37▌          │
│                                                         ├──────────────────────┤
│                                                         │  Rec   38            │
│                                                         │                      │
│  ▐ Hit Any Character to Continue ▌                      │                      │
│  Print Screen                                           │  Status Screen       │
├─────────────────────────────────────────────────────────┴──────────────────────┤
│  XTEL                                                                            │
│  >>>  Explain its recs.                                                          │
└─────────────────────────────────────────────────────────────────────────────────┘
```

Figure 18. XTEL explaining recommendation 37 on node 9.

```
┌─────────────────────────────────────────────────────────┬──────────────────────┐
│  Recommendation: 35                                     │  Printing...         │
│  Code: 35                                               ├──────────────────────┤
│  Recommended new link to DFF                            │  Rec   33            │
│  For                                                    ├──────────────────────┤
│  Node Code: 9 and                                       │  Rec   34            │
│  Link Code: 44                                          ├──────────────────────┤
│  New Facility:                                          │  ▐Rec   35▌          │
│  Node Code: 14                                          ├──────────────────────┤
│  Prospective Link Types:                                │  Rec   36            │
│  Type: HF                                               ├──────────────────────┤
│  Recommend Link be of type HF.                          │  Rec   37            │
│  Type:   Troposcatter                                   ├──────────────────────┤
│  Recommend install TROPOSCATTER link.                   │  Rec   38            │
│  ▐ Hit Any Character to Continue ▌                      │                      │
│  Print Screen                                           │  Status Screen       │
├─────────────────────────────────────────────────────────┴──────────────────────┤
│  XTEL                                                                            │
│  >>>  Show the recs.                                                             │
└─────────────────────────────────────────────────────────────────────────────────┘
```

Figure 19. XTEL displaying recommendation 35 on node 9—to add a new link.

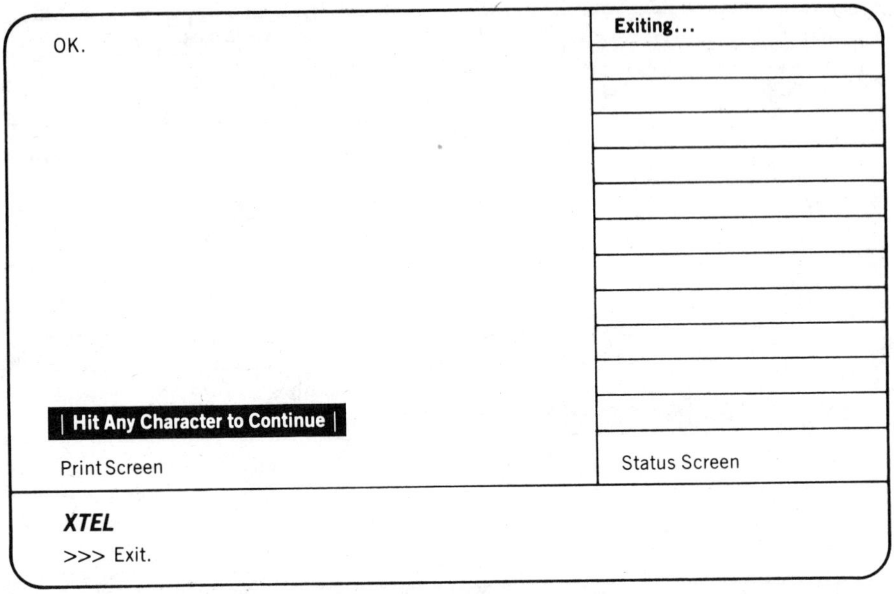

Figure 20. Exiting the XTEL environment.

Physical Protection. Measures to mitigate effects of sabotage, air strike, missile, chemical, and biological attacks.

- Minimal

  Each communications node assumed to have *minimal protection* at beginning of conflict

- Light

  If node is not overrun
  If node is colocated with critical users
  If at least one critical user is surviving
  If node does not have at least *light hardening*

- Moderate

  If node is not overrun
  If node is colocated with critical users
  If at least one critical user is surviving
  If node is member of two or more networks
  If node does not have at least *moderate hardening*

- Heavy

  If node is not overrun
  If node is colocated with critical users
  If at least one critical user is surviving
  If at least one critical user is buried
  If node is member of two or more networks
  If node does not have at least *heavy hardening*

Electronic Protection. Measures to mitigate effects of jamming and high-altitude nuclear burst.

- Antijamming

  If node at either end of link is not overrun

            If node at either end of link is colocated with critical
                users
            If at least one critical user is surviving
            If link is either *HF* or *Satellite*
            If reduced capacity capability meets capacity require-
                ments
            If link does not have *antijamming*

- EMP   If node is not overrun
            If node is colocated with Major C2 Headquarters,
                Pershing II/GLCM Base, Intelligence/Sensor Site,
                or Nuclear Weapon Storage Site
            If at least one critical user is surviving
            If node is member of two or more networks
            If node does not have *EMP* protection

Route and Media Diversity. Measures to enhance system capacity, coverage, and
survivability.

- Fiber Optic Cable   If node is not overrun
            If node is not connected to at least two other nodes
            If there is insufficient capacity on any link leaving
                node
            If media of any link leaving node is not *fiber optic
                cable*

- HF Link   If node is not overrun
            If node is not connected to at least two other nodes
            If there is insufficient capacity on any link leaving
                node
            If distance to another DCS node not overrun is >15
                miles
            If capacity requirement is ≤ 4 channels
            If media of any link leaving node is not *HF*

- Millimeter Wave Link If node is not overrun
            If node is not connected to at least two other nodes
            If there is insufficient capacity on any link leaving
                node
            If distance to another DCS node not overrun is ≤ 10
                miles
            If capacity requirement is ≤ 24 channels
            If media of any link leaving node is not *millimeter
                wave*

- Microwave LOS Link If node is not overrun
            If node is not connected to at least two other nodes
            If there is insufficient capacity on any link leaving
                node

If distance to another DCS node not overrun is ≤ 30 miles

If capacity requirement is ≤ 384 channels

If media of any link leaving node is not *microwave los*

- Tropospheric   If node is not overrun
  Scatter Link   If node is not connected to at least two other nodes

If there is insufficient capacity on any link leaving node

If distance to another DCS node not overrun is between 30 and 300 miles

If capacity requirement is ≤ 132 channels

If media of any link leaving node is not *tropospheric scatter*

- DSCS Satellite Link   If node is not overrun

If node is not connected to at least two other nodes

If there is insufficient capacity on any link leaving node

If distance to another DCS node not overrun is > 300 miles

If capacity requirement is < 1200 channels

If media of any link leaving node is not *satellite*

- Lease   If node is not overrun

If node is not connected to at least two other nodes

If there is insufficient capacity on any link leaving node

If nearest DCS node not overrun is within the same country

- Transmission   If node is not overrun
  Interconnect   If node is not connected to at least two other nodes

If there is insufficient capacity on any link leaving node

If distance to another node not overrun is ≤ 30 miles

If capacity requirement is < 24 channels

Extension and Reconstitution. Measures to enhance system coverage and survivability.

- Mobile HF System   If node is not overrun
  in Place   If node is colocated with critical users

If at least one critical user is surviving

If distance to nearest DCS node not overrun is > 15 miles

If capacity requirement is ≤ 4 channels

New Location

- If node is overrun
- If node was colocated with critical users
- If at least one critical user survives by moving
- If distance to nearest DCS node not overrun is > 15 miles
- If capacity requirement is ≤ 4 channels

- **Mobile Millimeter Wave System in Place**

- If node is not overrun
- If node is colocated with critical users
- If at least one critical user is surviving
- If distance to nearest DCS node not overrun is ≤ 10 miles
- If capacity requirement is ≤ 24 channels

New Location

- If node is overrun
- If node was colocated with critical users
- If at least one critical user survives by moving
- If distance to nearest DCS node not overrun is ≤ 10 miles
- If capacity requirement is ≤ 24 channels

- **Mobile Microwave LOS System in Place**

- If node is not overrun
- If node is colocated with critical users
- If at least one critical user is surviving
- If distance to nearest DCS node not overrun is ≤ 30 miles
- If capacity requirement is ≤ 384 channels

New Location

- If node is overrun
- If node was colocated with critical users
- If at least one critical user survives by moving
- If distance to nearest DCS node not overrun is ≤ 30 miles
- If capacity requirement is ≤ 384 channels

- **Mobile Tropospheric Scatter System in Place**

- If node is not overrun
- If node is colocated with critical users
- If at least one critical user is surviving
- If distance to nearest DCS node not overrun is between 30 and 300 miles
- If capacity requirement is ≤ 132 channels

New Location

- If node is overrun
- If node was colocated with critical users
- If at least one critical user survives by moving
- If distance to nearest DCS node not overrun is between 30 and 300 miles
- If capacity requirement is ≤ 132 channels

- **Mobile Satellite Ground Terminal in**

- If node is not overrun
- If node is colocated with critical users

Place	If at least one critical user is surviving
	If distance to nearest DCS node not overrun is > 300 miles
	If capacity requirement is ≤ 24 channels
New Location	If node is overrun
	If node was colocated with critical users
	If at least one critical user survives by moving
	If distance to nearest DCS node not overrun is > 300 miles
	If capacity requirement is ≤ 24 channels
• DSCS-GMF Gateway Terminal	If node is selected as terminating node for link established by *mobile satellite ground terminal*
• Spare Equipment	If node is not overrun
	If node is destroyed
	If node is not colocated with critical users
	If distant end nodes are not overrun or destroyed

5. SYSTEM USE

5.1. Current Use

XTEL is currently being used to design telecommunications architectures. It is particularly efficient since each rule set defines a unique set or sets of architectures. The justification or explanation module makes certain that the reasoning behind each resource expenditure is never forgotten. An architecture designed by XTEL is very easy to brief since every aspect of its design can be traced back to one or more design rules. If basic assumptions change through new management or are driven by new technology, by changing only the relevant design rules, a new architecture can be designed overnight. Prior to XTEL, this redesign process could last typically 6 months or longer. XTEL is an approach to telecommunication architecture design that is practical, efficient, and makes sense.

5.2. Future Development

XTEL is being redesigned to run on an IBM PC using a sophisticated graphics-oriented interface. Object-oriented graphics with pull-down menus will speed the design of complicated architectures. The attribute referenced memory (a variant of content addressable memory) will result in speeds high enough to reconfigure combat-damaged networks in real time. Thus, XTEL methodology will become an integral part of communications battle management.

Other applications of XTEL include designing systems having an inherent network structure such as power, pipeline, transportation, and other distribution networks.

REFERENCES

1. S. Fast, An Expert System for Initial Component Placement, *Printed Circuit Design*, October 1986.
2. H. Herz, An Attribute-Referenced Production System, 2nd ORSA Conference on Artificial Intelligence, 1986.

GENERAL REFERENCES

S. Andriole, *High Technology Initiatives in C31—Communications, Artificial Intelligence, and Strategic Defense*, AFCEA Press, Washington, DC, 1986.

J. Boys (ed.), *Issues in C3I Program Management—Requirements, Systems, and Operations*, AFCEA Press, Washington, DC, 1984.

P. Bracken, *The Command and Control of Nuclear Forces*, Yale University Press, New Haven, 1983.

D. Chuang, Telecommunications Resource Allocation: A Knowledge Based System. In *Proceedings of the Expert Systems in Government Symposium,* IEEE Computer Society, Washington, DC, 1985.

S. Conry, Distributed Artificial Intelligence in Communications Systems. In *Proceedings of the Expert Systems in Government Symposium*, IEEE Computer Society, Washington, DC, 1986.

J. H. Cushman, *Command and Control of Theater Forces: Adequacy*, AFCEA Press, Washington, DC, 1985.

M. W. Davis, Anatomy of Decision Support, *Datamation*, pp. 201–210, 15 June 1984.

R. Enter and D. Tosh, Expert System Architecture for Battle Management, In *Proceedings of the Expert Systems in Government Symposium*, IEEE Computer Society, Washington, DC, 1986.

A. George, *Presidential Decisionmaking in Foreign Policy*, Westville Press, Boulder, CO, 1980.

S. Goyal et al., COMPASS: An Expert System for Telephone Switch Maintenance. In *Proceedings of the Expert Systems in Government Symposium*, IEEE Computer Society, Washington, DC, 1985.

S. Guattery and F. Villarreal, NEMESYS: An Expert System for Fighting Congestion in the Long Distance Network. In *Proceedings of the Expert Systems in Government Symposium*, IEEE Computer Society, Washington, DC, 1985.

E. Hausen-Tropper, An Application of Learning Algorithms to Telecommunications Networks. In *Proceedings of the 6th International Workshop on Expert Systems and Their Applications*, Vol. II. Agency de l'Informatique, Paris, 1986.

F. Hayes-Roth, D. Waterman, and D. Lenat, *Building Expert Systems*, Addison-Wesley, Reading, MA, 1983.

H. H. Miller-Jacobs, ACES: Airborne Communications Expert System—A Proposed Expert System for Managing Airborne Military Communications. In *Proceedings of the Expert Systems in Government Symposium*, IEEE Computer Society, Washington, DC, 1985.

R. Pfeifer, On The Use of Experience in Expert Systems. In *Proceedings of the 6th International Workshop on Expert Systems and Their Applications*, Vol. 1, Agency de l'Informatique, Paris, 1986.

J. Psotka, Intelligent Design Environments and Assistant Systems. In *Proceedings of the Expert Systems in Government Symposium*, IEEE Computer Society, Washington, DC, 1985.

R. Reinman, National Emergency Telecommunications Policy: Who's in Charge? National Security Affairs Monograph Series 84-2, 1984.

E. Sykes and C. White III, Specifications of a Knowledge System for Packet-Switched Data Network Topological Design. In *Proceedings of the Expert Systems in Government Symposium*, IEEE Computer Society.

S. Thorsen, Intentional Inferencing in Foreign Policy: An AI Approach, *Foreign Policy Decision Making (Prager)*, pp. 280–309, 1984.

K. Whang, S. Brady, and R. Gilbert. Artificial Intelligence in Network Management Systems: A Total System Viewpoint. In *Proceedings of the Expert Systems in Government Symposium*, IEEE Computer Society, Washington, DC, 1986.

L. Zadeh and K. Fukanaka (eds.) *Fuzzy Sets and Their Application to Cognitive Decision Processes*, Academic Press, New York, 1975.

EXPERT SYSTEMS FOR NETWORK MANAGEMENT AND CONTROL IN TELECOMMUNICATIONS AT BELLCORE

Gary M. Slawsky and Dennis J. Sassa

Bell Communications Research, Inc., Red Bank, New Jersey

1. INTRODUCTION

Today's telecommunications network is evolving rapidly to include an increasingly diverse and complex set of switching equipment and supporting operations systems (OSs). Operation of the telecommunications network, which includes all the activities for planning, engineering, provisioning, installing, maintaining, and managing the network, requires a high degree of technical expertise. Highly trained personnel in network operations centers use their knowledge and the capabilities of OSs to perform the above activities.

Knowledge-based expert systems (KBESs) promise to improve network operations productivity and decrease operations costs. The technology provides a means for effectively using knowledge from diverse sources to offer fast, accurate, and complete analysis of information. To deploy KBESs successfully, they must integrate smoothly with existing network operations. That is, to maintain the evolving intelligent digital network, today's technicians must access information from many sources:

- The network elements that provide performance monitoring and self-diagnosis data.
- The test equipment strategically placed in the network that provides test results.
- Customers who report troubles.
- Experts who provide assistance in analyzing complex network troubles.

This chapter discusses two concept prototypes that provide expert assistance to personnel responsible for maintaining stored program control switches as examples of KBES technology being applied to support network operations.

Today, personnel in a switching operations center monitor several switches simultaneously as shown in Figure 1. Incoming switch messages are collected and analyzed by an OS and resulting alarm conditions alert control/analysis personnel to possible troubles. A trouble is analyzed and tests are performed until a faulty component has been isolated. If the problem can be corrected from the operations center, the appropriate fixes are applied. If hands-on repair is required, the work and force administration personnel dispatch a crew accompanied by repair recommendations. Control/analysis personnel are the first line of defense against network problems.

When a trouble cannot be cleared by the control/analysis operations personnel in a prescribed time, expert consultants residing in expert consultant centers are called in to help. Since these expert consultants serve a larger span of the network, they are often involved in trouble cases infrequently observed at any single operations center. The expert consultants review observed symptoms and recent switching operations center activities and advise them on additional tests and analyses to perform. Their recommendations almost always lead to a successful repair.

The first KBES described here intercepts and offloads problems often referred to the expert consultants. Knowledge engineers at Bell Communications Research, Inc. (Bellcore) have captured the troubleshooting knowledge of several expert consultants and made it accessible to control/analysis personnel. Rather than call an expert consultant, control/analysis personnel initiate a consultation with a KBES that for the most part mimics the dialogue that occurs between themselves and the expert consultant. The major difference is that the KBES accesses and analyzes most of the data that is verbally communicated in the human dialogue.

The second KBES described here performs real-time monitoring. The real-time system supports control/analysis personnel by intercepting OS data, autonomously processing the data, initiating tests, and recommending corrective action. The average expected daytime message rate, after prefiltering, is approximately 3 per minute. Knowledge engineers at Bellcore have captured the knowledge of several control/analysis personnel and incorporated it into a KBES that eliminates many of the existing manual procedures that require a high level of proficiency.

2. KNOWLEDGE-BASED EXPERT SYSTEM APPLICATIONS

2.1. Switching Maintenance Analysis and Repair Tool (SMART)

In recent years, the Bell Operating Companies (BOCs) have been replacing analog switches with digital switch technology. As digital switches become more widespread, the persons responsible for switch maintenance are receiving their training and experience in this new area. As a consequence, the pool of experts knowledgeable in analog switch maintenance is becoming smaller as time progresses.

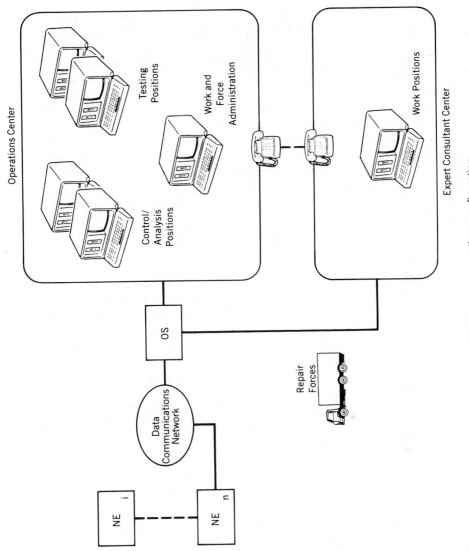

Figure 1. Maintenance operations configuration.

SMART is a KBES concept prototype being constructed at Bellcore using KBES technology to capture and preserve the dwindling analog switch maintenance expertise.

The objective of SMART is to capture the knowledge of persons who excel at troubleshooting a specific type of analog stored program control switch and to verify and improve its utility by field testing the system as a concept prototype. Within the scope of switch maintenance, as described earlier in this chapter, SMART captures the knowledge of expert consultants. The implementation strategy is to deploy SMART in switching operations centers as a consultation system to assist control/analysis personnel in troubleshooting complex switch faults much the same as they interact with the expert consultants today. SMART uses information about the environment surrounding a fault, switch output message data, and results of recommended tests to perform its diagnosis. If SMART can diagnose a problem successfully, it will identify the failed switch component and recommend corrective actions to the user at the conclusion of a consultation session for a particular fault.

2.2. SMART Knowledge Base

The strategy first used by SMART to diagnose troubles is to gather data about initial symptoms and recent activities in the switching operations center. SMART then tries to resolve the fault via use of this information and switch output message data. If resolution is not achieved, additional symptoms data are accumulated and a list of candidate troubles is formulated. The list is refined through testing until the cause of trouble is found. The trouble cause and recommended repair procedure(s) are then provided to control/analysis personnel. This strategy is implemented in SMART through the use of approximately 250 rules.

A sample SMART consultation session is shown in Figure 2. Each session contains a user interaction section and an analysis summation section. In the user interaction section, SMART presents questions to the user (shown as numbers followed by a :) and user responses to these questions (shown as corresponding numbers followed by a >) as initialization data and as information to satisfy the premises of rules. Questions 1–3 in Figure 2 are initialization questions that are presented for all cases. Questions 4 and 5 are presented to the user for the purpose of gathering answers for use in satisfying the rule premise.

The answer of "audits" as a message type to question 4 and of "32 21" as an audit type to question 5 completely satisfy the premise of a rule whose conclusion is that a translations' fault exists. This information is presented below the answer to question 5. Once the cause of a problem is determined, a review of the consultation session is presented in the analysis summation section. First, the output message data used to determine the cause is presented in the "output message data" category. In Figure 2 this is shown as "audits" and "32 21". Next, observations of the user are displayed in the "user observations" category. For this example the only user observation was that the "harv1" office is operational. Now that the problem has been identified, suggestions for the cause(s) are presented in the final recommendations category. In this example, the suggestion is that audits

1:    What is your last name?
1>   Jones
2:    Which office has a problem?
2>   "harv1"
3:    Is the harv1 office currently operational (i.e., is the PC Complete Lamp on)?
3>   yes
4:    What kinds of output messages (select any or all from the menu) has the harvl office generated since the problem first arose?
4>   "audits"
5:    What type of audit is being generated?
5>   "32 21"
The fault is definitely located to the translations.
The following report outlines SMART's intermediate findings and final recommendations.
****

HARV1 Trouble Report

Output Message Data

Output messages generated by the harv1 office found to be audits ⟨1.0⟩. The type of audit being generated found to be 32 21 ⟨1.0⟩.

User Observations

The harv1 office is currently operational

Final Recommendations

These audits are causing the CI-LIST to be zeroed. This is usually due to garbage being in the NOGR-RAC translator. There should only be data in words that correspond to assigned rate centers.

Figure 2. SMART consultation session sample.

are causing the CI-LIST to be zeroed, which is likely due to data in words not corresponding to assigned rate centers existing in the NOGR-RAC translator. SMART then stores this information and is prepared for another case to be initiated by the user.

SMART uses backward chaining to perform its reasoning. Figure 3 shows one rule used in the consultation session described above. The goal of this rule is to determine that the location of fault is in translations. To achieve this goal there must exist a fault whose output message symptoms is audits and whose audit type equals "32 21". If both conditions are proved true, the conclusion is asserted. Since both conditions of the premise were satisfied in the above example, the conclusion that audits are causing the CI-LIST to be zeroed, with data in words

::PREMISE already.existing(f:fault:output.message.symptoms[f] is audits and audit.type[f]
is "32 21")

::CONCLUSION begin
location.of.fault[h] = translations:
final.recommendations[h] = new.line() !"These audits are causing
the CI-LIST to be zeroed. This is usually due to garbage being in the
NOGR-RAC translator. There should only be data in words that correspond to assigned rate centers." !new.line()

Figure 3. SMART rule sample.

in words not corresponding to assigned rate centers existing in the NOGR-RAC translator as a likely cause, is reported to the user as a final recommendation.

2.3. Building the SMART Concept Prototype

The first task in building a SMART concept prototype was to analyze the domain of switch maintenance to determine if it was suitable for application of KBES technology and, if so, to narrow this domain to a subset of all output messages from a specific type of switch to identify achievable objectives. This task was performed by reading available documentation describing switching operations and interviewing Bellcore persons and BOC experts with experience in this area. Once the application domain was selected and narrowed, S.1* was chosen as concept design software and the Xerox 1108 LISP Machine was selected as concept design hardware. Use of hardware and software tools designed for building expert systems reduced the time required to build a concept prototype.

Initial encounters with domain experts were used to design the basic reasoning strategy and to identify the sources of knowledge to which the domain experts refer in solving switch faults. Detailed domain knowledge was then gathered from three switch maintenance experts, each from a different BOC, to populate the knowledge base. Once the knowledge base contained enough information to allow field evaluation, the software was ported to a C version for implementation on a personal computer to obtain a cost-effective and efficient system. A field evaluation plan was then developed to determine the utility of SMART based on actual operations experience.

2.4. Real-Time System (RTS)

The Real-Time System (RTS) is also a KBES concept prototype being constructed at Bellcore to support switch maintenance operations. However, its application domain is the initial trouble analysis performed by control/analysis persons shown earlier in Figure 1. The functional difference between the RTS and SMART is that the RTS will initiate processing autonomously upon arrival of switch messages. In addition, the RTS must always monitor the overall switch environment while processing a case in order to establish trouble analysis priorities. The RTS will use current switch output messages from a specific type of digital switch to initiate processing. It will also have the functional capability to request historical output message data and initiate switch diagnostic routines to complete its analysis of a switch fault. If the RTS can diagnose a problem successfully, it will recommend corrective actions to the user at the conclusion of each diagnostic session. When fully mature, the RTS will autonomously execute the recommended actions without human intervention.

As with SMART, switch maintenance operations documentation, Bellcore persons, and BOC switch maintenance experts were used to analyze the applicability

---

*S.1 is a trademark of Teknowledge, Inc.

of KBES technology and to narrow the application domain. Knowledge Engineering Environment (KEE)* is used as concept design software and a Symbolics 3640 Lisp Machine as concept design hardware. BOC experts are being used to develop the reasoning strategy. As with SMART, the RTS will eventually be ported to a system more suitable for operations use and field tested when the knowledge base is mature enough to be evaluated in an operations environment.

Future plans are for both SMART and the RTS to be integrated fully into a common system. Should this become a reality, RTS processing will attempt to resolve each switch fault in a short period of time and automatically establish a consultation session with SMART when complex problems occur.

3. APPLICATIONS EVALUATION

It is important to the success of a KBES project to evaluate the system. For both projects described in this chapter we use empirical performance assessments from domain experts, knowledge engineers, operations center personnel, and management. These persons will evaluate each KBES in the following areas:

- Start-up operation
- Integration into existing operations center work flow
- Human–machine interface
- Quality of advice
- Reasoning strategy correctness
- User acceptance
- Cost effectiveness

Although the evaluations of KBESs described in this chapter have not been completed, important lessons related to building KBESs that support telecommunications operations have been learned. The following is a compilation of the lessons we have learned to date from prototyping the SMART and RTS KBESs:

Systems engineering	To achieve the efficiencies inherent in using KBES technology, it is important to integrate the typical systems engineering role of function definitions with the knowledge engineering role when building large KBESs and/or a KBES requiring reasoning about data in real-time.
Feasibility	Although traditional rules used for assessing KBES applicability to a particular domain are also appropriate for telecommunications applications, it is important to have the knowledge engineer and systems engineer collaborate on the initial assessment.

*KEE is a trademark of Intellicorp, Inc.

Multiple experts   If an individual expert cannot be obtained, the use of multiple experts in a group environment should be considered. However, the data-gathering team must be prepared with techniques to resolve differences among members. In addition, the systems engineer–knowledge engineer team should meet with the group of domain experts before committing to use them as experts in order to assess their mutual compatibility.

Concept selling   To obtain meaningful data, the domain experts must be convinced of the KBES's utility before data acquisition begins. This can be obtained by building a demonstrator version of the prototype using the systems engineer's knowledge of the environment and introducing it to the experts prior to holding formal data acquisition sessions.

Identify scope   The field prototype users must be informed about the domain tasks the KBES does and does not address before they use the KBES in an operations environment. Domain experts should participate actively in the selection of domain tasks to be addressed by the field prototype.

Field support   User documentation and on-site field support are extremely important to the success of a concept prototype field test.

Local control   The system should allow for some local control of the KBES so that it can provide adequate support for needs that are unique to an individual operations center.

System response   The system response must be at least as fast as the expert consultant.

System integration   The KBES must be integrated effectively with the existing operations systems supporting network operations such that the resulting synergy provides productivity gains not achievable in a nonintegrated environment.

Technology assessment   It has successfully been demonstrated that expert systems technology is capable of supporting switch maintenance operations.

4. SUMMARY

Today's rapidly evolving telecommunications network is administered and maintained by persons who are experts at real-time and consultative analysis of switching systems' faults. To improve network operations and decrease operations costs,

KBESs are currently being integrated into this fault analysis environment. A consultation type KBES known as the Switching Maintenance Analysis and Repair Tool, which contains the knowledge of persons expert at troubleshooting complex switch problems, is being field tested. In addition, a real-time system concept prototype is under construction to monitor switch output messages, analyze switch problems, and recommend network control and repair actions.

EXPERT SYSTEMS FOR SCHEDULING: SURVEY AND PRELIMINARY DESIGN CONCEPTS**

Jay Liebowitz

Department of Management Science, George Washington University, Washington, DC

Patricia Lightfoot

Spacecraft Control Programs Branch, NASA Goddard Space Flight Center, Greenbelt, Maryland

1. INTRODUCTION

Scheduling is an important part of today's society. Most individuals base their daily events in terms of a schedule, either formal or informal. Businesses run their operations based on some allocation of resources. According to O'Brien [1], scheduling is the arrangement, coordination, and planning of the use of resources to achieve an objective. These resources can be time, labor, capital, information, machinery, and land. To maximize or satisfy these resources, various scheduling techniques have been developed over the years. The traditional scheduling methods used for time and resource scheduling include: PERT (Program Evaluation and Review Technique), CPM (Critical Path Method), PERT/Cost, Gantt Charts, Precedence diagrams, Close-order, Inventory Control, Linear Programming, and Transportation/Assignment methods. These methods are power-based approaches, which typically produce the optimum solution. Other scheduling techniques are being developed that employ knowledge-based or expert systems concepts. One

**Adapted from J. Liebowitz and P. Lightfoot, "Expert Systems for Scheduling: Survey and Preliminary Design Concepts," *Applied Artificial Intelligence Journal*, Hemisphere Publishing, Wash., D.C., 1987.

reason for their development is to have a tool in one's arsenal that will address scheduling of ill-defined domains. These domains typically have informal specifications that are possibly incomplete, inconsistent, and qualitative. Another reason for having expert systems for scheduling is to provide an easy vehicle for user interaction of resource allocation problems.

This chapter addresses expert systems used for scheduling problems. It focuses first on a survey of expert systems for scheduling, both NASA related and others. Then a case study is presented that deals with developing scheduling requests of NASA Goddard Space Flight Center principal investigators (i.e., satellite experimenters). Components of this scheduling domain are discussed, and then suggestions for requirements and preliminary design concepts for a generalized expert system scheduler are explained.

2. SURVEY OF EXPERT SYSTEMS FOR SCHEDULING

The following subsections address many of the expert systems designed for scheduling. Both NASA-related and other expert systems for scheduling are explained. At the end of each description, lessons learned from the development of the respective expert systems are cited.

2.1. NASA-Related Expert Systems for Scheduling

2.1.1. DEVISER. DEVISER [2, 3] is an expert system designed for the planning and scheduling of deep-space missions. It was developed by Vere at the Jet Propulsion Laboratory (JPL). It automatically plans and schedules spacecraft actions to achieve goals. Its major functions are to plan all spacecraft actions, manage spacecraft resources, check constraints, resolve conflicts, and create a time-ordered "sequence of events." DEVISER is written in INTERLISP and uses preconditions to determine consequences. The inputs to DEVISER include a start state description and goals description. The knowledge base is composed of (1) action, event, and inference descriptions (e.g., roll, slew, and platform setting) and (2) scheduled event descriptions (e.g., occultations and data rate capability changes). DEVISER then uses its production rules and search strategies to develop a parallel plan and a sequence of events with times and actions. The user may specify a linear ordering of relation names for priorities. Greater control over the search is further strengthened as DEVISER will attach the preconditions in the order in which they are listed in the individual productions.

The lessons learned from DEVISER include the following:

- There is a need for a modular knowledge base describing spacecraft actions and events.
- Output can be viewed more easily as a sequence of events: time and action/event.

- The user should be able to specify priorities.
- There should be a judicious ordering of preconditions to reduce search time.

2.1.2. KNEECAP. KNEECAP [4, 5] was developed by MITRE Corporation and serves as a planning aid for constraint-based crew activity scheduling. It is a frame-based system first developed in INTERLISP-10 and later translated into ZETA-LISP. The test environment is to assign pilots and crew to the Space Shuttle. It uses a daemon-driven architecture to lubricate the user interface. KNEECAP requires a substantial number of constraints and daemons, referenced by a hierarchy of templates representing different partial plans. The five templates, which contain constraints, are: (1) Mission template, (2) Pilot template, (3) Commander–Crew template, (4) Mission Specialists template, and (5) Payloads/Activities template. KNEECAP first assembles information about the "elements" that make up the plan. These include vehicle or platform in orbit, vehicle capabilities and house-keeping requirements, goals handled by a sequence of activities to be achieved during the interval, goals related to specific payloads, payload-independent goals, crewmembers, and constraints relating to the payload-specific activity, general constraints to the plan as a whole, and platform and crew constraints. KNEECAP next begins actual activity scheduling. Here it selects the performing crewmember and activity start time and checks three constraints. These constraints are the open space on the crewmember's time line to accommodate activity, satisfaction of special constraints pertaining to the activity, and satisfaction of concurrent activities. Last, KNEECAP performs replanning since substantial replanning is usually necessary. Station equipment failures, crew health problems, new priorities, and changes in constraints could render the original plan infeasible.

Lessons learned from KNEECAP include the following:

- Daemons might be helpful in the user interface.
- Frames could be helpful in a NASA scheduling environment.
- Two kinds of planning exist: (1) adding new information items until the plan is completed and (2) manipulating information items already in place ("manifesting").
- Substantial effort is needed to develop information-gathering aspects of the system before concentrating on the scheduling itself.
- The user needs to see the timeline *as a timeline* and needs to be able to move forward or backward along the time dimension and see how the activity blocks fit together.

2.1.3. PLAN-IT. PLAN-IT [3, 6] is an expert system for schedule planning, still under development at NASA JPL. The user interface has received the most attention in PLAN-IT's development. PLAN-IT uses hierarchical menus and has easy editing tools if, for example, the user wants to edit an event. A number of different strategies to perform scheduling are supplied to the user. Some of these strategies include localizing a shuffling window, a shuffle strategy modification, switching station choice to reduce conflicts, a shuffle to reduce station over subscription, a shuffle to synchronize events on viewperiods, a shuffle for both of the above reasons, moving events from beyond the plan, moving events to viewperiod beginnings, island building, split tracking, shrinking tracks to fit viewperiod, merging split tracks, shrinking tracks to minimum size, expanding tracks without causing conflicts, resurrecting events, and bringing events back into the schedule. Each of these activities can be accessed by simply "mousing."

Lessons learned from using PLAN-IT include the following:

- There is a need for colors to indicate if a resource is being used, consumed, or oversubscribed.
- There is a need for "mouseable" menus and a limitation on the amount of data on the screen.
- There is a need for various strategies that the user could employ to perform scheduling.
- Hierarchical menus are helpful but have programmed shortcuts for knowledgeable users.
- There is a need for easy editing tools.

2.1.4. EMPRESS. EMPRESS [7] stands for Expert Mission Planning and Replanning Scheduling System and was developed by MITRE Corporation for the Kennedy Space Center. EMPRESS helps in constructing and maintaining particular mission schedules on a schedule called the Master-MultiFlow. EMPRESS supports the Kennedy Space Center planner in planning schedule activities by defining the time, resource, and task requirements associated with processing a payload manifested to fly on the Space Shuttle. EMPRESS uses FLAVORS, an object-oriented programming language. The software structure of EMPRESS is shown in Figure 1. The constraint module contains scheduling heuristics derived from the expert. The resource module contains facilities, flight hardware, nonflight hardware, and people.

EMPRESS performs the following prime functions [7]:

- It chooses the appropriate standard flows for a mission payload as a function of carrier type.
- It stipulates the activities or critical path that comprises the mission.
- It assigns start and end times to each task defined in the standard flow.
- It posts requests for resources requested through the standard flow.
- It allocates resources to tasks when the user requests it.
- It deallocates and reallocates resources associated with tasks that are moved by the user.
- It attempts to resolve requests for resources that are unavailable, either by offering substitutions or by changing the time of the request.

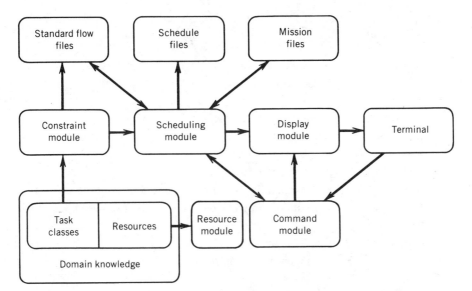

Figure 1. Software Structure of EMPRESS.

- It checks for constraints among payload schedules on the Master-MultiFlow;
- It identifies existing constraints within a schedule and suggests resolution alternatives.
- It supports the capability to generate alternative schedules to plan for "what-if" situations.

Lessons learned from EMPRESS include the following:

- FLAVORS is similar to a frame-based system.
- It is better to have a modular design.
- The system must be able to handle rescheduling and replanning easily.
- The system should allow what-if scenarios to be generated for the planner.

2.1.5.   CAPS. CAPS [5] is an expert system at the NASA Johnson Space Center and is a planning generator. It uses two large graphics display screens simultaneously to prepare a plan. One screen is for entry typing and option selection, and the other displays the timeline. CAPS does no constraint checking and expects the user to be the expert. The lesson learned from CAPS is that it is better to eliminate entry typing and to perform scheduling graphically on a single screen.

2.1.6.   IEPS. IEPS (Interactive Experimenter Planning System) [8, 9] is being developed by Bendix for NASA Goddard. It is being designed as a generalized expert system scheduling tool to aid the satellite experimenters in their request generation. (Suggestions in the last section of this chapter will be considered for incorporation into IEPS.) IEPS has the following major functions thus far [8]:

- It checks for conflicts between tape dumps and instrument usage.
- It checks for TDRSS (Tracking and Data Relay Satellite System) viewing availability.
- It performs tape remaining calculations.
- It checks for daylight available when scheduling an instrument other than tape recorders.
- It checks for magnetic-sensitive instruments.
- It checks for TDRSS availability when scheduling a tape dump.
- It checks for ground station viewing period availability when scheduling a tape dump.
- It checks for valid instrument start and stop times.
- It checks for start time less than stop time.

Lessons learned from IEPS include the following:

- Availability of source code is important.
- Increased generalization of user interface is important.
- C language should be used for portability.

2.1.7. *RPMS.* RPMS [18] assists users with general planning and scheduling tasks. It was developed by Ford Aerospace for the NASA Johnson Space Center. It is written in OPS5 and uses FLAVORS, where all payloads and missions are objects in the FLAVORS system. RPMS has a graphical interface in which the user can graphically model and reason about a problem. RPMS displays a PERT chart, and warning rules operate to warn the user as constraints are violated. An interesting feature of RPMS is its metaphor-based interface. It uses graphics, icons, and text to display the program's "world" to the user. In other words, the display on the screen represents the state of the expert system's knowledge base, so the manifest that the user sees and manipulates is the same one that the expert system reasons about [18]. There is two-way communication between the expert system and the interface via the user interaction mode and the expert system operate mode.
   Lessons learned from RPMS include the following:

- It indicates when constraints are violated.
- It uses a metaphor-based interface that communicates with the expert system.
- It uses FLAVORS.

2.1.8. *EXEPS.* EXEPS, developed at the NASA Johnson Space Center, is an expert system for timelining electrical power system activity blocks. EXEPS [19] uses modular design techniques, and it was constructed using ART and FLAVORS.

With the Shuttle, there are over 2400 components to schedule for performing electrical power system (EPS) analyses; thus, an expert system might be helpful in allocating and scheduling these parts. There are two parts of EXEPS: (1) a *timeliner* that derives an activity block timeline given input events and (2) a *planner* that reasons about the acceptability of the power profile derived from the activity block timeline and then replans the input events as needed. Phase I of EXEPS deals only with the timeliner.

EXEPS uses semantic networks as its knowledge representation scheme. Its search strategy uses the Match search strategy [20], which does not examine alternatives (i.e., no backtracking), and the data drives the search to a solution rather than being used to test hypotheses. The Match strategy can be used if [20]:

1. The problem must be ordered such that no decision need be made before all the information relevant to that decision has been gathered.
2. At any point in the problem-solving process, the program must have enough knowledge to take the next correct action.
3. Decisions must affect only parts of the solution not yet developed.

Future work on EXEPS involves creating a constraint monitor and developing a method to translate telemetry data into facts that rules could reason about.

Lessons learned from EXEPS include the following:

- Modular design techniques should be used.
- The MATCH strategy, if appropriate, should be used.
- A constraint monitor is needed.
- The system uses FLAVORS.

2.1.9. Scheduling Expert System at NASA Ames.

Cheeseman [21] at NASA Ames Research Center is developing an expert system to handle generic scheduling. It allows for a continuously changing world to be represented, so that queries about the truth of a proposition at an instant or over an interval can be answered. It uses a least commitment approach for its search strategy, and a learning algorithm is being incorporated into the expert system based on STRIPS by SRI. This expert system requires mechanisms to detect the effects of world changes on previous deductions (truth maintenance) [21].

An important lesson learned from this expert system development process is to use a deduction mechanism that can answer the common queries necessary in planning as well as that employed for deducing all other information. By having the same deduction mechanism, the need for a specialized time expert is avoided.

2.1.10. Expert System for Ground Support of the Space Telescope.

An expert system is being developed at the Johns Hopkins University Space Telescope Science Institute to assist in the planning and scheduling component of the Space Telescope ground support system. It is a rule-based system implemented in OPS5. The scheduling system requires a detailed description of the spacecraft functions, which can then be placed on a timeline and converted into command loads [22]. The scheduling software is organized into the following hierarchy [22]:

- An *exposure* is a single instrument operation.
- An *alignment* is a set of exposures that can be taken without moving the telescope.
- An *observation set* is a set of alignments that can be performed without affecting the guidance system.
- A *scheduling unit* is the smallest schedulable entity and is made up of observation sets.
- *Scheduling unit links* are scheduling units linked in time.

An important lesson learned from this work is that a hierarchical arrangement of the scheduling software is very useful.

There are other NASA-related scheduling expert systems being developed besides those already discussed. AMPASS, by General Electric, is being developed for the Space Station. PLANS/PLUS [23] is a scheduling language that has been developed to aid in expert scheduling systems development. STALEX [24] is being developed by McDonnell–Douglas for performing mission planning for the Space Shuttle.

2.1.11. NASA-Related Nonscheduling Expert Systems.

NASA has been developing expert systems in other areas besides scheduling. Some examples of these expert systems are:

- Software Development Workstation (NASA Johnson Space Center)—used to catalog, reuse, and manage NASA existing code and add new code as it is generated.
- LES (NASA Kennedy Space Center)—performs real-time diagnostics of the liquid oxygen loading system of the Shuttle.
- RENEX (NASA Johnson Space Center)—performs on-orbit determination of the Shuttle.
- NAVEX (NASA Johnson Space Center)—monitors navigation console for the Shuttle.
- KATE (NASA Kennedy Space Center)—acts as intelligent controller of liquid oxygen loading system of the Shuttle.
- Expert system to predict thunderstorms (NASA Kennedy Space Center).
- ECESIS—application of an expert system to space stations with personnel onboard.

- Space Shuttle Hazard Analysis (NASA Johnson Space Center)—analyzes potential applications between experiments on the Shuttle.
- IUIS (NASA Goddard Space Flight Center)—acts as an intelligent user interface for NASA's scientific databases.
- EPMS (NASA Goddard Space Flight Center)—acts as an intelligent project manager.
- READ (NASA Goddard Space Flight Center)—acts as an expert system prototype for generating command management software functional requirements.
- TRAPS (NASA Goddard Space Flight Center)—expert system prototype for data error detection.

2.2. Military and Industrial-Related Expert Systems Used for Scheduling

Besides those expert systems designed specifically for NASA-related scheduling problems, there are other expert systems that have been developed for resource allocation and scheduling problems that have been used in the military and industry. Some of these expert systems have similar problems in the scheduling environment as those developed for NASA. This section describes the expert systems that have been developed for resource allocation and scheduling in the military and industrial environments.

2.2.1. BATTLE. BATTLE [10, 11] is an expert system developed by the Navy Center for Applied Research in Artificial Intelligence to allocate weapons to targets for battle management purposes. BATTLE uses a computation network similar to Prospector's [28] and determines weapon-to-target allocation in two phases. First, effectiveness is determined by a complex calculation of 55 factors of the weapon, target, and battlefield situation. Then, it uses effectiveness to evaluate complete allocation plans. It computes expected total destruction, D, for that plan. Of course, in a battle management situation, there is a trade-off between destruction value, D, and time. In a research setting [10], for an allocation of 8 weapons to 17 targets, BATTLE took about 12 min to determine the *optimum* solution; whereas, the 98% suboptimal solution took 7 s.

BATTLE uses a best-first questioning strategy based on the merit system. The pruning algorithm for BATTLE is as follows [10]:

> To see if a partial allocation plan should be pruned, its expected destruction is added to the combined fighting capacities (maximum destruction by that weapon type against any target in any circumstance) of the weapons remaining to be used in completing that partial plan. If the sum is less than the expected destruction from the least destructive of the k complete plans cur-

rently on the tentative solution list, no attempt is made to complete the partial plan. This results in substantial savings of time during the traversal.

Lessons learned from BATTLE include the following:

- There is a need to determine effectiveness and this involves complex calculation.
- There is a need for best-first strategy and appropriate pruning algorithm.

2.2.2.   *ISA.* ISA (Intelligent Scheduling Assistant) is an expert system developed and used by Digital Equipment Corporation (DEC) to schedule orders for manufacturing and delivery. ISA [12, 13] was originally written in the LISP version of OPS5 and was later converted to BLISS, a standard VMS language. It is a rule-based system, with about 300 rules. It provides the capability of scheduling customer system orders against the current and planned material allocations. It is part of DEC's Common Scheduling System and can schedule at "orders per second," whereas traditional systems for manufacturing order schedulers require at least 10–15 min per system [12].

ISA uses several strategies for scheduling. The first strategy is to overload on the basis of expected cancellations. The second strategy is to roll forward within a quarter. The third main strategy used is to ship partials. If the order cannot be scheduled using these strategies, ISA will move the target date forward 1 month and will reapply the strategies. If the order still cannot be scheduled, ISA will reset to the request date and will try by relaxing the second and third constraints (i.e., strategies) above [13]. The acceptance rate was designated as 80%, but over 90% of the schedules have been correct.

Lessons learned from ISA include the following:

- Schedule to satisfy various loading constraints.
- Reschedule when relaxing the loading constraints to get alternative schedules.

2.2.3.   *KNOBS.* KNOBS [4, 5] is an expert system developed by MITRE Corporation for the U.S. Army to perform mission planning. It is a constraint- and frame-based system. KNOBS uses the FRL implementation of frames developed at MIT, and it also uses rules, but less than most expert system architectures. KNOBS has a constraint interpreter that interacts with daemons and constraints to enumerate and order suggestions for mission planning assignments. Templates are also used, as in KNEECAP, to aid in the generation of constraints. Lessons learned from KNOBS are similar to those learned from the KNEECAP experience.

2.2.4.   *ISIS.* ISIS [14–16] is an expert system prototype developed by Carnegie–Mellon University and Westinghouse to schedule manufacturing steps in job shops. It is a constraint-directed, distributed problem-solving type expert system that is designed to perform a job-shop scheduling task in a manufacturing plant. ISIS uses SRL as a knowledge representation language for modeling organizations and their constraints. ISIS uses a hierarchical, constraint-directed search paradigm and allows the user to construct and alter schedules interactively. Various constraints are taken into account [15]:

1. Organizational constraints to assure profitability.
2. Physical constraints to check the capability of the machine.
3. Gating constraints to check if a particular machine or tool can be used.
4. Preference constraints to enable the shop supervisor to override the expert system.

Schedules are influenced by due date requirements, cost restrictions, production levels, machine capabilities, operating precedences, resource requirements, and resource availability. ISIS checks all other constraints relevant to a scheduling decision imposed by the user and signals the user as to their satisfaction or violation.

Lessons learned from ISIS include the following:

- It helps to have a constraint-directed search paradigm.
- Hierarchical planning and scheduling should be used.
- There should be interfaces for updating and to provide incremental scheduling in response to changes.
- There should be interactive scheduling to flag poorly satisfied constraints.
- The constraints should act as independent knowledge sources to cooperate opportunistically to produce a schedule.

2.2.5. NUDGE. NUDGE [17] is a frame-based expert system used for scheduling. It was developed at MIT and is based on a knowledge representation language, FRL-0. NUDGE accepts informal requests and produces a calendar containing possible conflicts and an associated set of strategies for resolving those conflicts. It uses a domain-independent search algorithm, BARGAIN, to resolve these conflicts by traditional decision analysis techniques. The knowledge base consists of a hierarchical set of concepts that provide generic descriptions of the typical activities, agents, plans, times, and purposes of the domain to be scheduled. NUDGE converts an informal scheduling request into a formal request and then uses BARGAIN to develop the schedule using conventional techniques. NUDGE employs a best-first search.

Lessons learned from NUDGE include the following:

- A hierarchical set of concepts should be used.
- For well-defined formal situations, traditional power-based techniques should be used to find optimal schedules.
- For less-defined domains where informal specifications are present (i.e., scheduling requests that are potentially incomplete, possibly inconsistent, and qualitative), a knowledge-based system approach should be used.

- Frames should be used.
- A best-first search should be performed.

2.2.6. *Other Military and Industrial-Related Expert Scheduling Systems.* Besides the expert systems mentioned above, other expert systems for scheduling and planning exist:

- CSS—aids in planning relocation, reinstallation, and rearrangement of IBM mainframes (IBM–San Jose).
- DISPATCHER—schedules dispatching of parts for robots (DEC/Carnegie Group).
- Callisto—experimental expert system for management of large projects (CMU).
- Scheduling Craft—expert system shell for both interactive and automatic scheduling and the reactive supervision and repair of scheduled activities on the factory floor (Carnegie Group).

Some expert systems for planning include NOAH (Sacerdoti), NONLIN (Tate), PLANX10 (Sridharan), STRIPS (SRI), and SIPE (Wilkens/SRI). SIPE is particularly interesting as it uses hierarchical planning to perform metascheduling and metaplanning. ROME (CMU), ARIADNE (UVa), RPA (Systems Control Technology), and OPPLAN-CONSULTANT (Rutgers) are other examples of expert systems used for planning.

After examining the expert systems that have been developed for scheduling, the next step is to explore the domain at NASA Goddard Space Flight Center to understand the current way of handling the scheduling of experimenter requests. Afterward, requirements and a preliminary design for an expert scheduling system will be recommended.

3. DEVELOPING SATELLITE SCHEDULING REQUESTS OF EXPERIMENTERS AT NASA GODDARD SPACE FLIGHT CENTER

When developing the schedule for experimenters to request the use of a satellite for experiments, there are two primary ways of performing the scheduling. One method is block scheduling, where a block of time is devoted to an experimenter for using the satellite in a real-time mode. Block scheduling is usually used for geosynchronous satellites because the targets can be seen and observed 100% of the time. The satellite IUE (International Ultraviolet Explorer) is an example of this approach. The experimenters submit a target list that indicates the name of objects, exposure times, and observation specifications for each target that the experimenters would like to observe. NASA Goddard takes all these target lists from the various experimenters and decides when an experimenter can get the maximum number of observations during the year. This scheduling committee would then notify the experimenter, and usually no more than two experimenters will use the satellite during a 24-hour period. The other method for scheduling is interactive scheduling, where experimenters meet to determine whose experiments will be scheduled and when. Interactive scheduling can be accomplished using a centralized location or through a distributed environment. The next sections discuss the interactive scheduling of SMM (Solar Maximum Mission satellite), which uses a centralized scheduling location, and ST (Space Telescope), which has a distributed experimenter environment.

3.1. Experimenter Scheduling of SMM

Mission planning sessions with the SMM experimenters take place every Monday–Friday, where the formal planning sessions occur on Mondays and Thursdays. The meetings on Mondays and Thursdays last $\frac{1}{2}$–1 hour, and the informal meetings last 10–15 minutes. The formal mission planning meetings are when the schedules are planned for the week or weekend, and the informal meetings are established for any last-minute changes if, for example, a new solar activity appears. SMM takes pictures of the sun and transmits data on the sun's solar flare and related activities.

The experimenters of SMM are typically on-site at NASA Goddard. During a formal planning meeting, there are about six experimenters who attend the meeting, with the Chief Solar Observer and SMM Mission Engineer also in attendance. The Monday meeting is used to schedule events for the week, and the Thursday meeting is used to schedule events for the weekend. The Chief Solar Observer acts as the chairperson of the mission planning meeting and first gives an update via informal comments relating to the health of the satellite and any unexpected solar activity. Each experimenter then talks briefly about any sensor or data retrieval problems that he or she has experienced during the week. Any problem is noted, and then the Chief Solar Observer gives a slide show on areas of the sun that have recently been active or passive. After the short presentation, the Chief Solar Observer will schedule the experiments for SMM to perform. Scheduling strictly depends on the targets of opportunities. The Chief Solar Observer asks the experimenters if they want to continue with their experiments from the previous week, and, if so, how long they want to continue them. The Chief Solar Observer uses the chalkboard to fill in the experiments for the following week in the slots referring to the spacecraft revolutions around the Earth. If an experimenter wants a time slot, the Chief Solar Observer asks if anyone else wants that time slot for his or her experiment. If so, a compromise is worked out among the experimenters. The SMM Mission Engineer has an important role during the meeting: that is, telling the experimenters what is the best satellite revolution to transmit data, or to do "4 points", or to perform slewing. The Engineer is knowledgeable on the constraints dealing with the sensors, magnetic regions of the Earth (e.g., South Atlantic Anomaly), satellite revolutions around the Earth, and the data-gathering and transmission activities for ground support of the satellite. The experimenters usually go along with the Engineer. For example, the Engineer might say that it is best to transmit data during the 89–90 revolution. The principal concerns of the experimenters are for the safety of their instrument and satellite as a whole and the transmission and receipt of "good-quality" data from the observations.

3.2. Developing Experimenter Schedules for the Space Telescope (ST)

The Space Telescope is an orbiting optical observatory to be launched in 1989 [22]. Scheduling of astronomer (experimenter) requests begins when the astronomers send in a target list and exposure logsheet that collectively indicate the type and constraints of their observations. The exposure logsheets and target lists are then used to generate a "script" by the ST Operations personnel, which describes the hierarchical organization for that proposal. This script is a listing of assignments of exposure logsheet lines to scheduling system exposures, alignments, observations sets, and scheduling units [22]. The calculated total alignment time and any timing links that exist between scheduling units are also included in the script. After the script is made, both the script and proposal are taken by the Console Operators to a terminal connected to the planning system, and the details of the hierarchy are entered into the project management database. To aid in these steps, an expert system implemented in OPS5 has been constructed [22] to retrieve the input data from the database, transform the target data, merge exposures into alignments where possible and desirable, merge alignments into observation sets, merge observation into scheduling units, fill in project management database attributes, and write the data to the assignment file. This expert system helps in the scheduling procedure for handling astronomer requests to use ST.

3.3. Components of Scheduling in the Mission Planning Environment

Scheduling refers to the selection of activities to perform (if more than one exists) and the assignment of actual times and resources [25]. Scheduling is the process of sequencing a known set of goals, whereas planning achieves high-level goals by generating subgoals [26]. In the mission planning environment, the project engineer's primary scheduling objective is to improve scientific return from the mission while avoiding such failures as inadvertent pointing of sensitive instruments at the Sun and overuse of components [27]. Mission planning is an overconstrained domain owing to the amount of safety conditions that must be followed. When scheduling in mission planning, one must consider jobs (events in a schedule), resources, and constraints. There are three general scheduling techniques used in considering these components. One approach is job scheduling, which places jobs on a minimum timeline (PERT, CPM). The second method is activity scheduling in which the most important or most constraining jobs are usually scheduled first. The last generally used method for scheduling is enumeration of alternatives. This allows the planner to choose the best of several alternatives and allows a comparison of several alternative schedules. Both the activity scheduling and enumeration of alternatives are typically used in an overconstrained environment [26].

The next section presents the requirements for developing an expert scheduling system for the NASA Goddard environment.

4. REQUIREMENTS FOR AN EXPERT SCHEDULING SYSTEM FOR NASA GODDARD SPACE FLIGHT CENTER

The following is a list of preliminary requirements for developing an expert system for scheduling of experimenter requests at NASA Goddard (part of this roster is derived from Boarnet [26]):

Requirements for Expert Scheduling System

1. A modular design should be used.
2. A hierarchy of schedules should be used that corresponds to different levels of abstraction.
3. A constraint monitor (constraint-directed search) should be used.
4. Some deduction mechanism that can answer the common queries necessary in scheduling as well as that employed for deducing all other information should be available.
5. Metascheduling should be used.
6. Tools for a distributed environment should be developed.
7. What-if scenarios should be allowed.
8. Provision must be made for optimum and suboptimum solutions and trade-offs between time versus completeness of schedule.
9. The ability to trace back from implementation item to requirement and vice versa should be provided.
10. A system should be provided that will reduce the time needed to learn how to use the system.
11. A good model should exist of what jobs cause what constraint violations.
12. A tool should show the user constraint satisfaction and violation.
13. Comparison of several alternative schedules should be allowed.
14. Rescheduling must be handled easily.
15. Constraints must be modeled separately from job–resource interactions so that nontechnical, "political" constraints can be represented.
16. Similar resources, jobs, and constraints must each be able to be grouped.
17. A user should be able to specify priorities.
18. Precedence relations between jobs must be handled both qualitatively and quantitatively.
19. Resources must be represented in a fashion that allows unique association with jobs, pooling of resources, or partial pooling of resources.

20. Resources must be allowed to be created, consumed, and refurbished as required by the various jobs in the schedule.

21. Constraints must be represented in a manner that allows constraints to be associated with particular jobs and resources.

22. Grouping capability requires an object description language and preferably full object-oriented programming.

23. Object description language should have the ability to represent user-defined relations between objects and to allow the user to tailor the inheritance of properties along all relation links.

24. The system must be able to support the reasoning necessary to collect and classify the scheduling elements.

25. The system must be able to represent the time variance of the scheduling elements, describing each element's behavior in time.

26. The system must be able to define high-level schedule phases.

27. It should be possible for the programmer to scope all elements individually and use phases only as a program organization tool.

28. The system should support both single and multiple resource leveling and both threshold violation correction and resource smoothing.

29. For activity scheduling, the system should be able to use a window-filling technique to schedule those jobs.

30. The system must be able to represent heuristics that can intelligently guide the use of algorithmic scheduling techniques and short-circuit expensive searches.

31. The system must be able to combine the techniques of job scheduling, activity scheduling, and enumeration of alternatives so that the most appropriate technique can be used at any time in the schedule formation process.

32. The algorithmic, heuristic (rule-based), hypothetical world and hierarchical representations must all cooperate.

33. The system should be able to represent intelligence that can operate either automatically or interactively, at the user's discretion.

34. The system must allow user intervention at any time in the mission planning process.

35. The system should emphasize graphical representations of the schedule, and the tool should support generating timelines and other graphical displays.

36. Timeline displays should have the ability to zoom in and out and pan across a display that is larger than the terminal's screen.

37. A ''logical'' zoom in and out should be provided for viewing schedule hierarchies.

38. Menu, mouse, and other user-friendly input facilities should be supported by the tool.

39. A user ''override'' feature should be supported.

40. Some ''automatic'' rescheduling capability should be provided.

5. PRELIMINARY DESIGN CONCEPTS FOR AN EXPERT SYSTEM TO SCHEDULE EXPERIMENTER REQUESTS (SCHEDULER)

In designing SCHEDULER for handling experimenter requests for satellite usage, there are two major templates that act as frames in determining a timeline for satellite usage. These templates are the Experimenter templates and the Schedule Requests template.

The Experimenter templates are completed by each experimenter and consist of slots for the activity to be scheduled, requested activity start time, requested activity/event end time, window (tolerable range for starting the activity), and the priority (Pr) of how urgent the activity is when compared with other experimenter requests. The requests are sent to a Request Checker, which is a set of rules to see if the requests are valid. The Request Checker will make sure that the requests are not improper, undoable, unhealthful, unsafe, inefficient, or contradictory. A sample of rules for the Request Checker are:

IF request is incomplete or contradictory or redundant
THEN request is improper and invalid.

IF request calls for or implies operations beyond the capability of the space-
    craft
THEN request is undoable and invalid.

IF request stresses the spacecraft or uses up its consumable items
THEN request is unhealthful and invalid.

IF request greatly reduces the amount of value of scientific data gathered
THEN request is inefficient and invalid.

IF request contradicts each other with respect to a spacecraft operation or
    mode
THEN request is not mutually exclusive and invalid.

The experimenter is alerted to an invalid request.

Valid requests are sent to the Schedule Requests template, which consists of five subtemplates. These subtemplates are the Time, Satellite Usage, Environmental Activity, Satellite Health & Safety, and Satellite Position templates. The Time template consists of slots for each day of the week with hour time slots. This template will show a timeline based on the input of the experimenters and the interactions with the other subtemplates. The Schedule Requests template interacts with these templates to check for availability of resources. Rules are used to connect the templates and check for constraints, as well as to define relations and constraints between the schedules of various requests. Rules are also needed for (1) defining particular attributes and maintaining explanatory information as each attribute is filled, (2) supplying information about all requests scheduled at a particular time, and (3) defining the domain predicates and functions.

The Satellite Usage template consists of slots for previously and currently run experiments, STDN and TDRSS schedules, on-board computer usage, and other command management and satellite usage-related information, as shown in Table 1. The Environmental Activity template refers to changes in the satellite's environment such as new unexpected solar activity or important weather information based on NOAA. A sample rule is:

IF solar activity increases in northern part of the sun
THEN experiments centered on the northern part should have top priority.

The Satellite Health & Safety template refers to the engineering status of the satellite. A sample rule for this template might be:

IF sensor is malfunctioning
THEN do not schedule experiment dealing with that sensor.

The Satellite Position template deals with the orbit and attitude data affecting the satellite's position. A sample rule might be:

IF satellite is approaching the South Atlantic Anomaly
THEN turn off sensors and do not run experiments.

To decide on which experimenter requests should be scheduled first, a priority system is established. The priority (Pr) that the experimenter uses to determine how urgent his or her request is compared with the other experimenter requests is multiplied by an initial priority (Pi) for each experimenter. The initial priority is transparent to the experimenter and is a fixed priority already established according to the importance of the sensor and the seniority of the experimenter. The initial priority and the request priority (Pr) are rated from 1 to 10, with 10 being the highest rating. The product of the initial priority and the request priority is then multiplied by an environmental priority (Pe). The environmental priority is also rated from 1 to 10, and it would be given a high rating if, for example, the request refers to a continuation of a previously scheduled experiment or if a new environmental activity occurs that favors a particular satellite sensor. The product of (Pi)(Pr)(Pe) gives the overall scheduled priority (Ps) of the experimenter requests to be scheduled.

Various constraints exist when scheduling these experimenter requests. Examples of these constraints are shown in Table 2; they would be accounted for in the aforementioned templates. Conflict resolution strategies are needed to schedule the experimenter requests. There are four conflict resolution strategies that could be used:

1. Schedule request according to the experimenter's requested window (i.e., tolerable range for starting the experiment).
2. Schedule request by moving ongoing active experiments within tolerable range.

TABLE 1   Command-Management- and Satellite-Related Attributes

Command-Management-Related Attributes and Characteristics

Functions:
  Preliminary processing
    Input
      Command request
      On-board computer changes
      Command description table
      Orbital data
      Previous load history
    Output
      Command argument list
    Subfunctions
      Command request generation
      Command editing
      Command merging
      Command assembling
  Command load processing
    Input
      Previous load history data
      Orbital event data
      Command description table
      Command argument list
    Output
      New load history data
      Command load data
      OBC loads
      Timeline report
    Subfunctions
      Station scheduling
      Load organization
      Command fabrication
      On-board computer load generation
      Timeline validation and constraint checking
Performance Characteristics:
  Batch mode versus express mode
  On-line operations
Operational Characteristics:
  Batch mode and express mode timelines
  On-line operations
Commanding Information:
  Preamble and postamble for transmission

TABLE 1   *(Continued)*

Commanding Information (Continued):

Real-time commands
Types of stored command loads
    Attitude loads
    Memory command loads
    Microprocessor loads
    Stored command programs
    Command execution criteria
Commands of the OBC
S/C clock reset capability
S/C clock dump capability
S/C clock command format
    Sync pattern(s)
    Vehicle address
Critical commands
    Type
    Procedure for transmitting
Command verification (validation)
Command time-out notification
Priority system (command conflict)
    Ground-generated commands
    OBC-generated commands
Tape playback commands
    Non-real-time
    Time-tagged delay commands
Commands needed to load stored commands
    Alter the SCP
Procedure to verify SCP loads
Commands needed to execute loads or stored commands
OBC
    The total number of commands per pass
    Memory loads and dumps
    Control of BOC processing
    Special monitoring
Maximum size of command loads
Specific address for stored commands
Bit rate of uplinked commands
Commands required for the instruments
    Aspect sensors
    Bright object detectors
    South Atlantic Anomaly (SAA) detectors
    Other sensors

TABLE 1   (*Continued*)

Commanding Information (Continued):

Commands required to support electronics
    Focal plane transport assembly
Commands required for conducting experiments
    Configure
    View
    Home
    Raster
    Repeat
    Filter
    Telemetry format change
Safe memory conditions
Command formats
Manual versus autonomous control of S/C
Method for patching a command memory load
Special purpose computers (SPC)
    Memory size
    Clock rate
    Arithmetic
    Processor
SPC central processing unit
    Word length
    Number of instructions
    Execution time
    Number of registers
SPC I/O
    Number of channels
    Interrupt levels
Number of SPCs
    Operation constraints
        Cross-strapped
        Single operation
        Asynchronous
Computation cycle
    Major frame
    Minor frame
Memory usage
    Scratch pad
    Buffer loads
    Memory protection
    Scratch pad and buffer verification
Normal program load considerations

TABLE 1 *(Continued)*

Commanding Information (Continued):

Program modify considerations
SPC memory dump considerations

Time Constraints:

Loading the OBC while RT commanding the S/C
The number of commands executed at a given time
The number of sequencing commands needed to recover from an on-board error condition
Command retransmission in the event of verification error
Sequence of commands
Any cross-strapping of redundant instrument power supplies that would complicate commanding
OBC angular momentum and attitude control zones for magnetic torque control
Users load data
  That all RTS commands are valid for that specific user
  That all RTS counts are as specified in a project-defined users count table
  That all commands with the same "count" in a single RTS satisfy project-specified characteristics
  That all critical commands are flagged
  That all user data lengths are as predefined in a project-specified table
  That all user load data input identifications comply with a predefined project-provided table indicating user resource allocations
Users control data
  That all RTSs microprocessor data and OBC tables exist and are valid for that specific user
  That all load directive parameters are valid
  That load directives to be processed are within the specified operational day
  That RTS initiation is at valid orbital events
  That preplanned inputs are checked so that not more than one RTS is in active status at any time for a unique user
STDN and TDRSS schedules

Satellite-Related Attributes

Mission Unique Components:

Spacecraft bus
  Structure
  Power subsystem

TABLE 1   *(Continued)*

Satellite-Related Attributes (Continued):

    Attitude control subsystem
    Communications and data handling subsystem
Spacecraft Configuration:
  Sensors
  On-board computer (OBC)
    Execution time (cycle time)
    Word size
    Negative number representation
    Storage protection
    Number of hardware interrupts
    Asynchronous I/O
    Multiprogramming capability
    Command priority structure
      Ability to change priorities
      Asynchronous command loading and dumping
    Ability to change telemetry formats
    Memory protection
      Loops
      Hangs
    Sequential ordering of commands
    Polling commands
    Operational characteristics
    Loading characteristics
    Memory size
    Split programmability
      Absolute time processor
      Relative time processor
    Executive request commands
      Jump option
      Scan all memory
    Ability to inhibit applications processors
      Control the mode of processors
    Number of channels of OBC data
      Constant/intermittent data dumps
    Memory addressing
      Memory divided
      Paging used
      Dedicated locations
      Any bank loaded or dumped
    Registers list

TABLE 1   (*Continued*)

Spacecraft Configuration (Continued):

  I/O operations
    Number of channels
    Program control
    Cycle-steal
   Interrupts list assignment
    Priority
   Instruction set
   Subroutine set
    Problems with paging
  Commands from ground control to OBC hardware commands
   Clear
   Load
   Dump
  OBC hardware interfaces
  OBC data sources
   Telemetry formats
  Command output formats from OBC
   Command stacks
   Timing (milliseconds between commands)
   Commands per block
  Stored command processor
   Command formats
    Real, pseudocode, or both
   Timing of stored commands
   Pseudocommands
    Format
   Scratch pad area
    Length
    Any pseudocommands allowed
    Absolute/relative time-tagged
    Processed sequentially/polled
   Interface with ground control
    Command modification while being processed
  Software loads and dumps
   Memory dump limits
   Memory load limits
  Special telemetry formats
   Read only memory controlled
   OBC functions
   Ground control functions

TABLE 1 *(Continued)*

Spacecraft Configuration (Continued):

    Special addressing arithmetic
    Addressability checks
    Relocatable/absolute
    Performance requirements
    OBC/attitude control capability
    OBC/worker programs
    OBC/hardware interface
    On-board orbit determination scenario
    OBC "control laws" that affect attitude control
    OBC attitude data processing algorithms
    OBC information downlinked in telemetry stream
        Memory banks
        Status buffer

Contact Schedule Interface:

    STDN schedule parameters
    TDRSS schedule parameters
    Network configuration message
    NCC unedited schedule interface
    Mission operations interface

Orbit Event Generation:

    Orbital data interface
    Continuity
        Orbit
        Epoch
    Orbital position
    Orbital event list
        Satellite day/night
        Subsatellite point day/night
        Earth occultation
        Radiation belts and the South Atlantic Anomoly

Attitude and Maneuver Functions:

    Attitude and maneuver calculations
        Attitude and maneuver constraint checking
        Attitude and maneuver rerun capability
    Preparation of command arguments
        Control system configuration
        Control system constraint checking
        Control system timing
        Control system rerun capability

TABLE 1 *(Continued)*

Attitude and Maneuver Functions (Continued):

   Input

      Merged request file

         Appropriate request selection

   Output

      Attitude configured request files

   Database Access

   Orbit and Contact Files Access

Time Constraints:

   Procedure for reinitialization to prevent complete loss of critical on-board references and pointing data, in case of hardware or software failure

   OBC constraints

   Telemetry constraints

      Can any combination of real-time, playback, or dump data be received from the S/C at any time?

      How is data validated after a temporary loss of signal?

      Is tape recorder data dumped in reverse order?

      Will the UTC, which is appended at the ground, appear to be decreasing?

      Is the tape recorder ever partially dumped?

      How are the dumps controlled?

      Is there a conflict between multi-instrument transmission?

      Are formats (e.g., data locations within the format) changeable?

      Do the bit rates specified pertain to the data being generated on board the S/C before encoding?

      What conditions may cause interruptions of the data stream or S/C clock resets?

      Are the S/C and instrument telemetry formats the same size and are they in sync?

---

   3. Have the experimenter modify the schedule request.

   4. Put the request on a waiting list until resources are available to schedule the event.

Rules could be established to handle these strategies:

   IF request is made and needed resources are allocated to other events

   THEN shift the requested event start time within user-specified tolerances.

   IF shifting the requested event start time within user-specified tolerances does not work

TABLE 2   Sample of Rules Identifying Constraints

IF schedule request is present
    and sun interference between the ground station
    with the satellite is present
THEN constraint violation is present.

IF schedule request is present
    and satellite in view of TDRS[a] is absent
THEN constraint violation is present.

IF schedule request is present
    and sun interference between TDRS and satellite
    or vice versa is present
THEN constraint violation is present.

IF schedule request is present and TDRS is not available
THEN conflict is present.

IF schedule request is present
    and selected resource is not available
THEN conflict is present.

IF schedule request is present
    and active period is present
    and selected resource is allocated to an event on the active schedule
THEN conflict is present.

IF schedule request is present
    and schedule generation period is present
    and selected resource could be used to satisfy other
    requests applicable to the same schedule generation
    period
THEN conflict is present.

IF schedule request is present
    and active period is present
    and selected resource that is allocated in increments
    is allocated to extent that its duty factor would be
    exceeded by addition of the requested event
THEN conflict is present.

IF schedule request is present
    and schedule generation period is present
    and selected resource that is allocated in increments has
    a duty factor that is not sufficient to satisfy all requests
    for that resource
THEN conflict is present.

[a]Tracking and Data Relay Satellite

THEN shift start times of events already in a working schedule within user-specified tolerances.

IF conflict cannot be resolved by shifting event start times within specified tolerances
THEN (if user agrees) modify the request or generic requirement parameters and attempt to schedule an alternate support opportunity.

IF a conflict cannot be resolved during the active schedule period
THEN put schedule request on wait list.

Scheduling should be available to the user in two representations. One is scheduling by orbit in which events are generated based on viewperiods and station parameters. The second representation is scheduling by time in which events are based on minimum and maximum periods between events or by time of day and

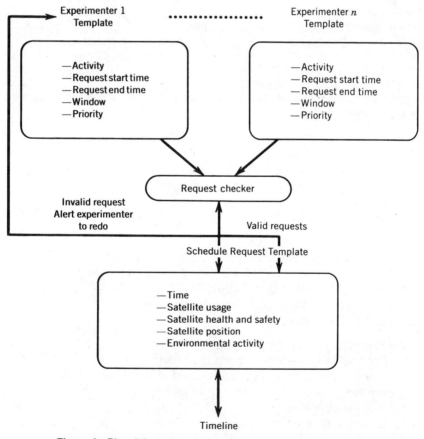

Figure 2. Pictorial representation of expert scheduling system.

specified periodicity. Schedule result messages should appear for the experimenter if:

1. Request fails validation.
2. Request is cancelled.
3. Request is queued for processing.
4. Final attempt to schedule requested event is unsuccessful.
5. Request is placed on waiting list.
6. Request is removed from waiting list without any attempt being made to schedule requested event.

These schedule result messages will ensure better human factors between the expert system and the experimenter.

Figure 2 shows a pictorial representation of the preliminary design, based on the discussions in this section. Implementation of this frame-based design, using TIE1 [9] as the expert system shell, is shown in the partial knowledge base in the Appendix of this chapter.

6. CONCLUSIONS

Developing an expert system for scheduling in the NASA environment has potentially great gains. When satellites and their ground support systems are being designed and built 7 years before satellite launch, there is a substantial need to allocate resources efficiently and effectively. One vehicle in helping toward better scheduling and performance is the use of expert systems. With the preliminary design concepts proposed here, future work will be conducted to implement these ideas and test the feasibility of this approach. It is hoped that an expert system to help schedule experimenter requests for satellite usage will be an important part in the mission and operations support of future satellites.

ACKNOWLEDGMENT

Jay Liebowitz is extremely grateful to have participated in the ASEE–NASA Summer Faculty Fellowship Program at NASA Goddard Space Flight Center. This would not have been possible without the kind and abundant support of Patricia Lightfoot, Bill Macoughtry, Gerald Soffen, Dan Fan, and the other competent personnel in Code 514, Bendix, and the Mission Operations and Data Systems Directorate, too numerous to mention here.

The views expressed in this chapter are solely those of the authors and are not intended to reflect the views of those at NASA Goddard Space Flight Center.

APPENDIX: PARTIAL KNOWLEDGE BASE FOR SCHEDULER USING TIE1

;   request

schedulerequest
;   default value:
    false
;   attributes:
     activity
       "What activity do you need scheduled?"
        tape dump
        slew
        take pictures

    orbit duration
    "What orbit(s) do you want to schedule the activity?"
     range: 80, 93

    requested activity start time
    "What time do you want to start the activity (use format xxyy for designating time,
     where x represents hours and y represents minutes)?"
    range: 0000, 2400

    requested activity end time
    "What time do you want to end the activity (use format xxyy for designating time,
     where x represents hours and y represents minutes)?"
    range: 0000, 2400

    beginning julian day
    "What julian day do you want to begin the activity (use last two digits)?"
    range: 60, 66

    ending julian day
    "What julian day do you want to end the activity (use last two digits)?"
    range: 60, 66

    window
    "What time would be the latest for starting your activity (use format xxyy for des-

ignating time, where x represents hours and y represents minutes)?''
range: 0000, 2400

request priority
''What priority for scheduling, ranging from 1 (lowest) to 10 (highest), would you give
   your request in terms of how urgent/important your request is, as compared with
   the other experimenter requests?''
range: 1, 10

request2 priority
''What priority for scheduling, ranging from 1 (lowest) to 10 (highest), would you give
   to experimenter2's request in terms of how urgent/important your request is, as
   compared with the other experimenter requests?''
range: 1, 10

; frames:
true
'' ''

activity   eq tape dump, slew, take pictures
orbit duration   ra 80, 93
beginning julian day   ra 60, 66
ending julian day   ra 60, 66
ending julian day ge beginning julian day
requested activity start time ra 0000, 2400
requested activity end time ra 0000, 2400
window   ra 0000, 2400
requested activity end time ge requested activity start time
window gt requested activity start time
request priority   ra 1, 10

false
'' ''

activity   ne tape dump, slew, take pictures
orbit duration   nr 80, 93
beginning julian day   nr 60, 66
ending julian day   nr 60, 66
ending julian day lt beginning julian day
requested activity start time nr 0000, 2400
requested activity end time nr 0000, 2400
window   nr 0000, 2400
requested activity end time lt requested activity start time
window le requested activity start time
request priority   nr 1, 10

constraintviolation
; default value:
    present
; attributes:
    schedulerequest
    〈INFERRED〉

satellite position
〈INFERRED〉

satellite usage
〈INFERRED〉

satellite health and safety
〈INFERRED〉

.
.
; frames:
present
" "

schedulerequest eq true, false
satellite position eq unacceptable
satellite usage eq unacceptable
satellite health and safety eq unacceptable

absent
" "

schedulerequest eq true, false
satellite position eq acceptable
satellite usage eq acceptable
satellite health and safety eq acceptable

.

satellite position
; default value:
unacceptable
; attributes:
sun interference between GS and satellite
〈INFERRED〉

satellite in view of TDRS
〈INFERRED〉

sun interference between TDRS and satellite
〈INFERRED〉

.

; frames:
acceptable
" "

 sun interference between GS and satellite eq no
 satellite in view of TDRS eq yes
 sun interference between TDRS and satellite eq no

unacceptable
" "

sun interference between GS and satellite eq yes
satellite in view of TDRS eq no
sun interference between TDRS and satellite eq yes

.

sun interference between GS and satellite

```
;   default value:
    yes
;   attributes:
        orbit duration
        "od"
        range: 80, 93

.
        requested activity start time
        "rast"
        range: 0000, 2400

.
        requested activity end time
        "raet"
        range: 0000, 2400

.
.
;   frames:
    yes
    " "
    orbit duration ra 80, 93
    requested activity start time ra 0000, 0400
    requested activity end time ra 0000, 0400

.
    no
    " "
    orbit duration ra 80, 93
    requested activity start time nr 0000, 0400
    requested activity end time nr 0000, 0400

.
.
satellite in view of TDRS
;   default value:
    no
;   attributes:
        orbit duration
        "od"
        range: 80, 93

.
        requested activity start time
        "rast"
        range: 0000, 2400

.
        requested activity end time
        "raet"
        range: 0000, 2400

.
.
;   frames:
    yes
    " "
    orbit duration ra 80, 93
    requested activity start time ra 1000, 1400
    requested activity end time ra 1000, 1400

.
    no
```

" "
   orbit duration ra 80, 93
   requested activity start time nr 1000, 1400
   requested activity end time nr 1000, 1400

.

.

sun interference between TDRS and satellite
;   default value:
   yes
;   attributes:
      orbit duration
      "od"
      range: 80, 93

.

      requested activity start time
      "rast"
      range: 0000, 2400

.

      requested activity end time
      "raet"
      range: 0000, 2400

.

.

;   frames:
   yes
   " "
   orbit duration ra 80, 93
   requested activity start time ra 1600, 1800
   requested activity end time ra 1600, 1800

.

   no
   " "
   orbit duration ra 80, 93
   requested activity start time nr 1600, 1800
   requested activity end time nr 1600, 1800

.

.

satellite usage
;   default value:
   unacceptable
;   attributes:
   TDRS is available
   ⟨INFERRED⟩

.

   selected resource available
   ⟨INFERRED⟩

   select resource allocated to event on active schedule
   "Is the selected resource allocated to an event on the active schedule?"
      yes
      no

.

   selected resource used to satisfy other requests

"Could the selected resource be used to satisfy other requests applicable to the same schedule generation period?"
yes
no

.

.

; frames:
acceptable
" "
TDRS is available eq yes
selected resource available eq yes
select resource allocated to event on active schedule eq no
selected resource used to satisfy other requests eq no

.

unacceptable
" "
TDRS is available eq no
selected resource available eq no
select resource allocated to event on active schedule eq yes
selected resource used to satisfy other requests eq yes

.

.

TDRS is available
; default value:
no
; attributes:
orbit duration
"od"
range: 80, 93

.

requested activity start time
"rast"
range: 0000, 2400

.

requested activity end time
"raet"
range: 0000, 2400

.

.

; frames:
yes
" "
orbit duration ra 80, 93
requested activity start time ra 1000, 1500
requested activity end time ra 1000, 1500

.

no
" "
orbit duration ra 80, 93
requested activity start time nr 1000, 1500
requested activity end time nr 1000, 1500

.

selected resource available

; default value:
  no
; attributes:
   orbit duration
   "od"
   range: 80, 93

 .

   requested activity start time
   "rast"
   range: 0000, 2400

 .

   requested activity end time
   "raet"
   range: 0000, 2400

 .
 .

; frames:
  yes
  " "

  orbit duration ra 80, 93
  requested activity start time ra 0000, 2200
  requested activity end time ra 0000, 2200

 .

  no
  " "

  orbit duration ra 80, 93
  requested activity start time nr 0000, 2200
  requested activity end time nr 0000, 2200

 .
 .

satellite health and safety
; default value:
  unacceptable
; attributes:
  duty factor exceeded by add of requested event
  "Is the selected resource that's allocated in increments allocated to the extent that
   its duty factor would be exceeded by addition of the requested event?"
  yes
  no

 .

  duty factor not sufficient to satisfy all requests
  "Does the selected resource that's allocated in increments have a duty factor that
   isn't sufficient to satisfy all requests for that resource?"
  yes
  no

 .
 .

; frames:
  acceptable
  " "

  duty factor exceeded by add of requested event eq no
  duty factor not sufficient to satisfy all requests eq no

 .

  unacceptable
  " "

duty factor exceeded by add of requested event eq yes
duty factor not sufficient to satisfy all requests eq yes

.
.

priority
;   default value:
        8
;   attributes:
    exper1 init priority
    "What is the initial priority, ranging from 1 (lowest) to 10 (highest), given to
    experimenter1 based on the importance of his or her instrument, seniority of
    experimenter1, and your other political considerations?"
    range: 1, 10

.

    exper2 init priority
    "What is the initial priority for experimenter2?"
    range: 1, 10

.

    exper1 env priority
    "What is the environmental priority for experimenter1, ranging from 1 (lowest) to 10
    (highest), based on continuing a previously scheduled experiment or if a new en-
    vironmental activity occurs that favors a particular sensor?"
    range: 1, 10

.

    exper2 env priority
    "What is the environmental priority for experimenter2?"
    range: 1, 10

.

    request priority
    " "

    range: 1, 10

.

    request2 priority
    " "

    range: 1, 10

.

    exper1 sched priority
    " "

    calc: exper1 init priority * request priority * exper1 env priority

.

    exper2 sched priority
    " "

    calc: exper2 init priority * request2 priority * exper2 env priority

.
.

;   frames:
    first
    " "

    exper1 sched priority ge exper2 sched priority

.

    second
    " "

    exper1 sched priority lt exper2 sched priority

.
.

experimenterrequest
; default value:
  invalid
; attributes:
  schedulerequest
  ⟨INFERRED⟩

  constraintviolation
  ⟨INFERRED⟩

  priority
  ⟨INFERRED⟩

.

; frames:
  invalid
  " "

    schedulerequest eq false
    constraintviolation eq present

  not meeting constraints
  " "

    schedulerequest eq true
    constraintviolation eq present

  not meeting all requested scheduling information
  " "

    schedulerequest eq false
    constraintviolation eq absent

  valid
  " "

    schedulerequest eq true
    constraintviolation eq absent

.
.

schedulefirst
; default value:
  unscheduled
; attributes:
  experimenterrequest
  ⟨INFERRED⟩

  priority
  ⟨INFERRED⟩

.

; frames:
  yes
  " "

    experimenterrequest eq valid
    priority eq first

no
" "

experimenterrequest eq valid
priority eq second

.

unscheduled
" "

experimenterrequest eq invalid, not meeting constraints
experimenterrequest eq not meeting all requested scheduling information

.

.

conflict
;   default value:
existent so try window
;   attributes:
schedulefirst
⟨INFERRED⟩

.

SAA start
"What is the South Atlantic Anomaly start time for the day that the experimenter
  wants the activity to be scheduled?"
range: 0000, 2400

.

SAA stop
"What is the South Atlantic Anomaly stop time for the day that the experimenter
  wants the activity to be scheduled?"
range: 0000, 2400

.

prev act start time
"What is the start time of the previous activity scheduled?"
range: 0000, 2400

.

prev act end time
"What is the stop time of the previous activity scheduled?"
range: 0000, 2400

.

requested activity start time
"What time do you want to start the activity (use format xxyy for designating time,
  where x represents hours and y represents minutes)?"
range: 0000, 2400

.

requested activity end time
"What time do you want to end the activity (use format xxyy for designating time,
  where x represents hours and y represents minutes)?"
range: 0000, 2400

.

.

;   frames:
nonexistent
" "

schedulefirst eq yes, no
requested activity start time nr SAA start, SAA stop
requested activity end time nr SAA start, SAA stop

requested activity start time nr prev act start time, prev act end time
requested activity end time nr prev act start time, prev act end time

.

existent so try window
" "

schedulefirst eq yes, no
requested activity start time ra SAA start, SAA stop
requested activity end time ra SAA start, SAA stop
requested activity start time ra prev act start time, prev act end time
requested activity end time ra prev act start time, prev act end time

.
.

req
;   default value:
not scheduled via window
;   attributes:
conflict
⟨INFERRED⟩

.

window
"What time would be the latest for starting your activity
    (use format xxyy for designating time, where x represents hours and y represents
    minutes)?"
range: 0000, 2400

.

;   frames:
scheduled via window
" "

conflict eq existent so try window
window nr SAA start, SAA stop
window nr prev act start time, prev act end time

not scheduled via window
" "

conflict eq existent so try window
window ra SAA start, SAA stop
window ra prev act start time, prev act end time

.

•
•
•

REFERENCES

1. J. J. O'Brien, *Scheduling Handbook*, McGraw-Hill, New York, 1969.
2. S. Vere, Presentation on DEVISER, Jet Propulsion Laboratory, May 1982.
3. S. Grenander, Toward the Fully Capable AI Space Mission Planner, *Aerospace America*, August 1985.

4. E. Scarl, Applications of a Non-Rule Knowledge-Based System to NASA Scheduling and Monitoring Problems. In *Proceedings of the 19th Intersociety Energy Conversion Conference*, 1984.

5. J. Mogilensky, E. A. Scarl, and R. E. Dalton, Manned Spaceflight Activity Planning with Knowledge-Based Systems. In *Proceedings of AIAA Computers in Aerospace IV*, Hartford, AIAA, New York, 1983.

6. NASA Goddard Space Flight Center, *Preliminary User's Guide for PLAN-IT*, Code 520, 1986.

7. G. B. Hankins, J. W. Jordan, J. N. Dumoulin, J. L. Katz, A. M. Mulvehill, and J. Ragusa, Expert Mission Planning and Replanning Scheduling System. In *Proceedings of Expert Systems in Government Symposium*, IEEE, Washington, D.C., 1985.

8. Bendix, Briefing, IEPS Phase II Research Prototype Features and Demo, NASA Goddard Space Flight Center, December 18, 1985.

9. D. McLean, The Design and Application of a Transportable Inference Engine. In *Proceedings of 1986 Conference on AI Applications*, NASA Goddard Space Flight Center, Greenbelt, MD, 1986.

10. J. R. Slagle, M. W. Gaynor, and H. Hamburger, Decision Support System for Fire Support Command and Control, NRL Report 8769, Naval Research Laboratory, December 30, 1983.

11. J. R. Slagle, and H. Hamburger, An Expert System for Resource Allocation Problems, *Communications of the ACM*, Vol. 28, No. 9, September 1985.

12. E. Orciuch and J. Frost, ISA: Intelligent Scheduling Assistant. In *IEEE Proceedings of First Conference on AI Applications*, IEEE/AAAI, New York, 1984.

13. D. E. O'Conner, Using Expert Systems to Manage Change and Complexity in Manufacturing. In *AI Applications for Business*, W. Reitman (ed.), Ablex Publishing, Norwood, NJ, 1984.

14. M. S. Fox, B. P. Allen, S. F. Smith, and G. A. Strohm, ISIS: A Constraint-Directed Reasoning Approach to Job Shop Scheduling System Summary, CMU Report, June 21, 1983.

15. M. S. Fox and G. Strohm, Job-Shop Scheduling: An Investigation in Constraint-Directed Reasoning. In *Proceedings of the National Conference on AI*, American Association for Artificial Intelligence, Menlo Park, CA, 1982.

16. M. S. Fox, Constraint-Directed Search: A Case Study of Job-Shop Scheduling, CMU-RI-TR-83-22 Report, December 1983.

17. I. P. Goldstein and R. B. Roberts, NUDGE: A Knowledge-Based Scheduling Program. In *Proceedings of the 5th International Joint Conference on AI*, American Association for Artificial Intelligence, Menlo Park, CA, 1977.

18. NASA Johnson Space Center, NASA Memorandum on Shuttle Manifesting Demo Program, FM 72/Applied Technology Section, January 10, 1985.

19. D. W. Heath and M. G. Boarnet, EXEPS: An Advisory Expert System for Timelining Electrical Power System Activity Blocks. In *Proceedings of ROBEXS '85*, Instrument Society of America, New York, 1985.

20. J. McDermott, R1: A Rule-Based Configurer of Computer Systems, *Artificial Intelligence*, Vol. 19, 1982.

21. P. Cheeseman, A Representation of Time for Planning, Technical Note 278, NASA Ames Research Center, February 1983.

22. D. Rosenthal, P. Monger, G. Miller, and M. Johnston, An Expert System for Ground Support of the Hubble Space Telescope. In *Proceedings of the 1986 Conference on AI Applications*, NASA Goddard Space Flight Center, Greenbelt, MD, 1986.

23. D. E. Wilkins, Domain-Independent Planning: Representation and Plan Generation, *Artificial Intelligence*, Vol. 22, pp. 269–301, 1984.

24. McDonnell–Douglas Technical Services Company, On-Orbit Mission Planning Using the Shuttle Trajectory and Launch Window Expert System, Houston, Texas, 1981.

25. A. Sathi, M. S. Fox, and M. Greenberg, Representation of Activity Knowledge for Project Management, *IEEE Transactions on Pattern Analysis and Machine Intelligence*, Vol. 7, No. 5, pp. 531–552, September 1985.

26. M. G. Boarnet, Requirements for a Scheduling Expert System Tool, NASA Johnson Space Center, April 1986.

27. L. R. Sayles and M. K. Chandler, *Managing Large Systems: Organizations for the Future*, Harper & Row, New York, 1971.

28. R. O. Duda, P. E. Hart, K. Konolige, and R. Reboh, A Computer-Based Consultant for Mineral Exploration, Artificial Intelligence Center, SRI International, Menlo Park, CA, September 1979.

METHODOLOGIES

STRATEGIC ASSESSMENT OF EXPERT SYSTEM TECHNOLOGY: GUIDELINES AND METHODOLOGY

Warren T. Jones

Department of Computer and Information Sciences, University of Alabama, Birmingham, Alabama

Robert L. Samuell III

Division of End User Computing, BellSouth Services, Inc., Atlanta, Georgia

1. INTRODUCTION

This chapter provides the technical manager or executive with information that can assist in the successful strategic planning and assessment of expert system applications within a telecommunications company.

Today, it is clear that expert system technology has the potential for increasing the productivity of organizations. The stages most frequently cited as necessary for the development of expert systems are:

Selection of an appropriate domain
Development tool selection
Knowledge engineering
Prototype development
Refinement of prototype
System maintenance

Our concerns in this chapter are not for this development process, but rather for the activities that should precede all of the above developmental stages—namely, a strategic technology assessment for the entire organization that appropriately sets the stage for the identification and development of expert system applications.

These predevelopmental planning activities are particularly important for at least three reasons:

1. Expert system technology is a new and emerging technology and therefore represents nontraditional ways of approaching computer applications. There are few individuals who are knowledgeable in the application of this technology.
2. The driving forces behind expert systems are more technology push than user pull [1]; therefore, one should be very sure where this new technology is to be used before beginning expenditures on a particular developmment project.
3. The loaded annual cost of technical expertise to a corporation has been estimated at over $120,000 for a single expert [2].

Our interest is in providing guidelines, discussion, and a methodology that will be useful in assessing the potential impact of the emerging technology of expert systems on a telecommunications company. A complete assessment of expert system technology would involve identifying all expert tasks performed in a company, determining their distribution and cost to the company,and estimating the cost of their mechanization. We have limited our discussion in this chapter to the identification of certain kinds of expertise and the determination of the cost of its provision to a company or any organizational component thereof.

We do this by providing a model of business task expertise and an approach to the assessment of this expertise within the context of factors that are known to underlie success in the transfer of any technology from the laboratory to successful commercial application. The results of the assessment can be used in connection with other information for the identification of specific application domains and for the computation of the cost of productivity gains resulting from the application of expert systems. Finally, we discuss how to apply the guidelines and methodology within an organization successfully and how universities can play an important role in interacting with the telecommunications industry and in facilitating the technology transfer process.

2. BUSINESS TASK MODEL

In general, a company is a goal-directed system. To meet the goals and objectives for which the company was established, business plans are developed. These plans are implemented via business tasks that are designed specifically to meet plan objectives. For purposes of our discussion, we define two types of business tasks as follows:

- *Routine tasks* are performed to meet the business plan objectives today, that is, current operations.

- *Exception-handling tasks* deal with problems that interrupt and impede the carrying out of routine tasks, that is, operational problems.

Routine tasks are typically well-structured activities that are carried out regularly by groups of employees. Exception-handling tasks, which the routine task performer is not trained to handle, often lack obvious structure and occur relatively infrequently and unpredictably.

Other business tasks can be defined, such as creative tasks, which are also subject to interruption in a way similar to routine tasks. But these tasks are typically less well specified as are their exceptions and thus they are not as readily subject to assessment. Greater opportunities for successful expert system solutions will be found in the mechanization of tasks that have some degree of structure [3].

For purpose of notation, we will let R and E, respectively, represent the routine and exception-handling task types. Obviously, each task type requires certain expertise on the part of the performers and in this sense can be viewed as candidate expertise for an expert system. However, we feel that a logical approach to a first pass at strategic assessment is to limit the definition of expertise to that of the exception-handling situation where the exception handler or expert is always another person or group of persons distinct from the routine task performer. That is, we are looking in our assessment for situations in which there is a task of type R standing in relation to a task of type E.

If we let $\rightarrow$ stand for "provides expertise to" and $P(\ )$ stand for the performer of some task, we can characterize in simple terms the situation we want to identify for the assessment as follows:

$$\{P(E)|P(E) \rightarrow P(R) \quad \text{and} \quad P(E) \neq P(R)\}.$$

If we call a performer of an exception-handling task an expert and a performer of a routine task a user (of expertise) within this model, then each situation satisfying the above relation can be viewed in terms of what we call a user–expert group (UEG), which is a pair:

$$\{(P(R), P(E))|P(E) \rightarrow P(R) \quad \text{and} \quad P(E) \neq P(R)\}.$$

For each category of exception-handling task, a user–expert group can be identified as typically consisting of one or more experts and a number of expertise users. An individual may belong to several user–expert groups in different roles. For example, an expert belonging to UEGx may also belong to UEGy as a user. Also, an expert may provide exception-handling expertise to the same group of users performing different routine tasks or to different groups of users performing different routine tasks. Figure 1 illustrates some of the possibilities: this matrix shows the possible roles of expert (E) and user (U) performed by eight employees (rows) who are members of seven different user–expert groups (columns).

MEMBER \ UEG	1	2	3	4	5	6	7
Ann	E	E			U	E	U
Bill	U	E	E	E	U	E	U
Chuck	U	U	U	U	U		U
Diane	U	U	U	U			U
Ed	U	U			U		E
Frank			U	U	U		
Gala					E	E	
Henry						U	

Figure 1. Employee Roles of Expert and User.

In addition to the particular nature of the expertise, some of the attributes of expertise within the user–expert group context include the job class and location of users and experts, the frequency of expertise utilization, and the officiality and availability of expertise. The users of expertise as well as the experts can be management, nonmanagement, or professional employees. The users and experts may or may not be colocated. For each individual employee or expertise user, exceptions occur relatively infrequently and unpredictably. However, for a group of users the frequency of exceptions may be quite high. The provision of expertise can be officially or formally a part of the expert's job description, for example, a technical support professional. Or the expertise can be provided informally, for example, an individual who has become the office guru on the voucher system. Expertise can be provided always by the same person or by different people at different times. The requirement to provide expertise can be only during business hours or it can be around the clock.

A simple heuristic or "rule of thumb" for identifying an expert is to answer the question: "Who do you ask when you have a business problem that you cannot solve yourself?" The answer to this question within the context of our business task model together with other associated information will identify a user–expert group. In the remainder of this chapter, we describe important aspects of expert systems technology and a simple methodology for assessing areas within a company that are candidates for the application of the technology.

3. EXPERT SYSTEM TECHNOLOGY

Expert system technology represents an approach to the mechanization of expertise. The ways in which expert systems can be applied to this mechanization and the costs of application development are beyond the scope of this chapter. Nevertheless, it is important to understand the benefits, technology transfer factors, strategic issues, and implementation considerations associated with the technology.

3.1 Benefits

The benefits of expert system technology are numerous and have the potential to impact corporate productivity significantly. These benefits include:

- Expert systems store information in an active form called a knowledge base rather than in a passive form such as a textbook or manual. Because of this characteristic, knowledge will be more responsive to a user's needs and can be kept up-to-date more easily.
- An expert system can be used to preserve knowledge that might otherwise be lost through the retirement, resignation, or death of a company's acknowledged expert in any field.
- An expert system can be developed that "clones" an expert mechanically so his or her knowledge can be disseminated, thus reducing the number of experts required in a given area while providing the remaining experts with the opportunity to concentrate on the more challenging problems in their field of expertise.
- From a training perspective, an expert system can be used to give novices an aid that will help them think the way more experienced professionals do. Also, training productivity and effectiveness can be increased by the use of expert system assistance for students that embodies aspects of the task expertise being taught in the classroom.
- Finally, in some environments, an expert system can be used to create a mechanism that is not subject to human failings like fatigue and can hold up in positions where information must flow constantly.

Having considered the benefits of expert system technology, we want to look next at the factors affecting its tranfer into an organization.

3.2. Technology Transfer Factors

The problems involved in the transfer of knowledge about the emerging technology of expert systems are a special case of the more general problem of the diffusion of any new technology within an organization or industry. A considerable body of knowledge is available as a result of research in the area that is known as the diffusion of innovations [4]. Examples of technologies that have been subjected to study are CAT scanners, telephone-based banking services and computer terminals in an established engineering environment [5], and software engineering methods [6].

The results of this research have provided us with factors that are common to all diffusion of innovation processes and thus applicable to the diffusion of expert system technology. The ideas involved provide a convenient and appropriate context and background for our discussion. In this section, we summarize the major concepts.

The diffusion of a new technology is known to involve four primary elements:

- The technology
- Communications channels
- Time
- Organization or industry being diffused

The technology is of course expert systems. The communications channels can be either formal or informal. From a strategic planning standpoint, the formal aspects are the most important since channels such as introductory seminars and workshops provide the ''local consciousness raising'' necessary for the early identification of appropriate domains of application.

Time is an important factor for at least two reasons. First, diffusion is a process that is characterized by a life cycle of distinct stages. Second, the level of adoption of an emerging technology over time is known to be an S-shaped curve that has certain implications that will be discussed later in this section.

The organization or industry being diffused offers opportunities that are functions of its own special properties. Telecommunications organizations can range from individual, privately owned networks to international networks from which individuals can lease services. As can be seen from other chapters in this volume, there are many opportunities for the application of expert systems which are related to the design and management of a telecommunications system itself. However, it should also be noted that any telecommunications company also has many aspects that are common to any business, and opportunities lie in this dimension as well. Our experience and concerns have been primarily with a large telecommunications company and the content of this chapter reflects this background, although most of what we have to say is generally applicable to the telecommunications industry and other business organizations as well.

Individuals who are participating in the diffusion process can be classified into three roles with regard to their function in the diffusion process:

- Innovators
- Diffusers
- Adopters

The effect of these three roles can be seen more clearly if we now identify the three organizational players in the diffusion game:

- Telecommunications company
- Expert systems software vendor
- Universities committed to expert systems research

As is the case for expert systems, universities are frequently the breeding ground for new ideas that form the foundation for commercial products that are then developed and marketed by expert systems software companies for application in telecommunications companies. Therefore, the innovators are usually represented by the university research community. The diffusers role can be found in all three of the above organizational players. Clearly, the company being diffused has employees involved in this process. The vendor has a vested interest in the successful diffusion of the new technology and thus is active through its promotions and presentations. Universities are also becoming more involved in the technology transfer process in a number of ways, as exemplified by the University of Alabama at Birmingham (UAB) Advanced Computer Technology Transfer Laboratory, which is discussed in a later section of this chapter. Finally, the adopter role is that of the expert system end user in a telecommunications company.

Thus, we can summarize the above discussion as follows:

	Innovators	Diffusers	Adopters
Telecommunications company		X	X
Expert systems software vendors	X	X	
University research community	X	X	

Five characteristics of innovations are known to affect the rate of diffusion directly:

- Relative advantage
- Compatibility
- Complexity
- Trialability
- Observability

Relative advantage is a measure of the extent to which the innovation is an improvement over the present methods. For the technology of expert systems, the relative advantages are those usually cited [7], namely:

- To preserve knowledge that might be lost
- To "clone" an expert to improve dissemination of expertise
- To store knowledge in an active form

- To help train novices
- To provide a facility not subject to human fatigue

All of the above translate into increased productivity and/or competitive advantage.

Compatibility is a measure of the degree to which an expert system is perceived to be consistent with the working environment within which it is integrated. Since some organizational restructuring may necessarily occur with the adoption of expert systems, there are issues of end-user acceptance that must be addressed. As a minimum, job descriptions could be redefined.

Complexity is a measure of the degree to which an expert system is perceived as difficult to learn how to use. This is another dimension of the possible end-user acceptance problem. The complexity as well as compatibility issues can be minimized by working closely with the end users during the planning stages and winning their support for the project early. Complexity, as defined here, is the ''user-friendly'' interface by another name and of course can also be minimized by careful system design criteria as well as expert system tool selection.

Trialability is a measure of the degree to which an innovation can be experimented with on a limited basis. Expert system technology is a natural for trialability because of the ease with which prototyping can be performed. The initial cost of experimenting with the technology can be minimized by use of personal computer (PC) workstations, which are already commonplace in many organizations. There are a number of high-quality development tools available for personal computer environnments. As the hardware technology of personal computers continues to grow more powerful, it will become even more attractive for expert system applications.

Observability is a measure of the degree to which the results of an expert system application are visible to others. Thus, if one selects a domain that is highly visible within the organization, it will likely have a positive effect on the identification of other appropriate domains.

We can summarize this discussion of the characteristics of innovations as follows:

Innovation Property	Value of Property for Positive Effect on the Diffusion Process
Relative advantage	High
Compatibility	High
Complexity	Low
Trialability	High
Observability	High

Now we can discuss the characteristics of adopters in the same way that we have presented the properties of the innovations themselves. In general, the rate of adoption of an innovation follows a bell-shaped normal curve when plotted over time on a frequency basis as shown below.

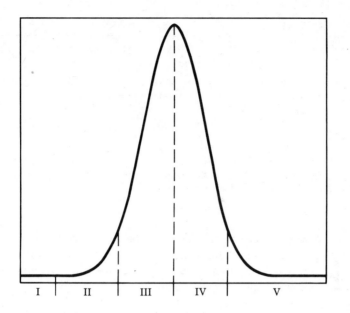

The corresponding cumulative distribution function (CDF) is the familiar sigmoid curve:

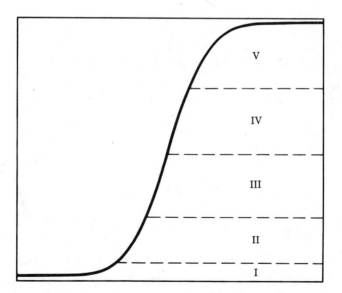

Five ideal adopter categories have been identified in diffusion research and are depicted on the curves above. Note that the classification is not symmetrical. These five categories are characterized as follows:

Adopter Category	Attributes
I. Innovators	First 2.5% of adopters: venturesome, first experiments
II. Early adopters	Next 13.5%: takes cues from first experiments
III. Early majority	Next 34%: deliberate willingness but seldom lead
IV. Late majority	Next 34%: skeptical
V. Laggards	Final 16%: traditionalists

The innovation adoption process in organizations can be characterized by the two stages of initiation and implementation with steps within each as follows.

Initiation

1. *Agenda Setting.* General organizational problems that may create the perceived problem that needs to be addressed in a more effective and different manner. For expert systems, the candidate problem symptoms might be among the following (knowledge bottlenecks):
   - Shortage of skilled personnel
   - Training problems
   - Need to distribute certain problem-solving skills
   - Loss of expertise because of employee turnover
2. *Matching.* Selection of a problem from the organization's agenda as a candidate for expert system development. This stage includes all the usual aforementioned expert system development stages (domain selection, tool selection, knowledge engineering, prototyping, and refinement).

Implementation. Implementation here refers to the implementation within the organization of the functions previously carried out only by the experts themselves and not the implementation of the expert system software.

3. *Redefining/Restructuring.* The expert system is assimilated into the organization and organizational structures directly relevant are altered to accommodate.
4. *Routinizing.* Loss of novelty of system and assimilation into work environment complete.

It should also be noted that the nature of the organizational structure is also a factor in the diffusion process. Relevant organizational properties are:

- Centralization—the degree to which power and control is concentrated in the hands of relatively few individuals.
- Complexity—the degree to which the members of an organization possess a relatively high level of knowledge and expertise.

- Formalization—the degree to which an organization emphasizes rules and procedures in the role performance of its employees.
- Interconnectedness—the degree to which the units in the organization are linked by interpersonal networks.
- Organizational slack—the degree to which uncommitted resources are available to organizational innovativeness.

The following table summarizes the effects of these organizational properties on the diffusion process:

Internal Characteristics of Organizational Structure	Effect on Diffusion Process
Centralization	Negative
Complexity	Positive
Formalization	Negative
Interconnectedness	Positive
Organizational slack	Positive

Given the above factors and their effects on the introduction and diffusion of new technology, we now examine some strategic issues that companies adopting expert system technology must address.

3.3. Strategic Issues

For companies considering the application of expert system technology, strategic issues include justifying expenditures for expert systems, deciding how to get started, choosing suitable applications, choosing appropriate expert system tools, and relating expert system activities to the rest of the organization [8].

Today, justifying expert systems expenditures can be a problem. The lack of visible operational systems, tested development methodologies, and false marketing claims have been a detriment. Thus, the investment in expert systems may still be viewed as somewhat speculative. Nevertheless, the entry cost of acquiring the technology is quite low [9]: experimentation leading to the development of relatively sophisticated applications can begin using a PC for about $6500. Basic demonstration systems can be found for as low as $40. By applying these PC-based tools to solve a modest problem, a developer can produce a working prototype in just a few months [10].

Deciding how to get started involves identifying pools of expertise, assessing the cost of this expertise to the company, and determining the availability of developmental resources. A strategic assessment of the type described in this chapter can assist in identifying expertise and estimating its cost to a company. Outside consultants can frequently assist in-house developers in training development personnel in the technology and in moderating other resource requirements.

Choosing suitable applications involves understanding criteria and the needs of the business, applying this knowledge to prioritizing pools of expertise for mechanization, determining the domain of an application, and assembling the best development team. A number of vendors can provide training in applying expert system technology. The results of a strategic assessment of the type described in this chapter can assist in prioritizing application candidates based on cost data. In assembling the development team, the key choice is identifying an expert who can appropriately articulate job expertise and devote a substantial amount of job time to the development effort.

Choosing appropriate expert system tools involves determining the degree of customizability, the kind of delivery system desired, the scope and complexity of the problem domain, and the characteristics of the application. In the area of customizability, tools range from packaged applications through shells and toolkits to general-purpose programming languages. Tools are available for all classes of processors from microcomputers to mainframes. Several reports have been published that compare and rate tools for all degrees of customizability and the range of processor classes [8, 11, 12]. These reports also describe methods for assessing the scope and complexity of expert system problems. Domain selection criteria are outlined later in this chapter.

Relating expert systems to the rest of the corporation involves determining the need for intersystem connection, compatibility, and integration of applications. Current trends suggest that expert system development tools will become widely available in traditional programming environments using conventional hardware [13]. This availability will bring the technology into the mainstream of computing and improve the capability for integration with other systems. Those companies with a significant investment in traditional facilities will then be able to move incrementally into applying the technology without acquiring specialized facilities.

Now that we have investigated issues impacting a company's decision to adopt expert system technology, we want to address some implementation concerns.

3.4. Implementation Considerations

Issues encompassing the implementation of expert systems include the attitude of the developers toward the technology, the commitment of management to the cost of development, and the concern of experts and users for the effects of the technology on their jobs.

When implementing an expert system, it is important for developers to realize that this technology represents only a new alternative to the development of computer applications: it is not a totally different approach to mechanization. Using the expert system technology still requires (1) the systems analysis of the problem domain, (2) the specification of a system design, (3) the programming of a computer systems solution, (4) the development of a set of test cases, (5) the testing and trialing of the program solution, (6) the review of human factors and the interface, (7) the maintenance of the program and databases, and (8) the transfer of the application model.

In developing expert systems, what differs from traditional application development is (1) the involvement of a subject matter expert, (2) the emphasis on prototyping and refinement, and (3) the applicative instead of procedural representation.

Although the cost of experimenting with the technology can be low, the successful implementation of significant expert systems will require a major commitment of corporate resources. Williamson [14] echoes others by saying:

> Developing the fully operational [significant] system . . . requires three years from inception to successful implementation, consumes 10 person-years of effort, and costs around $1,000,000.

However, the potential payoff can be enormous: beginning in 1978, Digital Equipment Corporation developed a proprietary expert system called R1 (now called R1/XCON), which configures minicomputers from custom orders [15]. Attempts to solve this configuration problem using traditional computing techniques had failed. Today, it is estimated that the annual savings to Digital are at least $20,000,000.

Expert systems are not designed to replace people. No expert system will be able to handle every problem submitted to it for handling: human experts will always be needed to handle those extraordinarily difficult or unique problems that arise. Concern for the implementation of expert systems should be tempered with a consideration of those important benefits of the technology: the storage and preservation of knowledge in an active form, improved access to and availability of expertise coupled with improved use of resources, and enhanced productivity in both formal and on-the-job training environments.

4. ASSESSMENT METHODOLOGY

The expertise embodied in the employees of an organization is one of the most important resources for achieving, enhancing, and maintaining its competitive position. The long-term success of a company depends on its competitive advantage over others. Expert systems provide the opportunity to leverage expertise and enhance this competitive advantage. Our objective here is to provide a systematic approach to the strategic assessment of expert system technology that will enable an organization to identify the appropriate domains of application and thus to maximize the potential leverage and productivity increases. We accomplish this objective through a process of data collection and analysis.

4.1. Data Collection Stage

The data collection stage of the strategic assessment involves the distribution and evaluation of a survey to potential users of expertise, the management and analysis of interviews of selected experts, and the accumulation of loaded salary and other cost information for users and experts.

The purpose of the survey is to identify the nature of routine business tasks and potential sources of exception-handling expertise within the survey domain. All management and nonmanagement users within the organization being assessed are asked to respond to the survey. Table 1 is a sample survey that can be customized for use in any organization.

The purpose of the interview of experts identified in the survey is to ascertain the characteristics of the expertise in terms of exceptions handled per unit of time, the amount of time to handle exceptions, and other information about the type of expertise. Table 2 is a sample interview guide that provides a set of questions to be asked a prospective expert.

TABLE 1   Sample Survey

Instructions:

You are being asked to participate in a survey that will assist in identifying the nature and distribution of certain kinds of problem-solving expertise that support the operation of your organization. This survey is organized into three parts. Section A requests general information. Section B requests information on one or more types of problems you encounter when you are performing some routine business task and the type of problem is one that you always seek assistance in solving. Section C requests information on the routine business tasks interrupted by the problems described in Section B of this survey.

The term "routine task" as used in this survey means a clearly defined activity that you carry out regularly and repeatedly as a part of your job. The term "problem" means an interruption of the routine task that you are not required or trained to handle yourself.

You have been provided with one copy of each section of the survey. Please fill out Section A first. Next, fill out one copy of Section B for each problem that you describe and assign it a problem number. Then, fill out one copy of Section C for each routine task interrupted by a problem or problems described in Section B. Please try to provide information on at least three problems.

A. General Information

A1. Your name?
_____

A2. Your title and organization?
_____
_____

A3. Your address?
_____
_____
_____

A4. Your telephone number?
_____

A5. Your Social Security number?
_____

A6. How long have you been in your present position?(Check only one)
   ☐ Six months or less
   ☐ More than 6 months but not more than 2 years
   ☐ More than 2 years

TABLE 1 (*Continued*)

B. Information on Problem #_____

B1. In the performance of some routine business task, when a problem related to the task is encountered that you cannot handle entirely yourself, who do you contact for assistance in solving the problem?
Contact name?_____
Contact telephone number?_____

B2. Briefly describe a sample instance of the problem.
_____
_____
_____

B3. How often does an instance of this problem interrupt your performance of the routine task? (Check only one)
☐ At least once a day
☐ At least twice a week
☐ At least once a week
☐ At least once a month
☐ At least once a quarter
☐ At least once a year
☐ Less than once a year

B4. What do you typically do while the problem is being worked on? (Check only one)
☐ Stay in direct contact with the person assisting
☐ Work productively on another task
☐ Work productively on the same task
☐ Cannot work until the problem is resolved

B5. How long typically before you can resume the routine task that has been interrupted? (Check only one)
☐ Thirty minutes or less
☐ More than 30 minutes but not more than 2 hours
☐ More than 2 hours but not more than 4 hours
☐ More than 4 hours but not more than 1 day
☐ More than 1 day

B6. How is the person assisting you with the problem contacted? (Check all that apply)
☐ In person
☐ By telephone
☐ By postal mail
☐ By computer mail
☐ Through another person
☐ Other: specify_____

B7. How does the person contacted typically handle the problem after you have described it? (Check all that apply)
☐ By himself/herself
☐ By referring you to another person(s)
☐ By delegating it to another person(s)
☐ By consultation with another person(s)
☐ Other: specify_____

B8. How is the person who provides assistance related to your position? (Check only one)
☐ Your peer
☐ Your supervisor
☐ Another superior

TABLE 1 (*Continued*)

☐ Your subordinate
☐ Another's subordinate
☐ Outside vendor employee
☐ Contracted employee
☐ Unknown

C. Information on Routine Task #_____

C1. Briefly describe the routine task that is interrupted by the problem(s) you have described.

_____
_____
_____
_____
_____

C2. How often do you perform the routine task? (Check only one)
☐ More than once a day
☐ At least once a day
☐ At least twice a week
☐ At least once a week
☐ At least once a month
☐ At least once a quarter
☐ At least once a year
☐ Other: specify_____

C3. How long typically does it take to perform the routine task? (Check only one)
☐ Thirty minutes or less
☐ More than 30 minutes but not more than 2 hours
☐ More than 2 hours but not more than 4 hours
☐ More than 4 hours but not more than 1 day
☐ More than 1 day
☐ Continually ongoing

C4. How long have you been performing the routine task? (Check only one)
☐ Six months or less
☐ More than 6 months but not more than 2 years
☐ More than 2 years

C5. What are the numbers of the problems that you have identified in Section B of this survey that can occur when performing this routine task? (List all)
Problem numbers?_____

4.2. Data Analysis Stage

The data analysis stage of the strategic assessment involves the determination of user–expert groups, the elimination of user–expert groups that are not associated with suitable expert system application domains, and the calculation of the cost of expertise for each group in terms of time and dollars.

From collected and analyzed data, it is possible to show the composition of each user–expert group and to identify the associated routine and exception tasks. It is also possible to compile information on how different user–expert groups relate to each other. This relation may be important in determining the order of expertise mechanization.

TABLE 2   Sample Interview Guide

Instructions:

To begin this interview, explain that the interviewee has been identified in the Strategic Assessment Survey as a provider of assistance to performers of routine business tasks who encounter problems that they are not trained to handle themselves.

Describe to the interviewee a problem and an associated routine task identified in the survey and ask the interviewee each question below as appropriate. Repeat this process for all problems identified in the survey as being handled by the interviewee.

Questions:

Is this an accurate description of the type of problem and the associated routine task? if no, what would you change in the description?

How often do you provide assistance in solving this type of problem?

How long do you typically take to handle an instance of this type of problem?

As a percentage of your total time on the job today, how much time do you spend handling this type of problem?

Do you ever handle more than one problem of this type at a time or are you able to perform other activities while handling this type of problem? If so, please describe.

Are you the only person who ever provides assistance for this type of problem? If no, who else provides assistance and under what circumstances do they provide assistance?

Do you ever call in others to assist you in handling this type of problem? If so, who are they, what is their function, and how often do you call them in?

Do you ever refer this type of problem to someone else? If so, who are they, why do you refer the problem, and how often do you refer it to them?

How long have you been assisting others in handling this type of problem?

Is providing assistance in handling this type of problem formally a part of your job? If no, please explain.

Have you ever performed the routine task associated with this type of problem yourself? If so, when and for how long?

After the survey and interview data have been collected on all user–expert groups, each candidate expert system domain will be assessed for appropriateness in accordance with criteria, the major aspects of which are summarized as follows:

Domain Selection Criteria [16]

- The domain is characterized by the use of expert knowledge, judgment, and experience.
- Conventional programming (algorithmic) approaches to the task are not satisfactory.
- The task primarily requires symbolic reasoning.
- The task requires the use of heuristics, for example, rules of thumb and strategies. It may require consideration of an extremely large number of pos-

sibilities or it may require decisions to be based on incomplete or uncertain information.

- The task does not require knowledge from a very large number of areas.
- The task is neither too easy (taking a human expert less than a few minutes) nor too difficult (requiring more than a few hours for an expert).
- The amount of knowledge required by the task is large enough to make the knowledge base developed interesting. (If it is too small, the task may be more amenable to another approach, for example, a decision tree.)
- The task is sufficiently narrow and self-contained.

For a given user–expert group and its associated set of problems, an estimate of the cost of providing expertise depends on the following variables.

P Mean number of instances of each type of problem solved
U Mean number of people with the problem or affected by the problem
E Mean number of experts solving each type of problem
T Mean time to solve each type of problem
L Mean time lost by the people with each type of problem
S Loaded salary of the experts and the people with the problem
O Other costs required to implement a solution for each type of problem

Most of these data can be obtained in survey responses and through the interviews of experts. Salary and other cost data must be obtained from other sources.

From the aforementioned data, calculating the cost of expertise for each user–expert group can be accomplished by applying the following formulas:

$$\text{COST}(\text{GROUP}_i) = \sum_{j=1}^{n} \text{COST}(\text{PROBLEM\_TYPE}_j);$$

$$\text{COST}(\text{PROBLEM\_TYPE}_j) = P_j * (T_j * E_j * S\_\text{EXPERT}_j$$
$$+ L_j * U_j * S\_\text{USER}_j + O_j).$$

4.3.   Assessment Results and Implications

The results of this strategic assessment are presented as a summary of user–expert groups. Ordering a list of user–expert groups based on various financial measures can be the basis for selecting the best candidates for expert system applications. A list of user–expert groups can be ordered by decreasing cost of expertise as derived directly from the assessment. Or lists can be ordered by increasing payback interval or by decreasing cost savings as a basis of determining expert system mechanization priorities.

Compilation of these other lists involves additional calculation beyond the assessment. The user–expert groups must be examined and estimates of development costs must be calculated based on the current cost of technology and development times. These data together with the cost of expertise are used to estimate the application payback period and an annual cost savings after payback for each user–expert group. Other information may also be provided such as the cost of expertise relative to the total cost of operations, which can be used to put the results of the assessment into an overall corporate perspective.

The process of selecting expert system applications can be approached in either of two ways. One approach involves selecting candidates that lie on the high-cost (or savings) end of the list. These candidates typically represent complex projects requiring a significant investment in development resources but are directly connected with the primary business mission of the company (e.g., network control and/or reconfiguration). This approach is said to be technology based. Conversely, the selection of a collection of smaller projects on the low-cost (or short payback) end of the list is referred to as a business needs approach. The financial and productivity impact of the business needs approach will require a number of applications and use locations of those applications to be equivalent to a single large project in a technology-based approach.

In either case, the mechanization of exception-handling tasks can be viewed as a least-cost alternative to the exploitation of expert system technology since it can be done independently of other efforts, particularly the mechanization of the associated routine tasks.

5. METHODOLOGY APPLICATION

The assessment methodology described in this chapter provides a realistic measurement of the cost of exception-handling expertise for a work group of any size and will allow management to prioritize expertise for mechanization. This section describes suggestions for the application of the methodology, a strategic assessment pilot, and the documentation associated with the assessment pilot.

5.1. Assessment Pilot

It is recommended that the assessment methodology outlined in this chapter be applied initially to one department within a company. If useful results are obtained then it can be applied to other organizations individually or the company as a whole.

The following characteristics should be sought in selecting an organization for the assessment pilot:

- In general, the business tasks performed in the organization are well defined.
- A good mix of routine tasks is required for day-to-day operations. No one task dominates all others.

- Exception-handling when it is needed is typically performed by someone other than the routine task performer.
- Some traditional mechanization of tasks has already been implemented in the organization.

To summarize the process of assessment: After selecting an organization for assessment and refining generic questionnaires and interview guides, a business research organization collects and summarizes survey data. Then, identified experts are screened and interviewed, and relevant loaded salary data are obtained. The survey, interview, and salary data may be transcribed into a database to facilitate calculation, manipulation, and historical record. The calculations required by the assessment methodology are performed and the results are appropriately summarized.

5.2. Assessment Documentation

Three documents should be produced as outputs of the assessment process: a report of assessments results, an evaluation of the assessment process, and a log of assessment activities.

The report of assessment results will provide a summary of user–expert groups in descending order of the cost of expertise. Additional orderings may be provided. As a consequence of this summary, several good candidates for mechanization may be identified and prototyped.

The evaluation of the assessment will catalog unforeseen benefits and drawbacks of the process for the organization being assessed. Improvements and enhancements to survey and interview material may be implemented in future assessments. Suitability of the assessment process will be determined for other organizations. Recommendations to assess specific organizations may be made.

A contemporaneous log of assessment activities will be kept by the assessment administrator. This record will provide data for the aforementioned evaluation.

6. ROLE OF THE UNIVERSITY

This section discusses the role of the university in the assessment process and in the introduction of expert system technology into a telecommunications company.

6.1. Potential for Universities in the Technology Transfer Process

There is an increasing trend of university involvement in research and development projects with business and industry. There are a number of reasons why such synergistic arrangements are mutually beneficial in the telecommunications field as well as with other industries. In the next subsection we present a model of the UAB Advanced Computer Technology Transfer Laboratory of the Department of Computer and Information Sciences, which may be useful to others in planning technology transfer activities.

6.2. University Technology Transfer Interface Model

We view the process as involving three entities: the university computer science department, local business and industry, and equipment and software vendors. The roles and benefits can be summarized as follows:

Organization	Role	Benefit
Computer Science Department	Transfer agent partner	Source of example domains for motivating research
Business/industry	Recipient of emerging expert systems technology	Increase in productivity and competitiveness
Equipment and software vendors	Transfer agent	Product sales

There are a number of secondary but very important benefits that are worthy of note. For example, the university laboratory environment offers the advanced equipment to explore and prototype potential applications of expert systems without investing initially in expensive hardware until after feasibility questions have been answered and directions for applications have been established.

This model offers the university computer science department the opportunity to obtain advanced equipment from vendors on the strength of the marketing value apparent from the visibility that such equipment would obtain from its presence and use in a technology transfer laboratory.

7. CONCLUSIONS

This chapter has provided the management of a telecommunications company with guidelines and a methodology for assessing the extent to which expert system technology may be exploited in the company's operations. Within the context of selected technology diffusion factors and a business task model, we have proposed an assessment methodology that can be used to identify and evaluate exception-handling expertise associated with user–expert groups. We have shown how the results of the assessment can be used together with other information to prioritize specific application domains for expertise mechanization. Finally, we have discussed how this assessment can be applied successfully and how a university can play an important role in the assessing of and the planning for expert system technology in a telecommunications company.

REFERENCES

1. R. E. Morley and R. A. Taylor, *Demystifying Artificial Intelligence*, Graeme Publishing Corporation, 1986.

2. L. Allen, In Depth—The Cost of an Expert, *Computerworld*, July 26, 1986.

3. J. Clifford, M. Jarke, and H. C. Lucas, Jr., Designing Expert Systems in a Business Environment. In *Artificial Intelligence in Economics and Management*, Elsevier Science Publishers, New York, 1986.

4. E. M. Rogers, *Diffusion of Innovations*, The Free Press, New York, 1983.

5. V. Mahajan and R. A. Peterson, *Models for Innovation Diffusion*, Sage Publications, Beverly Hills, 1985.

6. S. A. Raghavan and D. R. Chand, Diffusion of Software Engineering Methods, School of Information Technology Tech. Rep. TR-86-10, Wang Institute of Graduate Studies, November 1986.

7. H. P. Newquist, III, Executive Report—Expert Systems: The Promise of a Smart Machine, *Computerworld*, January 13, 1986.

8. J. Hewett and R. Sasson, *Expert Systems 1986—Volume 1: USA and Canada*, Ovum Limited, London, 1986.

9. R. C. Thibault, In Our Opinion: Expert System Shells—Ready for Retail?, *AI Today*, AAAI-86 Issue, 1986.

10. W. T. Jones, An Assessment of Artificial Intelligence Technology: The Potential of Expert Systems, BellSouth Services, Inc., March 1986.

11. P. Harmon and D. King, *Expert Systems: Artificial Intelligence in Business*, Wiley, New York, 1985.

12. J. F. Gilmore and K. Pulaski, A Survey of Expert System Tools. In *Proceedings of the Second Conference on AI Applications*, IEEE, Washington, D.C., 1985.

13. A. J. Symonds, Introduction to IBM's Knowledge-System Products, *IBM Systems Journal*, Vol. 25, No. 2, 1986.

14. M. Williamson, Focus on Artificial Intelligence—Rapid Growth is Forecast for Expert Systems, *PC Week*, October 21, 1986.

15. J. McDermott, Building Expert Systems. In *Artificial Intelligence Applications for Business*, W. Reitman (Ed.), Ablex Publishing Corporation, Norwood, NJ, 1984.

16. D. Prerau, Selection of an Appropriate Domain for an Expert System, *AI Magazine*, Vol. 6, No. 2, pp. 26–30, Summer 1985.

KNOWLEDGE ACQUISITION FOR KNOWLEDGE-BASED SYSTEMS

Daniel A. DeSalvo

MCI Telecommunications Corporation
McLean, Virginia

1. INTRODUCTION

This chapter discusses the activities involved in discovering, describing, and organizing knowledge so that it may be used in a *production* expert system—that is, one that supports a commercial or government organization's day-to-day operations.

In a production environment, expert systems do not exist in a vacuum: they may support or complement other systems, access corporate databases, or have a strategic effect on management. In the telecommunications world, planning for this interaction is particularly important, since telecommunications software

- may be very complex and computer intensive—that is expensive to run and maintain;
- usually processes a great deal of *time-critical* data that must be analyzed and acted on as quickly as possible;
- coexists and often interacts directly with *real-time* and *near-real-time* systems; and
- provides an organization with critical support in delivering or maintaining its telecommunications product.

This chapter draws heavily on conventional systems analysis techniques. The approach presented here should help deliver expert systems that meet the same strict design, operations, and documentation standards as other telecommunications systems.

1.1. The Reader

This chapter addresses readers with the following qualifications:

- Those who have had either classroom or practical exposure to data processing.
- Those who understand the basic data processing concepts of how languages and computers operate. The reader does not need to understand artificial intelligence or expert systems concepts, although some basic knowledge of the area would be very useful.
- Those who are passingly familiar with basic telecommunications theory. The concepts and techniques presented in this chapter have been selected for their usefulness in solving telecommunications problems.
- Those who recognize the need to apply the same kind of management and budget controls to expert system development as are applied to conventional projects.

1.2. Approach and Premises of This Chapter

This chapter approaches knowledge acquisition from a *systems analysis* viewpoint. In particular, the *systems life cycle* and extensive documentation play key roles in this approach, which relies on two practical premises:

1. Knowledge engineering, as noted by Hayes-Roth et al. [1], is not much different from conventional systems analysis.
2. A human expert, or experts, will be available to the software project. Although it is possible to build an expert system without a human expert, such a system should be referred to by the broader term of *knowledge-based system*.

1.3. Layout of This Chapter

This chapter has three main sections, along with this Introduction, a Conclusion and extensive Glossary:

- Section 2, on *preliminary concepts*, introduces some basic precepts of knowledge acquisition. It presents a working definition for knowledge, describes the participants in the knowledge acquisition process, and introduces the systems development life cycle. It describes a knowledge acquisition session and introduces some of the documents that the knowledge engineer develops during the course of knowledge acquisition.
- Section 3, on knowledge acquisition for systems specification, introduces the concept that an expert's knowledge can be organized and evaluated based on the tasks performed by that expert. It presents an approach to identifying that part of the expert's knowledge that is of most value to the organization. It

describes several key economic and tabular approaches to classifying knowledge and discusses how that knowledge should be documented.

- Section 4, on knowledge acquisition during the design, introduces the concepts that most actual expert systems are *hybrids* of both knowledge-based and conventional software. It presents an approach to modeling the entire hybrid system without regard to whether individual components will be implemented as knowledge-based or conventional components. It describes the use of *empirical modeling* techniques such as *inheritance graphs* to accomplish this.

This chapter approaches *knowledge engineering*—of which knowledge acquisition is a part—as a systems analysis activity, which therefore corresponds to the *systems development life cycle*. In particular, this chapter puts knowledge acquisition into the context of the first two major parts of the life cycle: the systems specification and system design.

2. PRELIMINARY CONCEPTS

Knowledge acquisition is the job of translating an expert's knowledge into a form that can be used in a computer. The resulting computer application will either support the expert or perform as a very limited surrogate under carefully defined conditions. Under most circumstances, expert systems cannot actually replace human beings, any more than an automatic teller machine can replace a human bank teller. However, like any computer application, an expert system can help us make better use of scarce human resources.

Knowledge acquisition comprises two basic tasks:

1. Identifying the knowledge that will go into the system. This contributes to the *system specification*, which identifies what the system will do but not how the system will do it.

2. Describing how that knowledge will be put to work. This contributes to the *system design*, which describes how the system will work.

Hayes-Roth et al. [1] make the point that *knowledge engineering*—the process of building a knowledge-based system—is essentially the same as conventional systems analysis. Those few differences that do exist between conventional and expert systems projects are rapidly disappearing. For example, rapid prototyping, object-oriented programming, and other knowledge-based systems techniques are finding their way quickly into the toolkits of conventional systems builders.

By the same token, in the last few years, we have dramatically improved our ability to plan, budget, and build expert systems within the hard constraints of the commercial world. A good deal of this improvement has come from adapting conventional *systems development life cycle* (SDLC) methods to expert systems projects.

The SDLC is a generalized schedule that describes the order and type of activities in a project. The literature of computer science, including several of our references, proposes a number of slightly different approaches to defining a life cycle [1–4]. However, these interpretations all have a common goal: to provide a step-by-step outline of the activities involved in taking a generally vague system concept and idea and turning it into functional software.

Figure 1 describes the first part of a common SDLC. As the exhibit shows, each stage of the SDLC produces two kinds of documents:

1. *Working documents* that the knowledge engineers and other system builders use among themselves.
2. *Major documents*, which are widely distributed throughout the organization to summarize the status of the project.

Since this chapter is not a treatise on project management, the exhibit shows only some of the documents that are involved. Any sizable software project will generate many more. Metzger [5], Yourdon and Constantine [6], Jensen and Tonies [7], Zelkowitz et al. [8], Boehm [9], and others discuss different aspects of the life cycle in detail.

2.1. Definition of an Expert System

Unfortunately, there is no uniform use for the term ''expert system'' within the data processing industry, which loves to churn out vague terms and then apply them loosely (e.g., fourth-generation language, English-like commands, user-friendly, and expert system). For our purposes, an *expert system* can be defined as a knowledge-based system that employs some part of the knowledge of a human expert. They are practical applications of some of the programming and design techniques developed by research into artificial intelligence. They are not necessarily more expensive or more difficult to build than conventional systems, nor are they necessarily the best tools for solving a particular problem.

Knowledge-based systems are characterized by their ability to process information that is more complex and that changes more rapidly than the information normally processed by conventional systems. As Figure 2 explains, a knowledge-based system is defined technically as one that explicitly and formally represents knowledge according to some semantic scheme or standard method for interpreting the meaning of information. The semantic scheme provides the following:

- A set of hard definitions for *declarative* knowledge, such as facts or data elements.
- A *syntax* or set of rules for the order and manner in which those declarative elements are presented.
- The *procedural* knowledge, such as algorithms or rules of thumb, which will process data elements to make decisions.

Some example components of a systems development methodology (SDM)

Systems Development Life Cycle	System Definition		Design		
Stage Purpose	Feasibility Preparatory study of business purpose, cost/benefit	Requirements Preliminary stmt. and justification of business purpose and concept	High-Level Design Functional description of how system will behave and look	Detailed Design Detailed description of how system will be built—"blueprint"	Code…

System Specification

Documents
Major documents
Supporting documents

Discovery notebooks, working papers (e.g., baseline, design approach, matching matrix, Ishikawa diagrams)

System Design

Major models document (e.g., predicate calculus, dataflows, inheritance graphs)

Analytical/Design Techniques

Discovery sessions
Proof-of-concept prototype(s)
......

This figure shows a few of the key deliverables associated with a knowledge-based software project. Several major premises went into this generalized version of an SDM:

1. Most expert systems applications will be hybrids of both knowledge-based and conventional software. For example, during the system definition phase, the knowledge engineer should allow time to identify the parameters for passing data between expert system and conventional components and extra time to evaluate them during system integration testing (not shown on this partial chart).

2. Most expert system applications will be built by or for ADP shops with an established SDLC. Expert system projects must therefore produce the same major documents and submit to the same budgetary and technical reviews as conventional software projects.

3. Many expert system applications will be integrated with preexisting applications and will therefore be subject to the specialized planning, accounting, and technical requirements imposed by the conventional application projects.

Ultimately, the client organization has the responsibility to monitor and guide the course of each project in their area of interest. Usually, each client organization establishes a standing committee to perform this review process; the committee may have oversight responsibility for a number of simultaneous processes.

Figure 1. A general SDLC showing some documents produced during each phase of a project.

A KNOWLEDGE-BASED SYSTEM EMPLOYS ABSTRACT PROBLEM-SOLVING TECHNIQUES

A knowledge-based system employs abstract problem-solving techniques, and it is often built in a language designed to express techniques like reasoning by analogy and the application of heuristics. Knowledge-based systems do not "know" anything, any more than a FORTRAN program understands mathematics.

For historical reasons, the execution of this logic is referred to as an "inference," and the software in which it is implemented is referred to as "knowledge," which resides in a "knowledge base." Instead of compilers or interpreters, they have "inference engines." Every discipline has its own terminology.

A TYPICAL KNOWLEDGE-BASED SYSTEM HAS THREE PARTS

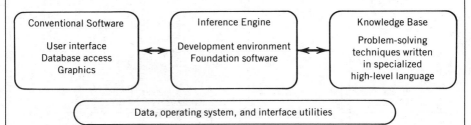

1. A knowledge base, which contains the explicit representation of the problem-solving logic.
2. An inference engine, so-called because it acts as a very sophisticated interpreter that executes the logic in the knowledge base.
3. Conventional components such as a graphical user interface.

As with any application, the "best" language for a given job is the one that offers the best overall match of features, compatability, and efficiency for the particular problem at hand. In fact, several of the development environments for knowledge-based systems are now available in languages like C or FORTRAN.

Two typical problem-solving schemes are frames and production rules. Frames are analogous to data structures and in fact may be implemented as dynamic arrays. They consist of slots, each of which names an object, such as "device," and object attributes, such as "out" or "downstream of B."

Production rules are IF-THEN program statements. In many implementations, recursion is the primary method for controlling program flow.

The inference engine manages the knowledge representation environment much as an interpreter manages the flow of logic through a BASIC program. It updates global and local variables, maintains pointers between programs and objects, and manages cache and buffer memory. Each inference engine offers its own unique set of features such as daemons, program monitors, and stepwise debugging.

Figure 2. A data processing view of knowledge.

THESE TECHNIQUES CAN BE REPRESENTED IN CONVENTIONAL LANGUAGES

The primary advantage of a knowledge-based system resides in its scheme—such as rules or frames—for representing abstract logic. Some languages, such as PROLOG, can represent that logic pretty easily. Other languages, such as C or FORTRAN, require sophisticated and complex constructs to represent some of the logic; in particular, most implementations require extremely complex linked-list arrangements and consequently complicated management software.

For example, a knowledge-based system may employ a heuristic (rule of thumb) stating that, "if a device on a network fails, the next one downstream will lose signal."

Part of a Pascal program implementing that heuristic might be:

```
for I := 1 to next do
begin
  if Device(I).Status = Down then
  begin
    for j :=1 to next do
    begin
      if (Relate(I.J) = DC) and
        (Device(J).Reason = '-- initial state --') then
      begin
        Device(J).Status := AtRisk;
        Device(J).Reason := Concat (Device(I).Name, 'is down.');
      end;
    end;
  end;
end;
```

MOST KNOWLEDGE-BASED SYSTEMS CLEARLY SHOW PROBLEM-SOLVING LOGIC

Even in the trivial example given above, the language obscures the designer's knowledge of network behavior. Knowledge-based system languages, however, are explicitly designed to represent that underlying knowledge. For example, in the M.1 language (from Teknowledge, Inc.), the heuristic can be represented as a production rule:

```
if
device__out = A
and device = B
and B is downstream of A
then signal__B is lost.
```

Obviously, this kind of representation is much clearer than the Pascal program: the code represents the designer's underlying logic, rather than the details of how the data get pushed around. Because of this clarity, this code can become a valuable document in its own right when it captures knowledge that is otherwise difficult to discern.

Figure 2. (*Continued*)

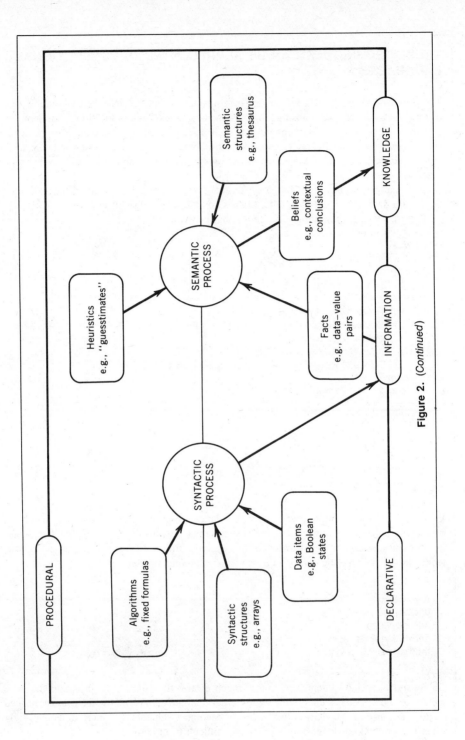

Figure 2. (Continued)

KNOWLEDGE CAN BE TREATED AS AN EXTENDED FORM OF INFORMATION

"Knowledge" can be treated as an extended form of information, just as information can be treated as an extended form of data. Both are based on procedural and declarative elements. The procedural elements define the logic that a system will use in its processes. The declarative elements are either parameters that guide the processes or the entities on which the processes act.

Conventional software operates syntactically; in other words, based on the position and form of the elements involved. Algorithms define the fixed steps for each logical process; programs implement the algorithms in fixed "sentence structures" and reserved instruction words; they moved fixed types of data elements such as integers into and out of ordered arrangements such as arrays.

Conventional systems represent information as data in context with other data. For example, a column of numbers on a tabular report is useless without a label.

Naturally, knowledge-based systems do the same. They do more, however, by projecting information into a more complex semantic relation, according to its use under given circumstances.

Typically, a knowledge-based system will use heuristics or rules of thumb or approximating formulas to process information. For example, a knowledge-based system might classify signal-to-noise ratios into approximate ranges like "high," "medium," or "low," according to different algorithms, depending on the type of signal or brand of radio involved.

THIS PROVIDES SEVERAL ADVANTAGES

A knowledge-based system has three distinct advantages in solving complex problems:

1. The problem-solving logic can be verified directly, since it is explicitly represented in the system's software.
2. Maintenance on a complex knowledge-based system is simpler than a comparable conventional system, because the core logic is explicitly represented all in one place, rather than hidden in a series of algorithms scattered throughout the software.
3. Knowledge-based system techniques include several approaches for accommodating uncertainty or ambiguity in source data.

As a result, a knowledge-based system may reliably and with lower maintenance, process more complex information than a comparable conventional system.

Figure 2. (*Continued*)

Also, a knowledge-based system manages and processes that knowledge according to one of the paradigms developed from research into artificial intelligence. For example, it may treat data and program elements as objects and may employ nonmonotonic logic.

Conventional and knowledge-based software each have their respective advantages. For example, conventional systems usually run faster than expert system applications on conventional hardware, while expert system applications often have very explicit logical structures that make them easy to maintain. Each kind of software can do things the other cannot. This chapter introduces an approach to knowledge acquisition that should help the designer choose those parts of an application that should be built as an expert system and those parts that should be built as a conventional system.

2.2. Participants in the Knowledge Acquisition Process

There are three key players in the knowledge acquisition process, each of whom plays effectively the same role in any systems development:

1. The *knowledge engineer* (KE) or *systems analyst* has the job of accurately and thoroughly describing the knowledge so that the rest of the project team can build a system around it. The KE works directly with the expert or experts during the *discovery sessions*. Also, the KE participates in designing the system. As with any large software effort, an extensive expert system project may employ a number of KEs, each working on some aspect of the problem to be solved, and a senior engineer who coordinates and directs their joint efforts.

2. The *domain expert* must accommodate the demands of normal activities and the demands of the project. Every hour that the expert spends on the project takes time away from his or her primary responsibilities. It is therefore vital that the expert have a fixed and accurate schedule for each session. The expert will almost inevitably have to put in time ''above and beyond the call'' of normal duties. In a project where multiple domain experts are involved, it is important that they have some common ground for working together; they may all have different areas of expertise within the same general field, may work together on a daily basis, or may have a common academic background.

3. The *client organization* has a twofold responsibility: first, to allow the expert time to participate in the project and second, to review and monitor the project's progress. Typically, the client organization establishes a formal process by which they review and accept or reject the results of each stage of a project. This review process relies on the information contained in major project documents, such as those shown in Figure 1. The organization usually assigns one or more individuals to a *review team* to review documents and monitor the course of the project. This review team represents the interests of two critical parts of the client organization: the group of individuals who will use the system and the managers who run the organization.

The KE's key to accomplishing these tasks lies in establishing a working relationship with the project's one or more domain experts. Most often, a *feasibility study* or other preliminary analysis will have been done to identify one or more candidate experts. If not, the current literature provides good examples of how to pick the right expert to work with [1, 4, 10], although his or her characteristics are usually apparent:

- Co-workers usually defer to the expert's judgment on issues relating to some *domain* or area of expertise that is critical to the organization's mission.
- The expert can articulate his or her job in unambiguous and largely nontechnical language.
- The expert is able to spend the necessary time with the KE(s) to develop the expert system.
- The expert can readily adjust to the knowledge acquisition process and to the one or more KEs with whom he or she will work.

2.3. Knowledge Acquisition and the SDLC

The SDLC is the core of a *systems development methodology* (SDM), which defines the following:

- The SDLC, which defines the phases and activities in a project, as they occur over time.
- The specific documents that must be produced at each stage of the system's development.
- The specific systems analysis (knowledge engineering) techniques that will be applied during the project.
- The relation between the knowledge engineer(s), domain expert(s), client organization, and the documents from which they all work.

Most of the "knowledge" that goes into a knowledge-based system is acquired during the first phases of the expert system life cycle. Each phase produces a set of major documents and a set of working documents. The KE uses working documents to support and record his or her analytical activities; they may be included as appendices to the major documents. The major documents summarize the state of the project at each phase and are the prime source of information the client organization uses to monitor and evaluate the project. In the general life cycle shown in Figure 1, the first two of these major documents are the system specification and the system design.

The client organization has the responsibility of reviewing the major documents associated with each system that they will use. If they find fault with the documents' contents, the client organization must work with the KEs to alter either the document or the conduct of the project, as necessary. Ultimately, the client organization must approve each major document before the project can continue from one phase to another.

2.4. A System Specification Defines "What" Not "How"

In the system specification, the KE must describe the behavior of the system, outline the basic knowledge and information the system will process, and discuss the interaction between the expert system and other existing or planned systems.

This chapter discusses only the knowledge acquisition techniques employed during the system specification or design. The KE applies these techniques during the discovery sessions, documents the sessions in the *discovery notebooks*, and records his or her analytical and design decisions in a series of working papers. The KE may include some or all of these findings as appendices to the system specification or design documents.

The system specification is normally preceded by some kind of study or studies, which have led the client organization to believe that they should pursue an expert system project. Typically, preliminary studies include at least *feasibility* and *cost-benefit* analyses, which suggest that it is possible to build the expert system and that it would provide some value to the organization. With luck, the organization will also have prepared a *system concept* or *conceptual design* document, which describes what they want the system to do.

The design document thus contains a description of the major parts of the expert system and some discussion of how they will work. Finally, the detailed design provides the actual "blueprint" from which the system will be built. Figure 3 shows this discovery–documentation–design process.

3. KNOWLEDGE ACQUISITION DURING THE SYSTEM SPECIFICATION

During the system specification, the KE has to (1) find out what the expert does that is valuable and reasonably amenable to automation, (2) outline the knowledge required to do those tasks, (3) validate that it is in fact the knowledge that should be acquired, and (4) verify that the knowledge has been recorded accurately. Having determined which parts of the expert's knowledge are valuable, the KE can select the parts to go into the expert system.

3.1. Job Classification: Finding Out What the Expert Does

The KE's ultimate goal is to define a system that performs certain functions. When working with an expert, the KE has to look at the tasks that the expert performs and translate some of them into functions that the system can perform. When there is no expert, the KE has to evaluate the tasks that need to be done and then translate those into a set of system functions.

The KE's goal in this should be to establish a *global perspective*: a set of terms, graphics, equations, or other descriptions that all parties to the project understand and that can be applied consistently to describing the entire project and its products.

Knowledge acquisition entails three kinds of task:

1. *Discovery* during which the expert works in conjunction with a *systems analyst* or *knowledge engineer* (KE). During the discovery sessions, the expert assumes two active roles. First, he or she provides the knowledge for the system, usually during interviews conducted by the KE. Second, the expert reviews and corrects the documented results of previous sessions.

2. *Documentation* of the discovery sessions and the KE's design decisions. Project documents store the technical and administrative history of a project; almost every important decision relating to the final product relies on this information. Knowledge acquisition directly produces two kinds of documents: *discovery notebooks*, which describe each discovery session, and *working papers*, which describe the KE's technical and design decisions. These documents provide the source material for the *major documents* and supporting documents, as shown in Exhibit 1. Two examples are provided under task 3. These documents are reviewed by the client organization as it monitors the course of the project.

3. *Design*, which transforms the expert's knowledge into a plan for a computer program. Design involves three participants: the KE develops graphical, numerical, or narrative representations of the knowledge as it will appear in the system; the expert examines, comments on, and corrects those representations; and the client organization, for whom the expert works, determines which parts of the knowledge should go into the final system. The KE also has the responsibility for suggesting which parts of the acquired knowledge should go into the system.

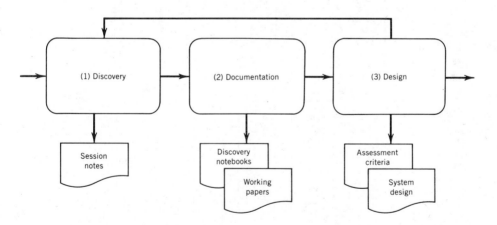

Each task assumes a slightly different character as the expert system project progresses. For example, in the early discovery sessions, the KE tends to ask the expert leading questions, recording the answers for later evaluation [10]. Later, the expert and the KE work closely together, with the expert commenting on and suggesting design approaches to the KE.

Figure 3. Knowledge acquisition tasks.

The KE should provide at least three views of this global perspective:

1. A *graphical description of how the expert's work tasks relate to each other.*
   Naughton [10] suggests that the KE can do this graphically, in particular
   with Ishikawa diagrams. Figure 4 provides an example of a modified Ishikawa diagram, which partially describes a hypothetical expert's knowledge
   of the tasks that he or she performs and shows which tasks are related to
   each other. The KE can develop these interactively with the expert during
   discovery sessions. This technique provides the engineer with an intuitive
   tool for guiding the session: at the start of each session, the expert can review
   and correct the diagrams from the last session, and the KE can continue on
   by filling in any areas that are missing. The highest-level diagram should
   reveal what Chandrasekaran [11, 12] calls ''generic tasks'' or those tasks
   basic to the expert's work.

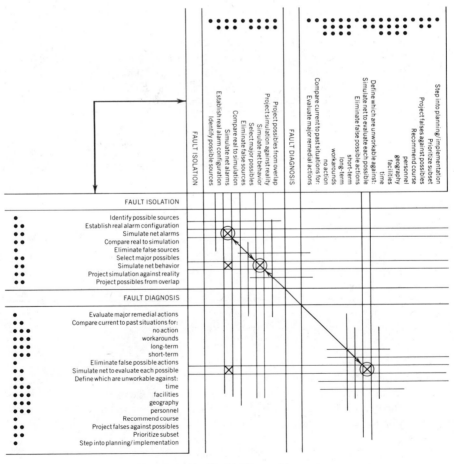

Figure 4. Modified Ishikawa Diagram.

2. A *controlled vocabulary and syntax*, which defines the terminology used in describing what the expert does and what the expert knows. Even knowledge-based systems tend to be vastly intolerant of ambiguity in terms and their use. *Faceted classification* techniques, as described by Batty [13], provide a straightforward means for identifying the major characteristics of an expert's domain or area of expertise. The KE can categorize the various terms used by the expert according to those primary characteristics. These terms are said to be *contained* in the various facets. In the final software, each facet may become a major program variable or object, whose permissible values are defined according to the terms contained in the facet.

3. An identification of *which tasks are amenable to automation*. Naughton [10] describes the use of a *transformation* or *matching matrix* to do this, such as the one shown in Figure 5. As the exhibit shows, some of the tasks performed by a hypothetical expert are so unstructured and unrepeatable that they cannot reasonably be automated. The same expert may also perform a number of very routine tasks, which could conceivably be automated in a very conventional fashion. Lying between these two kinds of tasks is a set of activities that may be amenable to automation in an expert or knowledge-based system. The KE should concentrate on identifying and describing these during the discovery sessions.

In addition, the KE may find it appropriate to develop other fundamental descriptions of how the expert views the organization and its operation. These fundamental views form the basis for the design and are discussed in the next section.

3.2. Outlining an Expert's Knowledge

Expert system software can be organized so that each module of software corresponds to a *chunk* of knowledge. By outlining the different chunks of knowledge that will go into the system, the KE can define the system's basic modules.

Chunk, naturally, is one of those horribly vague terms that KEs do not all agree on. For our purposes, a chunk has several characteristics:

- It can clearly be described according to some formal scheme, especially graphically or mathematically. The Horn clause, a predicate calculus expression described by Clocksin and Mellish [14], can be used to describe a chunk. Of course, chunks are comprised of smaller chunks, so the KE has to pay careful attention to consistently applying his or her particular definition of chunk.

- It is relevant to some task that the expert or the system will perform. For example, a chunk of knowledge might relate to fault isolation.

- It is complete and consistent. For example, a chunk of knowledge might deal with diagnosis. To be complete and consistent, it would have to treat all important aspects of diagnosis in equal depths and could not include components that relate to some other, unrelated task.

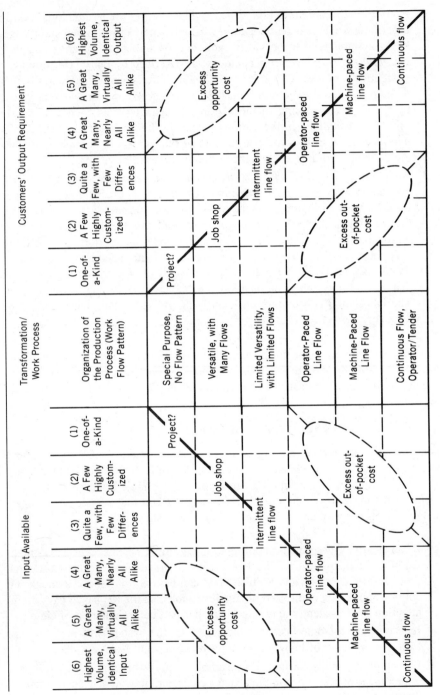

Figure 5.

These characteristics define a chunk as something very much like a software module. As you will see in the next section, chunks do in fact form the basis for expert system modules.

There are at least two steps to outlining an expert's knowledge:

1. Establishing a preliminary *scope* to the knowledge. In practice, this means describing each of the expert's tasks and outlining the knowledge required to do them. Figure 4, for example, outlines some of the procedural and declarative knowledge that a hypothetical expert might use to perform some tasks.

2. Describing some of the expert's knowledge of the *fundamental principles* behind the operation of the expert's world.

Step 1, setting a preliminary scope to the expert's knowledge, is a pretty straightforward systems analysis job, which starts with a description of the expert's work tasks. Figure 4 illustrates the use of an Ishikawa diagram to do this for a hypothetical expert's work tasks. From there, the KE can describe the data sources and data sinks needed for each of the tasks. These descriptions form a basis for determining the expert system's interface and performance requirements.

For example, the KE should identify what computer systems, persons, or other resources the expert uses to gather information is doing a particular task. *Dataflow diagrams* [3, 6] provide an excellent set of graphical tools for this job. In addition, the KE needs to establish a preliminary inventory of the kinds of knowledge the expert uses in performing key tasks. Chandrasekaran [11] and DeSalvo et al. [4] provide different approaches to organizing this preliminary inventory. In particular, Chandrasekaran suggests the use of *generic tasks* to describe what the expert does. For example, it might be feasible to organize an entire set of knowledge into a common classification for fault isolation or diagnosis. Whatever scheme you use,

---

Naughton [10] has suggested that the kind of work an organization does can be defined according to a *matching matrix* such as this one. Lowest on the matrix are those tasks that are continuous; the items they take in are all identical to each other, and the items they turn out are all identical. At the top of the matrix are those tasks that are performed only once; you cannot predict what the inputs or outputs will be ahead of time.

An optimal system matches the nature of its inputs to its outputs for the best possible cost efficiency, while a suboptimal system incurs undue expenses for its users and its owners. For example, a system that receives large quantities of the same type of data and produces exactly the same outputs based on that data is probably optimized to the task at hand. Jamming unstructured data into that system would result in an out-of-pocket cost to reorganize the data prior to input.

Figure 5. Transformation matching matrix. Reproduced by permission of EKS, Inc. Copyright 1986.

remember that these are preliminary judgments and subject to revision during the design stages.

In step 2, establishing some of the fundamental principles at work in the expert's knowledge, the KE can develop an *axiomatic description* of key parts of the knowledge. This approach has several advantages:

1. Axioms comprise a fundamental description of how the expert views his or her world within the client organization.
2. They can be described in the same terminology as the tasks performed by the expert, thereby linking the description of what the expert does to the description of the knowledge needed to do those tasks.
3. They provide an *empirical model* for describing and organizing the expert's knowledge.

Axioms may be described mathematically, logically, or graphically. Figure 9, to be discussed later, introduces the use of the *inheritance graph**, which describes the relationship between logical objects. In this case, it has been used to describe graphically the interaction of declarative and procedural knowledge. Inheritance graphs are a useful design tool and are discussed in the next section.

The KE can get a clear—if abstract—view of the expert's knowledge by identifying the major axioms associated with each of the expert's important tasks. Axioms provide a functional description of the "world" that should be equally understandable to the expert, the KE, and the client organization. Built into an expert system, they provide software for modeling or validating the expert system's information about its environment.

For example, Figure 7 shows a general outline of how a system might use a separate module to capture axiomatic logic. This hypothetical module contains a set of axioms about network behavior, such as the one discussed in Figure 9. Together, these axioms could form a model of the hypothetical network's behavior that other parts of an application could use to verify alarm data, fill-in missing parts of an alarm configuration, or check preliminary diagnostic conclusions.

In the design phase of a project, the KE and expert work together to identify and graph precisely and exhaustively the expert's axiomatic view of the world. These axiomatic descriptions can then serve as the basis for developing more detailed descriptions of the procedural and declarative knowledge used by the expert.

3.3. Preliminary Empirical Validation of Value of Knowledge

The KE can assign a reasonable value to a chunk of knowledge, based on how important it is in doing some task. The expert may be able to assign this value. However, the KE may face a situation where there is no expert, or the expert cannot evaluate how important a particular piece of knowledge is in doing a task.

*also referred to as an *inference graph*

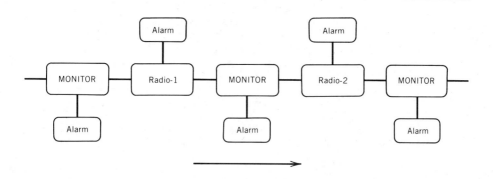

The block diagram above describes a part of a hypothetical network in which a signal flows into a receiver (Radio-1), is forwarded to a transmitter (Radio-2), and retransmitted. The signal is monitored as it comes into and leaves each radio. An event, such as a loss of signal, will set off an alarm specific to that event. For example, the loss of a signal on the receiving side of Radio-1 will cause "Signal-1-Lost" alarm to fire.

This network's behavior can be described by a set of basic axioms, or commonsense rules, that describe the engineer's view of how the laws of cause and effect operate in a network: for example, any device downstream of a failed radio will lose signal.

Each of these axioms, or rules, can be represented in a knowledge base. For example, the M.1 development environment from Teknowledge, Inc. provides a scheme for representing knowledge as a set of IF-THEN production rules.

In M.1, the axiom might look like this:

> if radio-out = A
> and downstream (B, A)
> then signal-lost-at B.

M.1, like PROLOG, operates on pattern matching. M.1's inference engine will search memory for character strings that match the program constructs. Here, it would look first for an entry that matches "radio-out = A," where A can be any string. Failing that, it will fire any rules that can infer the value of "device-out."

For example, if the system received the input "radio-out-radio-1," it would search next for a string that matches the form of the second rule condition. Finding "downstream (radio-2, radio-1)" in memory, the system would conclude or "infer" that "signal-to-lost-at radio-2." That conclusion would be stored in memory and made available to other rules.

Production rules are only one way to represent knowledge in a knowledge-based system: the designer has to choose the right representational scheme for an application and a specific vendor's implementation of that scheme. As with any software project, the developers still have to establish and document conventions for naming variables, using a database, and so on.

Figure 6. A tiny knowledge-based system program.

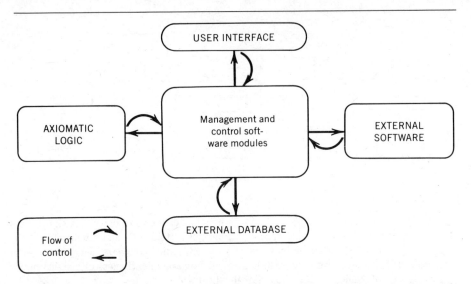

This shows one manner in which an expert system may employ a separate software module that performs axiomatic operations. Any of the other components may be implemented as knowledge-based software. Typically, the axiomatic logic module might implement a heuristic model (e.g., an approximating model of network behavior), specialized control logic (e.g., logic for heuristically searching the one or more likeliest paths for resolving a problem), or logic related to what Chandrasekaran calls a "generic task" (e.g., master methods for diagnosis).

Figure 7. Axiomatic logic as a program module.

In any case, the KE must assign a value to each chunk of knowledge, if for no other reason than to determine a schedule for coding it into the system.

Symbolically, this value can be described as

$$V = (U - C),$$

where V is an economic measure of the software's value to the organization, U is the software's *utility* or usefulness in performing some set of tasks, and C is the cost of implementing that knowledge as a computer program.

The cost C is a relatively straightforward quantity to assess. It consists of the costs for designing, implementing, and operating a particular chunk of knowledge on the system. The economics of software engineering have been covered in the computer science literature, in particular by Boehm [9].

For our purposes, the utility of a chunk of knowledge is a function of the tasks to which it contributes. This chapter cannot go into utility theory. However, we can take a shortcut by defining the utility of knowledge in terms of the number of tasks that cannot be done unless the knowledge is present.

Symbolically,

$$U(K_i) = \sum_{j=1}^{n} P(K_i \mid T_j) * (\text{Value of } T_j),$$

which reads: "Given n tasks, the utility of a chunk i of knowledge equals the sum over j of the product of the probability that chunk i will be used for task j and the value of task j.

In other words, for each chunk of knowledge K, you can:

1. Calculate the probability P that a given chunk of knowledge will be used when the system performs a particular task. If the system uses the knowledge every time it performs the tasks, the probability is 1.00 that this knowledge will be used. The probability can be derived from the case histories and a Bayesian prediction.
2. Determine a value for the task T and multiply T times P to get a result.
3. Repeat the first two steps, deriving a result for each task, T_1 through T_n, that might use that particular chunk of knowledge.
4. Sum all the results. The resulting quantity is the utility U of any given chunk of knowledge K.
5. Repeat steps 1–4 for each K, K_1 through K_i, until the utility for all chunks of knowledge is known.

Some assumptions underlie this example:

- The client organization bears the responsibility for assigning a value to any particular task. Ultimately, the value of a task that the expert or expert system performs is a function of how much good the organization thinks the task will do them. Determining that value can be a complex undertaking involving both tangible and intangible factors.
- This example assumes that all chunks of knowledge are equally *critical*. That is, we have assumed that the system's ability to perform a task will suffer equally no matter what piece of knowledge is missing. In real life, this is not true, but the actual criticality often cannot be determined prior to the system design.
- This description does not take the *volatility* of the knowledge into account. That is, we have assumed that the value of the tasks will not change over time and that the knowledge will remain equally valid over time. In practice, some tasks endure in value much longer than others. Typically, fundamental knowledge, such as axioms, have a very low volatility.
- It assumes that we can calculate directly the odds that any given chunk of knowledge will be used by the system.

For example, one of the KE's key discovery techniques is the elicitation of case histories from the expert. For each case, the KE catalogs each of the tasks that were performed and the knowledge that was used. Naughton [10] provides several explicit techniques for doing this from a transcript of the discovery sessions.

Referring back to Figure 4, one of our hypothetical expert's tasks is *fault isolation*. That task, according to the exhibit, depends on a knowledge of the "ripple effect" caused when one problem spawns others. The client organization might conclude that, for this particular system, the value of a fault isolation function is $20,000; that is, $T_n = 20,000$. The engineer might, in this hypothetical case, turn up the probability that for 2 out of every 100 fault isolations the expert uses the chunk of knowledge about ripple effects; that is, $P(K) = .02$, and therefore, $.02 * 20,000 = 400$.

If the same chunk of knowledge is used in other tasks, its value for each task can be calculated and the individual values totaled. But keep in mind that this is not a legitimate dollar value for a chunk of knowledge. It represents only a "guesstimate" as to its importance to the system.

3.4. Proof-of-Concept Prototypes and Preliminary Validation of Knowledge

During the system specification, the discovery sessions produce the knowledge that will serve as background for the rest of the project. The KE has to verify that the description is accurate but probably will not have enough detailed information to apply formal proofs, such as those provided by *predicate calculus* [14].

The expert, however, can verify this knowledge empirically. Referring back to Figure 3, the expert does this during the discovery sessions.

1. Prior to each working session, the expert reviews the transcript or detailed minutes that describe the previous session and prepares a list of items to be corrected and of topics that were overlooked.
2. Also prior to each session, the expert reviews the KE's working notes and prepares comments on them.
3. During each working session, the expert presents his or her comments to the KE and helps the KE make any necessary corrections.

As noted above, some of the expert's basic principles of operation, or axioms, may be uncovered during the system specification. If the expert does not believe that the KE has clearly, unambiguously, and correctly described those axioms then the KE must provide a more formal analysis of them.

At this stage, a logical or mathematical proof would serve little purpose; it would probably show only whether the axiom is properly phrased, rather than how applicable or useful it might be. A *proof-of-concept prototype* provides a very powerful tool for proving (or disproving) this kind of preliminary logic.

Boehm [9] makes a simple economic point: it costs more to go back and fix a software design mistake than it does to avoid that mistake in the first place, even at the cost of building a software prototype. He states that:

> late corrections involve a much more formal change approval and control process, and a much more extensive activity to revalidate the correction. These factors combine to make the error typically 100 times more expensive to correct in the maintenance phase on large projects than in the requirements phase.

He goes on to state that:

> An even stronger case for the prototype approach can be made for small, informal projects, with their 4–6:1 cost-to-fix increase, and for problem domains in which rapid-prototyping capabilities are available.

These are strong arguments for making an appropriate use of prototypes. But note that, within the context of production applications (government or commercial), ''appropriate use'' generally translates to mean ''controlled, managed, and pre-planned.''

As a result, the most appropriate use of prototypes during the systems definition is in helping to pin down any vague predesign concepts. Ultimately, a proof-of-concept prototype should be done only in those instances where there is a proven, practical need for one. Raw experimentation should be relegated to activities that occur prior to the real start of a project.

As shown in Figure 1, a proof-of-concept prototype is effectively a tiny project within the larger application project. The results of the prototype project must bear directly on some part of the requirements or design phases of the project, or the prototype is of no use in building the larger application.

The KE should ask several key questions about a proof-of-concept prototype: (1) Is there a specific problem that can be resolved by building the prototype? (2) Is there a scheme in place to exercise the prototype and evaluate the findings? (3) Can the cost, schedule, and benefits of the prototype be predefined?

If the answers to any of these questions are too vague, the prototype is probably not worth doing as part of an applications project.

4. KNOWLEDGE ACQUISITION DURING THE DESIGN

The design document describes what a system should do. It is a clear picture of all major system elements, their relation with one another, and the manner in which they are linked. However, except where pseudocode or other low-level descriptions are absolutely needed, the design document should be independent of any programming language, computer hardware, or actual program constructs.

Knowledge acquisition's contribution to this is a clear *abstract representation* of the knowledge that will go into the system and includes at least the following:

- *A Comprehensive Description of the System's Knowledge.* This comprises a set of logical descriptions of the knowledge as opposed to the physical representations that the detailed design covers. These descriptions should be presented together; Figure 1 shows this as the major models document.
- *A Method for Assessing the Behavior of the System.* This provides a scheme for evaluating how well the system is using its internal knowledge; Figure 1 puts this in the assessment criteria document. This document should become an important part of the client organization's larger, more comprehensive plans for testing the system.

4.1. Developing a Comprehensive Description of the System's Knowledge

This description guides the entire system development effort. It covers the knowledge that the system will use and the information it needs to operate.

This description is vital in designing the interfaces between the expert system and other systems and between the knowledge-based components of the system and any conventional components. It covers three critical views of the software that will embody the knowledge:

1. Its *modularity*, or how different chunks of knowledge are grouped together.
2. The *coupling* between modules, or the information that one module transfers to another.
3. The *processing* semantics, or how one module passes control to another.

4.2. Structuring Knowledge as Interdependent Modules

The KE can start this job by organizing the expert's knowledge into two broad areas: (1) knowledge about the expert's environment, such as procedural knowledge of how networks behave or declarative knowledge about the devices on the network, and (2) knowledge of how to work in that environment, such as procedural knowledge of how to perform different diagnostic tasks or declarative knowledge about the usefulness of particular tests or measurements.

Again, the structure of the system should conform to the expert's tasks. For example, Figure 8 shows a dataflow diagram derived from some of the information presented in Figure 4. Figure 8 shows that the fault isolation and network diagnosis task both share a common function that simulates the behavior of the network. In this fictitious case, we have made the assumption that one simulation can support both tasks when the system is built. In reality, of course, few networks lend themselves to a single model.

The expert system based on our example will derive some knowledge of the real world—specifically, of the network—from the simulation. This presents an interesting question: should the design describe a knowledge-based component to perform the simulation or a conventional program?

The KE will have to answer the same question about every part of the system. The answers directly affect the knowledge acquisition process:

- Where components will be implemented as conventional programs, the KE needs to describe how the knowledge-based software will interface to it, what parameters will be passed between the knowledge-based and conventional components, and the performance requirements for the conventional component.
- Where components will be implemented as knowledge-based software, the KE needs to define not only the interface to the module but the component itself.

Knowledge acquisition alone does not provide enough information to make this decision. It requires a careful analysis of the economic, performance, and structural merits of each kind of software. These issues go beyond the scope of this chapter, but keep the following in mind:

- Knowledge-based software usually suffices—that is, produces a nearly right answer most of the time, whereas conventional software optimizes—that is, produces a right answer or no answer at all.
- Conventional software usually executes instructions more quickly than knowledge-based software but often has to execute exhaustively many more instructions.
- The process of transferring control between conventional and knowledge-based components requires considerably more computer resources than transferring control between software components of the same type.

Inheritance graphs, such as the one in Figure 9, describe the structure of knowledge-based software in much the same way that structure charts describe conventional software. Each inheritance graph represents a *function*—a software component that emulates a particular chunk of knowledge.

Inheritance graphs are *empirical models*; that is, they present a nonprocedural view of the system that the client organization, the expert, and the KE can all agree on, even though the model may not be numerically precise.

For example, Figure 9 describes two functions and their relation. The graphs show the *objects* employed by each function, some of the values those objects may take on, and the *inheritance* of values between objects. The top graph, labeled Model, describes a *heuristic model* of the ripple effect described in Figure 6. The bottom graph, labeled Interface, describes a function that uses the model. Referring back to Figure 7, the actual software might implement Interface as a calling routine for the model.

Inheritance graphs provide an *object-oriented* representation of software in which vertical lines represent the objects. A line that crosses between functions indicates a shared object. For example, both functions share the object Alarm-Signal-1.

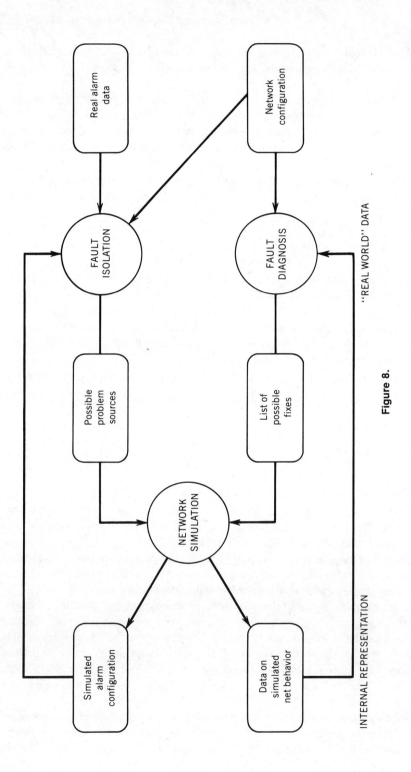

Figure 8.

292

Each line has a label at the top or bottom showing the name of the object it represents. For example, the physical object Radio-1 and the logical object Conclusion.

The circles and arrows define *inheritance*. The circles represent an object's value. An arrow shows the direction of inheritance from source object to the destination. For example, if Signal-1 is "lost," then Alarm-Signal-1 is "on." An empty circle indicates an unknown value. Boxes on the arrows indicate a *transform* operation, where the appearance of one value in an object causes a different value to appear in another object. For example, an unknown value in the object Signal-Test will cause the value "lost" to be instantiated in several other objects.

Boolean operators indicate how the collection or distribution of values takes place. In this example, the operator OR indicates that the transform may instantiate the value "lost" into one or more objects.

Inheritance graphs organize collections of functions into *modules* or *structures*. Modules are *bounded* in their ability to interact with other modules. One module can access another through only one entrance and one exit, for example, by passing values into the module through the object Signal-Test and extracting values through the object Signal-Test-Result.

Typically, modules should not comprise more than about seven functions. Also, a typical module should not have more than two or sometimes three *layers*.

Layers occur where shared objects terminate. For example, in Figure 9, an external module can share the object Signal-Test, but the Model function does not. Therefore, the module has two layers: the one where the shared object Signal-Test terminates and the one where the shared object Signal-1 terminates.

Layers can also define the break between knowledge-based and conventional software components. For example, the value of Signal-Test-Results could be displayed on a screen, printed, or processed by a conventional program. By the same token, the knowledge-based Model software in Figure 9 could be replaced by a conventional program. In both cases, the objects that form the entrance and exit to a knowledge-based module can represent software variables that pass parameters between conventional and knowledge-based components.

This diagram illustrates one hypothetical process in which an expert system collects data and compares that data to its own "knowledge"—in this case, the system's internal representation of how the real-world "should" act, as embodied in a simulation of part of that real world. This illustration fits the previous examples in that (1) the "network simulation" could have been defined according to the Ishikawa diagram discussed earlier, and (2) the simulation could properly be implemented as a knowledge-based program employing axiomatic logic about the behavior of some (hypothetical) network.

The inheritance graph discussed later in this chapter, presents an object-oriented approach to representing the data as values on objects that correspond to actual network components.

Figure 8. Dataflows for three chunks of knowledge.

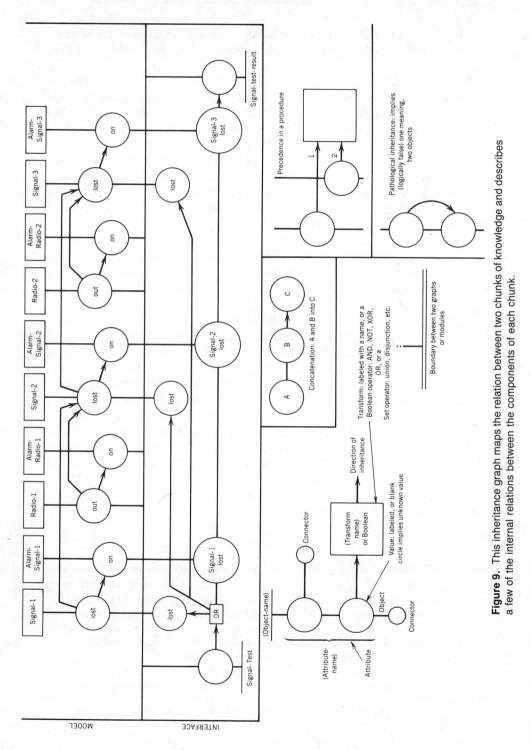

Figure 9. This inheritance graph maps the relation between two chunks of knowledge and describes a few of the internal relations between the components of each chunk.

294

Properly structured inheritance graphs must then have the following attributes:

- *Bounded.* A module has only one entrance and one exit. The paired graphs in Figure 9 obey this limit. Typically, a transform can be represented by a tightly coupled set of Horn clauses [13].
- *Regular.* A graph describes all inheritances unambiguously; for example, all transforms and inheritances have either a single source or a single destination. An inheritance that takes place between two values on a single object always interposes an object or transform between the two values.
- *Visible.* A graph should clearly represent all relations and inheritances that occur in the software. It should support other means of describing the same relation between objects, particularly with predicate calculus.

4.3. Developing a Method for Assessing the Behavior of the System

The system assessment criteria apply primarily to the system's knowledge base and its supporting software. For example, they would apply to the Application and Axiomatic Logic parts of the system described by Figure 7 but not to the External Software. These criteria provide an important part of the performance standards for the system as a whole. Together with conventional benchmarks, the assessment criteria yield a clear description of the system's behavior. In particular, assessment criteria measure the *integrity* of the knowledge base—that it properly performs all the functions of the design. Typically, assessment criteria should at least differentiate between flaws in design and in the implementation of the knowledge base.

For the most part, anyone familiar with software validation and validation techniques ought to be able to outline a reasonable set of expert system assessment criteria: for example, a set of sample inputs and outputs to the system, qualitative references for evaluating the user interface, and a list of key variables—objects—to record during system testing.

However, because of their complexity, expert systems are prone to *brittleness*—a vast intolerance of errors in data or processes. Even our simple examples have shown that a change in the value of one object may trigger a series of complex inheritances. In this environment, even a minor error has a lot of leverage; it may start a chain reaction that will bring the system down or cause it to start executing the wrong functions. The latter can be insidious, in that the operation of the system may appear normal until it has generated a whole set of false outputs.

Therefore, the KE needs to specify a set of criteria that will help (1) identify brittleness in the system and (2) indicate whether the source of error is in the design or the code. Ultimately, the KE cannot escape the need to walk through the system model, trying every reasonable configuration of system input and manually calculating the associated outputs. However, the KE does not have to generate every conceivable input to the system; the important inputs result from an analysis of those tasks that the client organization will expect the system to perform.

With luck, the expert can provide case histories of actual operations. Otherwise, the KE will have to project test data. Ultimately, the result comprises a set of data showing, for each task, the data that enter the system and the data that the system puts out.

In practice, these data can be very complex. In network applications, for example, the timing of an input can greatly affect its use by the system.

However, let us expand on the relatively simple example of a simulation task. The inputs to this fictitious system might come from the user or another process, indicating that one or more devices had changed state: for example, that Signal-1 was "lost." As Figure 9 shows, the input would travel through the object Signal-Test, while the output would travel through the object Signal-Test-Result and contain Signal-1-Lost, Signal-2-Lost, and Signal-3-Lost. We can also see that an input showing Signal-2 as "lost" would produce the output Signal-2-Lost and Signal-3-Lost.

This exercise reveals two things: the vocabulary terms that appear in the input and output and the number of inheritances generated by each input. From this information, the KE can construct at least two sets of important assessment criteria:

1. An ordered list of the cases that will cause the most inheritances to occur. The simplest scheme for deriving this list generates a "score" for each case, based on the number of inheritances it generates. These cases provide a useful basis for testing whole modules of software; in combination, they can help test the entire system when a new module comes on-line.

2. A selected sample of cases that represent the normal workload. This can be particularly helpful when the KE only has a few accurate case histories with which to work. Rather than exhaustively trapping case histories, the KE can first develop a normal distribution of input terms by counting their occurrence during cycles of a work task and then use terms from the middle and end points of the distribution curve to "score" the case histories that do exist.

These, of course, are not formal methods in that they are not mathematically exhaustive. However, they do cut down on the KE's potential workload.

This process supports an *iterative refinement* of the software model: the walk-throughs will demonstrate flaws in the model, which the KE can repeatedly modify, correct, and reorganize. The KE should feel comfortable with a software model that successfully supports the same case histories that will test the system.

In addition to the case histories, the assessment criteria should include the following:

• Subjective or qualitative criteria for evaluating the system. For example, the terms and order of questions put by the system to the user can be very important in some applications.

• Internal test data. For example, walk-throughs should indicate the values that some objects will take on during a given function for a given case. The programmer can monitor these values while debugging programs.

- A list of unknown object values and the instances where they occur. For example, Figure 9 does not specify the value of Signal-Test that triggers the instantiation of ''lost.''

5. CONCLUSION

This chapter has introduced several key concepts:

- The KE can decide what knowledge to acquire by evaluating the tasks performed by an expert.
- Expert systems that enter production environments must coexist with conventional systems and conventional data processing practices.
- There is a reasonable economic basis for determining the value of different kinds of knowledge.

In addition, we have looked at a few key techniques for putting these concepts into action:

- Analysis of the expert's work, particularly with the aid of Ishikawa diagrams and faceted classification techniques.
- Establishing a common frame of reference—global perspective—that the client organization, the domain expert, and the KE can all agree on, starting with the basic principles or axioms that the expert employs to describe the essential nature of his or her world.
- Describing the system's structure in a formal way, without reference to the actual language or development environment in which the system will be implemented, using the inheritance graph as a key design technique.

As we discussed at the start of this chapter, the body of technique presented here is not all-inclusive: many people are making continuous and substantive additions to the knowledge engineering field. We have tried to introduce a few practical techniques that apply to building expert systems in a production environment with the aid of human experts.

GLOSSARY

ADP. Automated data processing—a familiar term covering almost any job that has to do with computers.

Attribute. Classes of values that may be applied to an object, for example, color, model, and year of the object car. Usually, objects of a subclass inherit the attributes of the objects that define their class; for example, all birds have feathers. In practice, an object–attribute–value tuple in a knowledge-based system (KBS) can often be matched to a relation–attribute–value tuple in a relational database. Theoretically, an attribute may be declarative (e.g., a data element) or procedural (e.g., a program that produces a value for that attribute).

Axiom. Basic principle of a model that either guides or is used to interpret the behavior of a system—the highest level of logic in a knowledge-based system. In practice, an axiom is usually represented as a single heuristic and is a primary component of an empirical model—for example, describing one aspect of the behavior of a network model.

Behavior. The external manifestations of a system's processes. Behavior is the correspondence between inputs to the system and its outputs, usually expressed as a series of probabilities: for example, given configuration X of inputs and the expected output Y, $f(X) = P(Y)$.

Bounded. The property of having known limits: for inheritance graphs, the property of having only one entrance or exit to a graph or set of graphs.

Brittleness. An inability to tolerate faulty data or processes, a tendency to exhibit different levels of tolerance at different times, and serious outward manifestation of a bug, which shows up as a spurious or null conclusion. Brittleness can result from poorly designed inheritance in complex, unstructured systems.

Case history. Known example of input–process–output operation of a system that will be consistently valid under specified conditions.

Client organization. The organization that uses a system; usually the group that pays for and oversees the project to develop a system.

Compiled knowledge. Unwieldy term for a set of heuristics that operate in accord with several models at the same time; a heuristic that is only valid if one or more unstated assumptions are true.

Criticality. A rating for how important a particular chunk of knowledge is to the system; the probability that a task will abort or give a spurious result if a chunk of knowledge is absent. Criticality is a key indicator for the chunks of knowledge that prevent the system from exhibiting brittleness.

Daemon. A software module that becomes active when some predefined set of system conditions occur. It is usually not called directly by other modules.

Declarative. A value for an object or data item that a knowledge-based system assumes to be true; a value that is not subject to revision once it has been instantiated into a variable.

Design. The formal representation of a system; specifically, graphical, mathematical, and narrative descriptions of a system's inputs, outputs, structure, and behavior. A design is usually presented in several stages, from one showing preliminary concepts, to one showing the final product in exacting detail. This list becomes a blueprint for building the system.

Destination. Inheritance graphs describe the movement of values from a source object to a destination object.

Discovery. The process of finding all the raw "knowledge" that may go into a knowledge-based system. Most often, discovery refers to working with a human expert to uncover his or her knowledge.

Documentation. The written and pictorial descriptions of a project: its activities, products, and decisions.

Expert system. A form of knowledge-based system, built to solve essentially the same kinds of problems as a human expert would solve. It operates within much more limited environments and responds to much more limited circumstances than a human being but nonetheless can provide great value to a company where some particular, narrow capabilities are both rare and badly needed.

Function. A process performed by a system to complete a task. Function is a general term for the action a system takes to transform information from one form to another. In a knowledge-based system, a function is a software component that embodies a particular chunk of knowledge.

Heuristic. A rule of thumb, a procedure for processing information at the abstract or analogical level, an algorithm that produces the right answer most of the time rather than all of the time.

Heuristic model. A model that approximates the behavior of some logical or physical process; a collection of heuristics about the behavior of an object or event; a model of a system based on an analogous or abstract representation of the system.

Horn clause. A particular, limited form of clause in predicate calculus, which may have multiple clauses and multiple predicates—for example, $a:-b, c, d$.

Inference engine. Foundation software that underlies a knowledge-based system. An inference engine is usually implemented as a complex interpreter under a knowledge representation scheme, for example, the utility software that evaluates the production rules in a knowledge base.

Inheritance graph. A directed graph showing the inheritance and transformation of values between objects. An inheritance graph is useful in the iterative refinement of knowledge structures. Also known as *inference graph*.

Instantiate. To apply a value to an object. Instantiate is a software function that moves a value into a variable or area of memory that represents an object.

Integrity. A characteristic of a knowledge base wherein the knowledge base is (1) properly structured, (2) complete, and (3) bug-free.

Knowledge base. In a knowledge-based system application, the software that executes knowledge-based problem-solving techniques—for example, the production rules and facts in a rule-based knowledge-based system.

Knowledge-based system. A system that models certain kinds of associative, heuristic, or semantic logic. Most commonly, it employs frames, production rules, uncertainty, nonmonotonic logic, and object-oriented representation.

KE. Acronym for knowledge engineer.

Knowledge engineering. Directly akin to systems analysis, knowledge engineering comprises two jobs: (1) defining and organizing the knowledge that will go into a knowledge-based system and (2) developing a system design for the knowledge-based system.

Knowledge representation. The syntactic and semantic standards for representing problem-solving techniques in a particular knowledge-based system, for example, frames and rules.

Life cycle. See **Systems development life cycle.**

Major documents. Documents used by an organization to review the status or conduct of a project, for example, schedules and completed designs.

Module. A collection of system functions that serve a single purpose. Properly structured inheritance graphs provide one entrance and one exit to a module.

Nonmonotonic logic. A scheme of logic where conclusions are not fixed but may change to accommodate new facts or arguments. This logic permits different competing conclusions about the same set of circumstances or facts and employs rules for accommodating ambiguity or conflicts among conclusions.

Object. A logical software entity that may correspond to a relation–attribute–value tuple in a relational database; an untyped, autonomous variable that may represent one or more values or a software function that returns one or more values.

Payback. Ultimate value of a system, application, or product over its useful life. Payback can be predicted based on the probability of the product being useful or successful.

Predicate calculus. A mathematical notation for representing formal logic, principally as a set of well-formed formulas (wffs).

Procedural logic. Any part of a knowledge-based system that represents (1) a set of conditions and (2) a set of actions to be taken on the fulfillment of those conditions. Procedural logic does not necessarily imply serial execution of instructions; for example, daemons and the associated parameters that cause them to execute are procedural logic.

Properly structured. Complete, coherent, and consistent; an inheritance graph that describes only single entry or exit points for interfaces, only single changes in value for any one transform, and no inheritance between values on one object.

Regular. Unambiguous; a properly structured inference graph in that it has no ambiguous inheritance or complex transforms.

SDLC. Acronym for systems development life cycle.

Semantic. A relation defined by the meaning of the things being related; specifically, a scheme for dynamically assigning relations between objects according to their values. For example, a knowledge-based system may dynamically establish one set of relations for the object ''signal'' if its value is a signal-to-noise ratio, and a different set of relations if its value is ''lost.''

Simulation. A prediction of how a system will behave under certain circumstances. For the same inputs, simulation yields the same outputs as the system and may exhaustively mimic the actual workings of a system or present a sufficiently close analogy.

Source. Inheritance graphs describe the movement of values from a source object to a destination object.

Structure. In most cases, the same thing as a module; a discrete set of programs that serve one purpose and have only one entrance and one exit through which to pass values to other structures.

Systems analysis. The process of identifying, describing, and organizing all elements of a system, leading first to a design for the system; the process of analyzing the behavior or quality of an existing or planned system.

Systems analyst. Technical person who performs systems analysis; someone who is responsible for a particular part of a large systems analysis.

System assessment criteria. Specific technical measures against which the behavior of the knowledge base may be judged. These criteria are described in the system assessment criteria document.

System design. The process and documentation that describe how a system will work. It usually comprises at least a high-level and a detailed design.

Systems development life cycle (SDLC). The series of major stages in the orderly development of software, each of which is associated with a set of documents and tasks that must be produced before the next stage can begin.

System specification. The process and document that describe the functional aspects of a system—that is, what it should do rather than how it should accomplish the functions.

Task. Some job that a human being or a computer system can perform; a bit of work that can be quantified according to how long it will take, its prerequisites, and its value. A task may consist of subsidiary tasks.

Transform. The general term for a function that changes a value as that value is inherited from one object to another; the function that causes a value to be inherited from one object to another. A transform is represented by a box on an inheritance graph.

Utility. A measure of the usefulness of the knowledge in an expert or knowledge-based system; a combination of the value of the tasks that the system may be able to perform by using that knowledge and the long-term value of the knowledge as a capital asset.

Value. Benefits to the organization of a system or application after the organization has paid for using it. Mathematically, value is defined as $V = (U - C)$, where value V and cost C are real economic measures and U is some marginal utility that can include both tangible and intangible measures.

Volatility. The usefulness of a chunk of knowledge over time. Low volatility implies that the knowledge will be useful for a long time; fundamental or deep knowledge, such as axioms, generally has a low volatility.

Working documents. Documents generated by members of a programming project for their own internal use, for example, notes on design or internal memoranda.

ACKNOWLEDGMENT

Like most people in the data processing industry, I spend a lot of time talking over ideas and experiences with my colleagues. In a sense, the only *really* fair acknowledgment to this chapter would include my thanks to everyone with whom I have ever worked. Obviously, that is not a practical option, but there are a few folks right at the top of my list.

I would especially like to thank my chain of command at MCI Telecommunications Corporation, who were both encouraging and helpful: Dan Walters, VP; Kay Duggan, Director; Tom Onasch, Senior Manager; and Mike Jones, Manager.

A special thanks should go to Bradley Utz, my colleague at MCI. Brad is a fine mathematician, who contributed greatly to this chapter. He spent a good amount of his own time brainstorming with me about the right way to express the mathematical concepts presented here. In addition, he sat down one day and whipped up an expert system in Pascal that corresponds to one I wrote in Teknowledge's M.1 package. A piece of the source code from that program appears in Exhibit 6.

Certainly, Jay Liebowitz has to get credit for being a patient editor, who never cracked under the strain of missed deadlines. And, finally, I want to thank Jim Naughton, who let me draw on his significant background work in productivity evaluation, and David Batty, whose work on classification theory has been most useful.

REFERENCES

1. F. Hayes-Roth, D. A. Waterman, and D. B. Lenat, *Building Expert Systems*, Addison-Wesley, Reading, MA, 1983.
2. W. J. Clancey, Knowledge Acquisition for Classification Expert Systems, Stanford University Heuristic Programming Project Working Paper (HPP 85-18), July 1984.
3. T. DeMarco, *Structured Analysis and System Specification*, Yourdon, New York, 1979.
4. D. A. De Salvo, A. E. Glamm, and J. Liebowitz, Structured Design of an Expert System Prototype at the National Archives. In *Expert Systems for Business*, B. G. Silverman (ed.), Addison-Wesley, Reading, MA, 1987.
5. P. W. Metzger, *Managing a Programming Project*, Prentice-Hall, Englewood Cliffs, NJ, 1973.
6. E. Yourdon and L. L. Constantine, *Structured Design*, Prentice-Hall, Englewood Cliffs, NJ, 1979.
7. R. W. Jensen and C. C. Tonies, *Software Engineering*, Prentice-Hall, Englewood Cliffs, NJ, 1979.
8. M. V. Zelkowitz, A. C. Shaw, and J. D. Gannon, *Principles of Software Engineering and Design*, Prentice-Hall, Englewood Cliffs, NJ, 1979.
9. B. W. Boehm, *Software Engineering Economics*, Prentice-Hall, Englewood Cliffs, NJ, 1981.
10. M. J. Naughton, *Acquiring Expert Knowledge to Build Applied Expert Systems*, unpublished, Expert-Knowledge Systems, Inc., McLean, VA, 1987.

11. B. Chandrasekaran, Generic Tasks in Knowledge-Based Reasoning: High-Level Building Blocks for Expert System Design, *IEEE Expert*, Fall 1986.

12. S. B. Mittal. Chandrasekaran, and J. Sticklen, Patrec: A Knowledge-Directed Database for a Diagnostic Expert System, *IEEE Computer*, Vol. 17, No. 9, September 1984.

13. C. D. Batty, Origins and Development of Faceted Classification, report prepared for the Language of Data Project, Systems Development Foundation, 1983.

14. W. F. Clocksin and C. F. Mellish, *Programming in PROLOG*, Springer-Verlag, New York, 1984.

DISTRIBUTED EXPERT SYSTEMS: FACILITY ADVISOR

Barry G. Silverman

Institute for Artificial Intelligence, George Washington University, Washington, DC

Henry H. Hexmoor, Ravi Rastogi, and Joseph Chang

IntelliTek, Inc., Rockville, Maryland

1. INTRODUCTION

This chapter describes design considerations, progress to date, and next steps for developing a set of cooperating expert systems called the FACILITY ADVISOR that can support real-time operations, off-line planning, and adaptive behavior at facilities in general and at spacecraft ground facilities in particular. The focus of the FACILITY ADVISOR is to support the distributed problem protocols and behavior that traditional expert systems technology tends to ignore. The goal is to build a FACILITY ADVISOR shell that (1) consists of a number of validated, skeletal elements that can be tailored to the individual supervisory positions at any facility, (2) can support the distributed problem-solving aspects of these jobs, and (3) can successfully be extended (or integrated with any previously existing stand-alone supervisory expert system) to support the stand-alone nondistributed supervisory control problems encountered at that position.

Because of the relative newness of distributed expert system (DES) technology and the no-risk requirement of facility operations, a DES testbed activity for the FACILITY ADVISOR is described. Whether or not all the goals of the FACILITY ADVISOR can be met, the testbed is also expected to provide, at a minimum, a DES training ground, lessons learned, how-to-do-it manuals, and insights into integrating DESs into facility operations and planning activities.

An increasing number of facilities exist where a semiautomated process is operated and controlled by a team of human supervisory operators. For example, in a typical telecommunications network, three main facilities include (1) an orbit facility that has orbit equations concerning all orbiting platforms and that is the source of raw orbit information needed to support each spacecraft acquisition event; (2) a telecommunications control center that receives spacecraft acquisition schedule requests from various users (customers), which it in turn merges with raw orbit data to generate a message that the ground terminal can use to "acquire" the spacecraft at the appropriate time, location, and frequency; and (3) a telecommunications ground terminal that error checks incoming acquisition messages and, if they pass acceptability tests, proceeds to acquire the appropriate spacecraft at the scheduled interval. In each of these facilities, there is a hierarchy of human-staffed positions, each responsible for a subset of the overall task of running the process.

This chapter describes a set of expert systems (ESs) to be researched, built, and connected as a DES. The intent is to show a generic expert system approach (1) to certain classes of human supervisory positions commonly encountered in many facilities (e.g., facility schedulers, workstation operators, and facility hardware/software fault detection positions) and (2) to create a cooperating set of expert systems designed to operate in a loosely coupled hierarchy (i.e., a DES) that can serve as a FACILITY ADVISOR. The FACILITY ADVISOR is a set of ES kernels that potentially can be tailored to any facility. An overview of this chapter can be offered in terms of three principal areas of activity:

1. *Cognition and Protocol Analysis Studies.* The extensive results to date in studying human operators' protocols in ground facilities are being incorporated and extended, particularly in terms of adaptive problem-solving protocols that support the "telescience" concept.

2. *Logical Model of the DES.* The protocol and cognitive results have been formulated into an idealized facility level blackboard ES. The logical model as described in this chapter provides design guidelines for (1) each of the over one dozen components of that ES, (2) how these components interact on both an intra- and interfacility level, and (3) an idealized dual-calculi approach wherein real-time operations are supported by fast ESs and planning functions are off-loaded to more powerful plausible reasoning expert systems.

3. *Physical Implementation: DES Prototype Testbed.* Several of the key elements of the logical model have already been implemented on the VAX and LISP machine. These are explained as are the set of tasks anticipated to research and extend the prototype fully into a generic FACILITY ADVISOR that holds the potential to be used at actual facilities.

Because of the research nature of the FACILITY ADVISOR, it is hoped that it can serve as a training ground for new knowledge engineers and a testbed for demonstrating and teaching how ESs and DESs may be created. For each of the three areas of research just mentioned, a set of items are being generated that provide (1) how-to-do-it handbooks, (2) good design examples that can be emulated, (3) discussion of tools that have proved useful in the various knowledge engineering steps, and (4) lessons learned in the DES arena.

1.1. Hierarchical Framework Definition

Numerous metaphors exist in which *decentralized, loosely coupled* collections of entities *cooperate* in task execution and result syntheses. The entities *cooperate* in the sense that none of them has sufficient information to solve the entire problem and mutual sharing of information is necessary to allow the groups as a whole to produce an answer or result. By *decentralized*, it is meant that both control and data are logically and often spatially distributed; there is neither global control nor global data storage. There is often a *hierarchy* in which control is delegated along with subtasks responsibility. Finally, *loosely coupled* means that individual entities are free to spend more time in computation than in communication.

For example, the human brain is organized into a hierarchy, each level of which performs higher and higher mental functions:

1. The human brain is hypothesized to be a composite structure consisting of at least three layers: (a) a reptilian brain that provides basic reflexes and instinctive responses; (b) an old mammalian brain that is more sophisticated and capable of emotions and delayed responses; and (c) a new mammalian brain that can imagine, plan, and manipulate abstract symbols. The outer layers inhibit and modulate the more primitive tendencies of the inner layers.

2. Within each layer a hierarchy of distributed intelligent nodes is connected to each separate sensory–motor system. These become increasingly interrelated at the higher levels and eventually merge into a unified command and control structure. This enables a complex organism to coordinate its actions in pursuit of high-level goals.

It seems clear that intelligent human behavior is not achieved by one large "routine" but by numerous, small, distributed, and independent centers of intelligence working in harmony with each other.

By the same token, one could envision a FACILITY ADVISOR as a hierarchy of several levels with multiple, stand-alone nodes of intelligence distributed throughout each level. Figure 1 illustrates how the FACILITY ADVISOR will capture this distributed characteristic. The three lowest layers are what exist at present-day automated facilities, while the two higher layers are staffed by humans employed in these facilities. While many facilities are currently sponsoring stand-alone ES projects to support one or the other of the "example station positions," there is no attempt at present to approach the facility as a complete unit, which in fact it is.

As shown in Figure 1, the bottom three layers of a facility (i.e., existing automation, existing sensors/actuators, and actual facility hardware/software) can be viewed as corresponding to the reptilian brain, sensory system, and motor parts (body), respectively. These three levels already exist at various facilities (such as NASA Goddard Space Flight Center) as the automatic control execution and feedback and system parts.

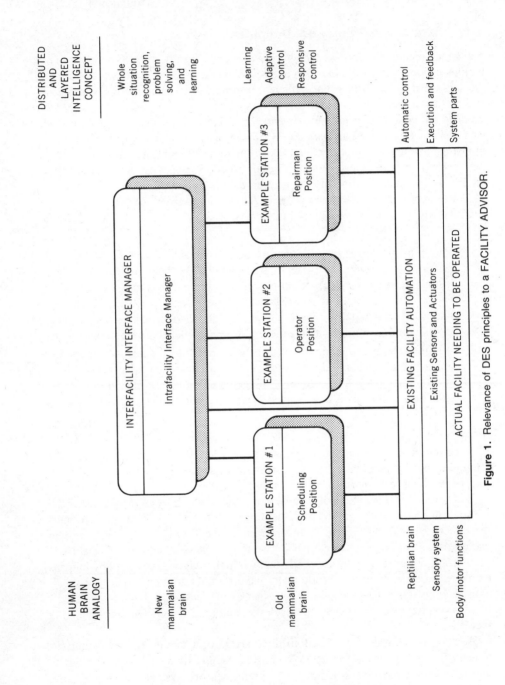

Figure 1. Relevance of DES principles to a FACILITY ADVISOR.

The goal of the FACILITY ADVISOR is to implement DES technology corresponding to the two upper layers. The two higher levels are not simply a collection of three or four stand-alone ESs. Like brain level counterparts, each of the four boxes (MANAGER plus three example stations) in fact contain a *set* of specialized but cooperating ESs each capable of performing a single, intelligent function.

1.2. Distributed Expert Systems

At this point it is useful to extend the DES capabilities discussion to a general view of DES advantages and disadvantages. This will hopefully set the stage for the reader to understand some of the research issues and motivations involved with any DES or hierarchy of ESs that might be attempted. To begin with, several of the potential advantages of a DES approach are summarized in the top half of Table 1. In short, DESs are achieved by relaxing central control, eliminating global knowledge, and permitting entities to select the tasks on which they will work. If this is carried too far, the individual entities could begin to encounter any of several pitfalls listed in the bottom half of Table 1 along with selected solution techniques.

The items in Table 1 have served to highlight a few of the reasons for choosing a DES approach and a few of the research questions that need to be considered carefully in order to build an effective DES such as a FACILITY ADVISOR. More will be said on each of these items in ensuing sections. At this point, it seems fruitful to introduce one final issue: the role of blackboards in a DES.

Traditionally, well-structured programs exhibit high degrees of modularity where each module performs a specific task. An important distinction, however, is the manner in which control is passed to perform a given task. Decentralized control is an essential feature of a system able to decompose a problem before it solves it.

To understand this distinction, it is useful to envision a trend from traditionally designed distributed software programs to DESs. For the sake of clarity, DESs will be discussed as a range from blackboard ESs to full DESs as displayed across the top of Table 2. The ESs focused on here are the more sophisticated because they use blackboards (e.g., HEARSAY II) for communicating knowledge between individual specialist ESs. ES nodes of fully decentralized DESs are generalists rather than specialists and all entities can perform any tasks.

Briefly, it can be seen that blackboard ESs impose less certainty in the control structure than traditional designs. One of the reasons to build blackboard ESs is to allow different points of view from different specialists to be aired, hypotheses to be tested, and conclusions to be reached on the basis of the best available (and uncertain) information. Despite the power of this approach, experiments have shown that it leads to potentially redundant and unnecessary processing and the formulation of answers that are ultimately rejected. This is a redundancy that, if not carefully controlled, can be deleterious to the speed and ability of real-time applications.

In the same context, fully decentralized DESs allow entities at different levels full freedom of choice in not only who to task but for whom they will work. The result is entities receiving commands from higher-level entities and deciding which task assignment to pursue. This permits busy nodes to shed workload and idle ones to pick up the slack. Finally, since an entity possesses internal metaknowledge, it will not process a task assignment it "knows" it cannot do well.

The lesson of this discussion is to permit multiple types of control ranging from centralized to fully decentralized DESs as appropriate to the application. It is possible also to consider an adaptive (learning) mechanism that can dynamically determine the appropriate combination: for example, an entity might start out fully decentralized and through experience recognize either a few specialists or possibly one it should always return to with a given problem. Empirical studies for each application will be necessary to determine which forms of control (three from Table 2 plus the adaptive) are most appropriate. An adaptive technique is elaborated in Section 1.3.3.

1.3.   Goals for the FACILITY ADVISOR

One of the goals for the FACILITY ADVISOR* is to explore how three worthy design guidelines can successfully be integrated.

1.3.1.   *Supervisory Controller Position (SCP) Expert Systems.*   Many of the ground operations personnel are employed at automated workstations. The person plus the workstation comprise three levels of intelligence at the position: one human supervisor plus two computerized lower levels of intelligence (see Figure 1). For convenience of discussion, all three level positions shall be referred to as SCPs: the reader can mentally replace the term SCP with any other word (e.g., scheduler, operator, analyst, or command controller). ESs built for facilities, be they stand-alone ESs or part of a DES, must carefully be integrated into the SCP tripartite if they are to be useful as suggested by the communication control lines in Figure 2.

1.3.2.   *Cooperative Interdependent Behavior.*   While most SCPs have relatively well-defined areas of responsiblity, in order to do their job they must interface and cooperate with other SCPs. For example, within a given facility there are generally at least three (and often many more) interacting positions: (1) the scheduler, who decides when equipment and other resources may be allocated to support each user, (2) the operator, who uses the resources to perform a user-requested service and who detects and corrects quality problems of the end product (e.g., message code errors and data set noises) by obtaining inputs from the equipment monitor to assist in problem isolation tasks, and (3) an equipment monitor, who detects and isolates equipment and resource problems and either corrects them

---

*It should be noted that not all elements of the FACILITY ADVISOR DES will be ESs. Some elements will use non-ES forms and algorithms of artificial intelligence (AI), and other elements will be objects, frames, and/or databases. The acronym DES, however, will be used in this chapter to encompass all the elements.

TABLE 1 Advantages and Research Issues of the DES Approach

Benefits of DES

Increased Reliability and Flexibility. Achieved through redundancy in communication paths and DES entities and through the modularity of design (which permits incremental addition of new entities and communication paths).

Enhanced Real-Time Response. Achieved through parallelism and through the placement of of DES entities near sensing devices and devices to be controlled.

Lower Communication Costs. Achieved by abstracting (preprocessing) data for transmission (lowering communication bandwidth requirements) and by placing DES entities near the data (reducing the distance over which the data must be transmitted).

Lower Processing Costs. Achieved through the use of cheaper, less-complex processors, which can be mass produced, and through load sharing (allowing relatively idle DES entitles to handle some of the work of a busy processing node).

Reduced Software Complexity. Achieved by decomposing the problem-solving task into subtasks, each more specialized than the overall task; the result of this decomposition is reduced software complexity at each DES entity (which performs a small number of subtasks) as compared to one piece of structured software performing the complete task.

Reduced Search Space. The decomposition minimizes potentials for combinatorial "explosion." Each DES entity only "worries about" a portion of the search space. This reduces solution time by an order of magnitude and increases near real-time capability.

Expert System Specialization. Complex behavior is achieved by the coordination of less complex, narrowly focused entities of "specialists." The nature of living entities can be emulated more accurately, a feature that at a minimum facilitates acquisition and management of the knowledge base.

Handling Incomplete, Uncertain, Conflicting Information. Like ESs, DES are adept at reaching the best possible conclusion in the presence of partial and uncertain information. One of their purposes, however, is to be better than ESs for handling conflicting information from alternate knowledge sources or sensors.

DES Limitations to Avoid

Weak Top-Level Control. If top-level control is extremely weak (or nonexistent), the subordinate specialists may speak up in different, possibly conflicting voices. Multiple control must not be allowed to substitute for unitary control and the decomposition function must be carefully and thoroughly tested.

Unnecessary Processing. Entities will accept and perform tasks that other entities are already doing unless a careful scheme to prevent this is incorporated. It is necessary to include some form of metalevel status exchange.

Lack of Synchronization. Without proper guidance, entities can get out of synch (timewise or functionwise) and be unable to understand each other. Again, it is necessary to exchange a metalevel view of their local problem-solving task.

Saturated Communication Channels. Interactions (communications) among entities in a distributed architecture are generally slower than computations. The framework for cooperation must minimize communication to avoid channel saturation and to avoid entities sitting idle while messages are being transmitted.

Suboptimal Results. Reduced search spaces of each specialist can lead them to less than optimal conclusions unless the decomposition and results synthesis functions provide robust and possibly parallel subtask allocations.

Repeating Mistakes/No Learning. The same problems, if always handled the same way, will lead to repetition of mistakes. Learning should be accomplished either by incorporating a "memory" or introducing it manually as in the Japanese quality control approach.[a]

---

[a] Quality is introduced into Japanese products by identifying each product defect as it occurs and by manually correcting the product line so it cannot occur again. Eventually, products are virtually defect-free.

TABLE 2 Transfer of Control (Selection)

	Traditional, Centralized Structured Program	Expert System (Early Blackboard)	Fully Distributed
1. Character of choice	None, predefined by the programmer (master, slave)	Caller (interpreter) chooses among respondents; respondents have no freedom of choice	Each node is aware of and able to choose between those nodes it might respond to and make requests of
2. Type of information for choosing	Subroutine name calls, preset	Patterns to be matched	Complex, dynamic
3. Information transfer and transmission	Caller to respondent transfer "directcast" to a single respondent	Caller to respondent and respondent to caller queries all with fixed format; broadcast to all potential respondents, each of whom must reply	Full opportunity for interactive conversation general transmission mechanism with freedom to reply or not
4. Evaluation of which respondent to choose	Centralized, predefined	Global evaluation function; metarule set is used	Localized and context-specific evaluations; can even decide that no one is currently suitable and reinitiate process later
5. Selection process	None except in the master or executive	Conflict resolution schemes: for example, evaluate priorities embedded in each rule. All selection is centralized in the rule interpreter. Respondents (rules) have no say in it	Mutual selection (symmetry on both sides based on evaluation of info from all requestors and respondents)

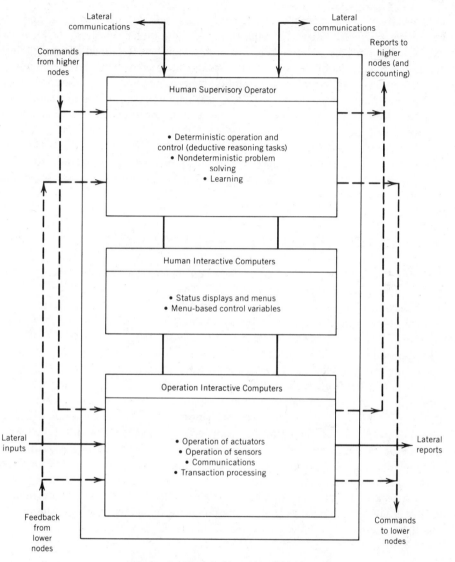

Figure 2. Model of local intelligence.

in time for a given service to be completed or suggests an alternative equipment pathway for the scheduler's consideration. In addition, each of these three SCPs individually must interact and cooperate with their counterparts at other control centers and facilities to solve problems and to perform their jobs.

1.3.3. Adaptive, Flexible Reasoning. The users of facilities desire and continuously make unusual requests for services: for example, these might include, among other requirements, (1) a large degree of flexibility in event scheduling, (2) dynamically varying spacecraft instrument commanding and controlling, and (3) alternative telemetry formats, frequencies, and durations. In short, SCPs must exhibit a great deal of adaptive behavior within their "well-defined" responsibility areas. The Space Station, as one example, is intended to be able to handle currently unforeseen activities, targets of opportunity, synergistic experiment operations, and adaptive instrument behavior and to allow user interactive use of the overall system in a flexible, transparent manner. (This has at times been called *telescience*: telescience is well documented in the CODMAC Report [1] and in Silverman et al., [2].) The implications for SCP ESs are in terms of two radically divergent modes of reasoning: at times SCP's must be capable of elaborate planning and adaptive behavior while at other times they must be prepared simply to execute the plans with great speed.

2.   DISTRIBUTED PROBLEM-SOLVING PROTOCOLS

The FACILITY ADVISOR is being designed to manage a generic version of a facility consisting of the three representative positions: Operator, Repairperson, and Scheduler. This generic facility is based on data collected over several years of knowledge engineering studies by the author at Goddard Space Flight Center facilities (i.e., NCC, POCCs, MORs, DCRs, NASCOM, WSGT, and FDF). In all these studies, the SCP has been described in terms of the three levels of intelligence portrayed earlier in Figure 1 and as further elaborated in Table 3 [3, 4].

As can be seen from Table 3, Supervisory Control Nodes tend to leave the most intellectually arduous cognitive functions up to the *human* supervisory operator: for example, (1) the anomaly troubleshooting of the Real-Time Controller, (2) the stochastic, plausible reasoning of the Problem Solver and Planner, or (3) the learning side of the Metaknowledge and Learning. Even so, with current day artificial intelligence (AI) and ES techniques it is becoming increasingly possible to replace many functions of the human at the third and highest level of local intelligence. For the sake of illustration, the human will be called a Specialist and the human tasks will not be explained as if his or her cognitive functions were separate, quasi-intelligent elements (as indeed they are) of his or her brain.

2.1.   Cognitive Functioning of a Specialist

Once a task is sent to the External Blackboard, any supervisory Specialist that takes responsibility for that task must be structured with the nine generic elements of Table 3. The task enters the Specialist as a message decoded by the Communicator/ Network Listener and is placed on the Internal Blackboard in queue with other tasks needing to be handled by that node. First, the Negotiator references the Metaknowledge and Learner to determine if the task can indeed be done internally and then Chair decides the sequence of tasks to be processed with the aid of the Fusion/Situation Recognizer. Anomaly-free tasks are generally handled by the Real-Time Controller, who takes the necesssary steps to complete the task, places the

TABLE 3 Handling of Cognitive Functions at Each Local SCP By Three Levels of Intelligence

Levels of Intelligence	COGNITIVE FUNCTIONS							
	Communicating & Negotiating	Blackboard Writing/Reading (Internal)	Chair/Task Scheduling	Fusion/Situation Recognition	Problem Solving & Planning	Controlling	Accounting & Logging	Meta-Knowledge & Learning
Task Level Computer	• Network Listener • Front End Processor • Code up Transmissions/Requests • Decode Responses	• General Display (Info Alerts Status, Action, Etc.) • Read Tasks	• Service Tasks in Priority Order Subject to On-going Constraint	• Automatic Sensing • Automatic Anomaly & Status Detection & Reporting	• Automatic Deduction (Check Meta-Knowledge & Pass Solutions to Controlling Problem to Human	• Semi Automatic Servo-Control	• Automatic Storage/Retrieval in Long Term Memory	• Execute Meta-Knowledge About Who to Call for Anomalies
Human Inter-Active Computer	• Display Organizer (Translate Machine to Menu Parameter) • Translate Human to Machine Language	• Hold/Display Info & Organize • Translate Human Input	• Fifo Run Scheduling Aids For Human	• Organizing Anomaly & Status Info Hierarchically	• Place Problem Alerts at Top of Information Hierarchy	Not Applicable	• Execute Retrieval Queries/Storage Requests	Not Applicable
Human Supervisory Operator	• Negotiate • Voice -in Room -over Phone -Keyboard	• Read Display • Write Cases • Make Mental Notes	• Reassign Task Priorities at Will	• React to Anomaly Alerts and Multiple Inputs • Remain Cognizant of System Status	• Full Range of Plausible Deductive Reasoning	• Implement Solutions & Exercise Interrupt Ability (Adjust, Takeover)	• Summarize, Account & Log	• Learn System Strengths & Weaknesses • Reprogram on Line as Needed

result along with tasks for other Specialists on the Internal Blackboard, and generates task results information useful to the Accounter/Logger. Anomalous tasks, on the other hand, if accepted, are preprocessed by the Problem Solver and Planner, who attempts to evaluate alternative solutions and to identify the proper sequence for the Real-Time Controller to then execute. Metaknowledge and Learning serves as the repository of information about what alternatives the Problem Solver and Planner should consider, including the possibility of referring the task to a completely separate Specialist for help, for result sharing, or for subtasks assignment. Negotiator is again used in subtask assignment interactions (i.e., subcontracting). Metaknowledge and Learning also "learns," as time progresses, which alternatives, which solutions, and which other Specialists are most useful and which are most counterproductive for each type of exchange.

2.2. The Multiple SCP Protocol for a Single Facility

The multiple SCP protocol is typified for one illustrative facility as shown in Figure 3, where there are three SCPs that specialize, respectively, in facility scheduling, facility operation, and facility repair. The Schedule Master is responsible for allocating the facility's equipment and other resources along a timeline that will

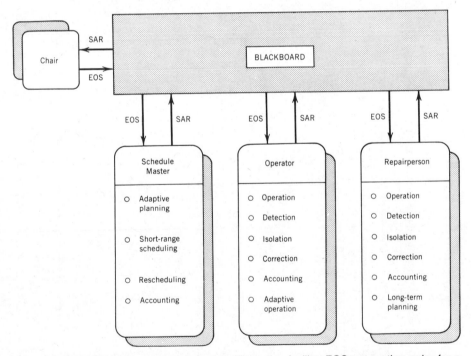

Figure 3. Multiple SCP blackboarding at an illustrative facility. EOS—execution order for a specialist; SAR—specialist activation request.

assure response to user service requests. The Operator in turn receives the schedule (authorization) and uses his or her local intelligence to assure the service is performed in a satisfactory fashion. If any problems arise that the Operator cannot correct, the Repairperson is contacted for assistance with the equipment or other resources and/or the Operator requests new schedules and/or resource allocations of the Schedule Master as needed. The Repairperson is constantly monitoring equipment operations and will alert the Operator and Schedule Master of new allocation requirements as needed. Other interactions exist as well. The Repairperson can learn more about the source of an equipment problem by asking the Operator about the symptoms. The Schedule Master in turn needs the Repairperson's recommendations for alternative (backup) equipment pathways that can be scheduled so as to minimize interruptions to other previously planned activities.

The intrafacility interactions are facilitated only *in part* by the existing automation at each Specialist's workstation. For example, the Operator can generally call up displays that show equipment sensor feedback data and thereby attempt to infer whether the source of a problem is equipment related (rather than operational). If so, the Operator would then compose a repair message to be sent to the Repairperson. However, the information is not always on the computer and voice interaction is often necessary. While current levels of automation can at times assist the Specialist, at other times it can actually contribute to increased workload and deteriorated performance.

2.3. Interfacility Cooperation and Protocols

In addition to the interactions within a given facility, each Specialist interacts with his or her counterpart at one or more other facilities. For example, the Schedule Master must exchange messages with a hierarchy of other Scheduler nodes in order to perform many of the planning responsibilities. The Operator may need to communicate with Operators at other facilities, for example, to isolate sources of message errors or, as another example, to obtain authority to assist in correcting an incorrect ID. The Repairperson in turn helps in the process of isolating which facility is the problem origination point in the event of a hard to isolate equipment problem.

While much interfacility exchange is facilitated by currently planned workstation automation, the human-to-human exchange is common and will probably remain so for the foreseeable future. These exchanges tend to be voice-based, although some of them seem to be migrating to teletype. For these reasons, it is essential to explore how much of the interfacility problem solving can be assumed by the DES when there are humans at the other facilities. To what extent will these individuals be able to migrate voice communications to teletype exchanges? Even more importantly, will they be willing to have natural language dialogues with an expert system and how can the effectiveness of these exchanges be maximized? These and other human factor engineering issues comprise some of the research tasks needed.

2.4.   Real-Time Execution Protocols

Real-time controlling is a continuous function, 24 hours a day, of monitoring and controlling activities, scanning a selection of critical parameters, seeking cautionary or out of limit conditions (or alarms), and low-level inferencing along cause–effect lines. For example, in terms of operator screen settings consider a *condition X* for which the logical and necessary *action* is *Y*. Here *X* might be an input that occurs in the presence of an initial or current system state while *Y* might be the outputs that lead to a final or next system state. In this fashion, chains of such deductive sequences can be envisioned where *Y*, for example, becomes a condition forcing yet another state transition action called *Z*. For the supervisory operator in a real-time setting, the deductive sequence just elaborated occupies the majority of the operator's time and there are a multitude of control variables to be managed in exactly this fashion, with rarely a need to call the Problem Solver and Planner.

Real-time controller functions require the human (or ES) to respond to each new "situation" and (1) to deduce that a set of rules or sequence of steps must now be attempted, (2) to recall those steps from memory (or from a look-up notebook), and (3) to execute those steps rapidly. A "situational" calculus can readily be conceptualized (although tedious to develop) in which human knowledge is organized into and replaced by one of five categories of (modus ponens) rules: transition, initialization, status, control, and accounting. Such a calculus has been demonstrated with the use of our Hierarchical Control System Environment (HCSE) [5].

2.5.   Alternative Planning Protocols

Planning and adaptive reasoning require repeated construction and testing of alternative plans and subplans, the weighing of different pieces of evidence, and much "milling over" the pros and cons of choices that can be made. In short, there is no valid reason to try and constrain SCPs to a single uniform calculus and the proposed approach involves two distinctly separate reasoning approaches (calculi) for the real-time and off-line functions, respectively. Furthermore, there is no uniform off-line calculus for all SCPs. However, a relatively limited number of planning calculi can be formulated that occur repeatedly across all facilities. In particular, each Specialist engages in three interrelated types of planning:

1. Routine operations planning that includes the preparation of ordered timelines for equipment allocations and services performed.
2. Active period planning (or replanning) that includes problem solving needed to continue operations when changes and/or anomalies occur.
3. Long-term adaptive planning that is responsible to relatively major shifts in user patterns and/or user service requests.

The first two of these levels currently are partially automated in many existing SCPs and one can envision relatively off-the-shelf ES technology, if creatively applied, offering substantial inroads into the human's domain (e.g., "mulling over" of pieces of evidence can be shown to include blackboarding, opportunistic reasoning by multiple modules, combinations of backward and forward chaining, and progressive deepening aided by heuristic search functions and dependency-directed backtracking techniques).

The adaptive planning is usually relegated to a system engineering team. However, there is no fundamental reason why this cannot be handled by the FACILITY ADVISOR via the use of intelligent assistant (IA) modules in each relevant Specialist, one for each desired adaptive planning capability. As an example, an IA might be created as an on-line software or data set assistant under the Operator SCP. This software (data set) assistant, in grossly simplified terms, could facilitate the facility's ability to adapt to new user message (or telemetry) frame formats and content meaning by (1) containing rules that query a user for the new formats and content meanings, (2) suggesting to a Human SCP how to alter the facility's software (or data set) to accommodate the new formats and content meanings *safely*, and (3) inserting those changes if given the authorization to do so.

The human would retain interactive as well as override capabilities in the event the IA's suggestions are naive or nonresponsive.

3. DES TECHNOLOGY FOR THE FACILITY ADVISOR

The FACILITY ADVISOR implies constructing a system with an architecture somewhat like that shown in Figure 4. The reader can see at this point that (1) the ES includes three representative Specialists plus a manager, (2) each Specialist includes nine generic elements that need be built only once and that handle all the cooperation and coordination needs, and (3) each Specialist includes a set of "modules" (unnumbered boxes) that are unique to its operation. There are thus certain generic elements to be added to the FACILITY ADVISOR and for any facility to which the FACILITY ADVISOR might ultimately be applied. Furthermore, the Specialist-unique module sets contain elements that can and should ideally be standardized so that any facility that wants a Specialist of that type (as part of its FACILITY ADVISOR or as a stand-alone entity) will receive a validated structure and certain validated knowledge base elements: the Specialist can thus be tailored to a given facility primarily by extending and tailoring its rule base.

One other factor critical to the FACILITY ADVISOR is that, because a number of stand-alone ESs are already under construction at existing facilities, the FACILITY ADVISOR must provide an open environment that maximizes the ease with which these third-party ESs can be incorporated into the FACILITY ADVISOR. It must provide application developers with utilities that support reuse of previously constructed components, integration of diverse components and modules, and interfaces to their favorite ES development shells (e.g., ART, KEE, or IntelliShell).

A DES and a testbed that supports cooperation yet more-or-less autonomous reasoning components are needed. A prototype of the FACILITY ADVISOR is

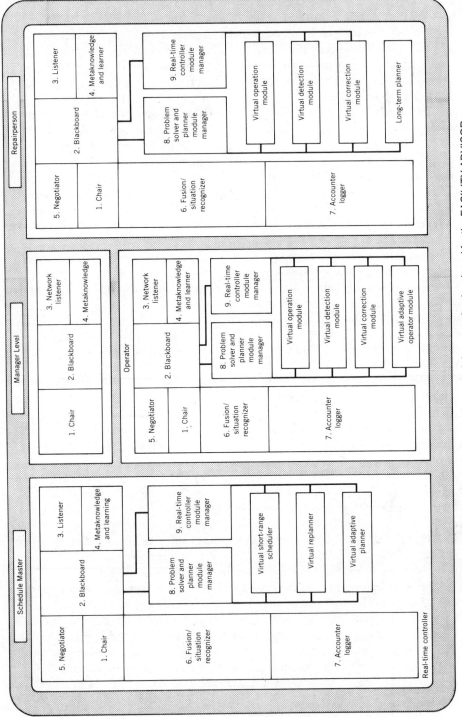

Figure 4. Nine generic elements and three module sets to be developed for the FACILITY ADVISOR.

already in place (see Section 4) and a number of the elements of the model have been described fully at a logical level in Section 2.0: for example, it must support a wide range of control schemes (slavelike to fully distributed), several levels of communication interfaces (intermodule, interprocess, intrafacility, interfacility), multiple reasoning schemes (situational calculus, belief-based fusion, and several planning calculi), and synchronization between numerous semiautonomous components not all of which use AI techniques. Since the FACILITY ADVISOR is ultimately targeted for transfer to a variety of facilities, the knowledge engineering effort must also provide a "virtual machine" that can be mapped into a wide range of underlying hardware/OS environments: primary targets are parallel and distributed environments.

In particular, the work to be completed and the technology to be used can be discussed in terms of the tailored modules, generic elements, and interentity coordination:

1. *Tailored Modules.* If the three representative specialists are considered equivalent to three stand-alone ESs, industrywide experience would suggest 10–20 work years of effort would be required to develop each of them fully. Clearly, that would be an enormous effort and in addition the DES aspects of the job would be ignored. To this end, the author and his staff have already invested close to 10 work years of effort on these modules and have already completed a substantial fraction of the knowledge elicitation effort required for the representative specialists' modules (see Section 4). Because of this preparation, the author believes they can generate and code rules for the Operator, Repairperson, and Schedule Master at the rate of about 200+ rules per month for several months.* In a short period of time, an extremely "interesting" FACILITY ADVISOR could be generated where "interesting" means it could handle a relatively large number of higher-level cognitive functions and protocols that are important to most SCPs. This would be a practical limit to place on effort expended in this direction as concerns real-time control and repetitive planning modules. At least an equal effort is contemplated, however, for collection, analysis, and coding of more complex protocols such as those encountered in intra- and interfacility problem-solving sessions, as well as for adaptive planning situations.

2. *Generic Elements.* The discussion thus far also suggests a substantial investment of effort for defining the generic elements and precisely how they would work. In addition, effort is needed for coding and validation testing

---

*For those modules in which the knowledge collection obstacles have already been overcome, the coding of rules should be roughly equivalent to normal programming rates. Two hundred rules per month is about 10 rules per work day. This is a fairly conservative estimate as most programming projects can generally generate code at the rate of 10–40 lines per work day.

of these generic elements so that they can be offered as customizable elements. The authors have had a chance to design, prototype, and test most of these elements by virtue of several DES and ES jobs they are doing. In particular, the off-line blackboard and chair have been developed for other work [6] while the real-time blackboard, chair, and module manager exist in a software environment called HCSE that already is part of the FACILITY ADVISOR prototype (see Section 4). Schedule Master planner and replanner techniques will be recycled from our prototype and from our Space Station Customer Scheduling Expert System currently being developed for Mc-Donnell–Douglas Astronautics Company. All remaining generic elements exist at the detailed design level as summarized in earlier reports [3, 4].

3. *Interentity Coordination.* Finally, the fifth level of knowledge engineering is intended to assure communications between diverse modules and elements, cooperation between operating systems of different machines on which the parts of the FACILITY ADVISOR will reside, and transportability for applications purposes. To leverage the effort, it would be fruitful to use techniques being developed elsewhere, to the extent possible, such as in the COP project at George Washington University. COP is a software effort to develop a cooperation between operating systems package for a separate DES project that the author is involved in at George Washington University, which will develop capabilities to be phased in over the next several years. COP presently offers very modest capabilities for affecting communications between parallel physical processes and resource management abilities. In summary, COP is a set of functions that an application (such as a FACILITY ADVISOR, specialists, blackboards, processes, or modules) can call on to establish logical networks to other applications and to select ways to send mail (e.g., point to point or broadcast).

COP also currently includes certain network listener and metaknowledge functions. That is, each local COP Controller monitors the "internal network" of the computer it's installed on for messages of interest to applications on its own board. It also monitors the interboard network(s) for messages of interest to applications on its own board. Upon finding such messages, it places them on the internal network for routing. In these regards, COP acts as an interboard daemon capability.

COP is thus a far less ambitious project than many other distributed operating system efforts. However, it is felt that not all DES applications need such power. In numerous DES applications (like the FACILITY ADVISOR), once design begins it is generally clear to programmers that certain subsystems deserve "privately held boards" with some capability for picking up added power during peak workload periods. Any application on a private board should be able to carry out operations without intervention by COP. This is thus taken as a currently planned extent of COP's capability: a goal that would seem to be sufficient as an entire goal for a DES such as the FACILITY ADVISOR.

4. CURRENT PROTOTYPE OF THE FACILITY ADVISOR

If the FACILITY ADVISOR is ultimately to be used, it must be capable of handling realistic workload levels with a minimum of computer investment. The fundamental problem common to both the interfacility situation and the across-user service request situation addressed here is that of managing processor resources to maintain the pace of the workload despite delays encountered while responding to a given user service request. For several reasons, it is necessary to be able to create and manage dynamically the SCP cognitive processes, modules, or module elements (subprocesses or IAs). Each of these entities must be a "virtual entity," that is, an entity that can create a clone capable of doing a task in the same fashion as the busy entity could have. A virtual entity occupies no memory when it is not needed.

It is inefficient to keep all these processes and their clones active in main memory simultaneously; however, for some problems there may not be a unique decomposition apparent to the higher levels of the hierarchy. The point of making all entities in the DES intelligent (they have metaknowledge) is to facilitate the ability of some entity to ask another whether it can offer a meaningful solution (or part of a solution) to the problem. That is, most entities must (1) keep some "listener" portion of themselves active and (2) in addition, an entity manager must exist that knows which additional entities to "awaken" for a response. This is a fully adaptive control formation and one that is supportable within the COP approach.

Progress already made toward the first version of the FACILITY ADVISOR is summarized in Figure 5 and described below:

The Virtual Machine Hardware. The virtual machine includes seven parallel boards plus a host. These boards are four Xerox LISP machines, one VAX 11/780, and an IBM PC. One of the LISP machines also contains a PC emulation board. The boards are physically connected via an EtherNet except the VAX, which is connected separately to the host.

The Virtual Machine Operating System (COP). The virtual machine straddles three distinct types of operating system (MESA, DOS, VMS) with the aid of the COP capability. A COP station exists on the host board and a local COP has been assigned a "beat" on each of the parallel boards.

FACILITY ADVISOR: Off-line Manager. The Off-line Manager position has been prototyped in LISP on a separate machine using an in-house blackboard technology (developed for the ARIEL and EPMS Shells). In brief, the Manager places a planning problem or goal on the blackboard, collects and evaluates Specialist Activation Requests (SARs) from the various position specialists who have offered to solve part of the problem, and issues Execution Orders for the Specialists (EOSs) that it feels can make the best contributions at the present time. These specialists, in the prototype, are on other boards of the virtual machine.

Schedule Master. The Off-line Master is prototyped on LISP machine #2 primarily in LISP. Objects are created for each piece of hardware, each user service request, service pathways, and for each of several types of constraint (e.g., priority, window, and service type). The LISP functions create a set of system states,

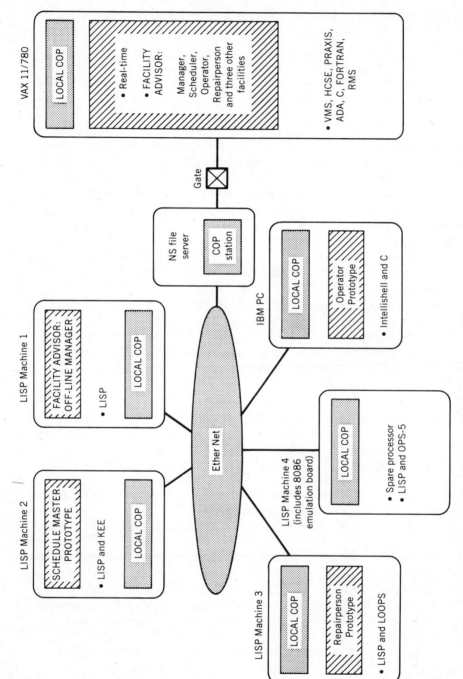

Figure 5. The FACILITY ADVISOR prototype. (*Indicates local COP not fully implemented.)

heuristically search the states, relax various constraints, and recommend feasible schedule alternatives to which the Repairperson, Operator, and User are asked to respond. The final selection is sent to the Real-Time FACILITY ADVISOR for execution (at present the Real-Time FACILITY ADVISOR only executes one schedule alternative).

Repairperson. The investigators have collected over 1000 rules used in the NASA Goddard Space Flight Center (GSFC) Repairperson positions; however, only a very simple prototype has yet been implemented. This Repairperson uses seven LOOPS rules and 21 LISP functions to operate and monitor one piece of equipment (currently an object). When it detects a failure, it uses a second set of rules to isolate and correct (or abort) the problem and it reports the result to the Off-line Manager.

Operator. Here too, the investigators have collected over 1000 rules used by GSFC Operators yet only about 15 or 20 rules have been implemented. The Operator is not presently integrated into the FACILITY ADVISOR; however, it demonstrates the detection, isolation, and correction of user request message errors as well as one of the explanation and accounting features. The Operator was originally written in M.1 but is currently being ported to IntelliShell, an in-house ES written in C and ultimately targeted to contain both forward and backward reasoning (it only offers backward at present).

The Real-Time FACILITY ADVISOR. A situational calculus capable of supporting the DES real-time elements has been tested on the VAX with the aid of a DES generator called Hierarchical Control System Environment (HCSE). HCSE provides a language in which to create fast, deterministic production-oriented specialists that communicate with each other via a blackboard mechanism. Specialists can be encoded with sets of condition–action rules and/or with more traditional procedures (in FORTRAN, C, PRAXIS, or ADA). The HCSE also permits hierarchies of specialists to be established and executed so that lower-level experts execute commands from and send results and feedback to higher-level experts. Specialists communicate through and are synchronized via the blackboard and chair. HCSE is thus a viable alternative for testbedding the FACILITY ADVISOR real-time elements. It may not be the ultimately chosen tool; however, skeletal elements can be prototyped rapidly within HCSE. To that end, seven ESs were built in HCSE corresponding to (1) a Facility Manager, (2) a Schedule Master (active period), (3) an Operator, (4) a Repairperson, and (5) three external facilities to emulate interfacility protocols. A busy entity cloning capability was also tested. The entire real-time DES is fully documented in an earlier report [5].

In summary, Figure 5 and its explanatory notes explain (1) the feasibility of off-line planning elements being constructed in different shells, languages, and machines, (2) the role of the HCSE for testbedding of real-time elements and modules, and (3) the cloning and virtual entity framework explained above. Albeit, each item in Figure 5 is in its relative infancy and most of the dedicated machine (private board) allocations have been made only for proof-of-concept purposes. In fact, only two boards are truly needed at this point: (1) the entire off-line FACIL-

ITY ADVISOR could easily have been implemented on a single LISP machine, and (2) the real-time FACILITY ADVISOR deserves a dedicated board. Nevertheless, the early prototype does demonstrate the fundamental precept of this chapter: the FACILITY ADVISOR concept works.

As a final note, the prototype of the FACILITY ADVISOR testbed has been devised in a fairly flexible, portable manner owing to a variety of techniques:

1. Common LISP is being used to the extent possible on individual machines.
2. Relatively portable shells are also being used (e.g., KEE, HCSE, COMMON LOOPS, and IntelliShell).
3. The C language is being integrated where feasible.
4. COP is open to many new hardware configurations (including a MIMD machine).
5. The distributed components and modules are being designed with parallel implementation in mind, thereby increasing the possibility of incorporating a massively parallel processor of some form.

5. NEXT STEPS

This chapter has described a DES approach called the FACILITY ADVISOR for supporting distributed problem-solving protocols commonly encountered in real-time control and operations. The FACILITY ADVISOR is suggested as an attempt to prevent individual facilities from reinventing the wheel and to create a way to share new, useful ES technology, techniques, lessons learned, and insights. If all FACILITY ADVISOR goals can be met, the results will be a set of validated skeletal elements that any facility can readily tailor to its domain and that can be extended "simply" by adding appropriate rules to individual specialist modules. To reach this goal, a testbed is needed to evaluate the viability of what is described herein. Specifically, this testbed for the FACILITY ADVISOR is depicted in Figure 6 in terms of an illustrative facility consisting of N supervisory controller positions existing in conjunction with other facilities. Figure 6 also shows how the various SCP expert systems (i.e., Specialists) will ultimately be integrated into the facility as advisors to the humans who currently perform those tasks and cognitive functions. In this advisory role the Specialist (1) watches what the task-level computer sends to each human, (2) formulates recommendations, (3) advises the humans if queried, and (4) alerts the humans if the Specialist "thinks" a given human's response is in error or if the human has failed to respond. Enormous amounts of validation testing are needed to reach this level of implementation to ensure that the various Specialists will help more than hurt the humans. Even more validation testing would be needed (e.g., several years of actual facility operation) to determine if the FACILITY ADVISOR's recommendations and performance are continually good enough to warrant collapsing the individual SCP humans into a single human position as shown at the very base of Figure 6.

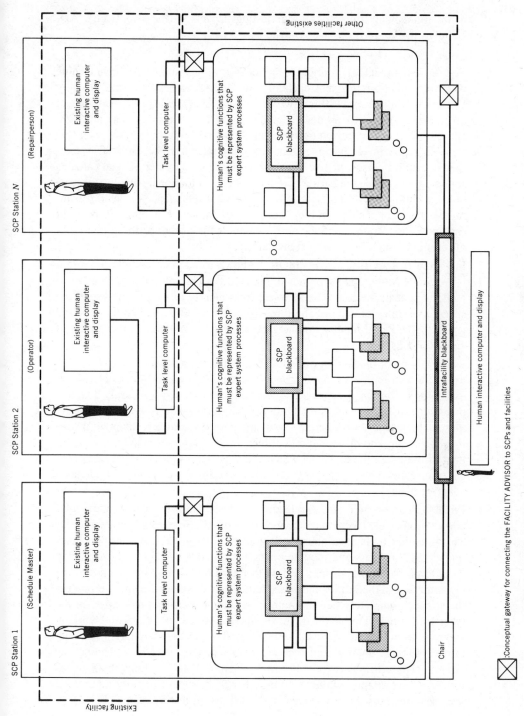

Figure 6. Overview of the FACILITY ADVISOR logical model and how it fits into existing SCPs and facilities.

327

Of more immediate concern are four testing aspects of the FACILITY ADVISOR shown in Figure 6:

1. The logical model of a single generic SCP ES is shown to include nine cognitive functions (boxes) each of which requires separate and possibly "parallel" ES process. All but two of the processes (real-time execution and off-line planning) as explained already are to be identical across all SCPs and probably will only require one version to be built and tested. The two remaining processes, however, capture the dual nature of each SCP: real-time execution versus off-line problem solving and planning. A dual calculus approach was discussed earlier: (a) deterministic situational calculus for real-time execution and (b) nondeterministic, belief-maintenance-oriented reasoning for the data fusion, problem-solving, and adaptive planning aspects of each position. How each Specialist's modules may best use these two types of reasoning must be tested extensively.

2. In Figure 6, FACILITY ADVISOR is shown to encompass three representative SCPs cooperating within a single facility. The intrafacility blackboard model and chair are felt to be identical from facility to facility; however, the specific modules of each of the three specialized SCPs need to be built and tested for SCP and facility-unique aspects. The same applies for modules of new SCP ESs.

3. Up to this point discussion of testing has concentrated on how the real-time execution and repetitive planning needs of facilities can be satisfied with ES technology. Earlier discussion has also indicated a need for a truly adaptive planning capability: that is the ability to handle previously unplanned activities such as (but not limited to) new targets of opportunity, adaptive instrument behavior, and mission redefinitions. While adaptive behavior is a design goal of the DES, the extent to which it can be achieved is a relatively open-ended research question; testing must also encompass validation of unplanned adaptive behavior.

4. Finally, Figure 6 intimates that testing must account for cases of interfacility cooperation as well as management of multiple user requests simultaneously. This is achieved via the dynamic creation and management of multiple copies of each SCP process and module on an as-needed basis. ESs are assigned to specific problems which they follow to their completion. For example, the Operator is assigned to a single user request. If the Operator fails to process the request completely before another user request arrives, a "copy" of the Operator is created to handle the next request. All ES operations and working memory elements are recorded on disk as they occur. This facilitates both the accounting function and the ability to manage processor resources by putting copies to sleep (out of virtual memory) and waking them up as needed—for example, while awaiting other SCP or other facility inputs. All such features must be considered in the validation testing plan.

In summary, DES technology holds much promise as this chapter has attempted to elaborate. On the other hand, facility operations need to be completed reliably and a no-risk approach is mandated. Since DES technology is relatively new, several years of exploratory development and testbedding are warranted to prove its capabilities. The next steps toward the integration of DESs into facility operations are to improve what we know and to determine what can in fact be delivered reliably.

ACKNOWLEDGMENT

The support of NAS5-28604, NAS5-30037, and NASA/GSFC/Code 520 are gratefully acknowledged.

REFERENCES

1. CODMAC Report, *Data Management and Computation*, National Academy Press, Washington, DC, 1982.
2. B. G. Silverman, V. S. Moustakis, and R. L. Robless, Ground Systems Autonomy Study for the Space Station Era, Technical Report of NAS5-28604, October 1984. This report is partially summarized in Expert Systems and Robotics for the Space Station Era, *Expert Systems in Government Conference Proceedings*, IEEE Computer Society, Washington, DC, 1985.
3. B. G. Silverman, *Distributed Expert Systems*, Technical Report prepared for NAS5-28604, NASA/GSFC/Code 520, August 1985.
4. B. G. Silverman, Fusion and Plausible Reasoning for Real Time Supervisory Controller Positions, presented at the *AI in Engineering Conference*, October 1985; reprinted in *AI in Manufacturing: Special Issue of the IEEE Transactions on Systems, Man and Cybernetics*, March/April 1987, IEEE, New York.
5. B. G. Silverman and Q. Ali, Blackboard and Distributed Expert Systems for Real Time Control Applications, prepared for NAS5-28604, GSFC/Code 520, 1986.
6. B. G. Silverman and C. Diakite, The Expert Project Management System. *In Proceedings of 1986 Conference on Artificial Intelligence Applications*, NASA/GSFC, Greenbelt, MD, Code 514, May 15, 1986.

FUTURE APPLICATIONS

EXPERT SYSTEMS FOR NETWORK CONTROL CENTER APPLICATIONS

John Lycas and Barbara A. Power

M/A-COM Telecommunications, Inc., Germantown, Maryland

1. INTRODUCTION

Previous chapters have discussed actual implementations of expert systems in conjunction with various aspects of telecommunications. This chapter takes a different track and looks at one part of a telecommunications system—the network control center—as a potential area for expert systems development.

The chapter starts with a review of the concept of a network control center and discusses some of its functions that are most often common to a number of implementations. It then moves to a specific system, the network control center of M/A-COM Telecommunications' Integrated Packet Network (IPN) Packet Switching Network. With this system as a model, the chapter identifies four candidates for expert systems methodology: network problem isolation and correction, network performance, network engineering, and training. For each of these areas it describes the candidate, how things are currently handled for that domain, why an expert system should be considered, and what the requirements for such a system would be. A summary concludes the discussion. A glossary is provided at the end of the chapter.

2. NETWORK CONTROL CENTERS

A network control center (NCC), as its name implies, is the central point for coordinating a network and providing services needed by a number of network components. This is achieved through the interaction of a number of functions that together form the network control system (NCS). The NCS operates primarily out of the NCC, with some of its capabilities distributed in the network.

The NCS generally provides the following functionalities: network configuration database management, including configuration update and verification as well as fallback and recovery mechanisms; report generation; network alarm detection and logging facilities; statistics collection; generation and logging of accurate records for billing; remote maintenance of network components; and secure NCS access via passwords [1–3]. Together, these capabilities form a basic NCS.

NCSs share other characteristics. Because a network is a distributed system, the NCS may be widely distributed geographically from the network components it supports. Given that much of the network expertise is probably located in the NCC, remote capabilities become very important. This expertise is shared among network operators, network engineers, and field service technicians. Responsibilities include day-to-day operations, network planning and installation, and troubleshooting.

3. EXPERT SYSTEMS

Expert system implementations meet with a greater degree of success when the following criteria are met [4–9]:

1. The problem is bounded. The task must be large enough to be of interest, but not so large as to be unmanageable. The problem definition can always be expanded to include more as the development continues, so it is advisable to start with a smaller subset of the desired goal.

2. There is an expert available. An expert must be willing and able to communicate his or her methodology to the knowledge engineers developing the system. The knowledge engineers in turn must be able to derive the required information to model the system.

3. There are almost as many exceptions as there are rules. Traditional programming is well suited for problems that can be defined completely from the start. Expert systems, on the other hand, are more appropriate for tasks that involve relying on incomplete or ambiguous information to make informed judgments.

4. Test data are readily available. Since expert system programming is an iterative procedure, where the system is continually being critiqued and updated, testing becomes part of the development process. Testing should be done by the expert to review the content of the response and by users to determine if the responses are both meaningful and useful.

It is important to emphasize that an expert system is not an expert, but rather an assistant that has a useful but restricted scope. If an expert system is rule based and if a real expert's rule or methodology is omitted from the knowledge base, an expert system may come up with a less optimal solution to the problem, or possibly none at all. The expert system is a machine application presented with a limited paradigm and limited data; it has no meaning outside these bounds.

If the desired application meets the four criteria outlined above, then an expert system implementation can achieve an increase in efficiency, reduction in cost, and a greater level of service. Later, this discussion will screen each candidate for these criteria.

4.   THE INTEGRATED PACKET NETWORK (IPN)

Any network will vary in its implementation of ''standard'' network functions and will provide its own set of unique features. The remainder of this discussion focuses on a single packet switching network product and how an expert system might be incorporated into it.

The IPN network is a packet switching network (PSN) developed at M/A-COM Telecommunications Division in Germantown, Maryland, and released in December 1985. The network provides reliable and efficient packet transmission and will connect users utilizing CCITT X.25 and X.75 packet interfaces and nonpacket mode users utilizing specified Packet Assemblers/Disassemblers. The IPN currently follows the 1980 recommendation for X.25 and is being updated for the 1984 standard [10].

4.1.   The Network Environment

The NCS consists of the network control processor (NCP), network operator console (NOC), and auxiliary service processor (ASP). The NCP is located in an NCC and can provide all network services and administrative and management functions. It also performs all requests entered at a NOC. The NOC may also reside in a NCC and is an easy-to-use forms-based interface between the operator and the network. The NOC is the place where the operator may view almost all available network information, configure components and users, and perform network debugging and control. The ASP is located in the switching nodes themselves and performs a subset of the NCP functions. It is located in the middle of the service path between switching clusters and the NCP and so attempts to accomplish service requests itself, thereby reducing the load on the NCP. If an ASP cannot service the request, the request is handed to the NCP.

Thus the NCP, ASP, and NOC together form the NCS, with its functionality distributed between the NCC and the switching nodes themselves. A general description of the rest of the network is needed to discuss how expert systems might enhance it.

The first level of subdivision of the IPN is the node. Nodes contain logically associated packet switching clusters (PSCs) and possibly one or more ASPs. The PSCs perform the switching function, while the ASPs provide basic network services to the PSCs. Nodes are joined to each other to form the network by means of connections called backbone links. When the network is fully operational, all these elements are connected in the manner shown in Figures 1 and 2.

The NCP provides an array of services important to sustained network operation. While data transmission would not be affected, functions such as configuration update and network event and summary status logging would be hampered by failure here. To lessen the impact of an NCP's failure, the network uses two NCPs in a redundant fashion. One is the master; it alone is responsible for things such as network configuration control and network time. The backup NCP is always ready to switch in for the master, should the need arise, but in the meantime it shares the service load with the master NCP. Thus, both NCPs perform functions such as call record and event logging, system maintenance and debugging, and more.

It would not make sense to colocate the NCPs and thereby subject them both to a single disaster such as fire, flood, or earthquake. Thus, the NCPs are frequently

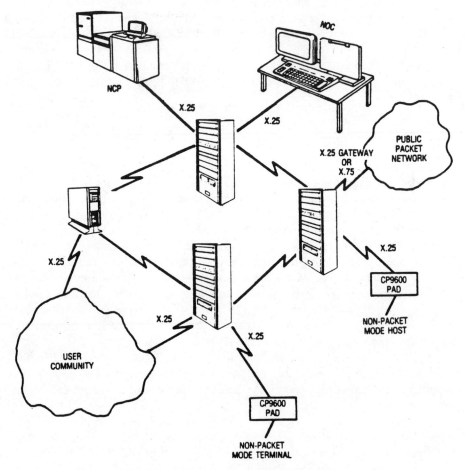

Figure 1. Integrated packet network.

The System

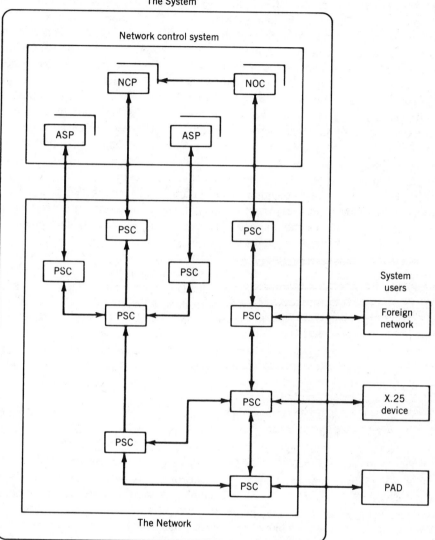

Figure 2. System components and system users.

geographically separated but maintain links to keep the backup NCP in synchronization and ready to take over.

4.2. IPN NCS Functions

4.2.1. NCS Administrative Functions.
The NCP and NOC of the IPN system provide all NCS administrative functions. A full description of the network is necessary both to control the network and to inform individual components as to

who and where they are, and whom they go to for service. This description is held in configuration databases, maintained in the NCP. Configuration changes are made at a NOC by an operator who has database change access. Operator change access is limited, and any changes desired are checked by the NCP for consistency and correctness. If a change has been made to an on-line configuration, the system components are notified by change notices sent down the entire network. A configuration database that is known to be operational may be designated as fallback to provide recovery in case of errors in a new on-line configuration database.

Events are informational messages describing specific occurrences within the network and are extremely important both for determining the health of the network and the cause of a fault. Events generated in the network and sent up to the NCP are therefore written to a log file and to a dedicated event printer attached to each NCP. Furthermore, NOC operator accounts are usually configured to monitor a specific set of event classes; if an event of high enough severity in one of the operator's event classes should occur, the event class indicator of that operator's console will flash until the operator acknowledges the event.

PSCs and ASPs are required to send summary status messages up to the NCPs on a periodic basis: this is the first level of determining overall network health. Summary status is stored at the NCP but displayed at the NOC. Should the NOC operator desire more information on a component, a detailed status report may be requested. The NCP retrieves the information for the NOC, and the NOC then displays it.

When a network user places a call, the PSC that is the source for that call creates a call record containing all route and billing information. Whenever a timer expires or the call is cleared, a copy of the record is sent to both NCPs for storage and later processing.

An operator may request a report on some predefined aspect of the network, such as users, operators, events, and cluster organization. The report is selected from the NOC and then generated and printed by the NCP in the NCC area.

The NCP operator (NCPOP) interface allows the user to view the status of the NCP's X.25 links and to change their state or configuration. Other component control is done from the NOC. For example, clusters may be put in or out of service, restarted, or a port may be put into camp-on state, whereby it refuses new calls and immediately goes into a maintenance state when its last call clears. Access to both the NCP and the NOC interfaces is controlled by the use of secure passwords.

4.2.2.   NCS Services. The NCP and ASP provide basic network services. When a cluster first starts up, it knows very little about itself and cannot operate as part of the network. Information necessary for operation is held originally at the NCP, with a copy possibly held later at a local ASP, and gets distributed to the clusters by a process known as downline load. Once loaded, the cluster becomes a functioning entity in the network.

The NCP is a participant in almost all call setup. With the exception of a special class of calls, any call entering the network must go up to the NCP for address translation and destination verification. ASPs can also perform call setup.

The last basic service is statistics collection. As in summary status, statistics on reliability, throughput, resource utilization, and response time are automatically sent to the NCP for storage. They can then be used later to analyze network performance.

4.2.3. NCS Management Functions.

The NCP manages three main information sources: the configuration, software, memory patch, operator, event, and system parameter databases that help control the network; the event, call record, trace, error, statistics, and operator command log files that help track the network's behavior and usage; and the downloadable software and software distribution groups. The NOC is the location for operator control of network components. From here, an operator may take ports in and out of service, change a cluster's software, and more.

4.3. M/A-COM's IPN and Expert Systems

The overview description given makes it clear that the network is a large and complex system. The sheer scale and intricacy automatically imply that some of the job functions to be performed by network personnel will be time consuming and often confusing. In addition, many of the tasks may be tedious and repetitive. Expert systems could alleviate some of this.

For example, a NOC operator must be available and alert to recognize an impending or actual failure. Furthermore, this information could be arriving from a number of sources (events, summary status, statistics) and be difficult to sort through for the root of the problem. An expert system would be able to sift through the numerous sources of information, determine significant occurrences or series of occurrences, and make a recommendation. Thus, it might have great potential in the area of fault prediction, isolation, and correction.

Continual monitoring of network statistics to see if the network configuration could be improved based on average traffic presented would be an expensive and boring job for a human. An expert system could review statistics logs in conjunction with the other logs and report on ways to improve network performance.

Network planning and installation, a part of network engineering, are based on facts and heuristics and are performed by a limited number of highly trained personnel, making it a prime expert system candidate.

Another possible enhancement for the current system would be an expert system to act as a network troubleshooting trainer, to speed the learning process for new network operators and engineers.

These situations, how they are handled now, why an expert system would be a useful adjunct, and what restrictions would be placed on such a system will be discussed in detail in the following sections.

5. DETECTING, ISOLATING, AND CORRECTING NETWORK PROBLEMS FROM THE NCC

5.1. Description

The goal of any network is to provide consistent, quality service to its customers; therefore, it is a high priority to catch faults as early as possible and to correct them swiftly. Often, a component may exhibit erratic or unstable behavior for some time before having a major fault, making it possible to correct the situation early. When failure occurs, a consistent and efficient problem-solving method should be applied.

Because a network is a distributed system, a fault may occur at various points in the system. The NCC serves as a central clearinghouse for network information and personnel, thereby facilitating efficient detection, isolation, and correction of problems. The centralization of information and expertise in a NCC results in dramatic savings in support costs. Down time or switch out time is greatly reduced if the field service people do not have to travel to the problem site. If travel is required, it is more efficient to know ahead of time what replacements, or even what test equipment, are necessary to take out to the site. Preliminary diagnosis done at the hub makes such preparation possible. Although there may be more than one NCC per network for distributed control, each has similar requirements.

Assembling all the necessary data that arrives at a NCC, determining what is pertinent, isolating cause and effect, and then choosing the right solution can be a difficult, tedious task, and one whose success is dependent on the competency of the person doing the analysis.

5.2. Current Approach

The NOC is the primary tool for detecting, isolating, and monitoring network problems. With over 90 screens associated in a tree-structured format, the NOC provides the ability to view a specific network component, perform route simulation, generate a report, and more. Once isolated, a problem can often be corrected from the NOC too. In addition, user observations and past performance provide important inputs to the problem-solving process.

Assimilating all the information coming from various sources is a formidable task—the support personnel must be able to understand each of the pieces and to access only the significant information in a systematic and efficient manner to meet response time requirements.

5.2.1. Problem Detection. Service degradation or disruption is reported by either a user or the NOC operator. If a user reports the problem, the NOC operator must identify the user, the user's destination, the time of the attempted call, and whether this exact call has ever succeeded before. The NOC generally signals trouble by an event being generated on the screen.

Over 110 events are generated by network occurrences. They fall into the following 12 categories [11]:

- Network operator events
- Packet assembler/dissassembler (PAD) management events
- Database administration events
- NCP redundancy events
- Downline load events
- Remote file management events
- Log file management events
- Summary status events
- State control events
- ASP events
- Link status events
- Miscellaneous cluster events

These categories are distributed into nine different classes for network control. If an event occurs, an indicator for that class begins to flash on the NOC's banner line to notify the operator. The indicator continues to flash until all major events in the class are cleared by the operator. Not all the events signify a critical problem. Some were included to monitor operational status, such as the occurrence of a routine downline load.

5.2.2. Problem Isolation.
When a problem is detected, the range of possible causes must be narrowed down to a smaller subset for closer scrutinization. Detailed information on each of the events and a set of five problem summary NOC screens aid this process.

The detailed information for each event number includes a text description of the problem, the source and object of the event, where to look for supporting data, when the event was generated, and the suggested general action to take. This information is not currently resident on the system but is documented in the user manuals. The problem summary screens, structured as shown in Figure 3, provide an overview of the network current operational status. For a general overall view, the problem summary status shows any components that are not fully operational. During normal network operation, one NOC should monitor the problem summary screen so that a problem may immediately be recognized. The remaining screens provide greater detail for the nodes, clusters, backbone links, and NCPs. Each provides an operational summary for that component in the network. For the node, cluster, and backbone links, a parameter can be set to show only the problem areas.

Once the event information and the summary screens are reviewed, a number of other sources may be explored for supporting information. The following are some possibilities [12]:

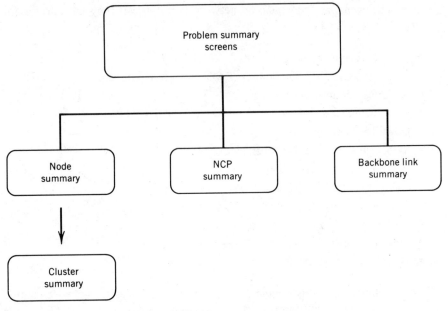

Figure 3. Problem summary screens.

- Detailed status and statistics
- Current and past call records
- Configuration database
- Reports
- Route simulation

Detailed status and statistics are available for every network component, containing the state, utilization, error statistics, and network servers (i.e., specific NCP or ASP) where applicable. Call records are present for both completed and active calls. The records specify the call route chosen, start and end times, per-call facilities, calling and called address, and the clearing cause code and diagnostic cause code if the call was cleared. The 11 clearing causes indicate why the call was cleared and where the problem was detected. The 106 diagnostic codes are used to report the details as to why the call was cleared. Often, first-time problems can be traced back to an incorrect configuration for the service attempted (such as an out-of-service destination), so the 35 screens available for reviewing various aspects of the configuration database are useful here. Reports can be generated for a hard-copy output of the configuration information. Route simulation is incorporated to explore the possibility that congestion is causing new subscriber's calls to be rejected. On the route simulation screen, the operator enters the class of service and source traffic parameter desired and the routing is then displayed.

5.2.3. *Problem Correction from the NCC.* The following actions can be initiated from the NOC to correct problems [11]:

- Forcing and clearing cluster sparing by the backup
- Restarting a cluster, ASP, or a port
- Changing the state of a cluster, ASP, or a port
- Resetting, reconfiguring, reinitializing, or loading a PAD

Often, clusters are placed in a group where there is an extra cluster available to stand in for any of the others. If a cluster is performing poorly, a NOC operator may force the spare to switch in, allowing desired network operation while a support person is dispatched to the site. An ASP or cluster restart will reset the hardware, clear any actions that are in process, and initiate a downline load of software and possibly configuration data. In the case of a port, all active calls are cleared and the link and packet level protocols are restarted. This might be desirable if a cluster displayed erratic behavior that precluded calls from passing through it. A state change, as in returning to in-service mode after having been in maintenance mode, assigns a new level of operation to the component. The five states are in-service, camped-on, maintenance, out-of-service, and undefined. The camped-on state is a transition state where all new calls are refused, and when the last active call clears, the port state changes from in-service to maintenance.

5.3. Expert Systems for Fault Isolation and Correction

Network fault isolation and correction is a prime candidate for an expert system development. As described in Section 5.2, extensive data are available from a variety of sources in a variety of forms. Development of a system could begin with a narrowly banded subset of faults, such as PSC failures caused by the hardware, software, or an incorrect configuration. As confidence in the system grew, other fault classes could be included. A number of experts are available to describe their analysis techniques, and they could additionally test the prototype system with real network data. Thus, this area meets all the criteria outlined for expert systems applications.

As an example of how a system might work, suppose that a small-scale expert system has been developed for the PSC failures mentioned above and that a log of user complaints shows a large number of users reporting dropped calls or inability to place a call. The following is a scenario of how the system might attack the problem. First, it would scan the log to see if there were a common node, cluster, line interface module (LIM), or port. All the calls are from the same cluster, so the system would now open the event log to search for events referring to this cluster. Relevant events are found in the following order:

- Cluster *not* reporting summary status
- Cluster start-up (supporting data)
- First reconciliation descriptor not found

Because a cluster should report summary status in all states, a failure to report from this cluster indicates a malfunction. The cluster start-up event means that either the cluster failed, decided to reset, or was reset externally; at any rate the start-up message explains why the summary status was not being reported.

The system would recognize that a "cluster start-up" event should soon be followed by a "cluster operational" event. Absence of this message indicates that the problem probably lies in its ability to restart. This leaves the "first reconciliation descriptor not found" message. A first reconciliation descriptor (FRD) is the first item exchanged in the downline load process and contains a brief description of all the information needed by the cluster. The NCP generates this event when it cannot find the FRD requested by the cluster, and it indicates a configuration problem. The expert system would now know to look for downline load events generated by the NCP indicating configuration problems. A second search through the event log turns up a "downline load (DLL) of unsupported software release requested" at about the same time as the FRD message. Since the software name is included in the descriptor, an error here would cause both messages.

The expert system has now determined that a cluster cannot start up because it cannot complete its downline load, which probably failed because of a problem with the software to be used. The expert system could stop here and print a report on the problem, the probable cause, and the reasoning behind it, or it could go on and search the configuration database for the name of the software requested by the cluster and the names of all the software supported on the NCP and find any misspelling candidates.

To determine why the cluster restarted in the first place, the expert system would have to look for events further back. In this case, an operator had put a new database on-line sometime earlier, and in the new configuration had misspelled the name of the software to be used by the cluster. After the cluster had gone a specified time without being able to verify its configuration (because it could not get its FRD), its reconciliation timer expired and it reset itself. Because it could not find its FRD, it could not successfully start up again. Note that the system conjectured the cause of the problem after it had happened: a fault prediction system would recognize the significance of repeated failures to find an FRD and could initiate action before the cluster restarted.

The sample situation points out some of the capabilities that would be necessary for a successful expert system implementation. The system would require a knowledge of general network structure and function (i.e., PSCs request downline load data from ASPs and NCPs), how the various log files and databases relate, and what the "normal" course of events are for things such as downline load and cluster start-up. It should know likely points of failure and component's capacity limitations. A pattern matching ability that could recognize spelling variations would be useful to help pinpoint things exactly. Additionally, an expert system application should be able to determine both the causes of specific situations and the expected outcome from a set of circumstances, implying both forward and backward chaining.

The addition of an expert system to this area of network operations could make the job of providing high-quality service more efficient and would ensure that problems were dealt with in a consistent fashion.

6. NETWORK PERFORMANCE IMPROVEMENTS

6.1. Description

The section on network engineering describes the process that goes on prior to and during the network installation to configure and initialize the network properly. At that time, assumptions are made on the traffic and service requirements. Once the network is in operation, additional steps can be taken to fine tune the network performance. This iterative process of monitoring and tweaking the on-line network is the subject of this section. Improvements are usually measured in terms of increased throughput, reduced transit delay, reduced cost, or greater availability. But, as is usually the case, it is a combination of the four that truly decides the performance.

6.2. Current Approach

The two major areas to consider are the utilization of the various components in the network and the call routing that takes place. Utilization is a barometer of the network performance, with an unexpected low utilization being of equal concern as a high utilization. Routing is also a key aspect, since the route chosen determines the resulting level of service and cost. The level of component usage is discussed first.

6.2.1. Component Usage. The network currently monitors the relative usage of the backbone links, clusters, and ASPs. All this information is available at the NOC in the summary status and the detail statistics screens. If usage is continually excessive, then the configuration should be reviewed. Users may have to be redistributed or the network expanded to handle higher than expected traffic requirements. The cause of the congestion could also be the result of database entry errors. If the capacity of a backbone link is overstated in the configuration database, then more traffic may be routed across it than is appropriate, resulting in poor service. Since network usage is dynamic and growing, such reviews of the network utilization are required on a routine basis. This is accomplished by monitoring both the utilization and the traffic statistics.

Congestion could also be caused by link errors on the backbones or access links, which would result in a high number of packet retransmissions. Since relative utilization and delay are monitored by the network, these conditions can be detected from the NOC. Take, for example, a backbone: if the utilization is normal and the delay is high relative to other similar backbones, then the backbone capacity could have been overstated as mentioned above, or there could be a high link-level error rate. The error rate can be determined by reviewing the port status screen for the number of cyclic redundancy check (CRC) errors that were detected. Another approach could be to monitor the CRC error numbers to predict when congestion will arise.

Although a high utilization of the network is often the focus, the inverse condition, underutilization, is also of concern. If a subsection of the network is underutilized, the average cost will be higher. Configuration errors may again be the problem. For instance, if a backbone port is placed out of service or if the capacity is understated, there is an obvious reduction in the level of use. Also the routing selection could be the cause. The routing is based on the class of service requested and the various link types available. If too high a "cost" is assigned to a specific link, traffic may continuously be routed across alternative paths.

This leads into the second major area—routing. Are calls being routed as anticipated? The route selected may result in over- or underutilization of the network, or the network load could be fine, but the connection did not follow the desired path.

6.2.2. Call Routing.

To understand better how performance improvements can be made, some background on the routing algorithm is required. In a PSN, which is typically a mesh configuration, there is usually more than one route between the source and the destination and more than one type of backbone link. For the network described here, the route that will be selected for a call is based on an estimation of how much traffic will result, the class or level of service desired, and the type, utilization, and queue delay of the backbone links available between the source and the destination. From this information the routing algorithm determines a shortest-path first tree, quantified in terms of the relative cost. If the resulting least-cost or shortest path is higher than that allowed for this call, the call is cleared. Otherwise, the route determined is used.

The primary configurable portion of this process is the class of service (COS) table. The table defines, for each level of service, the relative "length" or "cost" for each link type. Take, for example, a 56-kilobit per second (kbps) terrestrial link, a 9.6-kbps terrestrial link, and a 56-kbps satellite link as the only three link types defined for the network. If the goal of the first class of service is to minimize delay, 56-kbps terrestrial links would be assigned the least relative cost, followed by the 9.6-kbps links and then satellite links. The desire is to use high-speed, lower-delay terrestrial backbones where possible and satellite links only as a last choice. If the goal for the second class of service is minimum cost per bit transmitted, the least relative cost would possibly be assigned to satellite links, followed by 56-kbps terrestrial links and then 9.6-kbps links. In this fashion, the relative cost for each type of backbone is known for each type of "least-cost" service desired.

The path a call would take at the current time is available from the route simulator. The input to the route simulator mirrors that of a call. The user inputs the source and destination for the call, the desired COS, and the source traffic parameter. The assumptions made in assigning values during network configuration can then be verified.

The route that previous calls have taken is recorded in the call records. Each call record includes more than 40 details about the call including the start and stop times, the COS, and the route followed. All the call records are logged and archived for billing purposes and can be sorted any different number of ways to provide a look at the network service provided. For example, is the desired path used all the time? If not, was it because of a random spot problem, or are trends apparent? If a second route is chosen on a regular basis, is it the one wanted? These are the type of thought processes involved when attempting to refine the routing to improve the performance.

6.3. Expert Systems for Network Performance Optimization

Network performance or tuning meets all the criteria cited for expert systems applications. First, the problem of network performance can be broken up into two major categories that could be approached separately—component usage and call routing. Within each of these areas, the applications could be restricted further to involve only certain component types or calls of a specific class of service. As the expert system stabilized, the application could easily be broadened. The experts in this case are the network engineers. They could be relied on to test a system with data derived from a live network, as well as to supply the expertise for system development. While the data to be used in the statistics and call record logs are fairly standard in form, there are more data than an individual could work with comfortably. Finally, performance is an area that hinges on subjective expectations, which take a number of factors into consideration to form the overall picture of the network. This is something that cannot specifically be quantified and hard coded using standard programming techniques.

An expert system could review all the incoming data on component usage and congestion and flag problems. If it discovered an area of particularly high or low utilization, it could review the configuration to see if an unusually large number of users have been assigned to this area or if it is in the service path of many clusters. If either or both of these conditions were to arise, reduced performance could easily result.

Having identified an area of high usage, the expert system could then review other similar components in the geographical area of the component in question and postulate how the configuration might be adjusted to redistribute the traffic presented. The system would need to be able to discern average and peak uses and explain how the recommended configuration would handle both. It should also be able to review statistics logs from a predefined time period to identify trends and shifts.

The expert system would need to have the network topology in its knowledge base to track down the cause of the bottlenecks in the traffic flow. If the utilization for a component is abnormal, what is leading into and out of the area and its role in the network must be known. Both forward- and backward-chaining capabilities would be required both to project behavior and determine the cause of it.

In route simulation and call record monitoring, the expert compares the route chosen with the route desired. The keyword is "desired," a subjective term. An expert system must capture the framework of what is desirable for providing a data transmission service. One approach would be to incorporate the expert system in place of the routing algorithm for certain classes of calls, perhaps as presented by Stach [13]. Instead of reviewing the outcome, it would initiate the route selected. That is certainly a future possibility; however, the current least-cost or shortest-path algorithms are extremely fast and with the proper parameter selection produce the desired outcome. Thus, in this network, an expert system is more appropriate as the tool for tuning the current algorithmic approach rather than replacing it.

7. NETWORK ENGINEERING

7.1. Description

The IPN described earlier is M/A-COM Telecommunication's standard packet switching product. When a customer purchases the network, the customer's on-site configuration must be determined. The planning and implementation of a network installation are in the realm of network engineering.

The planning stage of a network's implementation is obviously very important: a topology unsuited to the customer's needs will undoubtedly perform below expectations. Although equipment can be changed and moved, installation is a time-consuming job that must be performed meticulously and doing it only once is certainly preferable.

Correct planning requires highly trained personnel who fully understand both the network and what the customer wants to achieve. They must perform a complete review of the customer's requirements and constraints and of the product's constraints to come up with a suitable implementation. Reliable and efficient methods must be used to examine the topology for inconsistencies when a plan is devised.

Once an acceptable plan is constructed, the network must be installed smoothly. This is the customer's first "live" experience with the network; therefore, it is important that the process go efficiently and correctly in order to make the customer feel confident and satisfied. To ensure success, the individuals performing the installation must be continually wary of errors and at the end should cross-check the implemented network against the planned one and verify that all aspects are working properly.

7.2. Current Approach

7.2.1. Planning. When a customer decides on a PSN to meet communications needs, that customer generally has a good idea of what the network will look like in terms of where the central points will be, how many users there will be and their locations, and any existing communications links. The network engineer's first step in planning the network is therefore to help the customer move from the general to the specific. To aid in this process, the customer normally fills out a questionnaire on intended network use. The questionnaire has three main parts: the expected use of the network, any site constraints, and network addressing issues.

Expected use includes issues such as the number of users and their types (i.e., terminal, host, or PAD users); the type of traffic profile likely to be presented, in terms of topology and traffic type (i.e., batch, interactive, or both); and any speed, delay, or availability requirements. Where the sites will be, how many users will be at each site and their type, and the locations of the NCPs and NOCs are just some of the site constraints. Addressing issues include identification of any special options desired and whether the customer plans any addresses that conflict with the IPN network's addressing scheme. By reviewing this for problems and then discussing it with the customer, the network engineer will have a good concept of the network from which to work.

Now the hardest part begins: the engineer must take the network description and turn it into a layout of hardware and software that will accomplish the desired ends. He or she first establishes the network subscriber configuration, as this part is driven from the outside world and is least able to change. A preliminary topology is then devised, involving attention to numerous rules and guidelines. (Rules can be considered to be restrictions that cannot be violated, guidelines as recommendations for improved performance.) For example, clusters may be placed together in something called a redundancy group, where there is a spare cluster that monitors the health of the others in the group and is ready to switch in for any cluster that fails. Because this spare must be able to assume the identity of any cluster, the rules require it to be fully loaded as a superset of all other clusters in the group. That is, if three PSCs in a redundancy group have three line interface modules (LIMs) each, and a single PSC has four LIMs, the spare must have four LIMs. The same reasoning extends to the number of I/O ports on a LIM. In addition, there are special addressing rules for redundancy groups as well [14]. For every location in the network, there are numerous rules concerning distances, relative configurations of clusters and cluster modules, and power and cooling requirements. The engineer must draw up a network plan, continually keeping all the rules in mind.

When a potentially suitable topology is found, users are mapped to physical components and user traffic assumptions are determined. At this point, the design can be tested for violations of the number of virtual circuits and packets per second required, and adjustments are made.

The intranetwork connections, known as the supervisory network, are designed next. This step delineates where network components will look for NCS services, and so it has a large impact on network performance. Design goals include the ability of the network to perform cold start-up and recovery without isolation of any part and in the least amount of time, rapidly executing call setup, minimizing backbone link loading for NCS services, continued operation with a single external failure, balancing traffic between ASPs and NCPs, and reducing virtual circuit fanout [14]. For each of these design goals there are a set of guidelines; the engineer designing the network must keep all of these in mind when assigning supervisory connections. Having made the assignments, the designer checks that the limits on servers, virtual circuits, and transport connections are not exceeded.

Other network items such as operating parameters and the NOC environment are determined and the design is ready for review. For this, the designer must construct diagrams and charts describing the network, as well as any supporting documentation. The plan is reviewed and adjusted until it is accepted by the customer and the review board.

7.2.2.   Installation.   The network is now ready for installation. Although much of the work is fairly methodical, it must be done carefully with a watchful eye for both configuration and installation errors. Those doing the installation must be well trained in network installation and operation.

The first step is to perform a site survey to make sure that there is enough space, power, air conditioning, and so on. Installation is scheduled for the NCP machines, and packet switching equipment is put in place. Once all the equipment is on site and powered up, a battery of diagnostics are run and release versions and media are checked. The components are now ready to be connected into a network.

In order for the network to function, its topology must be described fully in a configuration database located on the NCP. The installer enters that database from a description of the now partially installed network, all the time being alert to any deviations from the actual network. When the database is complete, it is brought on-line. The clusters, which have continually been requesting assistance, may now be downloaded and the internal network established.

When the network appears to be fully operational, the installers request all possible reports from the NCP. These are checked for errors against each other and then against the network installation plan. Finally, all the connections are checked from the NCP terminal and the NOC screens, and the summary and event screens are scanned for failures. When all these tests pass, the network is ready for customer acceptance.

7.3.   Expert Systems for Network Engineering

An expert system would be a valuable tool in network planning and installation for a number of reasons. First, both planning and installation are performed almost entirely by highly skilled network engineers and installers. Freeing some of their time for other tasks would be quite valuable. The simple task of verifying an order for completeness has been one place to start. For example, Digital Equipment Corporation's XCON is an expert configurer for VAX and PDP-11 based systems. It generally reduces the task of reviewing an order for consistency from $\frac{1}{2}$ hour down to less than 1 minute [15, 16].

A network planning application meets all four expert system criteria. Planning involves a large number of rules and guidelines in regard to hardware and software features, performance requirements, and budget limitations. The information collected is often incomplete (the third expert system criteria). Part of the configuration process is therefore developing a sensible topology based on a number of assumptions and informed predictions (criterion 3). Even the best planner must go back and review each of the rules during planning to make sure none has been violated. This is a lengthy process, and mistakes could easily be made and missed. Installation requires checking information from a number of sources and looking for conflict, a tedious task well suited for a computer application.

The application will be bounded initially by the current set of rules and guidelines considered. Inputs and results from past networks (test data) configured by the network engineers (the experts for this case) would be one check on the system's performance. From there, test cases could be constructed to test other possibilities. The installers would also be part of the review cycle to ensure that the system responses made sense to those who need to use the system.

For an expert system to be useful in the planning and installing of a network, it will need to have knowledge of the IPN's general network structure, philosophy, and terminology. It must be able to reason through the configuration rules and guidelines and come up with a viable topology or possibly a number of topologies. Furthermore, it must be able to use the information it has collated to format a report suitable for a design review. Design decisions must be explainable and well documented.

An expert system that would also assist the installation process should be able to cross-check the configuration database against the approved plan and flag deviations. Once the network is on-line, it should review the material in the reports and the status and event messages to confirm operation. Any suspected problems should invoke performance and fault analysis processes.

This aspect of network engineering could never be done entirely by an expert system, but it could facilitate the design and installation process, reduce some of the tedium involved in the verification procedures, and free the time of valuable employees for more creative, less methodical tasks.

8. TRAINING

8.1. Description

Instruction on the various aspects of network design and operation is an ongoing process for all employees directly involved with the product. Marketing representatives need to understand the network's capabilities in order to present it well. Network operators receive initial training on how to do their job and will have some slower moments in the NCC that would allow additional learning. Network engineers and field technicians must be fully versed in network design and operation for all aspects of their jobs but, in addition, should be skilled troubleshooters. As this is an ability that comes with experience, additional practice would be beneficial.

8.2. Current Approach

The following four courses are now being taught on a rotating basis [17]:

* Introduction to the Integrated Packet Network

- Integrated Packet Network Hardware Installation and Off-line Maintenance
- Integrated Packet Network Operations
- Integrated Packet Network On-line Maintenance

The introductory course provides a general overview of the network's functionality and operation. The hardware installation and off-line maintenance course takes the student from uncrating the equipment through the final verification tests once the installation is complete. The operations course presents the major duties of the NOC and NCP operators. And the on-line maintenance course tackles the area of maintenance of an on-line system. Each of the courses lasts 1 week and is a mixture of lecture and lab time. The lecture provides the time for the students to ask questions as the material is presented. Since all the information presented is contained in the associated course documentation, it can be reviewed outside the class. But as with any course, the lab time is by far the most productive segment.

8.3. Expert Systems for Providing Training

Two things stand out about the current approach to training in relation to expert system candidacy: courses are only available on a scheduled basis and hands-on experience is generally more effective than lecturing in teaching new material.

An expert system would always be available whenever an individual wanted training. Time could be set aside in blocks of hours instead of weeks. The system would be interactive, allowing the user to experiment with different ideas. It could allow the user to enter a skill level so that the system could be used by a range of employees. Particularly, the system could simulate a network fault and have the user find the cause and then propose how to correct it. If a better method existed according to the system's rule base, the system could point it out and present a case for why it is a better solution.

An expert system-based educational program would have many advantages over conventional on-line instructional systems. Conventional systems have two major restrictions that expert systems avoid. First, if the system is one where the students must type in information, then the student is limited to a very specific vocabulary in answering any questions, and the answers must be correct both in syntax and spelling. The conventional system has no way to understand what the student is getting at, and any deviation will be regarded as an error. If the system avoids this error by using a true/false or multiple choice format, then it has supplemented the student's own creative process by presenting specific choices. The students have been deprived of the opportunity to review the options and to come up with their own solutions. An expert system with natural language processing capabilities could forgive misspellings, understand synonyms, and follow a student's reasoning. This approach would be much more conducive to real learning.

Trying to lessen the requirement for personalized instruction is not a new concern. Much work has been done by the various defense agencies in the development of intelligent instructional systems. SOPHIE (Sophisticated Instructional Environment for Teaching Electronic Troubleshooting), initially sponsored by the U.S. Air Force, is one example [18].

An implementation for the system described would be bounded initially by the extent of information that is passed on in the current courses. Providing the instruction and labs currently taught would be the first step, since the courses have been taught a number of times and the instructor (the expert in this case) knows what the students would probably find confusing (test data). New employees could then further provide feedback by taking the expert system course, followed by an instructor-taught course to make a comparison.

An expert system that would be useful to individuals of various skill levels would need an overall knowledge of the network, some compartmentalized knowledge about operations, capabilities, and troubleshooting so as to be able to instruct in certain areas independently and be able to distinguish between basic and advanced operations in all these areas. The system should be able to explain operations and functions to users, to quiz them on the material, and to distinguish variations of correct answers. For troubleshooting, it should be able to simulate network faults and then analyze the user's process of isolating and correcting the fault. Because it should be able to handle scenarios of both the "why did this happen" and the "how can I make this happen" type, it should have both forward- and backward-chaining capabilities. Overall, it should have natural language processing capabilities sufficient for it to be able to understand a student's intent, perhaps asking questions that when answered could clarify vague statements.

An expert system for training is closely coupled with each of the other applications presented, though perhaps more difficult. An intelligent training system that can recall appropriate facts and details, advise and instruct students as to what actions to take in a specific case, and form hypotheses from incomplete facts would also form the groundwork for an intelligent network problem detection, isolation, and correction system. It is doubtful though that any expert system in the near future would negate the need for training.

9. SUMMARY

Each of the areas discussed meets all the criteria mentioned for expert systems applications. Of the four, network engineering is probably the most straightforward to implement because it follows such well-defined rules relative to the other applications. The knowledge bases for network performance and problem troubleshooting are based more on individual experience and so would be more difficult for the knowledge engineer to capture. The training applications are clearly delineated in the course material but would require a strong user interface, both in the amount of detail necessary to explain answers to students and in the natural language processing capabilities required. All four applications would be beneficial; however, rating them would be difficult because of the number of factors involved in gauging usefulness. The determination is subjective and driven by the perceived needs at the time.

None of the applications should be imbedded into the current system, since it is desirable to have only the IPN application running on the NCPs to maintain network integrity. However, all four would require access to the current databases and log files either directly or indirectly. Direct (or on-line) access necessitates a link to the system, with the capability for file transfers, similar to the redundant NCP. The thought there would be to add a third "host processor." Indirect (or off-line) access would be via tape and would require making sure the data needed are formatted onto the tape. This approach induces delays and is not recommended for instituting the network troubleshooting or the training programs. However, network performance and engineering are possible off-line candidates.

The NCC is a rich environment for expert system applications. In the specific system discussed, problem detection, isolation and correction, network performance, network engineering, and training are all areas where expert systems would be both interesting and beneficial. These areas, while well suited to an expert system application, are probably only a subset of the possible uses of such systems in conjunction with NCCs. The field is one with great potential.

ACKNOWLEDGMENTS

The authors would like to thank Professor John Carson for his comments and recommendations. The content of this chapter in no way reflects the opinions of M/A-COM Telecommunications, Inc. nor the direction the product discussed will take. M/A-COM Telecommunications Division, in Germantown, Maryland, is a subsidiary of M/A-COM, Inc.

GLOSSARY

ASP	Auxiliary service processor
COS	Class of service
CRC	Cyclic redundancy check
DLL	Downline load
FRD	First reconciliation descriptor
IPN	Integrated packet network
LIM	Line interface module
NCC	Network control center
NCP	Network control processor
NCPOP	Network control processor operator
NCS	Network control system
NOC	Network operator console
PAD	Packet assembler/disassembler
PSC	Packet switching cluster
PSN	Packet switching network

REFERENCES

1. T. M. Bauman and K. J. Lutz, Packet Switched Network Operations in a Multi-Supplier Environment. In *Proceedings of IEEE International Communications Conference*, pp. 1351–1354, IEEE, New York, 1985.

2. W. G. Hance and R. G. Schroeder, Experience and Requirements in Public Packet Switching Networks. In *Proceedings of IEEE International Communications Conference*, pp. 116–120, IEEE, New York, 1985.

3. J. J. Appel, Network Operations—A Major Opportunity in Evolving Digital Networks, *IEEE Communications*, Vol. 24, January 1986.

4. P. Haley and C. Williams, Expert System Development Requires Knowledge Engineering, *Computer Design*, February 1986.

5. B. Turpin, Artificial Intelligence: Project Needs, *Design News*, March 1986.

6. Y. T. Chien and J. Liebowitz, Expert Systems in the SDI Environment, *Computer*, IEEE, July 1986.

7. R. H. Michaelsen, D. Michie, and A. Boulanger, The Technology of Expert Systems, *BYTE*, April 1985.

8. J. D. Mosley, Expert Systems as Engineering Tools Will Broaden Productivity/Creativity Options, *EDN*, November 1986.

9. J. D. Daniels, Artificial Intelligence: A Brief Tutorial, *Signal*, June 1986.

10. T. H. Scholl, Packet Switching. In *Electronics Communications Handbook*, Chap. 14, McGraw-Hill, New York, in press.

11. *Network Operator Procedures Manual*, M/A-COM Telecommunications, Inc., Germantown, MD, 1985.

12. *Integrated Packet Network On-line Maintenance Course*, 2nd ed., M/A-COM Telecommunications, Inc., Germantown, MD, 1986.

13. F. Stach, Expert Systems Find a New Place in Data Networks, *Data Communications*, November 1985.

14. *IPN Configuration Manual*, M/A-COM Telecommunications, Inc., Germantown, MD, 1985.

15. W. E. Suydam, AI Becomes the Soul of the New Machines, *Computer Design*, February 1986.

16. T. C. Shannon, AI at Work, *Digital Review*, May 1986.

17. *Integrated Packet Network (IPN) Training Curricula*, M/A-COM Telecommunications, Inc., Germantown, MD, 1986.

18. J. D. Fletcher and J. Psotka, Intelligent Training Systems for Maintenance, *Signal*, June 1986.

EXPERT SYSTEMS IN RADIO SPECTRUM MANAGEMENT

George W. Garber

Office of Spectrum Management, National Telecommunications and
Information Administration, Washington, DC

Jay Liebowitz

Department of Management Science, George Washington University,
Washington, DC

1. INTRODUCTION

The radio spectrum is a limited natural resource accessible to and used by all nations
of the world. Because it is reusable, providing a wide variety of services, it requires
constant control and management to assure that the most effective and efficient use
is being made of it. Expert systems have significant potential for aiding in this
activity [1].

Increased demand for communications services both nationally and internation-
ally may soon bring about a serious shortage of radio spectrum availability, particularly in the key satellite and terrestrial microwave frequency bands [2]. The
factors influencing this increase in demand are many. One is an anticipated population growth in the United States of 10% over the next few years [3]. Another
is the rapid growth in demand for personal computers (PCs). The PC market is
expected to grow from the approximately 800,000 units shipped in 1982 to
5,500,000 units forecast to be shipped in 1987 [4]. A third factor is the increasing
use American business is making of telecommunications to transfer large quantities
of information on a daily basis.

With more PCs being used in the home and office, with an increasing percentage
of these computers engaging in communications, and with the certainty of major
increases in the amount of communications that will accompany the office of the
future, the availability of adequate frequency spectrum to accommodate the facilities that carry the information must be addressed [2].

In addition to the increase in commercial demand indicated above, U.S. government use of the spectrum is increasing at a rate roughly equal to that of the commercial sector. Federal spectrum use includes all conventional forms of communications, such as microwave point-to-point and land mobile and maritime mobile, as well as telemetry, radiolocation (radar), radionavigation, and other more exotic uses. To meet the disparate requirements of these different uses of radio and to make it possible to use the spectrum resource in a nonconflicting manner are a management problem of very significant dimension. Much information, both administrative and engineering in nature, must be integrated and evaluated to make appropriate decisions on even the simplest communications systems. Expert computer systems could prove very helpful in this regard.

This chapter will address some ideas for using expert systems in spectrum management. First, a brief description of current practice in radio spectrum management will be given. Second, some potential areas for using expert systems in spectrum management will be addressed. Finally, some of the research issues that need to be examined in developing and implementing expert systems for spectrum management will be identified.

2.   RADIO SPECTRUM MANAGEMENT

Management of the radio spectrum involves the cooperation of and agreement between the United States and many foreign countries. The radio frequency spectrum is susceptible to oversubscription and conflicting uses [5]. With many countries vying for spectrum usage, with the safety of life and property at stake, and with many billions of dollars involved, managing the spectrum is an important, complex, and difficult task.

There are several groups that are influential in affecting both national and international spectrum usage. The International Telecommunication Union (ITU), the Department of State, the National Telecommunications and Information Administration (NTIA) of the Department of Commerce, and the Federal Communications Commission (FCC) are the primary organizations of interest in the United States.

The ITU is the chief international coordinating body for spectrum use, organizing periodic World Administrative Radio Conferences (WARCs) and specialized conferences to develop and codify rules and regulations for international use of the spectrum. At these conferences, representatives of almost all the nations of the world decide on the use of the radio spectrum, allocating portions (bands) of the spectrum for each of the many radio services that have been defined. (Where appropriate, services may share the use of these bands.) These conferences result in agreements (Final Acts) that, when ratified by the administrations involved, have the force of international treaties.

As an ongoing task, the ITU coordinates the use of the spectrum in those bands where international conflicts are most likely to arise. High-frequency (HF) broadcasting, for example, is one portion of the spectrum about which the ITU maintains extensive records of spectrum use and for which it develops and periodically publishes schedules for transmission. Communications satellite frequency uses and orbit locations are other subject areas where the ITU is particularly active, coordinating spectrum and orbit usage in an expeditious manner.

The United States provides inputs to the ITU World and Regional Radio Conferences through the State Department. Working with State, NTIA provides input based on coordinated Executive Branch needs. The FCC represents private sector interests [5]. State, NTIA, FCC, and the private sector all provide members for the U.S. delegations to ITU conferences.

Domestically, the FCC coordinates and regulates the use of the radio spectrum by all nonfederal users including, but not limited to, such groups as state and local public safety organizations, AM, FM, and TV broadcasters, taxicab companies, cellular radio telephone companies, and others. The FCC does most of its spectrum management through the use of public Notices of Proposed Rule Making (NPRMs), whereby the public is invited to comment on proposed new rules or on proposed modifications to existing rules. Once rules or rule changes have been approved by the FCC, they are administered by the FCC staff through the issuance or denial of licenses to transmit.

NTIA manages the use of the radio spectrum by all branches of the federal government. This is done with the advice of the Interdepartment Radio Advisory Committee (IRAC) [5], a coordinating body established in 1922 to help avoid the radio interference problems even then being experienced. The IRAC, chaired by NTIA, is composed of representatives of those federal agencies having a significant interest in radio use. It currently has members representing the following agencies:

- U.S. Postal Service
- Department of Commerce
- Veteran's Administration
- U.S. Information Agency
- Federal Emergency Management Administration
- General Services Administration
- Department of State
- Department of Energy
- Department of Army
- Department of Agriculture
- Department of Navy
- Federal Communications Commission
- Health and Human Services
- Federal Aviation Administration
- U.S. Coast Guard
- Department of Air Force
- Department of Treasury
- Department of Justice

- Department of Interior
- NASA
- National Science Foundation

Although, in contrast to the FCC, IRAC meetings are not open to the public (for national security considerations), the public is represented at IRAC meetings by an FCC liaison representative charged with protecting the public interest from the point of view of the FCC. The representative participates in all activities of the IRAC and serves as a bridge with the FCC for the transfer of spectrum management related information.

IRAC members represent a wide range of federal missions and uses of the spectrum that cover all the radio services. Applications to use the spectrum are for services that include land mobile, fixed satellite, radiolocation (radar), aeronautical fixed, radio astronomy, and many others [5]. IRAC, through its Frequency Assignment Subcommittee (FAS), reviews these applications and submits the applications and their recommendations to NTIA for action. NTIA reviews the applications for adherence to the rules contained in the NTIA *Manual of Regulations and Procedures for Federal Radio Frequency Management* and for the probability of the proposed use creating harmful interference to existing installations. Those proposed uses that meet the necessary criteria are assigned and entered into the Government Master File of frequency assignments [6].

To support the IRAC functions and NTIA policy development, NTIA has set up the following internal program of activities [5]:

- Assignment of frequencies to federal agencies
- Computer support and database management
- Spectrum engineering and analysis
- Long-range spectrum planning
- Emergency spectrum planning
- International radio conference preparations

Frequency assignment is a daily function of spectrum management in which applications from the federal agencies are reviewed by NTIA for compliance with basic regulations [5]. Computer support is needed in this area to process, store, and retrieve data relating to the spectrum, system characteristics, propagation, and terrain. Spectrum engineering and analysis are used to help select frequencies that are appropriate for specific needs. This activity ranges from the specific calculations needed for the design and installation of a radio transmitter site to those computations needed to predict system performance in a given radio frequency environment. Long-range and emergency spectrum planning provide assurance that proposed uses of the spectrum will be feasible, that the spectrum will be available once the proposed uses become operational. International radio conferences are a forum for discussing, planning, and regulating the use of the radio spectrum and associated resources, such as the geostationary orbit [5], on a long-term basis.

2.1. Frequency Assignment and Selection

Of the functions listed above, two are ripe for expert system development. These are frequency selection and assignment. These are activities where the rules and regulations have been spelled out in detail and voluminous records concerning current use are available. The development of an expert system prototype, a Frequency Assignment and Selection Tool (FAST), to assist in frequency selection and assignment has been proposed [7]. FAST is intended (1) to tap the professional experience and knowledge of experts in the frequency selection domain, (2) to apply the rules contained in the NTIA manual, and (3) to consider the existing electromagnetic environment when recommending a choice of one or more frequencies for use in a specific location.

To test the feasibility of using an expert system for this purpose, FAST would be limited to providing help for federal agencies in the selection and assignment of frequencies in the 162–174- and 406.1–420-MHz bands. These bands (specifically 162.0125–173.2-, 173.4–174, and 406.1–420 MHz) are allocated in the United States to Government Fixed Service and Government Mobile Service, with the exception that the Radio Astronomy Service enjoys some limited protection in the 406.1–410 MHz subband also.

The rules for these bands are explicit and are relatively few in number. The number of users in these bands is large and the interest in these bands is and will continue at a high level. Consequently, any expert system developed for use with these bands should provide immediate proof-of-concept. If this expert system prototype proves to be useful in this limited application, it could serve as the basis for using expert systems generally for frequency selection.

2.1.1. *Statement of the Problem.* Applications for permission to use radio are prepared by individual member agencies of the FAS and propose the use of specific frequencies (selected by the applicant), usually in specific locations, having specific technical characteristics. NTIA reviews these applications for technical appropriateness, to ensure compliance with policy and regulations and to determine if there is a possibility of conflict with agencies not members of the FAS. The FAS, including a representative member of the FCC, considers these applications each month and takes agreed action within policy guidelines. When additional policy guidance is needed or agreement cannot be reached, the matter may be referred to the Office of Spectrum Management in NTIA, the Administrator of NTIA, or even to the Office of Management and Budget in the Executive Office of the President, for resolution.

A significant problem with the present approach to performing frequency selection is that an institutional memory of how to do the job is not being preserved. Experienced spectrum managers are always in short supply. There are only a few experts who have gained the needed experience and expertise to be able to integrate from a variety of sources the information needed for the selection of frequencies. When these individuals retire or leave the federal spectrum management community, their experiential learning is lost. It would be beneficial to capture these experts' knowledge before they leave or retire. The lessons they have learned over the years, through successes and failures, may be applied through an expert system both to select frequencies and to train future experts in frequency selection.

Another problem with the present technique of frequency selection is the difficulty experienced by frequency managers, particularly neophytes in the frequency selection field, in remembering the contents of the NTIA manual. The manual, over 500 pages in length, is organized in terms of rules, and it would be helpful to have an automated way of capturing and representing these rules for easy access, updating, and application by frequency selection personnel. Developing an expert system is one approach that lends itself to capturing and applying, in a systematic fashion, the professional experience and knowledge of experts and the rules and regulations contained in the NTIA manual.

Finally, a systematic approach to the consideration of the existing environment is needed. NTIA maintains the Government Master File (GMF), a file of over 200,000 records, describing the current use of the spectrum. The individual federal agencies, when selecting frequencies, use this information resource in a variety of ways. Some, such as the military, have available the labor and techniques needed to perform detailed engineering analyses using the GMF. These analyses help predict the effect proposed frequency assignments will have on the environment and the effect the environment will have on proposed assignments. This type of prediction effort helps avoid potential conflicts with existing installations and enhances the application process. Other agencies with more limited resources must rely on less elaborate means to consider the environment in their selection processes, increasing the possibility for selecting incompatible frequencies for assignment. An expert system incorporating the latest and best techniques for consideration of the environment could improve significantly the frequency selection process of all government agencies. This, in turn, would improve the effectiveness with which we use the available spectrum.

2.1.2. Approach. In developing the expert system prototype (FAST) to help in the selection of frequencies in the 162–174- and 406.1–420-MHz bands for federal agencies, the following iterative, rapid prototyping approach would be used:

1. *Problem Analysis.* Analyze the current approach and its components to frequency selection. Define the acronyms, terminology, and concepts in the frequency selection domain. Select the expert(s) from the federal spectrum management community. Determine the acceptance rate of the prototype and the prototype evaluation criteria.
2. *Knowledge Acquisition.* Acquire the knowledge for knowledge base development from the following sources:
   a. Interviews with the frequency selection experts and users.
   b. The NTIA manual (and footnotes).
   c. Existing channeling plans.
   d. Frequency assignment principles.

    e. Coordination procedures for use of specialized channels.

    f. The Government Master File.

3. *Select Test Cases.* Develop attribute hierarchy that serves as the framework for constructing the knowledge base.

4. *Knowledge Representation.* Determine the best way to represent knowledge (production rules and possibly frames) for the frequency selection domain. Determine the reasoning approach (i.e., the inference mechanism) that most closely matches the way the frequency selection expert performs his or her task. Select an expert system shell (with hooks to an effective database system). Write out the rules for the knowledge base.

5. *Knowledge Programming.* Encode the knowledge into the knowledge base. Have the expert(s) and users employ the expert system to identify strengths and weaknesses. Refine the knowledge base by going through steps 2–4 above.

6. *Knowledge Testing and Evaluation.* Perform backcasting to test the expert system prototype. Perform a modified Turing test as a blind verification study for evaluation. Have expert(s) and users evaluate the expert system prototype.

FAST would be designed and implemented on an industry-standard MS-DOS PC to make possible wide distribution and use of the program. FAST first would be developed to help in frequency selection in the major fixed and mobile bands for federal agencies. Once experience in that domain has been gained, the program may be enlarged to encompass other parts of the spectrum, or expert systems tailored to the requirements of other radio services could be developed. The prototype would be developed using the iterative approach for refining the knowledge in the knowledge base.

The main benefits of using an expert system to assist in frequency selection and assignment would be to (1) capture professional experience and knowledge to build an institutional memory, (2) improve the quality and speed of frequency selections, (3) help to standardize the frequency selection process, (4) assist in the training of new experts, and (5) save and avoid costs.

In addition to frequency selection, there are other potentially rewarding areas for developing expert systems for spectrum management functions. Some of these are discussed in the following sections.

2.2. Spectrum Planning

Planning requires designing actions to achieve desired results [8]. Short-term reactive planning may be needed to certify a new routing strategy, for example [8]. Long-range spectrum planning may be necessary to consider executive branch agency needs in conjunction with the projected needs of the private sector for effective use of the spectrum in the national interest. Emergency spectrum planning may also be needed during national disaster or wartime emergencies.

Developing planning expert systems for these functions may be very fruitful for providing expertise for capacity planning, network expansion, and multinetwork integration strategies. Planning expert systems are already being developed to help in emergency situations, such as oil spills, handled by the Federal Emergency Management Administration. Planning expert systems have been developed in other domains also. CSS is an expert system developed by IBM for planning relocation, reinstallation, and rearrangement of IBM mainframes [9]. PLANPOWER, by Applied Expert Systems, is an expert system developed to aid professional financial planners in managing clients' accounts [9]. AALPS is an expert system developed by the U.S. Army to plan optimal loading of equipment and cargo on aircraft. The technology is already available to develop planning expert systems. Spectrum management is one more domain where such expert systems could be useful.

2.3. Interpretation and Diagnosis

Interpretation and diagnosis involve inferring system malfunction from sensor data and observables [8]. This expertise is helpful in assessing network performance, network fault isolation, and recovery from an outage by observing sensory information and alarms [8]. Several interpretation and diagnosis expert systems have already been developed in the telecommunications area. ACE, by Bell Laboratories, is an expert system used to diagnosis telephone cable maintenance problems. COMPASS, by GTE Laboratories, is an expert system used to determine switch problems. TRACKER, by British Telecom, is an expert system for diagnosing faults in electronic PABX power supplies. FIS, by the Navy Center for Applied Research in Artificial Intelligence, is an expert system for diagnosing faults in equipment. By using these expert systems and by developing other related diagnosis expert systems for spectrum management purposes, management of the spectrum could be greatly facilitated.

2.4. Monitoring

Another fruitful function for expert systems development in the spectrum management area is monitoring. Monitoring involves comparing observables to predictions [8]. On-line monitoring of observables is used in assessing network performance and in planning corrective actions [8]. Expert systems have been developed for monitoring a number of process flow activities. One of these is REACTOR, by EG&G Idaho [10], which assists reactor operators in the diagnosis and treatment of nuclear reactor accidents by monitoring instrument readings, looking for deviations from normal operating conditions. Likewise, expert systems for monitoring networks and spectrum congestion might also be useful for analyzing sensor and traffic information.

2.5. Analysis

Expert systems may also be helpful in the areas of spectrum engineering and analysis. The spectrum manager and policy maker use mathematical modeling and computer simulations to aid in their decision processes. The use of an expert system as an intelligent front end to the spectrum management databases could allow for easy access, interfacing, and retrieval of information.

Expert systems could also provide the spectrum manager some heuristic information based on expert knowledge to accompany optimization and simulation techniques. The built-in explanation process of the expert system could provide a better understanding of the factors involved in performing spectrum engineering and analysis.

2.6. Control

Control, taking action to bring a system state to the desired level [8], is another function of spectrum management where expert systems may be helpful to the spectrum manager and policymaker. Expert systems used for controlling purposes at the operational level have been developed, such as the expert system by Hitachi for controlling railroad train braking for accuracy and comfort. Similarly, expert systems might be developed in the spectrum management area for indicating actions for network routing changes and repair suggestions. At the management and policy implementation level, expert systems might be used to assist in controlling the utilization of the frequency bands, indicating when frequency bands are over- or underutilized.

3. RESEARCH ISSUES FOR DEVELOPING EXPERT SYSTEMS IN SPECTRUM MANAGEMENT

There are many research issues that need to be addressed to further development and implementation of expert systems in the spectrum management domain. Although these issues do not have to be settled in advance, attention must be given to each of these as time goes on if useful expert systems are to be developed and used in a coherent fashion.

One such issue involves the use of multiple, cooperating expert systems. In the spectrum and network management environments, there is no single individual who is considered to be an expert on all aspects of the spectrum or network. The network or spectrum is so complex that it is virtually impossible for one person to be an expert on all parts of the system. Thus, current expert systems, generally based on the expertise of a single individual, are confined to very limited domains. Since one individual is not an expert on all segments of the system, multiple, cooperating expert systems must be developed by tapping many experts who are knowledgeable on their respective parts of the total system. The interaction between these expert systems and their performance in a real-time fashion are research issues that need further consideration.

Another major research issue in the spectrum management environment is very much related to the first and deals with distributed artificial intelligence. Typically, a spectrum or network management system will be a distributed system because the sites, users, equipment, and policymakers of the spectrum or network management systems likewise are distributed. Distributed problem solving is an area that must be addressed to have efficient and effective responses for spectrum management decisions. Distributed artificial intelligence, a particular instance of distributed problem solving, is a class of activities that permit several more or less autonomous processes to perform globally coherent intelligent acts solely through local computation and interprocess communication [8]. This is an important research area in spectrum or network management and one that has particular importance in spectrum management.

Learning also is a major research issue that needs greater consideration in expert systems development. The ability of expert systems to learn from their mistakes and to modify their own rules based on these mistakes and inconsistencies is in the infancy stage. More work is needed to understand learning and to apply this understanding to expert systems.

4. CONCLUSIONS

Expert systems have a great potential in the spectrum management domain. They could be used for many functions to help the spectrum manager, spectrum analyst, and policymaker. With today's technology, expert systems are limited to narrowly defined tasks, such as frequency assignment and selection. However, as the aforementioned research issues are addressed and resolved, the usefulness of expert systems in spectrum management will grow.

REFERENCES

1. *Manual of Regulations and Procedures for Federal Radio Frequency Management*, National Telecommunications and Information Administration, U.S. Department of Commerce, Washington, DC, May 1986.

2. G. L. Armes, The Frequency Spectrum Crisis—Issues and Answers, *Telematics and Informatics*, Pergamon Press, New York, Vol. 1, No. 2, 1984.

3. J. Naisbitt, *Megatrends: Ten New Directions Transforming Our Lives*, Warner Books, New York, 1982.

4. Computer Shock Hits the Office, *Business Week*, August 8, 1983.

5. R. D. Parlow, Management of the Radio Spectrum to Achieve More Efficient Utilization, Access, and Network Growth, *Telematics and Informatics*, Pergamon Press, New York, Vol. 2, No. 1, 1985.

6. G. W. Garber, Spectrum Management Data Bases, *IEEE Transactions on Electromagnetic Compatibility*, Vol. EMC-19, No. 3, August 1977.

7. J. Liebowitz, Frequency Assignment and Selection Tool (FAST): Development of an Expert System Prototype for Frequency Assignment and Selection, proposal submitted to NTIA.

8. S. R. Goyal, Expert Systems in Network Management. In *Proceedings of Expert Systems in Government Conference*, IEEE/MITRE, Washington, D.C., 1985.

9. B. G. Buchanan, Expert Systems: Working Systems and the Research Literature, *Expert Systems*, Vol. 3, No. 1, January 1986.

10. D. A. Waterman, *A Guide to Expert Systems*, Addison-Wesley, Reading, MA, 1986.

INDEX